D0390206

ALSO BY MICHAEL SCHUDSON

THE POWER OF NEWS

WATERGATE IN AMERICAN MEMORY

RETHINKING POPULAR CULTURE
(edited, with Chandra Mukerji)

READING THE NEWS
(edited, with Robert Manoff)

ADVERTISING, THE UNEASY PERSUASION

DISCOVERING THE NEWS

MARTIN KESSLER BOOKS

THE FREE PRESS

New York   London   Toronto   Sydney   Singapore

The

G·O·O·D

CITIZEN

A History of
American Civic Life

MICHAEL SCHUDSON

THE FREE PRESS
A Division of Simon & Schuster Inc.
1230 Avenue of the Americas
New York, NY 10020

Copyright © 1998 by Michael Schudson
All rights reserved,
including the right of reproduction
in whole or in part in any form.

THE FREE PRESS and colophon are trademarks
of Simon & Schuster Inc.

Designed by Carla Bolte

Manufactured in the United States of America

10 9 8 7 6 5 4 3 2 1

Library of Congress Cataloging in Publication Data

Schudson, Michael.
    The good citizen : a history of American civic life / Michael Schudson.
        p.   cm.
    Includes bibliographical references (p.   ) and index.
        1. Political participation—United States—History. 2. Political culture—
United States—History. 3. Citizenship—United States. 4. Civics. I. Title.
JK1764.S37 1998
323.6'0973—dc21   98-19991
                                                                        CIP

ISBN 978-1-4516-3162-3

FOR DANIEL, JENNA, AND ZACHARY

CONTENTS

Election Day

In 1996, I served as an election inspector in the San Diego precinct where I vote. Of the five volunteers, I was the only one not yet a grandparent. Though I turned fifty a few days before the election, I was the youngster of the group. The oldest was seventy-three, the same age as Republican candidate Bob Dole.

We worked for fifteen hours in a garage donated year after year by a law enforcement official and his family. He sees this as a part of his children's political education. He received $25 for his efforts, the clerks $35, and I, as supervisor of the clerks, $50.

Dozens of the 563 voters who cast ballots thanked us for our efforts on behalf of this democracy. When voters knew one of the clerks, there was friendly banter and, invariably, some indication that they were proud of their neighbor for volunteering. The labor required to run an election is substantial: with more than 25,000 precincts in California alone, each employing three to five poll workers, the outpouring of volunteer labor is enormous and their organization and training no mean feat.

People brought their children to the polls. Often they took them into the voting booths. A few times babies were handed to one of the clerks while a parent voted. All but the most stubborn of the small children would light up when a clerk offered them an "I Voted" sticker. Some of the kids took advantage of the "demonstrator" voting device. A clerk placed the sample computer punch card in the device and the child could then vote for George Washington, Albert Schweitzer, or Helen Keller for president, and select "yes" or "no" on the proposition that hot dogs should be served at all sporting events.

Not everyone came. Not everyone was registered. But more than seven of ten of those registered voted. It was not always easy. Several visually impaired people brought companions to provide assistance. A neighbor of mine voted and, his jaw drawn tight, observed that his wife, an Alzheimer's patient, was missing a presidential election for the first time.

The clerks divided their labors in an orderly fashion. The first clerk took the voter's name and had the voter sign in on the alphabetical roster. The second clerk marked the voter's name on a list of street addresses. The third clerk handed out the voting device and demonstrated it if the voter was unfamiliar with the punch-card contraption. The fourth clerk received the device back after the voter had voted, folded the ballot, and placed it in the ballot box in the presence of the voter.

Late in the afternoon the clerk who kept up the street address list began to wonder what she was doing. Every hour or two we used the street address list to cross off names on a duplicate list posted publicly at the entrance to the polling place. This was for the convenience of poll watchers from the parties or other organizations. If political workers wanted to know who among their loyalists had not yet voted, this provided them the information they needed.

But not a single poll watcher came. And as the day wore on and the clerk came to the realization that there was no other reason for her function to be performed, she was somewhat disheartened. Indeed, not long after four o'clock, I decided that we would not bother to update the public list any more unless a poll watcher turned up—and still no one did. The county hired hundreds of clerks to subsidize political parties and other voluntary political organizations. But at our precinct, as at increasing numbers of precincts, when parties choose to subsidize television stations rather than citizenship, this is wasted money and labor.

As a Democrat myself, I should probably have hoped for a low turnout in my heavily Republican district. But it was not possible to barter my preference about the election's outcome against my hope that the democratic process would work. There was a sense among the clerks and among the voters that right there, in that unassuming garage, democracy was happening. The question we were most frequently asked was, "How's the turnout?" When we declared that it was good (without much evidence except the sense that we were constantly busy), people were cheered. I was cheered, too.

A number of people, I assume Dole supporters, expressed doubt that their votes would do much good. A number of voters indicated that they had studied hard—or not hard enough to handle the remarkably complex California ballot. "I'll be right back, I left my crib sheet in the car," one voter declared, referring to the "sample ballot" that the county's Registrar of Voters mailed out several weeks before the election. Many voters brought the sample ballot into the voting booth after having marked it at home. One voter shook his head, having left parts of the ballot blank, presumably some of the more obscure local offices or some of the more bewildering state or local propositions, and said, "I shoulda done more homework." In California, at least, voting is not only an act of civic engagement but of cognitive challenge.

When the clerks and I counted the ballots at the end of the day before delivering them to the sheriff's department at the designated checkpoint, we were beat. We had spent more than thirteen hours at the polls (with two 45-minute breaks for each clerk, but none of them took their full breaks). We were cold from sitting in the garage, which got quite chilly after sunset. The seventy-three-year-old clerk's daughter brought by several blankets. The government worker's wife set up a Mr. Coffee for us. But mostly the clerks just persevered. In the end, there was a strong shared sense of a day well spent, especially when the number of ballots in the ballot box tallied perfectly with the number of signatures on the roster of voters.

So goes today's central act of democratic citizenship, a small ritual of neighborly cheer and personal disappointment. People want it to feel like a Frank Capra film, but the experience rarely obliges, if only because it is so forceful a reminder that in this last act of the campaign drama, there is no heroism left for the individual, only a small duty to perform. It takes some imagination to recognize that there is drama, if not spectacle, when tens of millions of people across a vast nation simultaneously engage in the same activity on the same day and with very similar sets of feelings. Apart from holiday observance, nothing else mobilizes so many people in this country to do the same thing at the same time, not even the massive rush to the shopping malls on the day after Christmas. There remains something compelling, even if perennially disappointing, in voting on election day.

Election day today is unlike election days in the American past; Americans have found different ways to establish a public life together over the past three centuries. There have been fundamental historical changes in the American experience of politics and in what Americans of different periods have taken a "good citizen" to be. Picture, for example, a very different scene of voting:

Imagine yourself a voter in colonial Virginia, where Washington, Jefferson, and Madison learned their politics. You are, first of all, a white male owning at least a modest amount of property. Your journey to vote may take several hours since there is probably only one polling place in the county. As you approach the courthouse, you see the sheriff supervising the outdoors election. Although elections are uncontested more often than not, in this case two candidates for the House of Burgesses stand before you, both of them members of prominent local families. You watch the most prominent members of the community, the leading landowner and clergyman, cast their votes, and you know whom they have supported because they announce their selections in loud, clear voices. You do the same, and then step over to the candidate you have voted for, and he treats you to a glass of rum punch. Your act of voting, though you did indeed have a choice of candidates, has been an act of restating and reaffirming the social hierarchy of the community in which no one but a local notable would think of standing for office.

Turning to New England rather than to colonial Virginia, a different model of voting prevails. Here you elect town selectmen and representatives at a town meeting. You are still necessarily a white male property owner or at least a white male taxpayer, but the format of the meeting stresses equality among the members rather than deference to authority. Still, like Virginia, the New England model reflects an organic view that the polity has a single common good and that the leaders of locally prominent, wealthy, and well-established families can be trusted to represent it. Dissent and conflict are no more acceptable in New England than in Virginia.

This is the context in which the founding fathers thought about citizenship. They were generally hostile to political parties and to any politically oriented associations. They expressed significant reservations about a free press, the open deliberation of legislative bodies, candidates' solicitation of the votes of citizens, and public education.

In the long parade from colonial Virginia or colonial New England to a secret ballot in a California garage, American citizenship has changed dramatically. There have been three distinct eras since the colonists first arrived, each with its own virtues and defects, and in the past forty years we have entered into a fourth era. The opening period of the founders, which can be labeled a politics of assent, gave way early in the nineteenth century to a new mass democracy, the world's first. Imagine yourself voting in the mid-nineteenth century. Here there is much more bustle around the polling place. The area is crowded with the banners and torches of rival parties. Election day is not set off from other days but is the culmination of a campaign of several months. You must still be a white male to vote, but not necessarily of property. During the campaign you have marched in torchlight processions, perhaps in military uniform, with a club of like-minded individuals from your party. If you were not active in the campaign, you may be roused on election day by a party worker to escort you to the polls on foot or by carriage. On the road you may encounter clubs or groups from rival parties, and it would not be unusual if fisticuffs or even guns were to dissuade you from casting a ballot after all.

If you do proceed to the ballot box, you may step more lively with the encouragement of a dollar or two from the party—not a bribe but an acknowledgment that voting is a service to your party. A party worker hands you a "ticket" with the printed names of the party's candidates.

The ticket is likely to be distinctive enough in shape and size that poll watchers can readily see what party you vote for as you place the ticket in the ballot box. You are not offended in the least by this openness; indeed, you want your party loyalty to be recognized. Your connection to the party derives not from a strong sense that it offers better public policies but that your party is your party, just as, in our own day, your high school is your high school. In any event, parties tend to be more devoted to distributing offices than to advocating policies. Very likely you have been drawn to your party by the complexion of the ethnocultural groups it favors; your act of voting is an act of solidarity with a partisan alliance. This is a politics of affiliation, not a politics of assent.

To reformers at the end of the nineteenth century, this mode of voting seemed not colorfully carnivalesque but corrupt, and they sought to clean it up. They made campaigning more educational and less emotional. They passed personal registration laws for voters. They enacted a secret ballot. They created an atmosphere in which traditionally loyal party newspapers "bolted" from party-endorsed candidates. They supported civil service reform to limit the rewards parties could offer their partisans. They prohibited electioneering close to the polling place. In short, they celebrated the private, rational "informed citizen" that remains the most cherished ideal in the American voting experience today.

Did they create a better system? They at least created a different one, which instructs us in what citizenship is and should be in novel ways. Political education comes to most people not only from history textbooks or recitations of the Pledge of Allegiance in school but from the presence and practice of political institutions themselves. Elections educate us. The ballot educates us. Parties educate us. The division among federal, state, and local jurisdictions educates us. The First Amendment educates us. The product of this education is our citizenship, the political expectations and aspirations people inherit and internalize.

When children go out to play Little League, their coach offers all sorts of verbal instructions and encouragements. Anyone who listens to the coach will hear that the point of Little League is that everyone should learn to play baseball and have a good time. Everyone will get to play. Every member of the team is just as valuable as any other member. Teamwork is essential and teammates should encourage one another. As soon as the game begins, however, the kids receive an even more powerful, but unspoken, set of instructions: the pitcher and the catcher are the key positions and only the best players will have a chance for those spots. The first baseman and the shortstop are the next most important positions and only the most skillful players will play there regularly. Relatively few balls are hit to the outfield, so that is where the weaker athletes are platooned. Baseball demands of all but the most ruthlessly egalitarian coaches that they submit their democratic aspirations to the logic of the game. No one will have any fun if the pitcher can't get the ball over the plate or if the first baseman can't catch a ball thrown right to her.

What values, then, are the children learning and who is their teacher? In part, the coach teaches. In part, the children teach one another, usually without mincing words. The most unrelenting teacher is the game of baseball itself, to which the coach's "Let's all just go out there and have fun" seems a feeble countercurrent.

To understand American political experience, I am directing attention to the instructions of the game itself. It is in this respect that I emphasize basic rules of political practice, including formal constitutional provisions, statutory laws, and conventional patterns of public electoral activity. This is not all there is to politics, but nothing more fundamentally shapes people's grasp of public life and their concept of citizenship.

The rules of the political game have obviously changed over our history. Eighteenth-century American political authority was rule by gentlemen; the nineteenth century brought rule by numbers, majorities of associated men organized in parties; and twentieth-century American politics is rule by everyone, and no one, all at once. This is expressed in government by the central importance of impersonal rules themselves—in civil service examinations, formal procedures of review and record-keeping in bureaucracies, requirements of public notice, and practices of parliamentary procedure. It is expressed in the life of the private citizen by the importance of rights, legally legitimated claims upon the government.

In fact, rights have grown so important since the civil rights movement that they define a fourth model of citizenship in our time. The "rights-bearing citizen" has not displaced the "informed citizen" at the ballot box, but the expansion of rights-consciousness has made the polling place less clearly the central act of political participation than it once was. The "political," carried on the wing of rights, has now diffused into everyday life.

Another way to characterize the past three hundred years of political change is to say that the type of authority by which society is governed shifted from personal authority (gentlemen) to interpersonal authority (parties, coalitions, and majorities), to impersonal authority (science, expertise, legal rights, and information). The locus of authority has moved from shared, generally religious, values located in the community to the formal polity and elections, to individual rights guaranteed by administrative fairness and the courts. The geographical center of politics has shifted from the countryside to the cities to the suburbs and perhaps, today, to "technoburbs," "postsuburbs," or "edge cities," or whatever we name our newer habitations.[1] Correspondingly, the kind of knowledge a good citizen requires has changed: in an age of gentlemen, the citizen's relatively rare entrances into public discussion or controversy could be guided by his knowledge of social position; in the era of rule by majorities, the citizens' voting could be led by the enthusiasm and rhetoric of parties and their most active partisans; in the era of experts and bureaucracies, the citizens had increasingly to learn to trust their own canvass of newspapers, interest groups, parties, and other sources of knowledge, only occasionally supported by the immediacy of human contact; and in the emerging age of rights, citizens learn to catalog what entitlements they may have and what forms of victimization they may knowingly or unknowingly have experienced.

We can also say that the "ownership" of the political sphere has shifted. In the eighteenth century, political activity was set in motion and controlled by gentlemen; in the nineteenth century, it was organized by parties; in the twentieth century, after democratization had reduced the authority of social class and reform had seriously weakened the parties, multiple claimants compete to set the standards of political life. The media, the political candidates set adrift from party, the increasingly important, well-funded, and professionally staffed interest groups, the government bureaucracies shielded in many respects from close public scrutiny, and individual citizens empowered by the expansion of "rights" all bid to define what counts as politics and what the experience of politics might mean.

Each reorganization of political experience has had its own virtues and defects. I do not join the common practice of beating up on our own era because it fails to live up to the standards of another day. It goes without saying that a democrat today, plunked down in colonial Virginia, would find slavery a savage practice and the exclusion of women and the propertyless from the franchise inexcusable. Likewise, a gentleman from colonial Virginia visiting our world during an election campaign would be appalled at how candidates readily reshape principles to appease public opinion or how they quickly shed a sense of the public good to win the financial backing of special interest groups. He might well wonder: whatever became of civic virtue?

Comparisons of this sort lack both a sense of history and a sense of sociology, an understanding of the complex coherence of a society at a given time. We do not have to accept a society, least of all our own, on its own terms, but we do have to know what those terms are. We can gain inspiration from the past, but we cannot import it. None of the older models of authority and of citizenship will suffice. We require a citizenship fit for our own day.[2]

The use of history should not be to condemn the present from some purportedly higher standard of the past, but to know where we stand in time. If my argument persuades, it will at least convince the reader that today's most honored notion of citizenship, the ideal of the "informed citizen," arose in the Progressive Era as part of a broad-gauge attack on the power of political parties. The nation's framers would not have recognized it. The institutional practices that were legislated to make it realizable were made deeply inadequate by the emergence of a complex, national industrial society. Moreover, the informed citizen model has had less influence on progress toward a society of free and equal citizens than the model of the "rights-bearing citizen" that began to displace it in recent decades. Even so, the rights-bearing model has curiously failed to win the cherished place in civic education or public discourse that the informed citizen has now held for nearly a century.

What can political experience be today? What should it be? What are the structures of power in society that bear most on defining it? The ideals of republican virtue, party loyalty, informed citizenship, and rights-conscious citizenship, by themselves, cannot adequately serve as moral guideposts for us today. I hold out the hope, nonetheless, that the sum of them, reconceived and reinvigorated, may still serve us well. What kind of citizenship, of the kinds that may be possible, should we strive for? What kinds of standards, of the kinds that can resonate with people's life experiences now, should be held up as ideals? I seek to anchor these questions so that they can be addressed critically and productively.

It is easy to wonder, thinking of California garages and comparable locations across the country, if the Grand Experiment that Jefferson inspired, Madison nursed into being, Washington protected, Lincoln rededicated, and King revitalized has come to no more than this. Has the great "choosing day" that Walt Whitman declared the Western world's "powerfulest scene and show," more splendid than Yosemite or Yellowstone or Niagara, been reduced to these drab scenes?[3]

It *has* come to this. But what *this* is, what this prosaic exercise in American polling places at the end of the twentieth century means and how we came to it, is deeper than at first appears, and nearer the rushing force of Niagara than one might imagine.

Chapter 1

Colonial Origins of American Political Practice

1690–1787

Prospectus

A deferential society in the classical—that is, eighteenth-century English and American—sense is usually conceived of as consisting of an elite and a nonelite, in which the nonelite regard the elite, without too much resentment, as being of a superior status and culture to their own and consider elite leadership in political matters to be something normal and natural.[1]

On September 25, 1690, Benjamin Harris published a newspaper. This Boston coffeehouse proprietor, formerly a politically controversial publisher and bookseller in London, intended his *Publick Occurrences Both Forreign and Domestick* to appear monthly or more often "if any Glut of Occurrences happen." Harris planned to give an account "of such considerable things as have arrived unto our Notice." This would include

11

"Memorable Occurents of Divine Providence" and other items to help people everywhere "better understand the Circumstances of Publique Affairs, both abroad and at home."

These lofty ambitions notwithstanding, Harris made a serious miscalculation: he neglected to get governmental approval for his publication. Military news in the first issue included criticism of the Iroquois Indians, England's allies against the French in King William's War. Harris attacked these "miserable Salvages [sic]" and hoped that the military effort to take Canada might triumph without Indian assistance so that with an all-Christian force "God alone will have all the Glory."[2] Most likely it was this article that led authorities to kill the paper, and it never saw a second issue. This was an inauspicious inauguration for American journalism. No other newspaper appeared in the American colonies until John Campbell, Boston's postmaster, began the first sustained newspaper in 1704, the Boston News-Letter.

The year 1690 is a somewhat arbitrary starting point for the history of American journalism and more arbitrary still if the beginnings of the newspaper are to symbolize the opening of an American public sphere. A "public sphere," as current academic discourse uses the term, refers both to a public forum independent of government and to private associations beyond the household where people come together to discuss public affairs. A public sphere may come to life in verbal give-and-take at a tavern, in a public square, on the courthouse steps—or in the pages of a newspaper or pamphlet.[3] It is the playing field for citizenship; democratic citizenship may bear fruit in the formal acts of voting or legislating, but it germinates in the soil of a free public life.

In Britain's North American colonies in the 1600s, written public communication about politics was scant. Elections were the exception, not the rule, and where there were elections it was taken for granted that results should be unanimous.[4] Early elections in Virginia and in Plymouth Colony were uncontested. New York did not even have a colony-wide elective assembly until 1683. The first seventy years of elections in America, one historian concludes, "produced few real encounters and generated little sustained interest among the populace."[5] Government was a modest enterprise; it operated in accord with and as an extension of social hierarchy, not as an expression of popular interests or passions. Public discussion of governmental affairs barely existed.

So the last decade of the seventeenth century is not too late a time to begin a history of a distinctly public political life for America. Is it too early? Governmental functions were few, governmental resources scant, political participation severely limited, and popular interest in government generally slight. Still, the 1690s saw not only the beginning of the American newspaper, abortive as it was, but the first stirring of an inter-colonial post office. Thomas Neale received a royal patent for an inter-colonial post in 1691 and by 1693 began service between New York, Massachusetts, and New Hampshire.[6] There was also significantly increased electoral activity in a number of the colonies in these years and the representative assembly was becoming "a fixed feature" of colonial government.[7]

Moreover, the Glorious Revolution of 1688 that deposed the Catholic James II, brought William of Orange to the throne, and brought forth the British Declaration of Rights, cheered the Protestant colonies, and brought to England and its territories a solidified faith in parliamentary government. It encouraged political thought that defined a place for representative institutions. Popular involvement in government increased at this time in dramatic episodes, including the ouster of the royal governor of New England in Boston and a bloody rebellion in New York. At the same time, the new regime in England integrated the colonies more tightly into the empire. Colonists were increasingly drawn into England's political affairs in King William's War (1689–97) and Queen Anne's War (1702–13).[8] England gained greater control over colonial affairs, but this enlarged as much as it constricted public life. A new charter for Massachusetts in 1691 reduced that colony's political autonomy, reserving to the king the right to appoint the governor, to veto laws, and to select the governor's council from a slate provided by the House. At the same time the new charter enforced greater secularism, providing voting rights and liberty of conscience to all Protestants, not just the Calvinist faithful.[9] Voting was tied to property rights, not to church membership. Citizens of

Massachusetts began to show greater interest in political participation and greater skepticism of constituted authority.[10]

The thirteen colonies, which began as a set of very different religious, commercial, and social experiments, became more alike in the eighteenth century—and more English. Urbanization, the spread of print, the development of professions, professional associations, colleges, and other institutions promoted a common culture more uniformly anglicized across the colonies. Maryland, for instance, founded as a haven for Roman Catholics, disenfranchised the Catholics and established the Church of England after the Glorious Revolution. Political aspirations and ideals throughout the colonies were anglicized as colonials increasingly praised the British constitution as the great political instrument of the age. They took the Revolution of 1688 as the fount of the British political heritage and the modern summit of human political experience.[11] In 1767, when John Dickinson wrote his famous *Letters from a Farmer in Pennsylvania*, he chose November 5 as the date for the first letter, the seventy-ninth anniversary of William's triumphant landing on the English coast.

By the early 1700s, despite continuing differences among the New England colonies, the middle colonies, and the Southern colonies, the political culture of colonial America, as a whole, differed from British or other political cultures of the day and from the political culture of the United States after 1776.[12] A number of central features were common to all:

1. Consensus: The political and social ideals of early colonial leaders stressed consensus and community.
2. Deference: Colonial politics and society operated by a practical ethic of deference and an assumption of social hierarchy.
3. Monarchy: Colonial societies took monarchy for granted, including both loyalty to the king and identification with the rights of Englishmen they believed it the king's obligation to protect.
4. Property, Virtue, and Independence: The colonies were, by English standards, relatively egalitarian and the franchise widely extended, but the colonists' political philosophy stressed the im-

portance of economic independence as a qualification for the franchise and took some forms of inequality for granted (the subordination of women and slaves).

5. Limited Government: Colonial governments retained the right to regulate all kinds of behaviors and even beliefs far beyond what would be acceptable today, but they reached affirmatively in only limited ways into people's everyday lives; they simply did not *do* much. The content of political dispute was rarely elevated, the ambition for political life was not differentiated from more general ambitions for advancement, and general interest in politics was low.

6. Oral, Dramatistic, and Print Culture: Colonial politics was conducted in oral and dramatistic modes as well as print, but print came to have a growing place that helped transform the very idea of politics.

As we examine these relatively enduring features of political culture for the period from 1690 to the 1760s, you will also see elements of social change, particularly those that moved toward the enlargement of a public sphere. In this three quarters of a century, there was significant growth in the number and power of representative institutions; expansion of print media and published reports of politics; growth of civil society—nongovernmental associations for the expression of political opinion, including the press, spurred especially by opposition to British colonial policy; and democratization of family, church, and social relations.

Not all of the social change was onward and upward. The movement toward representative institutions came in fits and starts. Competitiveness in Virginia elections was more common from 1720 to 1750 than in the 1760s and 1770s.[13] Representative government was in some respects more autonomous in Massachusetts in the seventeenth century than in the eighteenth century after the reincorporation of the colony as a royal province. The level of popular political interest and political participation grew with economic woes and military involvements only to die off again to lethargic levels in calmer times.[14] Had it not been for the anticolonial struggles after 1765 and the Revolution that consolidated republican tendencies and catapulted people into a new world where republican values were vigorously promoted, the gradual social transformation of the early eighteenth century might not be seen retrospectively as leading up to something. But, as events took the turn they did, it is now hard to view them otherwise.

Consensus and Community: The Mythic Town Meeting

The New England Town is one of the myths out of which Americans' conception of their history has been constructed, along with such others as The Liberty Bell, George Washington, and The Frontier.[15]

The Edenic quality of the town meeting myth makes it the inevitable starting point for anyone who thinks about political life in the colonial era. Colonial history is not New England history writ large, but whether or not we are genealogically children of the Puritans, we are ideological kin. The New England town as the fountainhead of modern democracy remains a potent ideal of how a democratic political system should function. In the late nineteenth century, critics of the party-dominated political system looked to the town meeting and a resurgence of direct democracy as a likely solution to political ills.[16] As recently as the 1992 election, Americans borrowed the notion of the town meeting to speak of electronic town meetings and electronic town halls to justify the experiment of presidential candidates appearing to listen to the public on televised talk shows.

Yet the actual colonial New England town meetings were a far cry from the myth they inspired. Town meetings were open only to property-owning adult males of the community and, early on, only those who were church members. In Dedham, Massachusetts, the requirement of property ownership for at least some periods in the seventeenth century disenfranchised about half of the male taxpayers. Besides restrictions on the franchise, there were limitations on the powers of the town meeting itself by the prerogatives routinely granted to the selectmen. Selectmen were invariably older, richer members of the church, regularly returned to office. They called the town meetings, but not often, and led discussion of an agenda they set themselves.[17]

The town meeting not only failed to include everyone but failed to govern everything. Towns in Rhode Island were practically autonomous republics early on, but in Massachusetts they were more closely supervised by the state government and in Connecticut the General Court of the state exercised even more control, legislating what officers the town meetings should elect and what functions they should serve. The General Court intervened directly in disputes between towns, whether the towns wanted such aid or not.

Within the Connecticut towns, the militia was not an arm of the town meeting but an independent institution answerable only to the General Court. Churches operated outside the town meeting, too. Church societies were empowered by the colony to levy taxes, build meetinghouses, and run primary schools. The town meetings were not even constituted to select representatives to the colony-wide government; the "freemen" of a town met twice a year for the purpose of electing deputies to the General Assembly.[18]

Further, not all of those eligible to vote in town meetings did so. Political scientist Jane Mansbridge concludes that voter turnout in eighteenth-century Massachusetts ranged from 20 to 60 percent of eligible voters for town elections. (Only 10 to 30 percent of adult males voted in colony-wide contests.)[19] As she puts it, using the example of Dedham, Massachusetts: "Even though no more than fifty-eight men were eligible to come to the Dedham town meeting and to make the decisions for the town, even though the decisions to which they addressed themselves were vital to their existence, even though every inhabitant was required to live within one mile of the meeting place, even though each absence from the meeting brought a fine, and even though a town crier personally visited the house of every latecomer half an hour after the meeting had begun, only 74 percent of those eligible actually showed up at the typical town meeting between 1636 and 1644."[20] For most of the eighteenth century, only 15 to 25 percent of adult male Bostonians went to the polls. In New England generally, turnout ranged from 10 to 25 percent. Turnout in the middle colonies was higher, 20 to 40 percent in New York and Pennsylvania.[21] Later in the century, where more records for more towns are available, attendance was rarely as high as 50 percent.

In Connecticut, levels of attendance at both town meetings and freemen's meetings were generally under 50 percent.[22] Many generations later, in the Concord where Ralph Waldo Emerson boasted of "the whole population of the town having a voice in the affair," attendance averaged 42 percent.[23]

The most telling point against the picture of the New England town meeting as the model democratic institution is not the limited participation in decision-making but the normative presumption that open discussion of differences was to be avoided at all costs. The object of the meeting was order, not representation. There was nothing in the town meeting to show special respect to the individual or to honor and respect differences of opinion. The New England town fathers praised "harmony, conformity, and consensus. Real freedom (though they would not have formulated it precisely in this way) was possible only within a community of like-minded men."[24]

The town meetings did change over time. In some cases, they became more participatory and more inclusive. In Massachusetts in 1691, the General Court reduced the property qualification for voting from 80 pounds to 20 pounds of taxable estate; in Dedham, this increased the percentage of males eligible to vote from 40 to over 70 percent.[25] In Dedham and Watertown, meetings became more powerful relative to the selectmen after 1680. There were more of them (three or four a year instead of only one), they grew more contentious, and selectmen were returned to office less and less regularly.[26] In other cases, as in Connecticut, the number of town meetings declined steadily during the 1700s (until the increasingly contentious political activity leading up to the Revolution revived them) and selectmen were steadily granted greater discretionary power by their towns.[27] Still, the emphasis on consensus was fundamental, even in voting. Voting was not an act of individual expression but "a sign of . . . collective union with the established interpreters and custodians of God's eternal law."[28]

The New England insistence on consensus remained high throughout the colonial period. The term "liberty" was most often applied to the liberty of the town against outside influence rather than liberties of the individual against the town.[29] In contrast, in New York, New Jersey, and

Pennsylvania, the elite cohesion that obtained in New England (and in the Southern colonies) was elusive. The middle colonies were by ethnicity and ethos the most diverse, and they experienced hard-fought political contention much earlier than the other colonies. There was even some defense of party rivalry. An essay in the *New-York Gazette* (in 1734) proclaimed that "Some Opposition, tho' it proceed not entirely from a public Spirit, is not only necessary in free Governments, but of great Service to the Public."[30] But this remained until well into the nineteenth century a minority view in American political life. Long after the "community" of the New England towns weakened or dissolved (for good as well as ill), the idea of a covenant, entered into by political equals, remained a potent emblem of political community in American life.

Deference: Gentlemen Take the Lead

In the American colonies, gentlemen called their social inferiors by their first names and expected to be addressed as "Mister" or "Your Honor" in return. The gentry could be very familiar with their inferiors, joking or teasing with them, but they were marked off by speech, dress, manners, and a presumption of gentility even if their learning and character did not live up to the presumption. Social hierarchy was less pronounced than in England, and the distance between ranks less steep, but colonists took for granted a natural hierarchy of people of different degrees. In Massachusetts, for instance, when the Puritans entered church for Sunday service, they found their seats assigned by a church committee according to their social rank in the community. Such signs of hierarchy were powerfully reinforced by systems of patronage; deference, as historian Gordon Wood puts it, "was not a mere habit of mind; it had real economic and social force behind it."[31] Men of property were not customers for artisans so much as their patrons, and not employers so much as masters. Society was small, it was conducted by personal relations, and these relations invariably served to reassert the naturalness of social distinction.

This certainly pertained to political relations. Even in politically volatile Boston, the most important offices in town government were filled by a small set of leaders of the highest social standing, men to whom others instinctively deferred.[32] American political democracy owes much to the Pilgrim fathers, to be sure, but there is as much separation as continuity between them and the founding fathers. New England shared with Western civilization generally the assumption of hierarchy, not the premise of political or social equality.

Deference influenced not only a conception of who was fit for leadership but what was owed leaders in office. One obligation was to trust leaders to make wise decisions. In Massachusetts, the House began publishing a journal of proceedings in 1715. From the journal an attentive reader could learn about the basic disputes between the governor and the House, but could not have established his own representative's position. A roll call vote would have made these views public, but the House rarely employed it.[33] The confidentiality of the proceedings reflected not only the legislature's fear of monarchical interference but its assumption that voters did not need to know just what their leaders were up to.

Deference affected every element in the political process. In nominating people for office, it helped support the norm of the noncompetitive election. In Virginia from 1728 to 1775, only a third of elections to the House of Burgesses were contested, and it is likely that this was higher than in most of the colonies.[34] Compared to some other colonies, Virginia had few elections of any sort, contested or otherwise. Before 1776 the only elections in the Commonwealth were for the House of Burgesses, and these were relatively rare. When the freeholders gathered on election day in Virginia, they were generally asked only to affirm the candidates who ran unopposed.[35] Colonial Virginians did not see representative government and aristocracy as incompatible but interpenetrating. The franchise was widely distributed among freeholders, but all candidates for office were chosen from a small set of gentlemen.[36] In New England, many offices at both the local and state level were elective and elections were held frequently, but patterns of deference persisted there, too.

Elections in Virginia were rituals for the reinforcement of gentry rule. Gentlemen were distinguished by family name, dress, the possession of a carriage, a large house, and ample holdings of land and slaves.

They were invariably Episcopalian by religion and frequently held public office.[37] Even though the outcome of an election was not normally in doubt, election day was exciting. Since there was only one polling place in each county, people came from miles away to vote. Elections were usually scheduled for court days, when people would come to the county seat to transact business in land or slaves, or to do other business in the court. (Do not let the term "court" conjure up magnificent Georgian architecture; civic buildings in the colonies were few and "courts" frequently met in taverns.)[38] Voters would proclaim their vote orally when the clerk called their names. As the clerk wrote down the freeholder's vote, the candidate for whom he had voted would often rise, bow, and thank him.

The election was conducted in a very personal way and was understood in terms of personal loyalties to community notables. The county was the largest constituency in Virginia, and most counties had less than a thousand voters. In an election at Frederick Court House in 1758, once the sheriff, clerks, and four candidates for two seats in the House of Burgesses were assembled, the first voter to approach was Thomas Lord Fairfax, the leading figure in county affairs. The next voter, William Meldrum, was the chief clergyman in the area and, like Fairfax, he voted for George Washington and Fairfax's nephew, Colonel Thomas Bryan Martin. The next several voters were also local leaders. It was not difficult for those who followed them to know which way the wind was blowing.[39]

There was still more to the influence of the gentry. For one thing, gentlemen were entitled to vote in any county where their land ownership could meet the freehold requirement and therefore voted, if they chose, in several counties. A gentleman could stand for office in any county where he was eligible to vote and so could select the county where he had the best chance. As for influencing the votes of others, gentlemen not only voted early and audibly but "treated" other voters to liquor. Rum punch, sometimes cookies and cakes, and occasionally a barbecue were part of the festivities. George Washington paid for dinner and a ball during one election for the House of Burgesses; in another his agent provided 391 voters and various others with 160 gallons of rum,

rum punch, wine, and beer.[40] This was not a bribe but a ritual of deference—the freeholder offered a vote to the gentleman, the gentleman acknowledged the favor with "treating." Gentlemen would often treat all voters, regardless of their votes, to confirm their character as liberal and magnanimous.

Elections, then, reaffirmed the leading gentlemen's right to govern. Symbolic gestures earn their social keep not so much by their clarity but by their capacity to combine in persuasive ways apparently disparate or even contradictory cultural features. In this case, the same ritual that reconfirmed social hierarchy also reminded citizens that legitimate government must operate by consent.[41] If people willingly agreed to defer, they strenuously objected to any signs of coercion or, as they called it, influence. Leaders would be willingly selected from the group of natural leaders offered to the community, but they were themselves subject to common understandings of what kinds of power governmental officers should restrain themselves from exercising.[42]

In New England, voting took place in town meetings by voice vote, by raising hands, by a "division of the house" in which people bodily moved to one side or another of the meetinghouse to indicate their preference, or sometimes by paper ballot. The ritual of treating was not common, although in elections for militia officers treating and electioneering were usual.[43] The difference in voting method did not mean a difference, however, in the general practice of electing men of wealth, prominent social standing, and family connection.[44]

While election day could be festive, little in the system of elections anywhere in the colonies encouraged political interest or political attention as opposed to routine voting. Voter turnout was not high. Apathy was common throughout the colonies, as Bernard Bailyn suggests, "in part because of lack of real alternatives in a society dominated by the sense that the natural social leaders of society should be the political leaders. . . ."[45]

The voting process itself was in most colonies open and public, although a secret ballot existed in South Carolina and North Carolina during the first half of the eighteenth century while Pennsylvania and Connecticut law permitted secrecy.[46] Secrecy was not supported by the rationale that twentieth-century citizens would see as self-evident: that it protects the autonomy of the voter and the integrity of the vote. In fact, notable authorities judged secrecy in voting a danger to sound government. Montesquieu, a favorite political philosopher in the colonies, judged public voting a "fundamental law of democracy." He held that the lower class "ought to be directed by those of higher rank, and restrained within bounds by the gravity of eminent personages."[47]

Deferential though colonial society was, it was not an aristocracy. If England was unusually republican compared to the Continent, the colonies were unusually egalitarian compared to England. There was no legal support in the colonies for aristocratic titles or privileges, nor a branch of the colonial legislatures to specifically represent aristocratic interests. The better elements in colonial society did not have a clearly delineated function or even a sharply focused identity. In America, it was always possible to rise, Benjamin Franklin style, from obscurity to honored position.[48]

So compared to England, the colonies were renegade, individualistic, and distrustful of authority.[49] The Americans were a special breed. Well before the Revolution, they were said to possess a characteristic individualism, optimism, and enterprise. Even among the stern Puritans, belief in the primacy of self-control and self-mastery led to a form of child-rearing that emphasized the internalization of social norms rather than deference to external authority. Cotton Mather's 1710 *Bonifacius: Or Essays to Do Good*, borrowing directly from John Locke's writings on education, urged discipline of children based on the withdrawal of affection rather than on physical punishment. He wanted a practice of child-rearing so that children "shall fear to offend me, and yet heartily love to see me."[50]

The question of an aristocratic house in the legislature would later occasion debate in the Constitutional Convention. There was great support for a legislature of two branches but confusion over what the rationale for the second house should be. The classical view of balanced government, stated especially by Montesquieu, was that the best government was organized to represent the monarch, the aristocracy, and the general population each in a different institution within the government. The English model was, of course, the obvious one to adapt—executive, House of Lords, and House of Commons. But without an aristocracy or any interest in establishing one, what justified the upper house of the legislature? The best answer, although it is not clear that the founding fathers ever agreed on any answer, seems to have been that a representative assembly itself could be a source of tyranny and that it was best to provide two houses as brakes upon the presumption of either.[51] Even if the upper house had roots in a deferential society, this rationale brought it into alignment with the fundamental moral and civil equality of persons that democratic citizenship would one day presume.

How Republicans Could Love a King

Colonial Americans took great pride in their liberty and in their rights within the structure of royal government. They assumed that a degree of self-government was their rightful British heritage. This, indeed, was the source of the secrecy of legislative proceedings. In England, the House of Commons was very protective of its right to deliberate in secret—without kings or lords overlooking—and this pattern was borrowed in the colonies.[52] When the founding fathers referred to freedom of speech, they were more likely to mean the freedom of legislatures to deliberate than freedom of citizens to speak their minds.[53]

Notions of popular sovereignty or republicanism as such did not have to arise for a view of popular representation and popular rights to take hold. British conventions of monarchy in the seventeenth and eighteenth centuries were consistent with popular representation and popular protest. Monarchy had been "republicanized" long before the colonists gave any thought to throwing over monarchy altogether.[54] In the political culture of the British monarchy, the "king" and the "people" were both legitimate entities whose voices should be balanced within government—the jury for the people, the judge for the king; elected representatives for the people, a governor for the king. As the colonists understood this system, the king was obliged to be solicitous of the people's welfare because God had raised him up above the people to protect and serve them.[55] In Virginia, William Stith, chaplain to the

House of Burgesses, expressed this view in a sermon in 1745. He explained that the saying "The King can do no wrong" meant that the character of the British monarchy prevented him from doing wrong: "This is to say, his Prerogative can never extend so far, as to injure and oppress his People."[56]

Faith in the monarchy, then, did not preclude popular rebellion, nor did belief in popular rule preclude accommodation to royalty. As late as 1768, in Charleston, South Carolina, the king's birthday was widely celebrated, although the practice of illuminating houses for the occasion disappeared in the next two years. Almost until the outbreak of hostilities in 1775, colonists sought not an American revolution but a British one, understanding their cause to be the reclaiming of basic British rights under the protection of monarchy. Colonial leaders repeatedly argued that Parliament, not the king, oppressed them.[57]

The colonists were deeply British. More members of the Continental Congress of 1774 had traveled to London than had previously been to Philadelphia.[58] There was simply no readiness for, let alone inevitability about, the revolution soon to come. Even Samuel Adams, often pictured as a manipulative propagandist pushing toward independence, was seeking reform within the British system as late as 1774.[59] Colonial leaders did not easily envision a future in which they would not be British subjects. Their speculations in the 1760s and early 1770s are notable for what one historian has called their "essential tone of passivity."[60] The idea of government without a king was not on the political drawing boards.

Over the course of the eighteenth century, the practice of representation, especially in the lower house of colonial assemblies, became entrenched. In New England, elective assemblies had been important early, but in early Massachusetts elected officials were supposed to be superior men serving God, not representative men serving constituencies. That the freeholders voted in annual elections did not lead them to conclude that representatives should express popular desires. In other colonies, it was only after 1689 that the lower houses began to be the leading lawmakers. Between 1689 and 1763 the lower houses increasingly won the power to tax, to sit separately from the governor's council, to initiate legislation, to battle the governor and his council with assurance, and to come to speak authoritatively in the voice of the colonial population as a whole. The lower houses in Pennsylvania and Massachusetts attained dominance in their colonies by the 1730s or 1740s. In New York and South Carolina, the lower houses were powerful by 1750. In New Jersey and Virginia, the greater legislative demands and more frequent legislative sittings that came with the Seven Years' War (1756–63) helped the lower houses take control. During the war some of the assemblies demonstrated a "soaring self-confidence," and all of them, operating on the large field of play that war provided, gained vital political experience. This trained a generation of politicians who would be unwilling to return to a more dependent status when, after 1763, Parliament introduced harsh new measures to bring the colonies into line.[61]

All of this speaks to the successful efforts of local economic and social elites to gain control of their affairs.[62] Their power in the assemblies was not "democratic," but it operated through the forms of representative government and paid homage to a set of principles that, as they came to be articulated after 1765, would ultimately underwrite republican government.

What representation meant still differed across the colonies. In New England, where representation was by towns rather than by parish or shire—where, in other words, the constituency was corporately constituted and representatives were elected at town meetings—there was a tendency for the meetings to control representatives by providing them mandates or instructions to carry out. In the middle and Southern colonies, where elections were held not in a meetinghouse by a people assembled but on the green or outside the courthouse with people announcing their votes one at a time, there was no corporate form of organization that even could have offered instructions.[63]

Apart from the election itself, the representative was the primary medium of communication between government and citizenry. Citizens, even voting citizens, were not expected to keep informed, to follow the news, to monitor government through a political party or an interest group, or in any other way to be in continuous communication with the government. They were to elect their representatives, go about their business, and make another judgment about their representatives at the next election. In Britain, representation "did not mean communication with the electors, and only on the septennial occasions of a general election did it mean accountability to them."[64] Even in the colonies it was only after the Revolution that a second meaning of representation entered popular understanding, one that assumed legislators should keep the people informed of their work and that citizens should judge public servants on a continuing basis.[65]

All that said, representation in the colonies had begun to imply, as it did not in England, that the representative should not only use his own judgment but also speak for his constituency. This seems clear in the growing prevalence of residency requirements in the colonies. Representatives were expected to live among the people they represented. This practice was uncommon in Britain where, even in theory, members of Parliament did not "represent" the views of local constituencies. In the colonies, however, local representation was fundamental.[66] Representatives were expected to have wealth and the training and judgment social standing provided, but they were also expected to possess local knowledge and to identify with the interests of their constituents. This was historically new. Here the seeds of conflict were sown between the representatives' obligation to their own best judgment of the public good and their responsibility to the interests of the people.

Republican Virtue and a Theory of Voting

From the early colonial days until the 1760s, American politics was politics by assent, elections largely a communal ritual of reaffirming rule by gentlemen. In the seventeenth century there were no campaigns for office by rival candidates and in the eighteenth century they remained the exception. Only under the impact of urban life, the growing size and heterogeneity of populations, the increasing availability of print for political argumentation, and the ferment of the resistance to England did this substantially change. Open political controversy and electoral competition emerged first in the cities. As early as 1739 a pamphlet in Boston attacked Governor Jonathan Belcher and urged voters to know "the opinions and intentions" of candidates for office and to "survey their past behavior" in official positions. This was a somewhat daring suggestion, as a letter to the *Boston Gazette* indicated in criticizing the pamphlet. The letter denounced candidates who "attack characters of the highest station and influence the people by the meanest acts, and poorest scandal."[67] Open criticism of incumbent officeholders at that point was still far from accepted practice.

The guiding political ideal was that of a mixed government, one that would incorporate the strengths of both popular participation and aristocratic restraint. There was no question in the minds of colonial leaders that a property qualification for the suffrage was a necessary bulwark of good government. Eighteenth-century political thinkers understood that landowners would have an interest in and enduring attachment to society. People would be granted the vote if, in the words of Section 6 of the Declaration of Rights of the Virginia Constitution of 1776, there was "sufficient evidence of permanent common interest with, and attachment to, the community."[68] This reflected not so much a conservative approval of wealth but a romantic agrarianism, a devotion to the ideal of the yeoman farmer. The virtues of the farmer—independence, self-sufficiency, a permanent commitment to the community, and a high regard for protecting the same virtues in others—were also the virtues of the citizen. In a classic statement of this position, Thomas Jefferson wrote, "Those who labour in the earth are the chosen people of God, if ever He had a chosen people, whose breasts He has made his peculiar deposit for substantial and genuine virtue."[69] Eighteenth-century colonial thinkers believed farmers had the requisite virtues to sustain a republic, but they saw the rise of commerce and manufacturing on the horizon and feared that it would lead to the decay of the virtues on which republican government depended in America, as they believed it had in England.[70]

Six or seven colonies (New Jersey is a complicated mixed case) established a freehold qualification for voting, meaning that to vote one must own land of a certain value in income or rent. Other colonies used a taxpaying rather than freehold qualification.[71] Voting was restricted in other ways, too. Only three colonies specified that voting was limited to males; elsewhere, it went without saying. Republicanism was "gendered" from the outset. Women, like slaves and servants, were defined by their dependence; citizenship belonged only to those who were masters of their own lives.[72] But autonomy was not always enough. Free blacks were denied the vote by statute in North Carolina, South Carolina, Virginia, and Georgia. A statute of 1701 prohibited Catholics from voting in New York if they refused a special oath, and there were barriers to Catholic suffrage in other colonies, too. Jews were specifically barred from voting in Rhode Island, Maryland, New York, and South Carolina.[73]

All this applies to colony-wide voting; local provisions were frequently more liberal. Because property was much more widely disseminated in the colonies than in England, the proportion of men in the voting population was larger, too. While the formal limits to the suffrage testify to the colonists' general philosophy, imported from England, actual enfranchisement by these rules was unusually high. In Rhode Island, for instance, 75 percent of free adult males met the property qualifications for voting, although this was probably higher than in most colonies.[74] Besides, in practice, the suffrage regulations were not rigidly enforced. So it is a matter of interpretation whether to emphasize that colonial belief in the virtues of property continued a premodern, antidemocratic worldview or to emphasize that relatively broad enfranchisement was the nursery of a more egalitarian political society.[75]

It is equally a matter of judgment whether to emphasize the continuing assumptions of hierarchy and social deference or, instead, the relative frequency with which people of modest means and no family standing rose to social respectability and prominence.[76] Likewise, is it more sensible to emphasize the acceptance of representative assemblies or the rarity with which colonists actually took advantage of them and voted? Colonial politics is, in some facets, preface to our own; in others, it stands on the other side of a great gulf, the democratic transition of the early nineteenth century.

The Blur of Politics and Society

It is not easy to locate "politics" as a separate institutional domain in the colonial era. To be sure, there were appointive and elective councils and assemblies. There were officers with power delegated by king or people to make public policies, though even here there was a lot of ambiguity about who or what institutions held what kind of sovereign authority.[77] But membership in these bodies or access to these offices derived from social standing near the upper reaches of the social hierarchy. The colonists understood politics as a responsibility attached to high social standing. One might imagine, as a rough modern comparison, a university community and ask, what is the distinctly political sphere within the faculty? Formally an elected faculty senate may govern, but by long established custom, senior faculty have greater obligation than junior to serve in it. There is little suspense about who will be nominated or elected. Senior faculty in prestigious departments have greater obligation than those in minor departments. Just as the role of the faculty in governing the university is an extension of its central function in the university's research and teaching, so were colonial legislatures simple extensions of the economic and social hierarchies of the time. In colonial days, gentlemen owned politics, and, generally speaking, no one doubted that this should be so.

In England, government was unobtrusive. There was no expectation that Parliament would legislate except to fill in the gaps or refine existing law. Before mid-century, government demanded very little in the way of taxes, operated on paltry budgets, employed very few people, and performed few tasks. In America, provincial governments were more ambitious in regulating the economy and providing some social services, but colonists still expected (and got) little from their governments. Royal governors did not generally have legislative programs, nor did colonial assemblies have legislative ambitions. In both Virginia and Pennsylvania in the eighteenth century, the majority of legislative acts originated not in initiatives of legislators but in citizen petitions.[78]

Legislation was, in any event, a secondary activity of the colonial assemblies. Their primary tasks, as in England, were to express the grievances of the people and to keep watch on the executive. Their activities often concerned adjudicating private and local disputes; government was only thinly divided from private affairs. Even later, in the first decade of the new nation, if some collective action seemed necessary, people were more likely to take up a voluntary subscription than to use the offices of government for general taxation. These subscriptions not only got a job done—establishing an academy or a library, for instance, but reconfirmed social hierarchies as the names and contributions of subscribers became public knowledge.[79]

One might conclude that the colonial assemblies' main purpose was to perpetuate themselves; certainly this was their main expense. The largest outlay for seventeenth-century taxpayers in Virginia was the salary and fees for the burgesses and the clerks of the House of Burgesses for the few weeks of their annual session.[80] Government was not charged with altering the basic structures of society but, at most, of assisting in and coordinating their perpetuation.

If government was small and ambitions for it constrained, not much more can be said for the politicians who ran it. Indeed, the term "politician" is something of a stretch. Colonial officials did not in any sense live for politics nor depend on political office for their livelihood. Politics in the eighteenth century (and on into the nineteenth) was an avocational activity for gentlemen. Benjamin Franklin felt himself fit for public office and service as a colonel of the militia only in his forties, when he had retired from his trade as printer with enough money and leisure to aspire to gentry status.[81] For a member of the colonial elite, public office could be advantageous, providing prestige, influence in the disposal of land, and reputation at the bar. But at the colony-wide level, the amount of time legislators actually spent on politics was modest, and an assembly's social season was probably as attractive to prospective officeholders as its political content. Turnover in the Continental Congress and early national Congresses was high because the demands on the legislator in time spent far from home were substantial and very few men had any ambition to make a career of such activity.

With even politicians only seasonally committed to governance, it is little wonder that the citizenry at large had few resources for keeping abreast of current affairs and little incentive to attend to civic life.

The Media of Public Life

Politics, then as now, was essentially an oral art. The tavern, boarding-
house, legislative chamber, and private parlor were the natural milieu of the
politician, not because he craved secrecy, but rather because he thrived on
the amiable sociability such surroundings offered.[82]

On the eve of the Revolution there were some forty newspapers in a society that boasted only one sixty years before, but that number pales
when put up against, say, the 3200 churches existing at the same time.[83]
As late as the 1790s, when newspapers were still not easily acquired in
many rural areas, there was nonetheless a Protestant minister in nearly
every village.[84]

Print was not widely circulated early in the eighteenth century. It
was used for political purposes only under severe constraint of both law
and custom. People's lives were overwhelmingly local and their cultural
worlds overwhelmingly oral. Nevertheless, print played a growing role in
colonial politics as the century moved on, and, in the decade before the
Revolution, it would become a central institution of the public sphere.[85]

The role of print in colonial life is illuminated in the autobiography
of the greatest colonial entrepreneur of print (as of so much else), Benjamin Franklin. No reader of the *Autobiography* can doubt that there was,
at least in Philadelphia, something properly called a public sphere.
Franklin was himself a walking public sphere—a constructor, projector,
and inventor of publicness. There is no equivalent figure for the nineteenth century nor for our own era, although the energy with which
Ralph Nader has pursued the construction of public institutions and
found ways to make them proliferate, one spinning off from the next, at
least hints at the flavor of Franklin. But Nader's projects have aggressively and self-righteously claimed the title of "public interest" whereas
Franklin's worked toward public good with stealth, slowly gathering up
support, disarming potential opposition before proceeding, and never
disavowing benefits to himself.

Franklin's *Autobiography* is a window on the cultural world of the literate colonists. That world was remarkably small. Franklin, though a
very young man, an artisan and the son of an artisan, of no known ac-

complishments and no social standing, was twice befriended by colonial governors. Once it was Sir William Keith, who sought to encourage him as a promising printer. The other time it was Governor William Burnet of New York. Learning from the captain of the ship that had just brought Franklin to the city that "a young man, one of his passengers, had a great many books," he asked that Franklin come to see him. Franklin repeatedly describes the companions of his youth as "readers" or "lovers of reading," and this became the basis of lifelong friendships. He came to books with some family support. His father's library contained theological polemics and the Bible. Even as a child Ben used what little money he had to buy books, including the works of John Bunyan, later selling those to buy R. Burton's *Historical Collections*, some forty or fifty "chapmens books." Ben as a young man was exposed to *The Spectator*, John Locke, Xenophon, Daniel Defoe's *Essay on Projects*, and Mather's *Essays to Do Good*, not to mention a tract urging vegetarianism that he tried out for himself.[86]

If books were relatively scarce, newspapers were even more unusual in Franklin's youth. Ben's older brother James, to whom he became apprenticed, was a Boston printer whose idea of starting a newspaper in 1721 was ridiculed by friends, who believed John Campbell's solitary *Boston News-Letter* was enough for America.[87] There was no profession of journalism; there was only the craft of printing. Even when Ben moved to Philadelphia, already a skilled printer eager to set himself up in the trade, he attests to no sense of vocation or mission in printing. It was simply his trade. When he took on the publication of Samuel Keimer's *Pennsylvania Gazette* in 1729, the newspaper was not for him a public institution but a private business venture.

This is not to say it was without public purpose—he saw it, he wrote in the *Autobiography*, as "another means of communicating instruction" and so reprinted extracts from *The Spectator*, and "other moral writers."[88] Still, when he explains the success of the *Pennsylvania Gazette*, he understands success in economic terms. The *Gazette*, in Franklin's own judgment, had better type and was better printed than other Philadelphia papers. It also quickly won the interest of "the principal people" of the city when Franklin ran an article on the dispute in Massachusetts between the assembly and the governor (in 1729) over the governor's salary; Franklin speaks of his "spirited remarks" on the subject that led the paper to be "much talked of." He is not concerned to have persuaded anyone of anything except the liveliness of the paper. This led "the leading men" to encourage him in his enterprise.[89]

There is no grandiose claim about the press here; even the claim that his paper was intended to serve the public enlightenment is mentioned matter-of-factly. When Franklin had occasion to defend printing, he did so on minimalist grounds. Having been attacked in 1731 for printing an offensive advertisement, he published an "Apology for Printers" that defended the printing business as a neutral vessel. Men are of varied opinions, he observed. Since printing is a trade that "has chiefly to do with Mens Opinions," it followed that a reader would find "most things that are printed tending to promote some, or oppose others." The printer necessarily offends, then, just by sticking to his last, so to speak, where the shoemaker does not. This arises from the currency of the printer's trade, not the content of his views. "Printers are educated in the Belief that when Men differ in Opinion, both Sides ought equally to have the Advantage of being heard by the Publick; and that when Truth and Error have fair Play, the former is always an overmatch for the latter: Hence they chearfully serve all contending Writers that pay them well, without regarding on which side they are of the Question in Dispute."

It follows from this, Franklin argues, that a printer cannot be held responsible for the opinions he prints. But he then turns around to insist that printers do "discourage the Printing of great Numbers of bad things, and stifle them in the Birth." He himself has "refused to print any thing that might countenance Vice, or promote Immorality; tho' by complying in such Cases with the corrupt Taste of the Majority, I might have got much Money."[90] In the *Autobiography*, Franklin similarly recalls that he refused to print matter he judged libelous or personally abusive. If the writers "pleaded, as they generally did, the liberty of the press, and that a newspaper was like a stagecoach in which any one who would pay had a right to a place, my answer was, that I would print the piece separately if desired . . . but that I would not take upon me to spread his detraction" by printing it in the newspaper.[91] The newspaper was more closely identified with the printer himself than a pamphlet could be; it was his signature. Franklin advised young printers "not to pollute their presses and disgrace their profession" by printing private altercations, false accusations of character, or scurrilous reflections on the government of neighboring states.[92]

How well did printers follow Franklin's advice? In the first half of the eighteenth century, there seemed nearly as many models of what a newspaper should be as there were printers. Clearly printers did not imagine their newspapers to be either political instruments, or professional news gatherers. None of the early papers took any action to gather news. They printed what came to them. John Campbell's sense of purpose in the *Boston News-Letter* was a kind of documentary one. He was recording recent history, maintaining a record of the "thread of occurences." He kept his reports chronological, but because he had little space and occasionally suspended publication, he could not print all the news he received from London. He fell further and further behind. By 1718, he was running news more than a year old.[93]

The newspaper Benjamin Franklin came to in Philadelphia in 1729, Samuel Keimer's *Pennsylvania Gazette*, proposed to offer "the best and most authentic Accounts of the most remarkable Transactions in Europe." Keimer sought "to please all, and offend none," and to do so at a reasonable subscription price.[94] The full title of his sheet was *The Universal Instructor in All Arts and Sciences and Pennsylvania Gazette*. This revealed Keimer's plan to print serially Ephraim Chambers's *Cyclopaedia, a* through *z*. Keimer's paper began in 1728 and just before Franklin bought it late in 1729, it was still on the *a*'s, the entry for "air" taking up almost the entire paper for two months running, from May 17 through July 25.

Colonial printers, more than their London brethren, were public figures—running the post office, serving as clerks for the government, and printing the laws.[95] But they were equally small businessmen and there was at first little to indicate that the newspaper would become a central forum for political discourse. At the time Franklin penned his "Apology for Printers," a party newspaper did not yet exist in the colonies. The first such paper was born in 1733 in the print shop of John Peter Zenger in New York. Zenger was a struggling tradesman, not a political person.

Until a political faction led by Lewis Morris sought out his services in its campaign to discredit Governor William Cosby, he had printed primarily sermons and theological works in Dutch. The *New-York Weekly Journal* that he began producing under the direction of the Morrisites criticized the policies of Governor Cosby. Cosby, who had become governor in 1732, seemed a perfect embodiment of exactly the kind of corruption colonials feared (but expected) from officeholders—the use of public office for private financial gain.[96]

Zenger's published attacks brought him to trial on the charge of seditious libel in 1735, and in a celebrated case, the jury found him not guilty. Andrew Hamilton, Zenger's attorney, argued that Zenger could not be guilty of libel if he printed only the truth—an argument that would become a part of the American legal tradition in the wake of the Alien and Sedition Acts of 1798. But in 1735, Hamilton did not have a legal leg to stand on; the common law doctrine of seditious libel declared any words libelous that tended to injure the reputation of government. Hamilton had the good luck to take up a popular cause in front of a jury willing to exercise the broadest authority it could, taking the interpretation of law as well as facts into its hands. Although the Zenger trial gave support to popular sentiment favoring liberty of the press, it created no legal precedent. The Morrisite opposition evaporated. While Zenger continued in the printing trade, and maintained the *Weekly Journal* until his death in 1746, he never again tested the limits of political toleration.

This was not surprising. Colonial printers avoided controversy when they could, preached the printer's neutrality in the style of Franklin's apology when they had to, and printed primarily foreign news because it afforded local readers and local authorities no grounds for grumbling. Foreign news overwhelmed everything else in the colonial papers. Local political news remained a small part of newspaper content until after 1765. In a sample of 1,907 stories from the *Pennsylvania Gazette* from 1728 to 1765, just thirty-four touched on politics in Philadelphia or Pennsylvania. Of all news items on all subjects, only 6 percent concerned Philadelphia or Pennsylvania.[97]

Early in the century there was only a trickle of politics in print. In Pennsylvania, opponents of the proprietor distributed copies of the governor's speech and the Assembly's reply in Philadelphia coffeehouses in 1707. In 1710, the Assembly began to publish twice weekly its acts and laws to make it possible for citizens to appeal the acts before a legislative session ended. In Virginia, the House of Burgesses journals and enacted laws began to be published soon after the colony acquired its first printing press in the 1730s.[98] In Massachusetts, as we have seen, the House of Representatives printed its journals for the first time in 1715 to vindicate itself before the citizenry in a dispute with the governor. Since newspapers could be fined for printing more about the legislative proceedings than did the *Journal* itself, the press generally did little more than paraphrase what was already available in the *Journal*. In times of crisis and heated controversy, roll calls increased and pamphlets dared provide information not in the *Journal*, but otherwise, there was no way for citizens to learn from printed sources about the activity of the colonial legislature.[99]

In times of economic dislocation or war or both, political controversies enlarged; elites, in efforts to defeat rival elites, began to address campaign pamphlets directly to freemen at election time. In Boston, New York, and Philadelphia combined, there were thirty political pamphlets published from 1695 to 1714, compared to 145 in the next two decades and 149 in the two decades thereafter. Leaders turned to print to recruit support from people who had traditionally been outside politics altogether or whose loyalty to traditional elite interests could be taken for granted. The irony was that leaders of elite factions, none of them democrats in any respect, nonetheless felt driven to solicit the votes of ordinary freeholders. They might object to the new practices and worry that the pamphlets would "breed and nourish Discontent," and dangerously mislead "ignorant people & others who are not well acquainted with the publick affairs," but they could not refuse to make use of print themselves.[100]

How did political talk begin to flow from the presses of the surprisingly apolitical printers? It may be that the very neutrality of the colonial newspaper and the cautious ideology of its printers was a liberating force. The printers' self-serving, defensive posture provided a foundation for a new sort of public forum, one in which opposing views could indeed enter into the same newspaper and be tolerated.[101] The public realm that commercialism and commercial sentiments shape is different from one dominated by political principle or partisan engagement, but it is not necessarily retrograde. The newspapers' neutral space was revolutionary in its own way. That the printers' ambitions were commercial rather than political may have been a critical step in a growing toleration for conflicting points of view.

While pamphlet publication, generally speaking, could be more spirited, partisan, and controversial, it was the newspaper and not the pamphlet that created a continuity, coordination, and periodicity around the news. Newspapers created a space that demanded to be filled and an expectation for novelty about current affairs that stimulated writers and readers alike. The newspaper, in contrast to the pamphlet, helped to build a market for political controversy.

The newspapers advanced a public discourse also because they were connected to one another; they helped promote a colonies-wide consciousness. Newspapers constituted a powerful *network* of communications. Interconnections among newspapers grew not only because the papers' continual need for items to fill their space led them to borrow from one another's pages, but also because relations of kinship and friendship bound printers from distant places into a kind of extended family. Franklin, a master at the conventional political art of patronage, upon becoming deputy postmaster general for North America in 1753, appointed his son postmaster in Philadelphia, a brother postmaster in Boston (and later the brother's stepson), a nephew in New Haven, the son of a friend in Charleston, and another friend as controller in New York.[102] Franklin's kin, former apprentices, or business partners ran newspapers in New York, South Carolina, and Rhode Island. Along with the Bradford family (whose members printed newspapers in Pennsylvania, New York, and New Jersey and whose former apprentices included John Peter Zenger) and the Green family of Boston (whose family members operated printing establishments in Annapolis, New London, New Haven, and Philadelphia), the Franklins were a dominant force in colonial printing. There were frequent interconnections, through the mobility of apprentices, among the Green, Bradford, and Franklin clans.[103]

The newspaper created a public forum in yet another respect: it was available in taverns and suitable for reading aloud there. It may be that more people read newspapers at taverns or coffeehouses than at home, and many others could hear them read aloud or discussed.[104] In the social locations of its reading, as well as in the periodical form of its publication, the newspaper seemed well suited to accommodating and advancing public discourse.

This is certainly not to suggest that political discourse grew more elevated. On the contrary, it seems the press lived up to and exceeded the worst fears of elites as political discourse shifted from attacks on the opposition's policies to assaults on the opposition's leaders, and each salvo in a political skirmish would then bring an "increase in the brutality of language" from the other side.[105]

As for the redoubtable Benjamin Franklin, he developed a position in Philadelphia society that no other printer matched anywhere. Though he took printing to be a business and the newspaper to be a relatively nonpartisan instrument of both business and enlightenment, he also made use of it to promote civic betterment. A one-man band of civic pride, he was full of ideas for community improvement. When he came up with an idea, he would first discuss it with the Junto, the reading and discussion group he had organized with other tradesmen and artisans of the town. He read a paper about the night watch to the Junto (and to other, similarly constituted clubs). He read his ideas on fire prevention to the Junto, publishing them only later. Alternatively, or sometimes subsequently, he wrote and printed a pamphlet proposing his views on a subject. He did this on the question of paper currency and on his ideas regarding the militia. But he might also write in the newspapers, as he did with an idea for establishing a public hospital in Philadelphia, holding in his *Autobiography* that it was his "usual custom" to "prepare the minds of the people" in this way. At that point, not resting on published laurels, he used his contacts and his political muscle in the Assembly to advance his cause.

The newspaper was thus continuous with a variety of other communication devices in assisting his efforts at social change. Franklin neither neglected the newspaper's possibilities nor expected too much of them.

The newspaper's job was not to persuade but to publicize, to "prepare the minds of the people," to plant seeds that other forms of persuasion and pressure would then have to supplement. As an operator in Philadelphia's public sphere, Franklin sought to pursue his goals while putting himself "as much as I could out of sight" and offering his various projects as the proposals of a group of people rather than a single man.[106]

Print thus enlarged Franklin's political arsenal, but it also had a political influence far beyond Franklin's intentions. The very impersonality of print encouraged a faith in norms of rational discourse.[107] The reproducibility of print and its impersonal address made the audience potentially and in conception unlimited. This new audience, the republican public, was not the traditional face-to-face gathering of the church assembly or town meeting. It was an imagined rather than territorially concrete community. As it was more abstract, it was also more dangerous to traditional social relations, less bound to the subtle self-abnegations of daily life in a hierarchical society. It was difficult to control who would see something in print and it was difficult to contain the meanings to which print could give rise when read, as it increasingly was, in private and for secular rather than religious purposes. Print was inherently scandalous; Governor William Berkeley of Virginia had recognized this in 1671 when he wrote, "I thank God, there are no free schools nor printing and I hope we shall not have these hundred years; for learning has brought disobedience, and heresy, and sects into the world, and printing has divulged them, and libels against the best government. God keep us from both!"[108] God did not long cooperate.

After 1765: A Farmer and a Staymaker

John Dickinson first published his "Farmer's Letters" in Philadelphia on December 2, 1767. The first of the letters began with an affecting and ingratiating self-characterization: "I am a Farmer, settled, after a variety of fortunes, near the banks of the river Delaware. . . . I received a liberal education, and have been engaged in the busy scenes of life; but am now convinced, that a man may be as happy without bustle, as with it. My farm is small; my servants are few, and good; I have a little money at interest; I wish for no more. . . ."[109]

While Dickinson could have printed his letters in pamphlet form (they were later republished in seven different pamphlet editions) the decision to publish first in the weekly press enabled him to reach a wider and less sophisticated audience than a pamphlet by itself would have allowed. Dickinson was among a new brand of popular party leaders who used the press to become "public figures." They appealed to a wider public through the public prints, not only to the Assembly through petitions, speeches, and letters. Dickinson's series of "letters" spread rapidly throughout the colonies, appearing in nineteen of the twenty-three existing English-language newspapers by the end of January 1768.[110]

"Farmer's Letters" were distributed more widely than any prior political writing in the colonies, even though newspapers probably reached no more than 5 percent of the population even incidentally.[111] Because events seemed to many people at a point of crisis, the papers felt an obligation to print. Indeed, papers that failed to run the letters were pressured to do so in both Boston and Philadelphia and perhaps elsewhere.[112] Clearly, Dickinson was a propagandist of no mean skill. He developed an important idea in the letters about taxation that came to influence political discussion for years to come. He made use of the most popular Whig ideas. Not least important was his choice of the yeoman farmer as his pseudonym. For all the attribution of virtue to the farmer, Dickinson was the first American political writer to identify himself as one.[113]

The printing history of Dickinson's essays indicates a growing politicization of printers. As recently as 1765, printers had failed to resist the Stamp Act, even when it directly impeded their businesses. David Hall, Benjamin Franklin's partner and his successor at the *Pennsylvania Gazette*, complained later to Franklin that he should have opposed the Stamp Act more vigorously; the truth is that he lagged behind the outrage of public opinion. The printers were reluctant partisans.[114] As politics grew more intense and as printers engaged in it themselves, there was also a multiplication of printing establishments. In 1764, twenty-three newspapers were published in fifteen locations; by 1775, forty-four papers in twenty-four communities and by 1783, fifty-eight papers in twenty-six places.[115]

The newspaper press was by 1765 a large enough and well enough established institution to provide significant continuity to political discussion even beyond the specific outbursts of political protest. Nothing that a newspaper could do was as forceful for mobilization as actual participation in an uprising or dumping of tea in the harbor. But because the newspapers had space to fill on a weekly basis, at a time when more and more minds were aflame with political talk, they recurrently gave vent to political discussion.

With a political crisis looming, the colonists made use of their various means of communication, of which newspapers were only the most visible. Colonial elites knew one another through trade; businessmen in one colony might buy real estate in another. They knew one another through college experience; Yale attracted many students from New York and Massachusetts as well as Connecticut, and a scattering of students from Rhode Island, New Jersey, and Pennsylvania, too. Students who went off to Yale did not necessarily return to their home colonies but chose to settle elsewhere. In the 1760s, religious connections crossed colonies, too. Out of fears that the Anglican Church might establish an American bishop, Presbyterian and Congregationalist ministers representing most of the colonies banded together with annual meetings and committees of correspondence. The bishop was the "ultimate symbol" of religious oppression for dissenters; their intercolonial organization contributed its ideas and its leadership to the more general political struggle.[116] A wide variety of social, economic, educational, and religious contacts transcended colonial borders, and so did common interests in science, medicine, or the arts.

By 1774, leading figures in the Continental Congress were widely known by reputation through the colonies. Many members of the Congress had never met before, but the Congress provided a reunion for William Livingston of New Jersey with his old Yale classmate Eliphalet Dyer of Connecticut, while Silas Deane of Connecticut, lawyer and merchant, encountered New Yorkers he knew well. Thomas Mifflin of Pennsylvania had met John Adams of Massachusetts a year before when he visited relatives in Boston, and in Boston Adams had also met socially Thomas Lynch of South Carolina.[117]

As for communication within a colony, formal and informal organizations operated as well as newspapers. Boston's social clubs and Masonic lodges became centers where people could come together to talk politics (among other things). A caucus system coordinated Boston artisans and prepared them to vote as a bloc at town meetings. While New York had no similarly focused system, its taverns were a regular site for political talk.[118]

Meanwhile, printer William Goddard proposed and organized a colonial postal system as alternative to and in opposition to the royal post. In March 1774, he received the support of the Boston Committee of Correspondence, which then solicited other committees to support the plan. "When we consider the Importance of a Post," declared a letter from the Boston Committee, most likely written by Samuel Adams, "by which not only private Letters of Friendship and Commerce but *publick Intelligence* is conveyd from Colony to Colony, it seems at once proper & necessary that such an one should be established as shall be under the Direction of the Colonies. . . ."[119]

In a subsequent broadside urging subscription to the new private postal system, proponents pointed to the dangers of continued dependence on the royal postal system. "It is not only our Letters that are liable to be stopt and opened by a Ministerial Mandate, and their Contents construed into treasonable Conspiracies, but our News-Papers, those necessary & important Alarms in Time of public Danger, may be rendered of little Consequence for want of Circulation."[120] The colonial post office was adopted by the Continental Congress on July 26, 1775; a year before the Declaration of Independence, the Revolution began to be institutionalized.

Dickinson's public, assembled through the newspapers, represents one arena of public communications; Thomas Paine's pamphlet *Common Sense* constitutes another. Between 1764 and 1776, 195 political pamphlets were printed in the colonies, 150 of them in Massachusetts, Pennsylvania, and New York alone.[121] Much has been claimed for *Common Sense*, not least of all by Paine himself. But historians believe he was not immodest when he wrote in 1779 that 150,000 copies had been printed and sold in America. The success was international, with seventeen printings in London in 1776 and French and German editions as well. *Common Sense* was very important in making the unthinkable—independence and a republican government without a monarch—thinkable. As its title suggests, it turned heresy into common sense. Paine turned assumptions about American life that the colonists took to be evidence of colonial inferiority into signs of America's special mission. Paine saw the newness, the raw and rustic quality of colonial life not to be faults but virtues. If Americans were inexperienced, at least they were not corrupted by the ways of the Old World; indeed, he wrote, "We have it in our power to begin the world over again. A situation, similar to the present, hath not happened since the days of Noah until now."[122]

Common Sense, which went through twenty-five American editions in 1776 alone, was an amazing literary success. And a literary success of a sort with powerful political implications. In it, Paine pioneered a plain style of political writing: "As it is my design to make those that can scarcely read understand, I shall therefore avoid every literary ornament and put it in language as plain as the alphabet."[123] There was little conceptually new in *Common Sense*. John Adams grumbled that it was no more than "a tolerable summary of the arguments which I had been repeating again and again in Congress for nine months."[124] But to make such arguments available to a wider readership, in a new popular idiom, woven together into a single coherent narrative, was a major contribution to the quickening of American public life.

Paine himself had been an artisan—a staymaker, making corsets for wealthy women; unlike almost all earlier pamphleteers, he did not come from the elite of lawyers, ministers, and merchants. He was of, and wrote for, the ordinary person. Dickinson posed as a common man; Paine, like Franklin, actually was one. Again like Franklin, he counted among his friends the likes of George Washington and Thomas Jefferson. He was in this sense part of a newly emerging class of professionals, the intellectuals, divorced from narrow class allegiances and free to think of themselves as speakers bound by no loyalties of class or party.[125]

In the American Revolution, thirteen separate political entities, tied to London and without formal political ties to one another, came together with political and military unity of purpose. The leadership that effected this unity did so while retaining the loyalty of the vast majority of the citizenry at large, even though relatively few of the leaders and few of the citizens generally had contemplated, let alone intended, a break from British rule.

The American Revolution transformed colonial political culture. The emphasis on a consensual politics did not die, but increasingly, with the thirteen disparate post-colonial states banded together, the governing image was James Madison's of an orchestration of competing interests. Madison would guide the Constitutional Convention toward political institutions designed to withstand, and even profit from, the pitting of interest against interest. No longer was it easy to imagine that deliberation might lead to consensus.

Likewise, the Revolution did not mark the end of deference or of hierarchical social relations, but it was the beginning of the end. In the new nation, the rationale for an upper house in the legislatures was more than ever in dispute. What reason could an upper house have if there was no "aristocratic principle" for it to embody? When the states after the Revolution instituted two-house legislatures (except for unicameral Georgia), there were sometimes higher property qualifications for voters for the upper house or for membership in it.[126] Clearly there was some sort of view that the upper house was more like the Lords than the Commons, but the weight placed on popular sovereignty and the power soon to be vested in the "we the people" formulation of the Constitution marked a decisive shift.

As for the assumption of monarchy, it disappeared with astonishing speed and finality. Even the Declaration of Independence, historian Richard Bushman has observed, was a document of monarchical culture: "It was a bill of treason, indicting the king for assaulting his people rather than protecting them. The Lockean language in the Declaration simply stated explicitly the right to revolt which was always implicit in the monarchical covenant."[127] Yet as the colonies, now become independent states, wrote constitutions in wartime America and joined together in the Articles of Confederation, republican principles were taken for granted.

One of the most reliable lessons of political history is that new and explosive movements build on the framework of old institutions. Republicanism, if that means a faith in and the practice of representative institutions, was something the colonists had experience with. And when they moved from petitions and remonstrances in their assemblies to demonstrations in the streets, they did even this within the framework of established practices. The difference between authorized exercises of power within duly constituted bodies and unauthorized exercises of power by mobs in the streets was not sharp. In colonial America, the police power was not exercised by any permanent or professional corps of officials; law enforcement was often in the hands of posses. The power of government was exercised by the sheriff's calling together able-bodied men of the community, the same people who between 1765 and 1775 assembled in extra-legal protests. The "mobs" who protested the Stamp Act and other British initiatives could understand themselves as a quasi-legal force. Indeed, the experience of the participants in the militia and in a *posse commitatus* gave to their protests a kind of enforced restraint and moderation. The popular uprisings that became the Revolution built on a heritage of quasi-legitimacy.[128]

Popular protest and military mobilization notwithstanding, the revolutionary leadership did not seek to involve the general public in political debate. The Continental Congress swore members to secrecy at first, and of course there was military justification for doing so. The Congress that met under the Articles of Confederation understood itself to be a council of states, not a popular assembly, so it made its actions public only through communiqués to state governments. Occasional efforts to make congressional debate public were unsuccessful. Still, by 1779 the Continental Congress authorized weekly publication of its proceedings. New York and Pennsylvania required in their new constitutions that legislative sessions be public.[129]

Should we judge the glass of public life by the 1780s half empty or half full? The important point is to recognize that it was half a world away from our own. Certainly representation became more and more a cardinal principle. Every state except South Carolina required annual election of the lower house. "Where ANNUAL ELECTION ends, TYRANNY begins" was a maxim of the radical Whigs, and the new state constitutions made it a practice of government, too.[130] State constitutions generally enlarged the size of the legislature, reducing the size of the local constituency that elected each representative.

The suffrage was extended, too. In part, this was a by-product of the depreciation of paper money, a factor great enough in several states to all but nullify the property qualifications for voting. But it also came from a shift in a number of states from a property-owning to a taxpaying qualification for the suffrage—in Pennsylvania (1776), New Hampshire (1784), Delaware (1791), Georgia (1775), and North Carolina (1776). Because of nominal poll taxes, the taxpaying qualification was very close to universal white manhood suffrage although, technically, only Vermont adopted manhood suffrage (in 1777), establishing neither taxpaying nor property-owning as a requirement for the vote. Apart from Vermont, some form of financial requirement for voting survived, but the movement was clearly toward liberalizing the franchise.[131] Liberalization took other forms, too. New Jersey and New York made provision for an increase in the number of polling places at elections, and that may have made a great deal of difference when travel even over short distances could be arduous.[132]

On the other hand, the voting public was not encouraged to take a strong interest in government. On the eve of the new nation, politics remained in the hands of gentlemen. The gentry ruled, notwithstanding representative institutions and a relatively broad electorate; printed accounts of political affairs were occasional, notwithstanding the growth of newspapers; the expectations of what government should undertake were low as were the resources of state power for what it could undertake, notwithstanding the rhetorical assault on the tyranny of the monarchy. Looking back from beyond the democratic transition, colonial political practice still appears an extension of the social life and comfortable consensus of a gentlemanly elite.

Chapter 2

The Constitutional Moment

1787–1801

Prospectus
Rules of Order
Private Associations: "Self-Created Bodies Under the Shade of Night"
The Rage of Party and the Mischief of Faction
The Press, the Post, and the Parties
The Informed Citizen
"How Do You Like the Election?"
Representation in an Extended Republic
The Perfection of the Republic

Prospectus

"We the people," begins the preamble to the Constitution, but "the people" were not present at the Constitutional Convention in Philadelphia in 1787. The "call" for a convention was at best obscure. The legal or institutional standing of the convention did not derive strictly from the national government under the Articles of Confederation; it was much more a voluntary gathering initiated by nationalist leaders from several prominent states and eventually prompting twelve of the thirteen states to send delegates.

The delegates were elected by state legislatures, not by the people directly. They were closer to representing "we the states" than "we the people." All voting at the convention was by state delegation, not by individual delegates.

Not only was the general public not directly involved in calling for a convention or in selecting delegates to it, but, once constituted, the convention operated behind closed doors. When Thomas Jefferson, safely settled in Paris, learned that delegates were sworn to secrecy, he objected to "so abominable a precedent as that of tying up the tongues of their members."[1] But secrecy prevailed and was taken very seriously. When it was at one point breached, presiding officer George Washington issued a warning: "I must entreat Gentlemen to be more careful least our transactions get into News Papers, and disturb the public repose by premature speculations. . . ."[2] Delegates believed they should operate beyond the public eye; the public would have the opportunity later, in the struggle for ratification, to make their views known.

Even so, "the people" were very much present in the minds of the delegates. Rhetorically, the people were out in force. References to "the people" and "the genius of the people" and what the people will or will not do, what they will or will not approve, were accepted as legitimate arguments (with some notable and interesting exceptions) as delegates batted proposals back and forth before the convention. Often the people's support was invoked to make a case for adopting or rejecting a particular proposal. The delegates often referred not just to the people but to "the genius of the people" to argue that deep sentiment and tradition, much more than transitory opinion, favored or opposed a particular recommendation. George Mason of Virginia urged democracy because "the genius of the people is in favor of it."[3] Oliver Ellsworth of Connecticut argued that a national militia could not accommodate "the local genius of the people."[4] Without adopting that particular phrase, others made similar points. Massachusetts delegate Elbridge Gerry held that "the people of New England will never give up the point of annual elections."[5] (He was wrong.) He held also that a term in the Senate of more than four to five years "never would be adopted by the people."[6] (Wrong again.)

Delegates sometimes conceded great wisdom to the people. When Pennsylvania's Gouverneur Morris argued that the executive should be the guardian of the people against the aggrandizement of the legislature, he asked, who could judge the officers of the executive? And he answered, "The people at large, who will know, will see, will feel the effects of them. Again who can judge so well of the discharge of military duties for the protection and security of the people, as the people themselves who are to be protected and secured?"[7] Delaware's John Dickinson argued that the people will be best suited to elect the executive. "The people will know the most eminent characters of their own States, and the people of different States will feel an emulation in selecting those of which they will have the greatest reason to be proud."[8]

The delegates did not believe the people's judgment was always to be trusted. The people could be uninformed. Roger Sherman argued that it would be better for the legislatures rather than the people at large to elect the president. "The latter will never be sufficiently informed of characters," he held.[9] Likewise, in arguing that the House of Representatives should be elected by state legislatures rather than the people, Sherman declared that the people "should have as little to do as may be about the Government. They want information and are constantly liable to be misled."[10] Even an ardent republican like George Mason, suspicious of central governmental powers, could observe the limitations to the public's knowledge. He did not think the people suited to choose the president any more than it would make sense to "refer a trial of colours to a blind man. The extent of the Country renders it impossible that the people can have the requisite capacity to judge of the respective pretensions of the Candidates."[11] Mason believed that people were best qualified as electors when they could choose among candidates with whom they were personally acquainted. Knowledge of politics meant, most of all, knowledge of men.

It was not only ignorance that limited the people's capacity for governing but their inclination toward emotion. Gouverneur Morris argued that one of the difficulties of constitutional structure was to find a way to limit the influence of the rich, who are often able to manipulate the people. "We should remember that the people never act from reason alone. The Rich will take advantage of their passions and make these the instruments for oppressing them."[12]

The people may not have constituted the convention, then, but the convention constituted or constructed "the people"—with both respect and a degree of contempt, with both reverence for their underlying potential and distaste for their vulnerability to manipulation and emotion.

What did the men who drafted the Constitution expect of citizens? And what kind of citizenship did they mean to encourage? "The people," as the Constitution's framers conceived them, were ultimately sovereign but, in the daily operation of government, should be, and necessarily had to be, distant onlookers. The test of the political process would be how their representatives, in Congress assembled, would comport themselves, not how much the citizenry at large knew of government or what that citizenry might seek from politics. At one revealing moment in the proceedings Elbridge Gerry invoked "the people" to oppose biennial elections for the House. James Madison called his rhetorical bluff. He observed that the opinions of the people could not be ascertained and, indeed, that a notion of the opinion of the people was not finally coherent:

> . . . if the opinions of the people were to be our guide, it would be difficult to say what course we ought to take. No member of the Convention could say what the opinions of his Constituents were at this time; much less could he say what they would think if possessed of the information and lights possessed by the members here; and still less what would be their way of thinking six or twelve months hence. We ought to consider what was right and necessary in itself. . . .[13]

For Madison, as for most of those who supported the Constitution, a republic could work not because every white man of property had a say in it but because these people would have a constitutional mechanism for delegating their authority to representatives who would deliberate together. The founders' world of less than four million people may look tiny to us, but to them it was a dauntingly large, "extended" republic, a new nation of enormous size and of considerable heterogeneity in ethnicities, classes, religions, and economies. The founders' political thought spared little time over the obligations or virtues of the general citizenry and labored instead over the details of representation. This chapter seeks to explain why.

Rules of Order

The Constitutional Convention presented the would-be leaders of a new nation a complex chicken-and-egg problem. They were trying to establish a republican form of government, a system in which the people rather than a crown or a parliament would be sovereign, but how were they to put the people rather than themselves at the point of origin? Even when, by different procedures in different states, delegates to the convention were chosen, there were no rules for conducting the convention itself. The convention, like the nation, had to invent itself.

On Friday, May 25, 1787, the Constitutional Convention met for the first time. Its opening business was promptly taken care of—George Washington was selected president of the convention, and a committee was appointed to prepare rules of procedure. On Monday the committee reported back. Among its proposed rules were that when one member of the meeting held the floor, other members should not talk with one another "or read a book, pamphlet or paper, printed or manuscript." No one could speak more than twice on the same question without special permission and could speak the second time only if all others who wanted to speak had had a chance to do so. These rules of equal respect and equal opportunity for participation were supplemented with rules to encourage deliberate consideration of issues. A complicated question could be divided at the request of any member. Any state could have a vote postponed until the next day even if debate was concluded. Any written document to be considered was to be read through once for information and then debated by paragraphs. Rules of civility were also proposed. Any member could be called to order by any other member and would then "be allowed to explain his conduct or expressions, supposed to be reprehensible." The president would decide questions of order without appeal or debate.

One rule that members would later chafe at was that nothing that was said at the meetings could be "printed, published, or communicated without leave."[14] George Mason of Virginia would endorse this in a letter to his son as "a proper precaution to prevent mistakes and misrepresentation until the business shall have been completed." James Madison, writing Jefferson in Paris a week after the convention opened, listed members of the convention but declined to relay news of discussions because no disclosure in "even a confidential communication" was allowed by the rules.[15]

Jefferson, as we have seen, was not pleased about the secrecy, but he probably would have sympathized with the other rules adopted. He had a lifelong interest in parliamentary procedure. As vice president from 1797 to 1801 and presiding officer of the Senate, he wrote A Manual of Parliamentary Practice, published first in 1801 and in hundreds of editions since then (it is still in use today). Jefferson began the brief volume with a section on "The Importance of Adhering to Rules." He opens it by quoting Arthur Onslow, Speaker of the House of Commons, who said that the rules of proceeding "operated as a check and controul on the actions of the majority, and that they were in many instances, a shelter and protection to the minority, against the attempts of power." Jefferson endorsed this as "certainly true, and . . . founded in good sense." The substance of the rules mattered less than the fact that there were rules at all so that "there may be an uniformity of proceeding in business, not subject to the caprice of the Speaker, or captiousness of the members."[16] In a democracy, the people or their representatives make the rules, but no democracy can work without rules to shelter minorities during the course of rule-making.

All the recommendations of the convention's rules committee met with general approval except one: the proposal that any member could call for yeas and nays and have them entered into the minutes. Because the acts of the convention did not bind the delegates' constituents in any way, Rufus King of Massachusetts argued that it was unnecessary to show the votes to them. George Mason added that keeping a written record of the votes would prejudice members against changing their votes even when their convictions changed. An astute social psychologist, Mason suggested that recording votes would force people toward self-consistency even when reason led them to change their minds. Besides, Mason added, the record would hand over to adversaries of the convention a lethal weapon. These objections won the day.

Notice, then, how complicated, subtle, and local are the issues in designing a democratic public life. Even the rules of design must be designated, and by what rule is that to be done? There must necessarily be, as the sociologist Emile Durkheim urged, a precontractual basis of contract.[17] In the case of the founding fathers, a common culture emerged from British political thought and from a century and a half of colonial experience. At the same time, substantial cultural differences existed, too, between the New England Puritans, the Dutch landowners along the Hudson, the German shopkeepers of Philadelphia, and the planters of Virginia and the Carolinas. In the convention, all would have to agree on the rules for arriving at the rules for the nation.

The framers believed that the science of politics they worked on was a science of governmental systems and structures that would be, once constituted, a perfect mechanism for the deliberation of public issues. Much has been written about the character of the government they designed and their views on checks and balances, federalism, mixed government, and so forth. Less attention has been paid to what the framers expected to happen outside government in the public sphere, where citizens would gather and public opinion would be formed. What would take place outside the formal political system itself to support its work— indeed, to give it life?

Were there to be political parties to crystallize and consolidate opinion? Certainly not. On this point at least the founders agreed among themselves. Eighteenth-century political thought in England and in the colonies came down hard against parties; attachment to party was taken to be the very opposite of the public-spirited virtue sought in both citizens and leaders.[18] This, at any rate, was the theory.

Were there to be private associations, short of fully formed parties, to articulate views and to petition the legislature? Here the founding generation was more equivocal, followers of Washington and followers of Jefferson having significant divisions, as we shall see.

Was there to be unbridled criticism in the newspapers? The weight of evidence tends to the negative, but certainly the framers can be quoted on both sides of the question. Probably none of the founders expected much from the press, at first, and many of them were willing to throw contentious editors in jail for criticizing the government.

The founders, in short, conceived and established a republican government, but outside the central requirement of frequent elections, they did not readily tolerate the private institutions that twentieth-century thinkers have found necessary requirements in the formation of a public sphere of opinion and public communication. Some of the founders straightforwardly condemned private political associations. They had little enough regard for a free press to pass the Sedition Act of 1798. They discouraged candidates from presenting themselves to the voting public. They made no provision for publicly supported political education.

The founders' vision of a civil society or a public sphere was very limited. Not only were these leaders skeptical of democracy in the sense of opposing the enfranchisement of all but propertied white males; they also disapproved of general public discussion among the propertied white males. They were far from sharing a pluralist vision, still attached as they were to the notions of consensus, property, virtue, and deference that came naturally to them.

Of course, the founders were not armchair philosophers but practicing politicians, and their positions shifted with circumstance. Some of the same men who opposed parties in theory set about to create them in practice. Thomas Jefferson, who generally refused to write for the newspapers, nonetheless secured financial support to underwrite them. As for the general benefits of private associations, it is misleading to read twentieth-century notions of pluralism into *Federalist* No. 10, to read recent praise of civil society into Tocqueville's well-known remarks on voluntary associations (which were not, as we shall see in the next chapter, so celebratory as some interpreters have suggested), or even to read Tocqueville back into the world of Washington, Adams, and Jefferson. The proper place of private associations in conducting public affairs was very much in doubt in the 1790s, as the battle over the Whiskey Rebellion quickly and bitterly demonstrated.

Private Associations: "Self-Created Bodies Under the Shade of Night"

Beginning in 1793, popular associations sprang up in the new republic to debate public questions, criticize government, and influence public policy. More than forty of these "Democratic" or "Republican" or "Democratic-Republican" societies were founded between 1793 and 1798 (although most of them died out after 1796). The most influential of them, the Democratic Society of Pennsylvania, was also probably the largest, with more than three hundred members. Several others had upwards of one hundred participants; most had twenty or twenty-five. The clubs collectively, and sometimes even individually, were socially heterogeneous, including merchants, lawyers, landowners, artisans, and people of middling or lower status.[19]

Some of the clubs even encouraged the formation of groups similarly constituted with different political philosophies. The Political Society at Mount Prospect (New Jersey) wrote in its constitution: "Are several of you disposed to advocate an aristocratical or monarchical government? Where there is real opposition of sentiment, in a well regulated discussion, the righteous cause will probably shine with an additional lustre. Come forward, then, with your arguments; we are more generous than cowardly; liberty is yours, as well as ours. . . ."[20] A number of societies welcomed spectators at their meetings or invited nonmembers to take part in forums or discussions.[21] The societies self-consciously acted as a counterweight to the overwhelmingly Federalist press. In Maine, for example, in 1794, all newspapers were Federalist. The Constitutional Society in Boston sent to the Republican Society of Portland a bundle of papers in which they could get and spread news that could not get into the Federalist papers. The clubs distributed their own constitutions and helped print and distribute patriotic orations or pamphlets with which they sympathized.

The Republican clubs engaged in a variety of activities besides discussion. Societies in Baltimore, Norfolk, and Charleston watched English ships to see they did not violate Washington's neutrality proclamation; a Charleston group even disarmed a British ship in Charleston harbor. Others engaged in electioneering—publicizing anti-democratic statements of Federalists and poll watching. The societies also kept tabs on legislators in office; Kentucky societies had their congressional representatives face questions at their meetings or sent pointed questions to them in Philadelphia, reading and discussing the answers in their meetings. Others undertook philanthropic activity. Their ardent sympathies for the French Revolution received material expression when the Carlisle, Pennsylvania, society sent flour to France. Many of the societies passed resolutions supporting the Revolution and urging the American government to honor its treaty obligations to France.

The Democratic-Republican clubs insisted that they served to make government more responsive to the people. The security of the people, one advocate remarked, should not be "confined to the check which a constitution affords" nor to the "periodical return of elections," but should depend also on "a zealous examination of all the proceedings of administration," presumably to be carried out by voluntary bodies of citizens.[22]

That may sound like the heart and soul of an appropriately civic-minded population today, but to many at the time it smacked of the violence and anarchy of the French Revolution itself, that earthshaking event that frightened even republican upholders of property and order. Political societies were strongly criticized. An address at a meeting of the Democratic Society of New York defended them against their critics. Printed as a broadside in 1794, it declared that under republican government, "it becomes a duty" for citizens "to acquire a perfect knowledge of the government and political institutions of their country, in the administration of which they may one day be called upon to take an active share." Societies like the Democratic Society are an avenue toward this. "If, then, by the institution of our society, or of others similar to our own, we acquire a knowledge of one single political point, we benefit ourselves; if we publish it for your inspection, we render you a service the most essential." And this was why the society was founded:

> Such was the pure, such the patriotic purpose for which the Society that now addresses you was instituted: To obtain a more perfect knowledge of the fundamental principles of our own constitution; to diffuse political information; to form a more intimate acquaintance with the sacred and unalienable Rights of mankind; to cherish in our breasts the pure and holy flame of Liberty, and to cultivate the love of our country as the most noble of human virtues, were the great and ruling objects of its formation.[23]

Federalists were not convinced. Their views, like so much else in early American political thought, echoed British sentiments. In England, parliamentary sovereignty was jealously guarded, not only from the monarch but also from the voting public. The right of constituents to "instruct" their representatives—that is, to bind them to specific policy stances—was controversial. Even the right to petition was restrained by an act of 1664 against "tumultuous petitioning." Further, defenders of parliamentary sovereignty "looked still more jealously on any unofficial political organization which could claim to represent the public."[24] In the British case, fear of private associations may have been inspired by anxiety that the House of Commons did not truly represent the citizenry; private associations implicitly challenged its legitimacy. In the American case, the concern was more that the Congress *was* representative—and deliberative—and that no other body could match it on either count.

Federalist objection to the societies came to a head at the time of the Whiskey Rebellion in 1794. This critical episode in the early republic began in 1791 when, with the urgings of Treasury secretary Alexander Hamilton, Congress passed an excise tax on whiskey. The tax was unwelcome among farmers whose whiskey production was one of their few sources of cash and so an entree into a broader market economy. The tax was doubly unwelcome, however, because it was to be collected by federal tax collectors and tax evasion would be prosecuted in federal courts. Farmers responded to the new law with petitions and occasionally with violent protest—tax collectors were tarred and feathered, as were local citizens sympathetic to the law, some of whom found their houses or barns pulled down. President Washington denounced the protests and a period of calm followed. Congress reduced the tax rate and made the collection process less onerous. In 1794, Hamilton proposed a further modification—that tax delinquents living more than fifty miles from a federal district court could be tried in state courts. But while Congress considered this provision, which eventually passed, tax collectors in western Pennsylvania vigorously pursued farmers under the existing terms of the law. This meant alleged violators had to appear in federal court in Philadelphia, the nearest district court. At this point, shots were fired, western Pennsylvania district tax inspector John Neville's house was burned to the ground, and federal troops guarding his house gave way to the rebels.

Protests accelerated, aided and abetted, Federalists charged, by the Democratic-Republican clubs. Some of the Pennsylvania rebels were members of a Democratic-Republican club. They had a hand in passing resolutions at public meetings pledging opposition to the whiskey tax. Seven thousand protestors marched through Pittsburgh. Spontaneous protest began to shift toward organized resistance, although historians doubt that this could have gone very far, in part because the protestors themselves shared the prevailing distrust of organized associations.[25] The Washington administration, anxious about any sign of popular discontent at a time when the French Revolution sent shivers even through a republican government, reacted sharply—though not before Washington assured himself of broad popular support, with even many of the Democratic societies weighing in on his side. The German Republican Society of Pennsylvania publicly declared that the resistance in western Pennsylvania was "contrary to the constitution of our country, and repugnant to every principle of liberty." The Democratic Society of Pennsylvania (in Philadelphia) likewise condemned the resisters. Despite finding the excise taxes "oppressive, hostile to the liberties of this Country, and a nursery of vice and sycophancy," they declared, "we, notwithstanding, highly disapprove of every opposition to them, not warranted by that frame of Government, which has received the sanction of the People of the United States."[26]

Only after such popular support became general did Washington call out the militia and, with Secretary Hamilton and Pennsylvania governor Thomas Mifflin beside him, led a force of 13,000 to confront the insurrection. By the time the militia arrived in western Pennsylvania, there was little insurrection left to face. The army brought rebels into custody and delivered twenty of them to Philadelphia to be tried for high treason. Two were convicted, but later pardoned by Washington.[27]

If this all seems, in retrospect, scarcely worth the name "rebellion," it looked otherwise to Federalists at the time. The allegiance of frontier regions was barely secured; as late as 1789, British officials seemed hopeful that parts of Virginia, western Pennsylvania, and Vermont would separate from the Union and join with Canada. John Marshall, in his 1804 biography of Washington, praised his hero's actions against the Whiskey

Rebellion for terminating "an insurrection, which . . . threatened to shake the government of the United States to its foundation."[28] Over-drawn this is. Still, more dramatically than any other moment in the early years of the new nation, the Democratic-Republican societies and the Whiskey Rebellion, separately and together, raised the question of what ways and means of political dissent, if any, would be legitimate in a republic.[29]

A central objection to the Democratic-Republican societies was that they were "self-created"—that is, voluntary and unauthorized by any governmental body. In a letter Washington spelled this out. Seeing the Democratic societies behind the "insurrection" in western Pennsylvania, he asked if anything could be

> more absurd, more arrogant, or more pernicious to the peace of Society than for self created bodies, forming themselves into *permanent* Censors, and under the shade of Night in a conclave resolving that acts of Congress, which have undergone the most deliberate and solemn discussion by the Representatives of the people, chosen for the express purpose and bringing with them from the different parts of the Union the sense of their Constituents, endeavoring as far as the nature of the thing will admit to form *that will* into Laws for the government of the whole; I say, under these circumstances, for a self created *permanent* body (for no one denies the right of the people to meet occasionally to petition for, or remonstrate against, any Act of the Legislature etc.) to declare that *this act* is unconstitutional and *that* act is pregnant of mischief, and that all, who vote contrary to their dogmas are actuated by selfish motives, or under foreign influence; nay, in plain terms are traitors to their Country, is such a stretch of arrogant presumption to be reconciled with laudable motives: especially when we see the same set of men endeavouring to destroy all confidence in the Administration, by arraigning all its acts, without knowing on what ground or with what information it proceeds and this without regard to decency or truth.[30]

Several weeks later Washington wrote to Edmund Randolph, his secretary of state, holding "if these self created societies cannot be discountenanced, that they will destroy the government of this Country. . . ."[31] Washington expressed the sense that the mechanics of government were complete in themselves and that the establishment of other political organizations could only be a way of highlighting "interest" over virtue, and faction over the mechanisms that enabled legislators to ascertain the public good. As George Cabot, another staunch Federalist, put this not long thereafter: "After all, where is the boasted advantage of a representation system . . . if the resort to popular meetings is necessary?"[32]

When Washington addressed the Congress on September 19, 1794, providing a postmortem on the rebellion, he made a critical reference to the role of the self-created societies. This precipitated debate in Congress over how, or whether, to mention this portion of Washington's address in drafting the ritually obligatory reply. At the time it was customary for the two houses of Congress to each draft a response to presidential communications that restated and reaffirmed what the president had said. In this case, that is just what the Senate did, over Aaron Burr's objections. In the House, some members were loath to appear to censure the societies, even though they were far from wanting to encourage them. James Madison, chairing the committee to draft a response, was by no means prepared to endorse party politics or proto-party politics, nor was he happy in censuring popular political activity. "If we advert to the nature of Republican Government," he said, "we shall, find that the censorial power is in the people over the Government, and not in the Government over the people."[33] The response of the House, after three days of debate, spoke only indirectly of the societies.

Washington's remarks produced as much outrage among the societies as the insurrection had produced condemnation. The same German Republican Society that had condemned the rebellion now declared in Philadelphia's *Federal Gazette* its shock at the president's criticism of the societies. "If Democrats have been the instruments of the western insurrection, how will it be explained that they were among the foremost to suppress it? Our brethren, the Democratic Society of Pennsylvania, could have made a quorum in the field, and they were among the number who received the commendations of the President of the United States."[34] Speaking for itself, the Democratic Society of Pennsylvania passed a motion in October observing that "The enemies of Liberty and Equality have never ceased to traduce us—even certain influential and public characters have ventured to publicly condemn all political societies." The society reiterated its commitment to public discussion: "If the laws of our Country are the echo of the sentiments of the people is it not of importance that those sentiments should be *generally* known? How can they be better understood than by a free discussion, publication and communication of them by means of political societies? And so long as they conduct their deliberations with prudence and moderation, they merit attention." [35] Jefferson, in self-imposed retirement from public affairs, wrote in outrage to Madison: "The denunciation of the democratic societies is one of the extraordinary acts of boldness of which we have seen so many from the fraction of monocrats. It is wonderful indeed, that the President should have permitted himself to be the organ of such an attack on the freedom of discussion, the freedom of writing, printing and publishing." [36] (By "wonderful" Jefferson clearly means "bewildering.")

The combination of the societies' sympathies for the French Revolution, their frequent unity with local militias, and their appearance in "faction"-like form thoroughly frightened and alienated Federalist leaders. There was no place in their political philosophy (their political practice was another matter) for permanent or semi-permanent agencies, institutions, or organizations oriented to the public life outside the government itself. [37] The fundamental protections for civil society were far from established in the political culture.

Washington returned to the subject in his Farewell Address two years later. When he contemplated leaving public life at the end of his first term, he wrote to James Madison asking for help in drafting a statement. He outlined his main theme—he wanted to impress upon citizens that "we are all the children of the same country, a country great and rich in itself, capable, and promising to be as prosperous and happy as any which the annals of history have ever brought to our view. . . ." He held that the government might very well, with experience, come "as near to perfection, as any human institution ever approximated, and therefore the only strife among us ought to be, who should be foremost in facilitating and finally accomplishing such great and desirable objects, by giving every possible support and cement to the Union; that, however necessary it may be to keep a watchful eye over public servants and public measures, yet there ought to be limits to it, for suspicions unfounded and jealousies too lively are irritating to honest feelings, and oftentimes are productive of more evil than good." Madison, in response, offered a draft in which the virtues of keeping a watchful eye were stressed equally with the defects of excess watchfulness, a notable shift in emphasis from Washington's sketch. Madison restated the issue this way: he urged that the government and Constitution be maintained, that its administration be wise and virtuous, "and that this character may be insured to it by that watchfulness over public servants and public measures, which on one hand will be necessary to prevent or correct a degeneracy, and that forbearance, on the other, from unfounded or indiscriminate jealousies, which would deprive the public of the best services, by depriving a conscious integrity of one of the noblest incitements to perform them. . . ."[38]

Washington finally published his farewell four years later (September 17, 1796). With further editorial assistance, this time from Alexander Hamilton, he moderated his tone in Madison's direction, but there is no question that he feared the spirit of party, faction, and disunion, not an insufficiently zealous public watchfulness. For him, it was important to remember, "The very idea of the power and the right of the people to establish government presupposes the duty of every individual to obey the established government." Thus he went on to urge that "all combinations and Associations, under whatever plausible character, with the real design to direct, controul, counteract, or awe the regular deliberation and action of the Constituted authorities, are distructive of this fundamental principle and of fatal tendency. They serve to organize faction, to give it an artificial and extraordinary force; to put in the place of the delegated will of the Nation, the will of a party; often a small but artful and enterprizing minority of the Community; and, according to the alternate triumphs of different parties, to make the public administration the Mirror of the ill concerted and incongruous projects of faction, rather than the organ of consistent and wholesome plans digested by common counsels and modified by mutual interests."[39]

Washington may have felt all this much more acutely than others; he was, after all, both the head of state and the symbolic linchpin in whose strength the nation had been able to come together in both war and peace. He no doubt felt, as no one else could have, the power of the forces that could tear the society apart. He grew anxious, as no one else could, over the battles within his own cabinet between Hamilton and Jefferson. Still, his views were in concert with a pervasive fear among the patriot leaders, that Madison had expressed so well in *Federalist* No. 10, of the mischiefs of faction and the spirit of party. Even Samuel Adams, who under British rule was a consummate political organizer, objected to parties *in a republic*. For him, once republican government was established and liberty of the people protected by annual elections, privately organized committees became "not only useless but dangerous."[40] If the founders were right in this, then the task of the good citizen, so far as keeping an eye on his delegated representatives, was to elect the best possible representatives—and then let them do their work without interference.

The Rage of Party and the Mischief of Faction

It is well known that the founders loathed parties, fearing that they would promote partial interests rather than the common good. In *Federalist* No. 10, Madison cautioned at once against the "violence of faction" and the "rage of party," using the terms interchangeably, meaning to suggest that they are corrupting to republican government. The present-day term "special interest" has something of the same connotation as Madison's "faction." But in the 1790s, different views of the new nation's proper course developed and each group, in an effort to win support for its own vision, began to organize. Ironically, party organizations developed precisely because each side took the other, but not itself, to be a faction, committed to a partial interest hostile to the nation and the general good. Madison, like most other American political thinkers of the day, believed parties were and should be temporary coalitions rather than enduring antagonists. One party or the other would ultimately triumph and represent the political consensus of society as a whole. John

Adams held to this eighteenth-century understanding of party even in old age. Party competition was inevitably a barrier to human betterment:

> ... parties and factions will not suffer improvements to be made. As soon as one man hints at an improvement, his rival opposes it. No sooner has one party discovered or invented any amelioration of the condition of man, or the order of society than the opposite party belies it, misconstrues it, misrepresents it, ridicules it, insults it, and persecutes it.[41]

Views of this sort notwithstanding, the beginnings of political organization can be traced to Washington's cabinet where Alexander Hamilton and Thomas Jefferson faced off as representatives of federalist and republican viewpoints—that is, positions more sympathetic (federalist) or less sympathetic (republican) to locating power in the national government, and more supportive (federalist) or less supportive (republican) of commercial expansion and transformation of a relatively homogeneous agrarian order. The bitterness of the rivalry was encouraged by the absence of any intellectual acceptance of parties or a party system as legitimate. When in 1800, Massachusetts Federalists used a caucus to nominate their candidate for governor, they did so with embarrassment. They protested that it was a "respectable convention" and not an effort to dictate how people should vote; Republicans attacked the meeting as a "caucus" and insisted that "*real* great men are always known and acknowledged" and so in no need of so artificial and factional a device.[42]

Though Jefferson held, "If I could not go to heaven but with a party, I would not go there at all," and he disclaimed himself either a Federalist or Antifederalist,[43] he joined with Madison to create an organized republican opposition. They began early in 1790 to seek out a newspaper voice for republicanism, the first step in building something like a "party." This was no small step in a political culture so allergic to the idea of party. But lines of cleavage were already forming in the Congress that paralleled the split between Hamilton and Jefferson in the cabinet. Candidates for presidential elector in the eight states where electors were popularly chosen began to publicly announce which presidential candidate they favored. In 1796, the candidacies of Adams and Jefferson for president

helped these two diverging inclinations in political opinion define
themselves. Even so, the partisan newspapers urged voters to line up behind the characters of the candidates and not their political views. The
"parties" were not named, did not formally exist, and did not issue any
platforms.[44]

Opposition to party was taken very seriously, even formalized in
election laws. In Pennsylvania, each voter had to turn in a handwritten
presidential ballot listing the fifteen electors he favored; to discourage
party slates, no printed tickets were accepted.[45] By 1800, Federalists condemned the Republican practice of distributing printed tickets of nominees before the freemen's meetings as undemocratic. Republicans replied
that it was at least more democratic than having a list made at the meeting, where "a significant *wink, nod*, or *shake of the head*" by "some *dictator*
of the meeting" would decide the outcome.[46]

Jefferson's turn to the newspapers to advance his own views, then, in
an atmosphere dominated by anti-party rhetoric, was a matter of some
daring and one he embarked on secretively. It was also a vital step in enlarging the public sphere, making public and distributing widely arguments that had tended to be aired behind closed doors.

The Press, the Post, and the Parties

Between 1763 and 1775 the number of master printers in the colonies
increased from forty-seven to eighty-two, and the number of newspapers doubled from twenty-one to forty-two.[47] There were more newspapers and at least some of them grew more attentive to local politics.
Philadelphia newspapers in 1794 provided 23 percent of news space to
local news, compared to 12 percent in 1764. The city by that date
boasted eight newspapers, including four dailies, compared to two
weeklies in 1764. The editor of Philadelphia's *Federal Gazette* held that
newspapers enable people to "feel, in solitude, a sympathy with
mankind. . . . Men stick to their business, and yet the public is addressed
as a town meeting."[48]

The founders saw possibilities as well as dangers in the press. Early
on they chose to underwrite the circulation of the press with the postal

service. In 1792, the Post Office Act provided for newspapers to be carried in the mail at rates much lower than those for letters. There was controversy about whether newspaper rates should be flat or graduated by the distance the newspaper was sent, not over providing preferred rates to newspapers. The argument for a flat rate was that a graduated rate would limit the flow of information to the more remote areas of the country. Elbridge Gerry argued for low and uniform newspaper postal rates "by which the information, contained in any one paper within the United States, might immediately spread from one extremity of the continent to the other."[49] Indeed, the law of 1792 would provide that every newspaper printer could send one copy of his paper to every other printer in the country, postage free.[50] Newspapers took liberal advantage of this; as much as a third of all items in provincial newspapers were simply reprinted from exchange papers.[51]

The plan finally adopted established two zones so that newspapers could be sent up to one hundred miles for one-cent postage, beyond one hundred miles for a penny and a half. This was a compromise between those who wanted information to circulate cheaply and those who wanted to protect a local press from competition: rural newspapers feared cheaper and more authoritative city sheets and Southern printers feared competition from the North.[52] John Steele, a representative from North Carolina, praised the law in a letter to his constituents. "The diffusion of knowledge," he wrote, "is productive of virtue, and the best security for our civil rights."[53] The federal government thus subsidized newspapers significantly; in 1794, for example, newspapers sent through the mails accounted for 70 percent of total weight the postal system handled while contributing only 3 percent of postal revenues.[54]

The price of postal service was not the only politics of the post. Some people assumed that Federalist postmasters tampered with the mails. During debates over ratification of the Constitution, Antifederalists in several states claimed that their correspondence and their newspapers were delayed in the mails by postmasters seeking to weigh the debates in favor of ratification. Even a decade later Madison wrote Jefferson that in the last mail he did not get a single newspaper. "That there is foul play with them I have no doubt. When it really happens that the entire Mass cannot be conveyed, I suspect that the favorite papers are selected, and the others laid by; and that when there is no real difficulty the pretext makes room for the same partiality."[55]

The line between letter and newspaper was easily crossed. It was not only a common practice for people to write letters to local newspapers but for private correspondents to include newspapers in their letters to friends in other parts of the country. When Madison wrote his father from Philadelphia, he often enclosed newspapers so that his father might follow the progress of congressional business.[56] Later it would become common to presume that the person one wrote to had been reading the papers: Madison makes the assumption writing to Monroe from Washington in 1801 ("You see by the papers . . .") and to Wilson Nicholas ("Little has occurred which you have not found in the newspapers.")[57] Jefferson urged Benjamin Franklin Bache to put all the ads in his *General Advertiser* on one leaf that could be torn off so the other leaf, with the news, could be sent through the mails easily.[58] Congressmen wrote directly to the newspapers and often saw to it that their speeches in Congress were printed in sympathetic newspapers (or sometimes printed by themselves for direct distribution). Even in the First Congress, a contemporary wrote, "it is generally agreed that many Speeches are calculated for the Gallery and the Gazette."[59]

The Federalist domination of the press concerned Jefferson, Madison, and their friends. As early as 1790, Jefferson searched for a reliable newspaper outlet for republican views. Meanwhile, poet and editor Philip Freneau was seeking to leave New York. His old Princeton classmate Henry Lee advised another Princeton classmate, James Madison, of Freneau's situation. In the summer of 1791, Madison and Jefferson at last tempted Freneau to Philadelphia to run a national republican journal.[60] Freneau's *National Gazette*, they hoped, would combat the influence of John Fenno's *Gazette of the United States,* a paper closely tied to Alexander Hamilton and for which Hamilton regularly wrote pseudonymous articles. Jefferson secured for Freneau a position in the State Department and promised him State Department contracts for public printing of laws and proclamations. He also provided news items from the department, sometimes editing and translating them himself.[61]

Fenno attacked Freneau for receiving a federal salary. Freneau retaliated with the charge that Fenno's government printing contract was won by a "vile sycophant."[62] A veritable newspaper war ensued, Hamilton attacking Jefferson in Fenno's paper and Freneau striking back on behalf of Jefferson. Jefferson worried that matters had gotten out of hand. Still, he continued to support Freneau, even as newspaper rhetoric heated up to uncomfortably factional temperatures.[63]

The Informed Citizen

Thomas Jefferson and James Madison, among others, believed public opinion must be actively engaged in the affairs of state. But just what did this mean? Whose opinions, expressed in what manner, and brought to bear on public questions on what occasions?

Madison seemed to fear that appeals to the people would tend to be appeals to the emotions, and this he opposed. In *Federalist* No. 49, he warned against "frequent" appeals to the public over constitutional issues, notably those where the different branches of the government were in conflict. For him, "every appeal to the people would carry an implication of some defect in the government" and "frequent appeals would, in great measure, deprive the government of that veneration which time bestows on everything." Madison was well aware that the success the states had had in forming new constitutions and new governments in the midst of the Revolution was a rare moment in history; the dangers of war "repressed the passions most unfriendly to order and concord" and "stifled the ordinary diversity of opinions on great national questions."[64] With the war behind them, the dangers of discord to the survival of the government increased.

Then what was the public's role and how was it to be played? At first, Jefferson and others opposed to the direction in which Hamilton was taking the country seemed to assume that "the people's basic republican virtue" would rouse them. But when this failed to do the job, what else might serve? John Taylor's pamphlets of 1793 and 1794 suggested that the state legislatures would play a key role in informing the public. They were "the people themselves in a state of refinement" and they had "superior information" about public issues. Of course, since the state legisla-tures elected the Senate, they would be particularly well placed to keep tabs on that body.

Others called for general public vigilance unmediated by legislatures or proto-parties. But how were people to inform themselves or watch over their leaders? This was nowhere spelled out. When the Democratic-Republican clubs presented themselves as watchdogs, Washington's re-action indicates that the virtues of such an organized expression of citizenship were far from self-evident.

The virtue of the press, on the other hand, was regularly noted, but the press became a subject of sharp conflict between Federalists and Re-publicans with the passage of the Alien and Sedition Acts of 1798 (as we will see in a moment). Newspapers did not merit the term "self-created so-cieties," of course: they were not societies. They were small businesses, not membership organizations; they spoke for political viewpoints, but they were not themselves political associations. Still, there was enough ambigu-ity in this to make many leaders more than a little doubtful about the value of the press to civil order. Incumbents in the new republic routinely com-plained that newspapers threatened order. George Washington wrote in 1792 that "if the government and the Officers of it are to be the constant theme for Newspaper abuse, and this too without condescending to inves-tigate the motives or the facts, it will be impossible, I conceive, for any man living to manage the helm or to keep the machine together."[65] He was still troubled in 1796. What would have appeared in the Farewell Address, but for the judicious editorial pruning of Hamilton, was a bitter attack on the "virulent abuse" Washington felt heaped upon himself by "some of the Gazettes of the United States."[66] Washington had ample reason to be put out. Benjamin Franklin Bache, Benjamin Franklin's own grandson and an ardent republican editor, regularly attacked Washington in the *Aurora* during his second term, accusing him of financial misdeeds in office and aristocratic and royal pretensions. He even urged impeachment.[67] "Diffu-sion of knowledge" was, for Washington, fine in principle; in practice, with the existing journals, it evoked his irritation and disgust.

If the press was not regarded as the happiest conduit of information from government to the people, provisions for the people to learn of government more directly were haphazard, at best. Many of the founders objected to opening governmental proceedings to the populace. The Senate's doors were closed to the public until 1795. When, in 1790, Virginia's senators sought to open the Senate doors, they could find only one vote besides their own. In 1791, after three other Southern states instructed their senators likewise, there was another attempt. It, too, failed. Senator William Maclay wrote in his journal that the main objection to open meetings was the fear that senators would only make "speeches for the gallery and for the public papers." When the Senate finally welcomed the public, it remained difficult for people in the newly built galleries to actually hear discussion and no provision was made for reporters to be admitted to the floor until 1801.[68]

It is easy to find among the founders great praise for the education of citizens and the general diffusion of ideas. It is even there in Washington's Farewell Address, a speech more imbued with a fear of faction and anxiety over public interest in politics than a wish for public enlightenment. The question is how to reconcile the rhetorical praise of the diffusion of information with the willingness in practice to limit or oppose the spread of knowledge.

This could be chalked up to hypocrisy; no halos protect the founders from the sins of lip service. Like many others, they may have professed on Sunday what they systematically undermined the rest of the week. In that case the libertarian rhetoric should simply be discounted. Alternatively, we may misunderstand the rhetoric. It may be that the diffusion of knowledge was so widely and willingly supported in principle because people believed it would engender obedient, not critical, citizens. This is probably true of the encouragement of formal schooling, for instance. In colonial America and afterward, schooling and reading were understood to be instruments of inducting citizens more firmly into the established order.[69] When people praised public enlightenment abstractly, this may be what they had in mind. When the diffusion of knowledge contributes to public order, it is praiseworthy; when it adds to contention and strife, it is dangerous.

In general, few of the founders supported government involvement in education (Benjamin Rush was a notable exception). Even the most

broad-minded of them, who did favor state-level planning for public enlightenment, conceived schemes of strictly limited objectives. Take Jefferson's proposal for "A Bill for the More General Diffusion of
Knowledge" in Virginia in 1778, perhaps the most farsighted proposal of
the era for general education. Its objective was to provide for the liberal
education of those who might ascend to the state's *leadership:* "Whence
it becomes expedient for promoting the public happiness that those persons, whom nature hath endowed with genius and virtue, should be rendered by liberal education worthy to receive, and able to guard the
sacred deposit of the rights and liberties of their fellow citizens, and that
they should be called to that charge without regard to wealth, birth, or
other accidental condition or circumstance." Education could help prevent "tyranny" by giving the people at large "knowledge of those facts,
which history exhibiteth, that, possessed thereby of the experience of
other ages and countries, they may be enabled to know ambition under
all its shapes, and prompt to exert their natural powers to defeat its purposes." [70] Political education was to be, in a sense, defensive. It should
help protect citizens against their own faulty judgments of character, but
there was no suggestion that it should positively induce them to greater
interest or activity in public affairs.

The liberality of Jefferson's proposal consisted in his provision that
elementary education be made generally available; he would cast the
net widely to discover his leaders of "genius and virtue." But Jefferson
did not doubt for a moment that governing should be undertaken by
this "natural aristocracy" rather than ordinary citizens. As for the latter,
the whole of their civic obligation was to recognize virtue well enough
to be able to know and defeat its counterfeit. As Thomas Pangle neatly
puts it, Jefferson hoped schooling would achieve an "informed popular
watchfulness." [71] But "informed" meant only to be informed about the
character of candidates for public office. Citizens were to be democratic
clinicians who could spot a rash of tyranny in a candidate. At the
polls—but not necessarily anywhere else—they would turn back the
ambitious and self-seeking. They were not to undertake their own eval-
uation of issues before the legislature. That was what representatives
were for.

As for the role of the press as a public educator, there seems to be an almost irresistible inclination today to believe that the founders understood the First Amendment and a "free press" very much the way we do—that is, as keystones of our entire political system and central, necessary guarantors of a democratic way of life. But this is wrong on at least six counts:

1.   The First Amendment set limits on the powers of Congress, but not on the powers of the states, to curtail free speech. The operative word in the First Amendment is "Congress"—Congress shall make no law abridging freedom of speech, not because freedom of speech is to be prized but because the powers of Congress are to be limited. It was originally an act of federalism more than of libertarianism; it protected the autonomy of state legislation against supervening national authority.[72] Framers of the Constitution had limited enthusiasm for the First Amendment. Madison finally led the fight for passage of the Bill of Rights in the Congress, but for him this was an act of political obligation more than personal conviction. The First Amendment was distinctly an afterthought for the leading framers of the Constitution.

2.   State constitutions also protected the liberty of the press, but the founding generation's intensely felt sense of the precariousness of governmental authority limited the reach of these formal guarantees. Leaders of the Revolution and of the early republic distinguished between the use of the press and its abuse. A free press could be defended insofar as it was "an instrument of liberty enabling a scattered people to make common cause against oppression." But it was no longer a free press if "perverted to the uses of power."[73] In colonial days, power lay with the Crown and its representatives and the press was taken to be an agency of the people that should weigh in on the other side. Once a government of the people was established, however, its preservation became the highest priority, and a people's government could survive only through the good opinion the people might have of it. "But," asked James Bayard in the Congress in 1799, "how is that good opinion to be preserved, if wicked and unprincipled men, men of inordinate and desperate ambition, are allowed to state facts to the people which are not

true, which they know at the time to be false, and which are stated with the criminal intention of bringing the Government into disrepute among the people? This was falsely and deceitfully stealing the public opinion; it was a felony of the worst and most dangerous nature."[74]

3. Holding to this politicized view of the press, political leaders seemed able to reconcile constitutional guarantees of a free press with vigorous prosecution of editors for seditious libel. Newspapers that criticized the government or officials of the government could be slapped with a criminal indictment. Even before passage of the Sedition Act in 1798, the Federalists prosecuted Republican editors under the common law of seditious libel, but the act sharply accelerated the trend. It made it a crime punishable by a fine of up to $2000 and imprisonment for up to two years to "write, print, utter or publish" anything "false, scandalous, and malicious" against the government, the president, the Senate, or the House "with intent to defame . . . or to bring them . . . into contempt or disrepute; or to excite against them, or either or any of them, the hatred of the good people of the United States. . . ." The law was strongly supported by Federalist editors, none of whom, apparently, imagined that the opposition would ever be in a position to turn the tables on them. The *Boston Centinel* simply declared that "whatever American is a friend of the present administration of the American Government is undoubtedly a true republican, a true Patriot. . . . Whatever American opposes the Administration is an Anarchist, a Jacobin and a Traitor."[75]

The Federalists engineered no less than fourteen indictments under the act.[76] At a time when there were only about two hundred newspapers in the country with less than a quarter of them manifesting strong republican sympathy, this was a considerable assault on the press. Under the Sedition Act from a quarter to a third of Republican editors were indicted.[77]

The Sedition Act, passed by the narrow vote of 44 to 41, was in force for two years. In 1801, an effort to extend it was narrowly defeated, 53 to 49, with six Southern Federalists joining the forty-seven supporters of the new president, Thomas Jefferson. Only at that point did Albert Gallatin articulate a broader defense of a free press, taking the First Amendment to mean that Congress could not pass any law punishing abuses of the press. At that point Madison added his voice, too, claiming that the Sedition Act was unconstitutional, that a free republican government could not be libeled, that the First Amendment superseded the common law of seditious libel, and that the freedom guaranteed the press by the Constitution was absolute. The Republicans in opposition found more freedom in the First Amendment than they had originally intended.

4. Apart from the important legislation establishing the post office, privileging newspapers in postal rates, and providing free franking privileges for congressmen, there is a notable absence of formal provisions for transmitting information to the public. Only two state constitutions opened the doors of the legislature to the public.[78] The Senate, as we have seen, deliberated in secret until late in Washington's second term. Initially, in 1789, Congress ordered the printing of all laws in at least five newspapers in the country and selected one each in Boston, New York, Philadelphia, Baltimore, and Charleston, but it seems unlikely that the Congress could have anticipated great consequences from this. Newspaper distribution was so irregular that, especially outside the coastal route of interurban travel, newspapers were not judged a particularly effective means of distribution. While leaders in government saw that the press could be threatening, they did not see clearly or consistently that it could play a positive, regular service in political communication.[79]

5. The actual practice of free expression in print was indeed widespread, but the founding generation rarely applauded, and frequently condemned, it. Washington, as we have seen, had little but criticism for the press. Even Jefferson, who set up Philip Freneau as an opposition journalist, recoiled at the language he then found in Freneau's paper. Of course, Jefferson can be quoted in praise of the press or in high dudgeon against it. Jefferson, well known for his statement that he would prefer newspapers without a government to a government without newspapers (1787), also declared (note that this observation comes when he was in office himself) that "the man who never looks into a newspaper is better

informed than he who reads them, inasmuch as he who knows nothing is nearer the truth than he whose mind is filled with falsehoods and errors." He complained that truth itself becomes suspicious when printed in the newspaper. He urged that newspapers be organized into four chapters— Truths, Probabilities, Possibilities, and Lies—but feared only that the first of these sections would be very short indeed.[80] As for the citizenry at large, enthusiasm for the press seemed to depend on whose ox was being gored. During state deliberations on ratification of the Constitution in Massachusetts, the papers would not publish unsigned articles for or against, "by which means," one Federalist admitted, "all freedom of writing was taken away," since anyone outspokenly opposed to ratification risked becoming a target for violence. Newspapers in Philadelphia, New York, and Boston that sought to report Antifederalist as well as Federalist views during the ratification conventions were forced by subscribers who stopped taking the papers to cease their coverage.[81]

Just as the founding generation praised an informed public, but took little effort at ensuring that public education might help bring it into existence, so the founders offered general praise of a free press but did little to make good on their approbation. Repeatedly the patriots applauded the free press as a bulwark of the people's liberty. But they also were convinced that a press operating against popular liberty endangered popular government itself.

6.   Finally, although the independent press has become a fixed part of the American heritage, in truth it figured little in the writings of the founders. In *The Federalist* papers, widely acknowledged as the greatest work of political philosophy ever penned in this country, Alexander Hamilton, John Jay, and James Madison defended the Constitution in hope of New York's ratification. *The Federalist* papers appeared in a series of New York newspapers (and were then reprinted widely elsewhere) in 1787 and 1788. In the course of these eighty-five essays, the press receives a total of four mentions, all in passing.[82] As we shall see in the next section, the issue of how to create a functioning representative system in a nation so geographically vast was very much in the minds of the framers as they constructed a governmental framework, but mention of

the role of print in accommodating geographic distance is rare. This is ironic, since many of the writings about the dangers of distance appeared as newspaper articles and reached people far beyond their point of origin. But the press remained the vehicle, not the subject of such discussions, and never took center stage in the founding generation's writings on the framework of government.[83]

Only in the wake of the Sedition Act did Americans boldly embrace a free press as a necessary bulwark of a liberal civil order. Historian Gordon Wood has judged this "the crucial turning point in the democratization of the American mind,"[84] and certainly it marked a shift of great magnitude. It was part of a multi-faceted drama of democratization, part of a package of changing attitudes and changing institutions that included the legitimation of parties, the growing political role of voluntary associations, and the democratization of election campaigning itself.

"How Do You Like the Election?"

Voting, as a writer argued in the Pennsylvania Gazette in 1788, "is the first concoction in politics; and if an error is committed here, it can never be corrected in any subsequent process. The certain consequence must be disease. Let no one say that he is but a single citizen; and that his ticket will be but one in the box. That one ticket may turn the election. In battle, every soldier should consider the public safety as depending on his single arm. At an election, every citizen should consider the public happiness as depending on his single vote."[85]

But what concretely was voting? The Constitution left the matter almost entirely to the states. Democratic reforms in the 1780s and 1790s changed electoral activity and elections from what they had been in colonial days. In New York, for instance, written ballots replaced viva voce voting, polling places were established in each township (rather than as few as one per county), there were more elective officers than in colonial days (governor, lieutenant governor, state senators, and U.S. congressmen were newly elective officers), and elections were held more frequently for many offices.

The necessity of electing persons to serve in statewide offices (governor and lieutenant governor, for instance) and the need to elect congressional representatives from large districts meant that people could not simply vote for leading community citizens, nor could candidates emerge spontaneously and informally as in the past. Awkwardly and haphazardly, nomination systems developed that forced political communication beyond the informal and hierarchical to the formal, public, and more democratic. In New York, committees of correspondence took the initiative in nominations for governor; in New Hampshire, members of the legislature took the lead in nominations for Congress. In Pennsylvania, efforts to nominate through open, popular meetings were at first decried as too readily subject to manipulation; the circularizing of names through private correspondence, handbills, and newspaper notices guided early campaigns.[86] But there, as elsewhere, public meetings for nomination grew more common.

Not that just anyone could be nominated, of course. Leading families continued to dominate. Candidates nurtured their "interest" through hints in letters to other local notables that their support would be welcome. In what one historian calls "a proliferating chain letter," friends wrote to friends who wrote to their friends to establish the basis for an "interest."[87] After a nominating meeting, where prior interest-building normally assured overwhelming support for one candidate, the meeting's secretary paid for newspaper publication of a statement that explained that so-and-so had been nominated at a well-advertised, "uncommonly large and numerous" gathering and listed the names of moderator, secretary, and committeemen, always local notables. A broadside from Albany, New York, in 1799 lists Federalist candidates selected "At a large and respectable Meeting of Freeholders and Electors of the City of Albany, convened at the Tontine Coffee-House on Saturday 13th April 1799—agreeable to previous notice in the *Albany Gazette*." The broadside identifies the nominated candidates, adding that in arriving at this ticket, "we experienced considerable embarrassment, by reason of opposite Nominations for Members of Assembly by our Friends in several Towns: This rendered the Business extremely painful. . . ."[88] This confession suggests that normally these grand meetings for nomination

had little to do but to confirm a slate of candidates that leading gentlemen had already agreed on.

During the campaign the local newspaper office was often a site for
submitting rival announcements and tracts and a meeting place for placing election bets. Odds taken in these bets provided a kind of ongoing
opinion poll. On election day itself, local gentlemen would gather to
drink and party and then gather up others of lower social station, treating them to liquor and shepherding them, sometimes in hired sleighs
during winter, to the polling place. They would give ballots to their
guests (of course, there were no standard, state-provided ballots), who
would then hand them on to the election official.

These New York electoral practices, reasonably typical of the middle
states, were more vigorous and convivial than in New England but less
rowdy than in the South.[89] In the South, election day was raucous. Candidates in Maryland for the legislature, Congress, and the electoral college all toured their districts, attended election meetings, and addressed
crowds wherever they gathered, be it at a cockfight or church meeting.[90]
New Englander Elkanah Watson, on moving to North Carolina, was
shocked at the rowdiness of elections, but he adapted quickly. With two
friends, he tried to disrupt a meeting two days before the election to elect
representatives to the convention for ratifying the Constitution. The
meeting was called by an anti-ratification candidate to air his views. Failing to break apart the meeting (and just barely escaping physical harm
themselves), Watson and friends made a caricature of the candidate and
found several "resolute fellows" to set it up and defend it at the polling
place. The young men were attacked and a battle royal raged, disrupting
the polling place and reducing turnout which, Watson confessed without shame, was just what he had wanted.[91]

Electoral practices in New York could be less than civil, too. In the
gubernatorial election of 1792, William Cooper, the leading landowner,
store owner, and judge of Otsego County, pressed ballots into the hands of
voters and, as one observer testified, took the voters by the arm, "dragging
them to the poll." Cooper's enemies said he threatened financial ruin to
those who would not vote his way.[92] Each side sought to portray itself as
free from electioneering and to show the other side utterly manipulative.

The ambivalence of Americans over electioneering was marked, no matter how cherished the election might be in principle. In the first federal election in 1788, a poem in a Trenton, New Jersey, newspaper summed it up:

Zealous Patriots heading rabbles,
Orators promoting squabbles;
Free Electors always swilling,
Candidates not worth a shilling!
Butchers, Farmers, and Carmen,
Half-pay Officers, and Chairmen;
Many Zealots, not worth nothing,
Many perjured Persons voting;
Candidates, with Tradesmen pissing,
Cleavers, Bagpipes, Clapping, Hissing;
Warmest Friends in Opposition,
Hottest Foes in Coalition!
Open Houses, paid to tempt the
Rotten Votes, with Bellies empty;
Boxing, Drinking Rhyming Swearing
Some Fools laughing, some despairing;
Fevers, Fractures, Inflammations,
Bonfires, Squibs, Illuminations;
Mur'rers, daring all detection,
Pray, Gentlemen, how do you like the Election?[93]

In this context of rowdy, increasingly public and increasingly contested elections, uneasiness about how much or whether a candidate should present himself before voters and actively solicit popular support persisted. Federalists tended to see electioneering as unbecoming. John Randolph complained as late as 1813 that a Republican opponent had "descended to the lowest and most disgraceful means—riding from house to house, and attending day and night meetings in the cabins and hovels of the lowest of the people. He was present at fourteen of these preachings (seven of them held at night) the week before the election."[94] Republicans, both as the opposition and as a group ideologically more friendly to popular politics, were more enthusiastic participants in electioneering. In the presidential election of 1800, candidate Thomas Jefferson urged his comrades to propagandize in the newspapers, although he himself would not do so. He articulated a "platform" for his party through writing his political ideas in private letters to political friends—but never in a public statement.[95] However cautiously, Jeffersonians or Republicans actively courted voters much more than Federalists, at least those of an older generation. The gentlemen of the old school "did not mingle with the mass: they might be suspected of electioneering," wrote one contemporary. They objected to "brawlers, who make popularity a trade" and judged the people who listened to such candidates a "swinish multitude."[96] Republicans, as the outsiders, organized more systematically and campaigned with more energy than Federalists in the 1790s, although the Federalists were not so ill organized as they liked to present themselves. Federalists, too, sponsored newspapers and wrote letters. "I trust that we may in one Instance imitate the Jacobins, I mean, Industry," wrote New York Federalist Peter Van Schaack.[97]

Little was expected in the way of political knowledge from voters, at least, little of the sort of knowledge that today's civic moralists urge upon people. The knowledge that citizens of the 1790s were expected to have was local knowledge—not of laws or principles, but of men. Voters were expected to be familiar with the character of candidates for office. What was true for citizens as voters was true equally when citizens served as jurors. To be judged by a "jury of one's peers" was to be judged by people well acquainted with the character of the defendant and very likely well acquainted with the particular situation for which someone found himself on trial. The failure of the framers of the Constitution to require that criminal defendants be tried by a jury "of the vicinage" may have reflected the anti-democratic views of the Federalists, but not a principled notion that a good juror is impartial. Controversy over this omission became an issue in constitutional ratification in four states. In the Judiciary Act of 1795, it was settled that in capital cases, trials would take place in and jurors would be selected from the county in which the crime was committed.[98] Although some of the founders were inspired by Enlightenment thought and a striving for universalistic values, all of them were embedded in a society that trusted in the local and the particular, a social world in which knowledge worth having came from experience and acquaintance rather than from information and reasoning.

Representation in an Extended Republic

For many patriot leaders, one of the great difficulties in imagining a federal system was their conviction that republican government could flourish only in small states. The state legislatures had the great advantage over the Congress that the representatives had more intimate contact with their constituents. "They are sent but a small distance from their respective homes: Their conduct is constantly known to their constituents. They frequently see, and are seen by the men whose servants they are. . . . They return, and mix with their neighbours of the lowest rank, see their poverty, and feel their wants."[99] Within the states, concern about distance expressed itself in controversy over the location of the state capitals. Between 1776 and 1812 there were efforts to relocate the original state capital in every one of the original thirteen states—and the effort succeeded in nine cases.[100] Communities far from the capital not only had a harder time communicating with their representatives but also more difficulty in even sending their full complement of representatives. A North Carolinian observed in 1789 that members of the legislature from the western part of the state lived nearly five hundred miles from the capital, a long and even hazardous journey. Since many states did not pay legislators salaries or even expenses, but asked each locale to support its own representatives, many of the more remote communities chose not to send representatives at all.[101]

If distance was an impediment at the state level, it was even more worrisome nationally. There the inconveniences in travel and communication were amplified by the vast size of the country. Moreover, the extent of the nation ensured that it would be less socially homogeneous and less a community of political interest than in a smaller territory. "Cato," one of the Antifederalist writers, put it this way:

> The strongest principle of union resides within our domestic walls. The ties of the parent exceed that of any other; as we depart from home, the

next general principle of union is amongst citizens of the same state, where acquaintance, habits, and fortunes nourish affection, and attachment; enlarge the circle still further, and, as citizens of different states, though we acknowledge the same national denomination, we lose the ties of acquaintance, habits, and fortunes, and thus, by degrees, we lessen in our attachments, till, at length, we no more than acknowledge a sameness of species.[102]

Cato's concern about the sympathies between a representative and his constituency arises particularly when the reigning theory of representation presumes "actual" rather than "virtual" representation. In England, there was no presumption that a community's representative must reside in that community. In contrast, representatives in colonial assemblies were expected to come from among the inhabitants of the constituencies that elected them.[103] This simple practice came to stand for one side of a larger debate about democracy: should representatives merely channel the views of constituents or should they make up their own minds about the public good of the nation? In the American model there was a notion of attorneyship or agency where it was vital that representatives "know and be known by the citizens," as "A Farmer" put it.[104] In what would be the First Congress, each member of the House would represent 30,000 or more people. The "Federal Farmer" complained that these representatives would not be "well informed as to the circumstances of the people, the members of it must be too far removed from the people, in general, to sympathize with them, and too few to communicate with them." The representative "can only mix, and be acquainted with a few respectable characters among his constituents."[105] So small a number of representatives, wrote "Brutus," "cannot possibly represent the feelings, opinions, and characters of a great multitude."[106] What was highly original in this discussion was the assumption that representatives *should* resemble the people. The means for effecting this resemblance might be debated, but the innovation of the American theory of representation was that the representative body was a condensed or distilled version of the people at large rather than a separate and independent body.[107]

This "mirror theory" of representation grew out of Radical Whig doctrine that presumed a community of interests among the people. Adequate representation could then be achieved through frequent elections, a broad franchise, modest requirements for officeholding, and at least occasional use of petitions and instructions.[108] But the Federalists were less enamored of the idea of resemblance than the Antifederalists. Madison eloquently articulates the view in *Federalist* No. 10 that the people would choose representatives who were not duplicates of themselves but better than themselves. They would choose people known for wisdom and virtue, people tested in their local communities. These people would be not only wise and virtuous but competent, with experience and training, and the ability to speak articulately and persuasively before an assembled group. The representatives would deliberate, not just decide. That is, they would listen to one another so that each could vote based upon a consideration of the public interest, not just the constituency's interest. Madison stressed the advantages of this filtering system—to have people represented indirectly rather than in person would ensure a coolness to legislative deliberation, a removal of the heat, passion, and emotion that might otherwise cloud judgment. *The Federalist* papers are full of praise of the "cool" and "calm" virtues of representative government. The representative process would "refine and enlarge" public views by "passing through the medium of a chosen body of citizens; whose wisdom may best discern the truest interest of their country."[109]

After the Declaration of Independence and the Constitution no document speaks more directly than *The Federalist* papers to the paradoxical purpose of American constitutional rule—to establish a system responsible to the people at large but at the same time to prevent majorities from working their will on minorities. Madison's *Federalist* No. 10 is especially revealing about how the framers, or at least this very self-conscious one, conceived the public sphere—and pictured its dangers. With almost mathematical elegance Madison makes the case that a representative democracy or "republic" provides better government than direct or pure democracy and that a large or extended republic will better guarantee the people's liberties than a small one.

This second point was the more original. Madison turned on its head the Montesquieuan presumption that a republic was a system fit only for small states. He adduced several reasons that the extended republic would work better. First, the larger the republic, the higher the ratio of citizens to representative since the size of an efficient representative assembly could not multiply without limit. But why should a higher ratio be a good thing? Contrary to common sense, Madison argued that the higher ratio could be a blessing for popular control. He argued that the relationship of citizen and representative is a two-way street, and that if a smaller constituency can better control a representative, a representative can also better tyrannize a smaller constituency. The smaller the constituency, the easier it is for the representative to use bribery or demagoguery to gain and retain office. In the large constituency, "it will be more difficult for unworthy candidates to practice with success the vicious arts by which elections are too often carried; and the suffrages of the people being more free, will be more likely to center on men who possess the most attractive merit and the most diffusive and established characters." (Madison added that, of course, "as in most other cases, there is a mean, on both sides of which inconveniences will be found to lie.")

Second, Madison makes his celebrated argument that the larger the society the greater the variety of parties and interests. The greater the variety of parties and interests, the more likely they will be to contend against one another, the less likely it will be for a majority to "have a common motive to invade the rights of other citizens." In a word, the pluralism of interests makes it difficult to establish a despotic majority. Madison incorporates in his argument not only the idea that a multiplicity of interests makes a majority more difficult to achieve but that it does so, in part, by making a majority more difficult to *recognize*. Even if a majority did have a common sentiment, the size and complexity of the extended republic would make it "more difficult for all who feel it to discover their own strength and to act in unison with each other." Madison is developing a political theory here that places communication at its center, a tendency in his thinking that he develops further in *Federalist* No. 51. There he adds that not only does the multiplicity of sects and interests in the extended republic make it difficult to establish a majority coalition, but that that same difficulty requires anyone who would form a majority to appeal to principles of "justice and the general good." When so many different groups must be won over to form a majority coalition, parochial rhetoric will not suffice—and so the extended republic, much more than the small republic, pushes at least the language of political actors, and very likely their policies as well, toward a broad concept of the public good.

Another question of representation divided the founders: should apportionment (a controversy at both state and federal levels) be on the basis of population or of "space"? Small states, of course, disagreed with large states for self-interested reasons, but "corporate" representation suggests something that "territorial" (population) representation does not: it suggests not only contiguity but community, a commonality of interests and a thickness of communication and contact that might enable a coherent character or "interest" to develop. Until the Revolution each colony had adopted some form of corporate representation. Equal representation, by this system, was equal representation not of individuals but of constituted communities.

Indeed, a notion of the indivisibility of state corporateness led some states initially to elect representatives to the House at large, by state, rather than in single-member districts within the state. This included both small states (New Hampshire) and large (Pennsylvania). Arguments in Pennsylvania newspapers (reprinted in Massachusetts as well) favored elections at large as affording people the widest selection of the most competent people and reducing the chances of "caballing and influencing." [110] On the other side, the argument was that district elections would significantly improve the closeness of the constituent to the representative and reduce the chance that one set of interests in the state would overwhelm the others. "Real Farmer," quoting an unnamed "eminent writer," argued that "'The end to be aimed at in the formation of a representative assembly, seems to be the sense of the people, the public voice: *The perfection of the portrait consists in its likeness.*'"[111] While this view would ultimately take hold in every state, it was not at first the obvious solution. Constructing a public sphere, even in terms of the basic electoral machinery, was an open-ended problem, with various alternatives that appeared on their face equally satisfactory or equally problematic.

Take, for instance, the debates in the Pennsylvania Assembly in 1788. Representative Findley of Westmoreland urged that the state be divided into eight election districts, each to elect one representative to Congress; only in this way could the eight "have a particular knowledge of the local and common interest of their constituents throughout the state." [112] On the other side, as "A Friend to Agriculture" wrote in the *Pennsylvania Gazette* in July 1788, district elections "would reduce me from an elector for a confederated state, to an elector for a part of a state." [113] As it turned out, Pennsylvania adopted statewide elections, a matter on which Madison commented in a letter to Thomas Jefferson: "This mode of election will confine the choice to characters of general notoriety, and so far be favorable to merit. It is however liable to some popular objections urged against the tendency of the new system." Madison believed that Virginia would adopt a district system (it did). He concluded hopefully that "various modes should be tried, as by that means only the best mode can be ascertained." [114]

The institutions that today people focus on in thinking about what makes a vibrant democratic public were for the founding generation either a secondary concern (the press) or positively discouraged (parties and, for some, voluntary associations). The founders looked first to the formal mechanisms that established the electoral relationship of citizens to their representatives, and the governmental mechanisms that regulated relationships among the representatives themselves. Nothing mattered more than the formal design of government. Both academic and popular thinking have strayed a long distance from this position, and for some good reasons, but the founders remind us that the character of the "public sphere" as an ordered and organized social arena for political discussion depends very much on the constitutional and electoral framework that undergirds it.

The Perfection of the Republic

The celebration of civil society that is universally associated with Tocqueville's writings of the 1830s had little precedent in American political thought of the 1790s. I have tried here to portray an absence, a missing chorus of praise for civil society, and even more than that, a hostility toward what would later be acclaimed as the very genius of American political culture. I intend by this neither to praise nor to condemn the founding fathers but to emphasize the distance we have traveled from them. There is much still to be learned about ourselves and our present possibilities from the founders, but they operated from premises a world away from our own. They wanted to squash institutions whose nurture nearly everyone today finds essential to democracy. If we can still gain guidance from the political thought of the framers, there are also obvious limitations to what we can learn, and anyone who seeks to rest too literally in their realm will experience an uncomfortable vertigo in trying to comprehend the ways of the world two hundred years later.

Many of the founders believed that the Constitution provided the framework for a "perfect" government. Washington, writing in 1790, suggested that "the government, though not absolutely perfect, is one of the best in the world." [115] Jefferson, to be sure, was much less satisfied. Writing to Madison in the fall of 1789, he proposed that a generation could not, or should not, pass on its laws as legacy to the next. "Between society and society, or generation and generation, there is no mutual obligation, no umpire but the law of nature." No law of society can be perpetual. Jefferson argued that "Every constitution and every law naturally expires at the end of nineteen years," the length of time he calculated for a political generation. [116]

For Madison, in contrast, hope lay not only in the mechanisms the Constitution established but in the prestige of the leaders who had created it. The Constitution would serve as a foundation for the country only if the country provided the Constitution a degree of deference. Early in 1788, the Constitutional Convention barely behind him, Madison argued vigorously against efforts to convene a second convention before ratification. Writing to Edmund Randolph, who in the end opposed the Constitution, he warned that a second convention would give vent to opinions "which must be as various and irreconcileable concerning theories of Government, as doctrines of Religion." Madison was supremely aware that the relative unity of elites standing behind the Constitution bolstered its chances for ratification. He cautioned Randolph:

Whatever respect may be due to the rights of private judgment, and no man feels more of it than I do, there can be no doubt that there are subjects to which the bulk of mankind are unequal, and on which they must and will be governed by those with whom they happen to have acquaintance and confidence. The proposed Constitution is of this description.[117]

The difference between Jefferson and Madison, friends and allies though they were, is significant. Jefferson valued liberty above all, but identified it with the democratic will, tempered by the filter of representation. Madison valued liberty, but believed it to be dependent on order, law, and a reverence for law. What they shared—and shared with Washington as well—was a focus on the institutions of government as the guarantor of both order and liberty. When they established a government, they did not mean to establish a new instrumentality to negotiate with other associations and opinions in society; they meant for opinion to be channeled into and formed in the institutions of government themselves.

Madison and Jefferson did not, by the standards of the nineteenth century, expect many people to be involved in the political process, nor did they expect, by the standards of the twentieth century, that national government would be an active presence in the daily lives of citizens. What they expected and hoped is that public opinion would find its voice in and through the formal institutions of government. Public opinion was as much something that government would make possible as it was the instrument to make a government.

Chapter 3

The Democratic Transition
in American Political Life

1801–1865

Prospectus
Electoral and Constitutional Reform
What Tocqueville Didn't Say About Voluntary Associations
Abolitionism and the Public Sphere
Embracing Parties
The Antebellum Press: "That Such Dry Bones May Live"
The Press as the Patron of Oratory
Politics as a Vocation

Prospectus

Since representative institutions and public participation advanced so greatly in the 1700s, it may come as a surprise that historians generally regard the early nineteenth century as the first flowering of American democracy. The eighteenth century saw the gradual emergence of popular control of government. In the revolutionary period, of course, there was a sea change in political life and the virtual "invention," to use James Madison's term, of republican government.[1] Nevertheless, politics on the eve of the nineteenth century was far from democratic. A deferential political culture endured. Voter turnout tended to be low and the gentry maintained their rule with little effort. Even on the frontier, long praised by some historians for its democratic mores, members of rich and well-connected families normally won political office without opposition.[2] The Constitution had not altered assumptions of deference and so-cial hierarchy, nor, really, had it been intended to. It is in this context that we can understand why Jefferson's coming to power in the election of 1800 began to turn the tide. Jefferson himself would later call it "the revolution of 1800."[3]

Of course, deferential habits did not disappear overnight. As histo-rian Joyce Appleby argues, the very content of political debate became the battle between deference and democracy.[4] The Federalists stood for social hierarchy in their combat with Jeffersonians, their battles raging in all spheres of life: in the family, in religion, in conflict over economic development and change, in contention over language, culture, and ed-ucation, and in constitutional struggles in the states. This broad and deep social transformation is more complex than I can describe here, but a few paragraphs can at least hint at how wide-ranging it was.

By 1800 and even more in the decades to follow, something new was in the air in family life; there was under way a democratization of parental, especially paternal, authority. The law and custom of primo-geniture, whereby the eldest son in a family received significant advan-tages in the inheritance of the family's estate, disappeared quickly after the Revolution as most states repealed existing laws of inheritance. After 1810 older sons lost all economic advantage over their younger brothers. One historian even speaks of a "revolution in age relations" taking place between 1770 and 1820. The advantages of age declined. Before about 1780 the father stood above the rest of the family in fam-ily portraits, the wife below him, the children below her; after 1780 it became increasingly common to place all family members on a hori-zontal plane; and from 1820 to 1890 every family painting is composed this way.[5]

In education, reform was growing by the 1820s, the view emerging that children could be trained to virtue and were not by nature sinful. McGuffey's sequenced readers, first published in 1836, featured stories about children rather than "long lists of often meaningless words" to teach reading.[6] Where teachers of rhetoric had insisted on a high style consistently from the 1760s into the 1820s, texts written from that point on promoted a democratized, "plain" style instead.[7]

School reformers began to argue that the state should provide public education and the "common school" movement spread, state by state, though not until the 1840s and 1850s. In Massachusetts, which was certainly the state with the best formal provision for public schooling, public education before the reforms was pitiful. In 1826 only a third of school-age children attended public schools for any part of the year. The teachers, generally young men of no training who saw schooling as a temporary position, were inadequate, some of them unable to multiply and divide themselves, let alone teach arithmetic to children. The state had ceded responsibility for the schools to the towns, and towns had passed responsibility on to districts or individuals. Horace Mann tried to persuade leaders in the state that "education has a market value; that it is so far an article of merchandise, that it may be turned to a pecuniary account."[8] At the same time, he was motivated by loftier goals: he sought to instill in new generations a public morality appropriate to citizenship. He would reform not only teaching but the very organization of classroom life:

> He who has been a serf until the day before he is twenty-one years of age cannot be an independent citizen the day after; and it makes no difference whether he has been a serf in Austria or in America. As the fitting apprenticeship for despotism consists in being trained to despotism, so the fitting apprenticeship for self-government consists in being trained for self-government.[9]

Mann's sense of morality in the schools was nonsectarian among the various Protestant denominations, but he insisted on Bible reading. The schools should be strictly nonpolitical—Mann was aghast when a normal school headmaster he had appointed took his students to an abolitionist meeting. Like other educational reformers of the day, he was a conservative reformer, using education to mold democracy and simultaneously to fend off the dangers of excessive democracy—that is, to prevent the newly enfranchised masses from threatening established authority by force. He believed universal education would be insurance "against mobocracy, confiscatory legislation, threats to judicial supremacy, and the spoils system which Jacksonism held so dear."[10]

Beyond New England the common school movement made little headway. Before compulsory attendance laws and the general rise of school attendance in the late nineteenth century, formal schooling remained the property of few. In theory, education was essential to republican life. If there are to be frequent elections and republican government, citizens must be educated well enough to vote intelligently and officeholders must be educated well enough to serve responsibly. In practice, antebellum efforts to expand public schooling were ideologically incoherent, sometimes appealing to republicanism, sometimes to an evangelical vision of personal transformation, and sometimes to a market-oriented dream of upward social and economic mobility.[11] Even as reformers promoted education for both rich and poor, black and white, male and female, the restriction of the franchise to white men came to be more explicitly defended, and the independence of school expansion from the requisites for an informed citizenry more apparent. When, in the late nineteenth century, state governments accepted responsibility for schooling, they did so with anxiety over the prospect of an unruly working class, the attendant threat to the virtues of an agrarian society, and the appearance on American shores of more and more non-Anglo-Saxon immigrants. Motives for school reform were mixed, to be sure, but the drive for social control seemed more powerful than the idea that democracy required that voting citizens be informed.

If educational change was slow, the spread of a democratic ethos in religion was explosive. Evangelical Christianity became a powerful agent of democratization in the first fifty years of the new nation. The second "great awakening" of that era was part of a broad alteration of Christianity. For one thing, there was just a lot more religion to go around; preachers per capita tripled from 1775 to 1845. In the proliferating evangelical sects, new leaders of little or no formal training preached a gospel that rejected Calvinist strictures and accepted popular spiritual aspirations at face value. Hierarchy and deference were of no account here; indeed, the new ministry "taught that divine insight was reserved for the poor and humble rather than the proud and learned."[12]

In the first decades of the nineteenth century, there were efforts, state by state, to extend the suffrage, eliminating the freehold qualification for voters. The number of offices that were elective rather than appointive grew. State senators and governors were elected directly rather than indirectly through the lower house of the legislature; legislative seats were apportioned more equitably by population.[13] These were just the most formal institutional signs of fundamental change in common understandings of politics, social life, and political communication.

The new egalitarian ethos provided a framework for American politics so much more democratic than that of the Federalist era that we can justifiably call this the democratic transition in American history. This transition was both profound and complex. At the same time that government became formally more democratized, powerful elements in society sought to exercise their influence in ways less accessible to the general public. Recent research on state and municipal government in this period finds that crucial matters of taxing and spending were carefully insulated from majoritarian decision-making.[14] At the same time that the halls of government became more open to all white men, the cultural significance of the distinctions between men and women, Protestants and Catholics, blacks and whites, immigrants and natives became more salient bases of political struggle. Simultaneously, as the nation grew not only more democratic but more populous, old, informal means of organization and influence broke down and new associations, including formally organized political parties, came into being. Organization supplanted deference. This, too, was part of the transition from the rule of gentlemen to the rule of majorities that fundamentally changed the ideals and practices of American citizenship.

Electoral and Constitutional Reform

"Democracy was the political talisman of the new age," one scholar observes, but that is not to say it worked its charms unerringly.[15] Political reform was enacted against opposition, and compromise made it less thoroughgoing than reformers intended. Conflicts over democracy were dramatically evident in the reforms of state constitutions. The constitutional convention in Massachusetts in 1820–21 prominently featured conservative arguments, notably from John Adams, Justice Joseph Story, and the young Daniel Webster. At first, the convention approved universal male suffrage, which was approximated in practice already, the property qualification for voting being so modest. But delegates reversed themselves when Josiah Quincy warned of an industrial rabble of the future arising in factory towns and outvoting those who respected property. The convention approved a compromise that extended voting rights to any male who paid any tax at all to state or county.

The Massachusetts Constitution of 1780 established that senatorial seats should be apportioned according to the amount of taxes paid in the different districts of the state. At first, the convention decided to retain this rule. But a powerful speech from Henry Dearborn inspired the delegates to propose reorganizing the Senate on a population rather than taxpaying basis. A motion to reconsider this decision brought forth leading conservatives to defend the role of property in a legislative system.[16] Daniel Webster argued in favor of a taxpaying basis for the state Senate. This part of the Constitution of 1780 was not a limit on the power of the people but only on "the authority of their agents." The Senate does not check the power of the people but the power of the lower house of the legislature. "And if it be wise to give one agent the power of checking or controlling another, it is equally wise, most manifestly, that there should be some difference of character, sentiment, feeling, or origin, in that agent, who is to possess this control. Otherwise, it is not at all probable that the control will ever be exercised." While Webster did not insist that the taxpaying qualification was the best such means of distinguishing the two legislative houses, he did hold that for forty years the laws produced by Massachusetts had been good ones, and that "it is entirely just that property should have its due weight and consideration in political arrangements. . . . We have no experience that teaches us, that any other rights are safe, where property is not safe."[17]

Webster's argument won the day, but when the convention's proposals were submitted one by one to the voters, Massachusetts citizens rejected the plan to keep the taxation basis for apportioning Senate seats while endorsing overwhelmingly the liberalized qualification for the franchise.

The most complex and perhaps also the most moving of the constitutional conventions was Virginia's. Especially moving, at least to the modern ear, was the "memorial" composed by the non-freeholders of Richmond that Chief Justice John Marshall presented to the convention on October 13, 1829. To these petitioners, ownership of property "no more proves him who has it, wiser or better, than it proves him taller or stronger, than him who has it not." For them, the question was patriotic attachment to the state, not property: "Virtue, intelligence, are not among the products of the soil. Attachment to property, often a sordid sentiment, is not to be confounded with the sacred flame of patriotism. The love of country, like that of parents and offspring, is engrafted in our nature. It exists in all climates, among all classes, under every possible form of Government. Riches oftener impair it than poverty. Who has it not is a monster." It was an affront to their dignity to be denied the vote. And it was inconsistent to deny the responsible attachment to society of the propertyless for the purpose of voting while entrusting these same irresponsible people with arms for defense of society. "The muster rolls have undergone no scrutiny, no comparison with the land books, with a view to expunge those who have been struck from the ranks of freemen. If the landless citizens have been ignominiously driven from the polls, in time of peace, they have at least been generously summoned, in war, to the battle-field. Nor have they disobeyed the summons, or, less profusely than others, poured out their blood in the defence of that country which is asked to disown them. Will it be said they owe allegiance to the Government that gives them protection? Be it so: and if they acknowledge the obligation; if privileges are really extended to them in defence of which they may reasonably be required to shed their blood, have they not motives, irresistible motives, of attachment to the community?"[18]

New state constitutions were not prompted by unselfish democratic reformers, nor by a cultural sweep of democratic spirit unpopulated by real striving souls. In New York, the "Bucktail" faction among Democrats, with Martin Van Buren in the lead, sought constitutional revision to gain greater leverage against the faction controlled by DeWitt Clinton that dominated the state government. Their success in making more offices elective rather than appointive reduced the power of the governor (Clinton was the incumbent) while increasing the role of the political party at a time when the Bucktails were the best organized in the state. Constitutional change helped Van Buren's organization control state politics for the next two decades.[19] As in the mid-eighteenth century, political insiders contending for power used democratization to gain political advantage. Yet in doing so, they left a legacy of democratic rhetoric and practice despite themselves. The nineteenth-century strategists were more comfortable than their colonial forebears with the egalitarian rhetoric that swept over all.

The written constitutions, both state and federal, and the recurrent efforts to rewrite or amend them, were novel political communications in themselves. England had no written constitution, nor did any other nation have a set of laws to which legislatures or other ruling bodies owed allegiance. The people in the United States were sovereign, through their appointed representatives, but not through their representatives alone. They were sovereign by the historical political contract written out in a constitution and revised or renewed through constitutional conventions. The nation was becoming more and more egalitarian socially and democratic politically, but not even in the heyday of the Jacksonian era was this democracy one of majoritarian principles alone. There was permanent tension between popular will as recorded at the polls and constitutional constraints as vouched for by written compact. This was a scribbling, editing, revising democracy that took its charter documents, state and federal, very seriously.

By 1824, every state provided suffrage to essentially all white male adults. The popular election of the president (through the electoral college) became standard practice. In 1800, electors in the electoral college were selected by a general popular vote in only two states; after 1832, South Carolina stood alone in having its state legislature choose electors. In 1824, six state legislatures selected governors for their states, by 1844 only two, as popular elections took over.[20] Lesser offices became elective, too, especially in the West. Illinois and Indiana provided for elective county offices in their first constitutions. Mississippi provided for elected justices of the peace and constables in 1832; Tennessee in 1834 did the same for county clerks and sheriffs. New York made more local officers elective in its constitutional revision of 1821. Delaware moved in the same direction in 1831, Pennsylvania in 1838.[21]

Constitutional change at the local level moved toward democracy, too. In Boston in the 1820s, Federalists who worried over the town meeting's potential for mob rule sought a city charter, but they got something very different from what they intended. Instead of citywide elections for a board of aldermen at a general meeting, a system of ward voting was approved. This was based on the growing assumption that a consensual public good, with a set of virtuous representatives to speak for it, could not be found but that representatives would reflect the contentious and conflicting interests of different groups in the city.[22]

This was already a long way from town meetings rooted in shared values and taken-for-granted social hierarchies, a long way from the assurance that leading notables could ascertain the public good. The change was not one of philosophy, though philosophy played its role, but of the democratic transformation of social experience in its every facet.

What Tocqueville Didn't Say About Voluntary Associations

Alexis de Tocqueville's celebration of voluntary associations is the best known of his many famous observations on American life. Americans formed associations at "all ages, all stations in life, and all types of disposition." These private nonpolitical associations had a variety Tocqueville found astounding—commercial, industrial, religious, "moral, serious, futile, very general, and very limited, immensely large and very minute. Americans combine to give fetes, found seminaries, build churches, distribute books, and send missionaries to the antipodes. Hospitals, prisons, and schools take shape in that way. . . . if they want to proclaim a truth or propagate some feeling by the encouragement of a great example, they form an association."[23] In the absence of an aristocracy that gave men the capacity and resources for great undertakings, the "art of association" was of supreme importance, the moral and intellectual associations quite as much as economic and political ones. "In democratic countries knowledge of how to combine is the mother of all other forms of knowledge; on its progress depends that of all the others."[24]

Washington's cautions against self-created societies seemed ancient history by 1840, made obsolete by the increasing size and heterogeneity

of society and by a growing spirit of democracy. Where once local notables led public opinion and dominated public life through the gestures
and habits of deference, increasingly organized associations of equals
came to play the leading role. Social control and social patterns were
shifting from the personal to the interpersonal. In economic life, banks
chartered by the states began to replace credit issued by individual merchants on a personal basis. Early temperance reformers, to take another
example, urged gentlemen to set the tone for the rest of society. From the
1830s however, middle-class temperance reformers, operating in a more
populous, heterogeneous, and class-conscious world, trusted not in paternalism but in organization. Taking its cue from the evangelical
churches of the Second Great Awakening, the American Temperance
Society (founded 1826) made extensive use of tracts, organized itself by
local chapters, and spoke to the broad middle class, urging upon it intelligent self-control.[25] Associations formalized what, in the older deferential society, did not require organization. Interpersonal organization was
in principle more democratic than personal social control, more divorced from assumed hierarchies of wealth and property. Social life, in
Max Weber's terms, was becoming rationalized.

In the early 1800s, various causes, especially religious ones, prompted
the organizing impulse. For instance, the federal government's policy of
delivering mail on the Sabbath spawned major protests between 1810
and 1830. A network of ministers mobilized church members, and in
1815 one hundred petitions came to Congress from Presbyterians and
Congregationalists all over the country. When this Sabbatarian movement was renewed a decade later, it was spearheaded by an organization of
ministers and laity, the General Union for the Promotion of the Christian
Sabbath. This group, determined to operate outside the churches, invited
membership of any person who pledged to honor the Sabbath and to
boycott all transportation companies that operated seven days a week. It
circulated 100,000 copies of leader Lyman Beecher's address through
pamphlet form or in newspapers. It established twenty-six branch offices.
It launched a drive that delivered more than nine hundred petitions to
Congress between 1829 and the spring of 1831. Most of these used standard texts the General Union provided, but others were homemade; more

than ninety differently worded petitions came in, typically with twenty to fifty signatures but some with as many as seven thousand.[26]

This movement, like many other antebellum voluntary organizations, had religious origins but a form much influenced by the political system, in this case, the focus on petitions. Middle-class temperance organizations, like so many other voluntary associations, borrowed from political life the practice of writing constitutions and bylaws, electing their own officers, and banding with comparable societies to form statewide organizations governed by decisions made at annual conventions by delegates from the local groups.[27] The voluntary benevolent associations, in turn, would provide models for the emerging political parties. Political parties at first nominated candidates in congressional caucuses; not until the Anti-Masons in 1831 nominated through a convention did parties begin to adopt the well-settled convention practice of the nonparty benevolent associations.[28]

Leaders of moral reform movements borrowed from the political system not only by adopting its organizational forms but by orienting their rhetoric, at least some of the time, toward constitutional rather than sectarian appeals.[29] Public life was by no means simply the sum of local, grassroots efforts. The public sphere of the early nation emerged not from the bottom up nor from the top down, neither from the provinces nor the capital, but in both directions at once. The existence of a broad franchise, of a legislature with elected, territorially based representatives, and the growing legitimacy (as we shall see) of parties and campaigns oriented to winning elections gave shape and body to private associations even as religion gave them breath.

The disadvantage of voluntary associations lay not in the word "association" but in the word "voluntary." By the twentieth century, while the voluntary association would continue to flourish, it also would come up against social problems to which its participatory form was not a very effective solution. As the locus of authoritative decision-making moved increasingly to Washington, national organizations that could act quickly and, just as important, act continuously, supplemented or sometimes supplanted voluntary associations. The petition, in other words, would in time give way to the lobby.

But in the early 1800s, voluntary associations were springing up everywhere. This included the volunteer fire companies in the cities. These fraternal organizations were, among other things, schools for democracy. The companies in New York elected their foremen annually and operated according to strict bylaws—but forbade any dissension or disputes among members. Other voluntary associations included many associations of artisans. New York boasted societies for tailors, hatters, shipwrights, coopers, masons, carpenters, printers, butchers, bakers, and cabinetmakers, some welcoming only journeymen, some inclusive of masters as well.[30] Where journeymen organized apart from and in some measure in opposition to masters, masters organized in return.[31] By the 1830s, workingmen even organized political parties.

Although Tocqueville was enraptured by the many moral and civic associations whose activities he witnessed, he expressed much more measured approval of *political* associations. There is an unmistakable echo in Tocqueville of Washington's distrust of self-created societies—voluntary associations with political purposes. Suppose, Tocqueville asks, that, in addition to the majority that makes the laws through elected officials, there is also a minority "which only deliberates and which gets laws ready for adoption." In that case, he writes, "I cannot help but think that then public order would be exposed to great risks." Unlimited freedom of association offers great dangers—it is "of all forms of liberty, the last that a nation can sustain. While it may not actually lead it into anarchy, it does constantly bring it to the verge thereof."[32] This observation in volume one of *Democracy in America* is important enough to Tocqueville that he quotes it in volume two and then re-asserts that the freedom of association is "a dangerous liberty."[33] It allows for the formation of political parties and pressure groups that can tear a country apart.

Nevertheless, because America had no aristocracy, some kind of social formation was necessary to bridge the gulf between the individual and the state, and political associations, specifically, parties, seemed the only possibility. So in America, Tocqueville concluded, political associations must be tolerated because they are the "great free schools to which all citizens come to be taught the general theory of association."[34] The parties provide instruction and inspiration to the plethora of community groups that Tocqueville marveled at. So, for instance, the Presbyterian preacher Charles Finney asked, "What do the politicians do? They get up meetings, circulate handbills and pamphlets, blast away in the newspapers, send their ships about the streets on wheels with flags and sailors, send coaches all over town, with handbills, to bring people up to the polls, all to gain attention to their cause and elect their candidate," and he proposed the churches learn from them: "The object of our measures is to gain attention and you must have something new." [35]

Tocqueville finds that political associations are rendered less dangerous in the United States than they might be in another democratic society for several reasons. First, the differences among American political parties and factions are relatively slight compared to Europe. Differences of view in America are "only matters of nuance." Moreover, because there is universal suffrage, the majority is known, it is measured, and no association that does not represent the majority can plausibly claim to do so—if they were a majority, they would be in office. So the Americans are relatively immune to the dangers of political associations—in America, political associations are destined to compete for majorities according to the legal forms rather than to venture direct action based on inflated and unverifiable claims of popular support. [36]

The dangers Tocqueville anticipated from political groups of strongly differentiated views would not be long in surfacing. Only, oddly enough, they would come not directly from political parties but from civil associations that over time developed strong political agendas.

It began in the churches. Out of the churches emerged groups to organize Sunday schools, to spread the Gospel, to end drinking, to abolish slavery, to work for peace. These voluntary associations developed statewide organization—the Missionary Society of Connecticut in 1798 and a General Association of Congregational Ministers in Massachusetts in 1799. These groups sent missionaries out to the frontier communities of Vermont, New Hampshire, Maine and west to New York, Ohio, and Pennsylvania. [37] New organizations sponsored charity work for the deaf, the colonization of American slaves in Africa, and improved treatment of the insane. Movements interpenetrated. The various associations met not only separately but together. In the 1830s, on "anniversary week," different reform organizations in Massachusetts all held meetings on the Boston Common. Large organizations set up tents and smaller ones met in churches around the Common, three or four different organizations each day holding meetings and giving speeches. Horace Mann invited his nephew to the event in 1837. "It is a most interesting week," he wrote, "full of instruction and of stimulus to a young mind."[38]

As the aims of the associations became more ardent and more politically defined, the groups were as often at one another's throats as at one another's sides. The abolitionists, in particular, sought to extend their influence through other religious societies. They tried to get the American Bible Society to distribute Bibles among Negroes, free and slave. They contributed funds to the Bible Society earmarked for Bibles for Negroes. They tried to persuade the American Home Missionary Society to withhold support from congregations that counted slaveholders among their members, and sought to get from the American Tract Society a condemnation of slavery.[39]

So long as the voluntary associations were oriented to religious or charity work removed from public debate or governmental policies, their relation to the "public sphere" was indirect. But they were scarcely cordoned off from public controversy. The Sabbatarians' goals were directly political—that is, they sought to change the laws governing Sabbath observance, and they insisted that the United States was fundamentally and essentially a Christian nation. The leaders of the reform societies were generally cultural conservatives. By the 1840s, many of them would tie the fortunes of moral reform to the success of the Whig Party. They saw political change as a serious obstacle to their efforts; as people moved westward, and as Westerners seemed to vote for Democrats rather than Whigs, the reform societies grew alarmed.

Senator Theodore Frelinghuysen (New Jersey), president of the Tract Society from 1842 to 1848 and the Bible Society from 1846 to 1862, was a founder of the Whig Party. He advised the benevolent societies that they must control the Westerners and not allow them to continue "with no moral culture." He made clear the dangers he saw in "King Andrew [Jackson] the First."[40] Frelinghuysen disputed the views of

Senator Richard Johnson, who asked the benevolent societies to keep out of politics: "Extensive religious combinations to effect a political object are . . . always dangerous."[41] Frelinghuysen, responding for the Sabbatarians, deplored an established church but asserted that the government should follow Christian principles, that a free people can flourish only when motivated by moral causes, and that "it is the Sabbath which gives vigor, and energy, and stability to these causes."[42]

The temperance movement at first stayed out of politics, but its stupendous growth pushed it into the political realm. The American Temperance Society reached 1.5 million members in more than eight thousand auxiliaries by 1835, as many as one in five members of the free adult population of the country. There were general community auxiliaries but also auxiliaries of African-Americans, of cotton factory employees, of college students, and even of taverngoers (since distilled but not fermented beverages were forsworn in the temperance society pledge).[43] The president of the Maine Temperance Union, Neal Dow, organized temperance voters into a disciplined unit, and in 1850 he ran successfully for mayor of Portland on the Whig ticket. He drafted and helped pass a statewide prohibition bill, "the Maine Law," that forbade the manufacture or sale of liquor except by bonded agents for medicinal or industrial use. This made Dow a national figure as efforts across the nation sought to duplicate his success. Temperance organizations would interrogate candidates of the leading parties and endorse those who supported their cause.

Much of the activity of moral reform was engineered by the energy of New England Puritan tradition and organization, but it was responsive equally to the broad rage for democratically minded improvement. If it was often backward-looking, an effort of its leaders to stave off what seemed to them the moral degradation of democratization, secularization, and the market, it was at the same time the incarnation of democratic ways and means. There was not only the Calvinist sense of stewardship but an "evangelical counteroffensive," and both fueled the proliferation of private organizations oriented to public service, from professional societies to libraries, schools, colleges, orphanages, and asylums.[44] Nothing illustrates this better than the explosion of abolitionism into American politics.

Abolitionism and the Public Sphere

There were forty-seven abolitionist societies in 1833, more than one thousand by 1837.[45] Traveling anti-slavery preachers moved from town to town, organizing new chapters and enlisting church women in petition drives. The abolitionists took advantage of the new efficiency of rotary steam presses and did their best to flood the country with newspapers and tracts.[46]

Southerners were stunned at this explosive attack on slavery, and their anger was exacerbated by hostility to the technical means with which abolitionists advanced their cause. "Yes, sir," said Virginia's Representative John Jones, "worked by steam, with the open and avowed object of effecting the immediate abolition of slavery in the Southern States." He objected to the use of steam power and the press, "these two great revolutionizers of the world," as he put it, harnessed to the task of publishing "newspapers, pamphlets, tracts, and pictures, calculated, in an eminent degree, to rouse and inflame the passions of the slaves against their masters, to urge them on to deeds of death, and to involve them all in the horrors of a servile war."[47]

The propaganda campaign and the petition drives, emerging on an unprecedented scale, intensified public life in deeply unsettling ways. In the South, opposition to the abolitionist propaganda campaign led to laws forbidding the distribution of incendiary literature, rewards for the arrest of abolitionist leaders, calls for arresting any abolitionist carrying the hated literature, and boycotting the businesses of abolitionists. Conflict came to a head in July 1835, when a vigilante group in Charleston broke into the post office, removed the abolitionist literature, and the next night burned it before an enthusiastic crowd of two thousand, about a seventh of the city's white population.

Public officials responded to the ensuing crisis on two levels. First, inside the postal service, the postmaster in Charleston faced a dilemma of how to carry out his federal responsibility to protect the mails without exacerbating his fear that abolitionist propaganda could spark a slave rebellion. He was rescued by Postmaster Samuel Gouverneur of New York, where the abolitionist materials had been placed in the mails. Gouverneur simply refused to accept further abolitionist materials, arguing that since receiving the materials was illegal in South Carolina (as in most Southern states), it was also illegal to enter it in the mails in New York.

On a second front, in Washington, Postmaster Amos Kendall resolved to keep abolitionist propaganda from the mails but without resort to federal law, arguing that the states of the Union were in many ways "twenty-six independent nations" and that one nation had no right to transmit subversive literature to another. Nonetheless, President Jackson, in his annual message to Congress in 1835, called for a national censorship law to bar "incendiary" materials from the mails. He was thwarted, ironically, by Senator John C. Calhoun (his former vice president and longtime political rival), who opposed a federal law, but sought federal legislation to place such power in the hands of the states.

Both Jackson's and Calhoun's proposals died, but their intentions were fulfilled. The post office under Jackson encouraged postmasters to exclude anti-slavery literature from the mails. Across the South old legislation was appealed to or new legislation passed to bar incendiary or inflammatory materials from circulation.[48] These efforts at censorship drew very little opposition, even in the North, where most newspaper editors and other leaders of opinion sided with efforts to keep abolitionists from threatening the nation's peace and union. One pamphleteering minister revived the Federalist language of opposition to self-created societies in denouncing the American Anti-Slavery Society as "a grand and permanent political organization, self-erected, self-governed, independent, and irresponsible." Such a permanent political machine, he argued, was unconstitutional on its face.[49]

At the same time hundreds of petitions with tens of thousands of signatures poured into Congress asking for the abolition of slavery in the District of Columbia and demanding that neither Florida nor Texas be added to the Union as slave states. Congressmen had routinely presented citizens' petitions to the Congress, stating on the floor their subjects, place of origin, and number of signatures, and then referring them to committee. This had happened with all variety of petitions, including anti-slavery petitions, from the beginning of the Republic. The abolitionist effort, however, sharply increased the visibility of petitioning. At the end of 1835, Southerners in both House and Senate asked that anti-slavery petitions be rejected rather than announced and tabled or referred to committee. This was an extreme position that split off a number of anti-abolitionist Northerners. Representative Samuel Beardsley of New York, who had himself led a mob against abolitionists, defended the "sacred right" of petitioning. In 1836, Henry Pinckney of South Carolina proposed referring all anti-slavery petitions to a select committee that would declare that Congress had no power to regulate slavery in the states and ought not to outlaw it in the District. A select committee was formed and reported back several resolutions, including one to prohibit the House from discussing or even mentioning the content of anti-slavery petitions. Pinckney said his main purpose was "to arrest discussion of the subject of slavery within these walls." [50]

This "gag rule" passed with ardent Jackson administration support. It was not a standing rule of the House but a resolution that had to be renewed in each congressional session. In 1837, near the beginning of the next session, the former president, John Quincy Adams, now serving as a representative from Massachusetts, read most of an anti-slavery petition before being gaveled down—and before the gag rule was renewed.

Meanwhile, petitions kept coming: 130,000 in 1837–38 asking for abolition of slavery in the District of Columbia, 32,000 asking for repeal of the gag rule, 21,000 to ban slavery from the Western territories, and 23,000 to end the interstate slave trade. In 1837–38, petitions and memorials fully occupied several clerks in the House and filled a large storage room.[51] In 1840, the gag order was replaced with a standing House rule that disallowed Congress from even receiving, let alone responding to, anti-slavery petitions.

John Quincy Adams, dubbed by a colleague Old Man Eloquent, played a stirring role in this phase of the anti-slavery movement; he boldly defended the right to petition and finally, in 1844, quarried enough votes to have the gag rule repealed. In his years of protest, Adams acted as a special tribune of civil society, a voice of the right of private citizens and private organizations to make themselves heard in the chief legislative assembly of the state. Again and again, he insisted on the sacred right of petition and insisted it belonged to all, white and black, free and slave. "Petition is supplication—it is entreaty—it is prayer," he reminded the Congress. Does the law say, he asked, that "before presenting a petition, you shall look into it, and see whether it comes from the virtuous, and the great and the mighty? No, sir, it says no such thing; the right of petition belongs to all."[52]

The effort to deny this right helped mobilize anti-slavery support; not a few people felt more strongly about preserving political liberties of citizens than about freeing slaves from bondage. The interaction between a relatively isolated gadfly in the Congress and a small, unpopular, but vigorous social movement suggests how critical is the relationship between the institutions of the state and the institutions of "civil society." The place of the Congress, particularly the directly elected House of Representatives, as the country's preeminent public forum, organized civil society and gave a focus and a force to voluntary activities. When the opposition to anti-slavery became also an opposition to open debate in Congress, anti-slavery drew new allies from those who, whatever their views on slavery, believed that Congress was the people's forum.[53]

The right of petition belongs to all; it was very important in the antebellum years that this included women as well as men, at least white women. Middle-class reform women frequently petitioned the legislatures on a wide range of issues, seeking especially financial and legal support, including corporate charters, for the charitable institutions they supported. Women, like men in the moral reform movements, looked contemptuously upon partisan politics. But if they shied from partisanship, their work was nonetheless political in the straightforward sense of seeking to influence the agencies of government. On the one hand, women frequently argued that they could exercise their greatest influence in politics by insisting on their moral superiority to and moral independence of parties, so they kept a sharp separation from "the dirty work of designing political partizans."[54] On the other hand, they sought by their own means to influence government. Angelina Grimké became the country's first woman to address a legislative hearing—in Massachusetts in 1838. Other women regularly spoke with legislators to advance their causes, like Lucretia Mott, who addressed legislators on the evils of slavery in Delaware, New Jersey, and Pennsylvania in 1841. One congressman objected to petitions from women, holding that they shamed themselves to address the Congress on political subjects, but the vigilant John Quincy Adams replied, "Why, sir, what does the gentleman understand by 'political subjects'? Every thing in which this House has an agency—every thing which relates to peace and relates to war, or to any other of the great interests of society, is a political subject. Are women to have no opinions or actions on subjects related to the general welfare?"[55]

But by virtue of what role was a woman to enter so directly into the political sphere? For John Quincy Adams, the answer was that every woman petitioner is "a mother, a wife, a daughter, or a sister of some constituents of mine." For women's groups, like the Boston Female Anti-Slavery Society, in contrast, the foundation of petitioning was not mediated by a woman's relationship to a man: "Remember that the representation of our country is based on the numbers of the population, irrespective of sex . . . . In vain it is said, this is nothing to us. Have we not a COUNTRY?"[56]

It may be that women, more than men, have a relational sense of morality rather than a morality based on abstract principles of justice, as psychologist Carol Gilligan has argued.[57] But their advocacy of a right to petition and to participate directly in politics, even before claiming a right to vote, embraced a universalistic and individualistic vision. Indeed, this seemed part of democratization itself. The very form of petitioning changed in the early republic, from one in which people signed petitions as members of organized churches or associations to one in which signing a petition was a radical expression of individual will.[58] As more and more of the business of politics came to be conducted by elected rather than appointed officials, nominated by open conventions rather than legislative caucuses, sponsored by parties with a mass constituency, and influenced by formally organized associations open to men and women of various backgrounds and interests rather than by the informal practices of influence by social elites, a majoritarian, egalitarian, and individualistic concept of citizenship radiated through the nation. It would reach its most remarkable, though gender-specific, nineteenth-century expression in the mass-based political party.

Embracing Parties

The most enduring organizational development of this period, and the one that would later be identified as a central and defining feature of American democracy, was the political party. The party was the agency through which the charismatic authority of the founders—and of the Constitution itself—became institutionalized. It was the vehicle for organizing democratic participation. It became the ladder on which political careers were made.

Central to any definition of political parties is that they exercise a preeminent role in electoral politics, lending their names, symbols, and resources to candidates for public office. But parties exist not only as formal organizations committed to winning elections. They exist also as collections of officials in government who work together and tend to vote together. Moreover, they exist as sources of identification and ideology among voters. Typically, parties are more enduring than other political organizations, more inclusive of heterogeneous groups of citizens, and generally defined by broad programs rather than by single issues. Parties thereby help to integrate a nation, to make public policy, to recruit political leaders, and to educate the citizenry. Clearly, then, parties are central agents of political education and political communication. They organize electoral activity, giving elections coherence and involving people in them, recruiting candidates, providing symbols to link candidates and voters, and helping candidates once in office to effect policy objectives. They also help citizens communicate their preferences to government; they help articulate, organize, and channel popular demands.[59]

Whether parties in this full sense—the party in government, the party as permanent campaign organization, and the party as a center of identification for voters—can be said to have existed before the Whigs and Democrats of the 1830s and 1840s is a matter on which historians have differed. Some find that the active electioneering of both Federalists and Republicans after 1800 signifies the arrival of the political party, others argue that the Federalists and Republicans failed to establish "durable" organizations that were "explicit ends in themselves," able to survive and thrive on their own, not dependent on a particular event or issue to call them into being.[60]

As we have seen, the founders viewed parties only as impediments to a republic. Jefferson was active in organizing a Republican party at the polls in 1800, but in 1796, when it appeared he and Adams were running even in the presidential race, he told Madison to urge Adams's election if there was a tie in the electoral college. The grounds he offered were not those of someone who gave much weight to party as such: Adams, he said, "has always been my senior, from the commencement of our public life, and the expression of the public will being equal, this circumstance ought to give him the preference."[61]

In a competitive party system, each party recognizes other parties not as enemies of the republic but as rivals for power. Competition may be bitter, much may be at stake, but the opposition party is not, apart from rhetorical flourishes, demonized.[62] A party system in this sense was an achievement of the Jacksonian era, not before. In the 1790s, the Federalists and Republicans did not understand themselves to be parties; each group understood itself as the only true vehicle of national destiny. "When out of office, their duty was to recapture power from those temporarily and illegitimately exercising it; when in office, their task was to keep it from those ready to usurp and misuse it."[63] That, at any rate, was how political insiders felt when the competitive juices flowed. At other moments, connection to "party" of any sort was remarkably superficial. It was easy for candidates to retire from political battle when the going got tough, or simply to switch to the opposing party, no matter how distant the political philosophies of Federalists and Republicans appeared to be.[64] The two groups, after all, had no consistent names, no formal organizations, and no consistent symbols with which voters could identify.

The party system of the 1790s, such as it was, withered in the first decade of the 1800s simply because there was no one dedicated to maintaining it. Even more, it remained the view of the first generation of American leaders that parties were to be positively discouraged. Upon his election Thomas Jefferson assured the citizens that "we are all republicans, we are federalists," and even much later, in 1817, he wrote that the best result of the War of 1812 was "the complete suppression of party." [65] When the Federalists were defeated in 1800, they learned Republican rule would not destroy the central government; indeed, the Republicans kept many Federalist policies in place and gained a new appreciation for centralized authority. The Federalists did not regroup to fight the battle anew in 1804; they just retired from the field.

From the point of view of an ordinary citizen, parties before the 1820s were of little psychological account. The Federalists, in particular, though well organized in some states, had no governing national organization and too small a following in Congress to justify an organized caucus. [66] Anti-party ideology was still profoundly important. Candidates routinely sought to present themselves as "above parties." [67] The idea that political office was an extension of privileged social position was still influential. [68]

With the sweeping Jeffersonian victory in 1800, Federalist power faded quickly. The Jeffersonians or Republicans had such a tight hold on political office by the second decade of the century that it is perhaps no great surprise that citizen political involvement declined. By the 1820s, one historian writes, "the vast majority of citizens had lost interest in politics. They had never voted much in presidential elections anyway, and now they involved themselves only sporadically in state and local affairs." [69]

Only with the "second party system" that developed in the 1820s did parties come to have—for the first time anywhere in the world—organizational permanence, ideological legitimacy, and a mass following. The mass-based, permanently organized political party is one of America's greatest gifts to the international world of politics, if gift it is. It includes as its chief features (1) the party as a mass-based institution, (2) the acknowledgment of the legitimacy of party for its own sake and a consequent attention to institutional development and institutional loyalty, (3) the cultivation and transmission across generations of party loyalty—a psychological attachment to party, and (4) the recognition that the opposition party or parties are also legitimate. The Albany Regency, Martin Van Buren's powerful clique of Democratic Party politicians in New York, according to one of its loyal newspapers, sought not to destroy its opponents but to accept a "tranquil though determined opposition."

The very word "opposition" came into more general use in politics in this period.[70]

American parties from the beginning had several distinctive features that would not be repeated in Europe. First, they were not membership organizations. No one pays membership dues to the Republicans or Democrats today, nor did anyone pay the Democrats or Whigs in the 1840s. American parties in the electorate are composed of party identifiers rather than party members, people who identify psychologically with a party and are potential recruits for campaign work but do not pay dues, do not attend regular meetings, and do not necessarily share political viewpoints.

Second, the American parties did not originate as local organizations but developed their identity first and most fully at the national and state levels. Local organizations, especially the urban machines that developed later in the century, might align themselves with a particular state and national party but would do so in an effort to serve local interests likely to have little or nothing to do with national party policies.

Third, American parties were candidate-centered. The separation of the presidency from the Congress made for a different pattern of party institutionalization in the United States than in European parliamentary systems, where control of the legislature necessarily meant control of the executive. In the United States, parties emerged to capture the presidency and have often been united by little more than support for their presidential candidate.[71]

With the organization of the Democratic Party behind the presidential candidacy of Andrew Jackson in 1828 and 1832, and within the next decade the organization of the National Republicans, or Whigs, in opposition to the Jackson and Van Buren administrations, the American political party had arrived. While the parties owed their identity to the competition for national office, they were organized at state and local levels, and nationally coordinated as a loose coalition. The national coordination gained institutional form with the development in the 1830s of the national party convention for nominating presidential and vice presidential candidates. Developing a set of positions rather than a set of candidates was a secondary task just as, still today, the party platform is normally in the background rather than foreground of politicking, but the beginning of platforms and platform committees also dates to this era. The National Republican and Anti-Masonic conventions of 1832 drafted addresses to the public, and in 1836 the Democrats drafted a similar address for the first time, coming out of a small committee that published the address three months after the national convention. In 1840, although the Whigs did not prepare a programmatic address, the Democrats not only drafted resolutions but also voted on them at the convention, establishing the basic pattern that would be passed down to the present.[72]

The elections of 1824, 1828, and 1832 were centered more on personalities than issues with "personal rivalries, elaborate intrigues, and calculated plots to 'destroy' opponents" occupying center stage in the political drama.[73] But this factional system gave way to a more fully elaborated party system in 1836 and 1840. With nomination by convention rather than caucus, candidates found it advisable to make public their views on political issues rather than to silently count on being judged for their general reputations. This did not lead to full-fledged campaigning by candidates, except in isolated cases; the unseemliness of electioneering and the dangers of taking stands that would give openings to the opposition were too great. But such restraint did not apply to party managers.

Thus the American presidential political campaign was born. The early efforts exploded in the full-throttle campaign of 1840. An anti–Van Buren convention met in Harrisburg in September 1839 and came out for William Henry Harrison, while a Democratic Whig National Convention assembled in the same city in December and likewise endorsed Harrison. There were no platforms; opposition to Van Buren provided unity enough. The candidates themselves were more active than ever before and the campaign was full of theatrical innovations and extravagant rhetoric. Most of the campaign efforts had been tried before, but never in a fully national contest by two well-matched parties with institutionalized party apparatus. The turnout was impressively greater than in any prior contest.[74]

By mid-century, the party was not only well established as the country's chief political organization but it was apparently very well estab-

lished in the hearts and minds of American voters. Voters were psychologically attached to their parties and passed party loyalty from fathers to
sons. Political campaigns were frenetic and fun-filled rituals of solidarity,
although historians have different views about just what community of
solidarity was being honored. Generally speaking, parties represented
coalitions of people united by ethnocultural loyalties; parties tended to
embody the stances or styles of different religious and ethnic groups. Parties also provided an important sphere for "male bonding." While
women participated in some political activities, their exclusion from the
suffrage kept them from the inner circles of party life.

In a world where public political argument was highly valued, the
making of that argument was not only part of the process of political activity but a precondition for it. That is, it was difficult to be a part of the
political arena if one did not have skill and experience in the forms of argumentation of the day. Women had difficulty entering the political
arena not only because they were formally deprived of the right to vote
or to serve in public office but also because they had little experience in
developing skills that could make their views known. At the famous
Seneca Falls Convention in 1848, the first organized effort to advance
women's rights in America on a broad front, no woman present was willing to chair the meeting—Lucretia Mott's husband finally took the post.
Nor were women typically experienced in political argument. An-
toinette Brown and Lucy Stone, early feminists who met as students at
Oberlin, organized other students into a debating and speaking society
that provided them practice in oratory, a skill that the "ladies" course at
Oberlin did not include. If Oberlin, as the first coeducational college in
the country, was unintentionally a resource for feminism, so was the abolitionist movement where women learned the subtleties of biblical exe-
gesis to refute scriptural justifications of slavery. One needed not only
skill in argumentation but also a set of values from which to argue, and
this, too, abolitionism provided women. Abolitionists in the mold of
William Lloyd Garrison insisted on "the absolute moral equality of all
human beings," and women in the movement were able to adopt this
principle to their purposes.[75] Thus associations bred associations, political activity bred political skill bred political activity.

The spirit of Max Weber must hover somewhere over a discussion of the early parties because they certainly represent in the truest Weberian sense a "rationalization" of political life—that is, a development of institutions and practices harnessed to the down-to-earth, efficient, and calculated pursuit of a goal. This can be seen, for instance, in the increasing formalization of candidate nominations, from the shifting, ad hoc, informal procedures of "interest" and "influence" in and around the congressional caucus to formally organized party conventions, made up of delegates elected by state, regional, and local conventions. This was a democratization of nomination, opening the process up to multitudes. Second, it was a decentralization of nomination, removing it from congressional leaders and placing it, for all practical purposes, in the hands of state- and county-level political leaders. Third, it was a process of making matters public. The process became not only formally more democratic but more visible, more open especially to the scrutiny of a newspaper-reading populace.

But what, at the opening of the party period in American political culture, did it mean to read a newspaper?

The Antebellum Press: "That Such Dry Bones May Live"

America's first daily newspaper appeared in Philadelphia in 1783. By 1800, there were six dailies in Philadelphia, five in New York, three in Baltimore, and two in Charleston, 241 papers of varying periodicity, most of them weeklies, in the country altogether. By the time Tocqueville visited, there were more than seven hundred papers, including sixty-five dailies. By 1850, there were two thousand papers, including two hundred dailies, and Americans were, as one British visitor put it, "the newspaper-reading animals." [76] Newspapers "penetrate to every crevice of the Union," wrote another visitor. [77] Increasingly, as competition between parties developed more clearly in the 1820s and after, the papers were identified with their editorial voice and known by their partisan affiliations.

At first, most news was foreign, as in colonial days, but the War of 1812 precipitated a gradual shift to domestic news. Foreign news in

Cincinnati newspapers, for instance, declined from 43 percent of all news items in 1795 to 14 percent in 1835.[78] By the 1820s, newspapers began to compete with each other to gather news, not just to express outrageous opinions. Some papers went so far as to hire reporters, a practice unknown before that time and one regarded by politicians of the old school, like President John Quincy Adams, with considerable suspicion. The Congress, after all, did not keep official records until the 1820s, and only Washington papers had regularly covered Congress. The *National Intelligencer*, founded in 1800, provided the best Washington news, especially after gaining the right to take notes on the floor in 1802. Reporting suffered, however, from inadequate stenographic skills; only the *Intelligencer*'s Samuel Smith had the requisite shorthand skills, and when he left the city for his health, as he frequently did, government news essentially stopped.

The newspapers were by no means the sole form, nor even the sole printed form, of communication between the government and the citizens. Of particular importance were the circular letters many congressmen sent to their constituents. These letters, generally printed on government stationery and addressed to individual constituents through the mails, were sometimes printed as pamphlets or broadsides, or occasionally sent to newspapers for first printing. More often, letters sent to constituents were reprinted in newspapers. Representatives who used this form of communication typically wrote one letter, though sometimes more, each congressional session. The letters were printed in quantities of four or five hundred—at a time when that represented from 10 to 40 percent of the number of votes cast in a congressional election.

The practice of sending circular letters was most common for representatives from Southern and Western states. This corresponds to the relative remoteness of these regions from Washington, the greater rarity of newspapers, and perhaps a more staunchly republican attitude toward government on the frontier. It had also to do with electoral practices. A circular letter would have been impractical in New Jersey, Connecticut, New Hampshire, or Georgia, where congressmen were elected at large. Moreover, electioneering—and there is no doubt that the circular letters tried to polish a representative's image—was more commonly accepted in the South and West than elsewhere.[79]

The circular letters, not unlike the newspapers of the day, provided little that was not available in government documents—indeed, they often did little more than offer extended excerpts from them. Others, however, analyzed the congressional session—from a partisan and interested viewpoint, of course. The very writing of the letters was often an attempt to burnish the representative's broadly republican credentials: "I have always conceived it to be among the most essential duties of a person honoured with a representative trust," Theodorus Bailey of New York began his letter in 1794, "to give his constituents every information in his power, on subjects which affect their interests." Samuel Conner, introducing the practice to his Massachusetts constituents in 1816, assured them it was "correct, & REPUBLICAN" to do so.[80] With great honesty, he explained that the use of the circular was the best way to diffuse information widely while also giving him "an economy of time in the necessary discharge of my duties."[81] There were some boilerplate phrases here; a few months later Francis Preston (Virginia) wrote, "I have always conceived it to be one among the most essential duties of the representative of a free people, to give them all the information in his power, and at as early a period as possible, on those subjects which effect their interest."[82] David Trimble of Kentucky praised the power of public opinion: ". . . in our political system we should never forget, that public opinion is the primary element of constitutional liberty—the great conservative principle of self-government. This opinion, however, 'to be rightful,' should be well informed; and hence a free people, if they intend to remain so, should take knowledge, from time to time, of their political affairs, and look into the conduct and course of policy pursued by the public agents and functionaries."[83]

The circular letter was a transitional form, neither personal, face-to-face communication nor private letter but still a letter with a personal voice sent without intermediary to constituents. While this form exists into our own day, its importance diminished rapidly in the nineteenth century as newspapers became the primary source of information about Washington politics. This is yet another expression of the movement from a personal and hierarchical to an institutionalized, public, and potentially more egalitarian social life.

The proportion of American households nationwide who subscribed to newspapers grew. Perhaps a third of households received a newspaper in the 1790s and half by the 1820s.[84] The newspapers helped spawn, even in rural areas, a newly fashionable habit of "keeping up with the world." Knowledge was being modernized—more secular than sacred, more timely than timeless, and more related to regional, national, and international communities of print than to locale.[85]

An institutional infrastructure grew to support reading. The Windsor, Vermont, district boasted three weekly newspapers, three printing offices, and four bookstores by 1810.[86] From 1790 to 1815, five hundred New England towns established libraries. New associations of people sprang up centered on reading and discussion. In Marlborough, Massachusetts, for instance, fourteen men got together to form the Society of Social Enquirers, discussing subjects from science to agriculture and beyond. The growing intensity of communications was made possible in New England and elsewhere in the nation by the rapid increase in post offices and post roads. In 1792, the country had seventy-five post offices; this number ballooned to 2610 by 1812. There were 1875 miles of post roads in 1792, 39,378 miles two decades later.[87]

It seemed no exaggeration when Justice Joseph Story, in an oration in 1826 in Cambridge, declared his times the "age of reading."[88] But reading took another leap forward in the 1830s. Beginning with the *New York Sun* in 1833, a new breed of newspaper sought commercial success and a mass readership in a way divorced from party preferences. Between 1833 and 1835, in New York, Boston, Baltimore, and Philadelphia, papers sprang up selling for a penny instead of the six cents at which they were commonly priced. The new papers were hawked on the streets by newsboys instead of being available exclusively by subscription. The penny papers were more aggressive than the standard papers in seeking out local news, assigning reporters to the courts, even covering "society." One study of Cincinnati newspapers traces a category of incidental topics fully outside politics—weddings, deaths, fires, crimes, and the like. This category represented 0 percent of items in 1795, 6 percent in 1805,

5 percent in 1815, 10 percent in 1825, 17 percent in 1835, and 23 percent by 1845.[89]

The penny papers aggressively solicited advertising at the same time that they engaged in vigorous competition to get the latest news as fast as they could. The New York Herald hired horse express riders that beat those of the most aggressive traditional papers in getting Jackson's annual message to New York from Washington in 1835. It also jumped into the newsboat competition that had developed in the 1820s, hiring small boats to go out to sea to meet incoming European ships, get their newspapers, and bring them back to port ahead of the ships themselves.

The Herald, run by James Gordon Bennett, was the most sustained commercial success of the penny papers, although Horace Greeley's New York Tribune (1841) would prosper, too, and Henry J. Raymond's New York Times (1851), with difficulty, would at least survive. Bennett, unlike most newspaper proprietors of his day, had never worked as a printer. Educated for the Roman Catholic priesthood in his native Scotland, he emigrated first to Canada, where he worked as a schoolteacher, and then to the United States, where he was a clerk in a Boston publishing house, then a proofreader, then an editorial assistant for a Charleston newspaper, then a freelance writer for the New York Enquirer and an associate editor writing on politics from Washington, Albany, and Saratoga Springs. He bounced from one party paper to another before establishing the Herald in 1835, sympathetic to the Democrats but without direct ties to any party.

The political independence of which penny papers boasted was the wave of the future in newspaper publishing, but it would be a long time coming. Newspaper editors preached independence but practiced partisanship. This included editors like the celebrated Horace Greeley. Greeley began his career on an old-style country weekly in the 1830s but moved to New York to run a literary magazine in 1834. In 1840, he ran the Whig campaign paper, the Log Cabin, with a circulation up to 80,000 for its brief life, and in 1841 began his own penny paper, the New York Tribune. This paper, with a circulation of some 10,000 at first, was strongly anti-slavery and clearly showed itself a journal of ideas, reporting on women's rights, socialist experiments, and other topics. Not an advocate of women's rights himself, Greeley nonetheless hired Margaret Fuller in 1844 as the first woman to be a regular staff employee on a major American newspaper. Karl Marx was a European correspondent.

Few papers in the country were so cosmopolitan. As late as 1846 only Baltimore and Washington papers assigned special correspondents to cover Congress. When politics heated up in the 1850s, however, more than fifty papers hired Washington reporters, most of whom wrote for half a dozen or more papers and supplemented their salaries with work as clerks for congressional committees or speechwriters for politicians. The occupational world of journalism was not well differentiated from politics.

In fact, the metropolitan press at mid-century was practically a subdivision of the political party. Party organs were taken as fundamental rallying points for political parties. Editors were intimately involved in patronage. This began with Jackson, who appointed at least fifty-nine journalists to office; as many as 10 percent of the appointments he made requiring Senate approval were journalists.[90] It continued with Lincoln. John W. Forney, editor of Philadelphia's *Press*, deepened a split in the Democratic Party in Pennsylvania by his support of Douglas. This helped elect Lincoln, enough for him to write Forney in thanks, gather support for his appointment as secretary of the Senate, and arrange a Marine Corps commission for his son. While the establishment of the Government Printing Office in 1861 ended the use of federal printing to reward faithful party editors, different government departments still subsidized newspapers with paid advertising, thousands of dollars going to Forney's Philadelphia and Washington papers.[91] Fortified by this support along with federal appointments for Forney's brother-in-law and cousin, Forney helped bring Pennsylvania's Douglas Democrats into the Republican Party.[92]

The editor of the Philadelphia *North American*, a pro-Lincoln paper, found favors extended in federal appointments or army promotions to four of his sons, not to mention substantial federal advertising directed to his paper. The editor of the Philadelphia *Evening Bulletin* and his seventy-three-year-old father received federal appointments. Editors were appointed as ministers, first secretaries of missions, or consuls in Switzerland, Holland, Ecuador, Russia, Turin, Hong Kong, Glasgow, Paris, London, Elsinore, Vienna, the Papal States, Bremen, Zurich, and Venice. They were appointed to customhouses or postmasterships in New Haven, Albany, Harrisburg, Wheeling, Puget Sound, Chicago, Cleveland, St. Louis, and Des Moines. Editors also claimed positions as Treasury agents and as governors of territories; others received military commissions; Charles A. Dana, of the *New York Tribune*, became assistant secretary of war.[93]

Newspaper work was not an independent calling so much as one path within the political world of the mid-nineteenth century. Horace Greeley would run for president in 1872. More commonly, newspaper publishers and editors worked the parties behind the scenes, although, as late as 1920, both parties would nominate publishers of small-town Ohio newspapers for president (Warren Harding for the Republicans and James Cox for the Democrats).

This was the press that Tocqueville judged both vulgar and irreplaceable for American democracy. He wrote that newspapers were a necessity in a democratic society: "We should underrate their importance if we thought they just guaranteed liberty; they maintain civilization."[94] But Tocqueville also wrote, "I admit that I do not feel toward freedom of the press that complete and instantaneous love which one accords to things by their nature supremely good. I love it more from considering the evils it prevents than on account of the good it does."[95] Tocqueville complained of the violence and vulgarity of American journalists. He later expressed satisfaction in noting that the greater the number of newspapers and the more they are dispersed around the country rather than concentrated in a capital city, the less influence journalism has. For Tocqueville, a great virtue of the American press was its weakness.[96]

For Tocqueville, the hallmark of the newspaper was its intimate connection to associations. "Newspapers make associations, and associations make newspapers" and both guard against the dangers of individualism and democratic despotism. Newspapers are an association of their readers. Some newspapers understood their role in these terms. An early African-American newspaper, *The Weekly Advocate* (later renamed *The Colored American*), wrote in 1837: "The Advocate will be like a chain, binding you together as ONE. Its columns will always be the organ of your wishes and feelings, and the proper medium for laying your claims before the Public."[97] The "you" here was the population of free blacks as the paper made clear in changing its name a few months later. Why, the editor asked, does the paper exist?

> Because our afflicted population in the free states are scattered in hand-fulls over nearly 5000 towns, and can only be reached by the Press—a public journal must therefore be sent down, at least weekly, to rouse them up. To call all their energies into action—and where they have been down-trodden, paralized and worn out, to create new energies for them, that such dry bones may live.[98]

Abolitionist William Lloyd Garrison saw *The Liberator* not only as a way to transmit his ideas to others about slavery, but also as an instrument of community, of conversation, of solidarity, a forum for a community of scattered reformers. It was this dispersed group's "weekly method of communicating with each other." So he encouraged readers to contribute. Letters from readers sometimes displaced his own communications to the subscribers. Garrison presented not only his own views of reform but other views as well, and when there were particularly lively controversies, the paper was "practically given over to publication of letters, articles, speeches, statements and rebuttals from all sides of the controversy."[99]

This associational model of the newspaper contrasts sharply with the new penny press that ostentatiously sought *not* to form a community. James Gordon Bennett emphasized for the *New York Herald* the "non-subscriber plan" of having newsboys sell his paper on the street. This, he insisted, would make the penny paper the only true free press "simply because it is subservient to none of its readers—known to none of its readers—and entirely ignorant who are its readers and who are not."[100]

The penny papers did not kill off the associational press then (or ever). They did more to expand than to close down a lively public discourse in print. They gave a new attention to local politics and society. And as the commercially vigorous and expansive penny papers sought readers beyond the city, they forced the country papers to take on more local coverage to compete.

On this point Tocqueville's common sense led him astray. Tocqueville was impressed by the quantity of American newspapers, as were other European visitors, but he did not understand why there were so many papers. He took the cause to be the multiple number of responsible governmental units in America. If citizens elected only members of Congress, Tocqueville suggested, there would not be a need for so many newspapers because there would be so few occasions on which people had to act together politically. But the multiplication of governmental units in each state and village "compelled" Americans to cooperate with one another and each one "needs a newspaper to tell him what the others are doing." [101]

In fact, local newspapers told readers very little about what others in their own communities were up to. Most of the papers in this period printed little local news. [102] Even in a thriving provincial city like Cincinnati, news of the city accounted for less than a fifth of all items in the press. [103] In the 1820s, when improved mail service brought urban papers more expeditiously to country towns, the country newspapers began for the first time to run local news in an effort to retain readers with something the urban papers could not provide. [104] In Kingston, New York, where village government was admittedly a modest affair, the press did not mention local elections in the early 1800s and did not cover village government at all until 1845. Where there were elections, they were generally without issues. If there was campaigning, no one reading the local paper in the 1820s or 1830s would ever have known. [105]

The multiplication of governmental units that caught Tocqueville's eye did afford one thing that helped support the press—government subsidy. Getting government printing contracts was a great boon to the partisan newspaper editor. The demand of a democratic audience for news had little to do with the proliferation of newspapers, but the supply of government advertising certainly helped.

What best explains the large numbers of provincial newspapers is not a popular demand for news but a large supply of would-be editors. Entrepreneurs began newspapers in hundreds of small towns in America not because a population demanded them but because the existence of the paper might attract a population. Country crossroads towns might have newspapers, small colleges, and grand hotels all on the prospect of future growth.[106] The anti-slavery leaders who founded the town of Emporia, Kansas, in 1857, for instance, began the *Emporia News* within a few months to help create an image of a prosperous community. Nearly all copies of the inaugural issues were mailed east, hoping to attract emigrants to buy town lots and make the fledgling town live up to its public relations efforts. Like the effort to attract the railroads or to win designation as a county seat or site for a state college, the establishment of a newspaper was a tool of real estate development.[107] The first two newspapers in Milwaukee, Wisconsin, for instance, were established in 1836 and 1837 by the leading landowners on either side of the Milwaukee River. Each man was eager to promote the new settlement, especially the advantages of his own side of the river.[108]

Local newspapers rarely took stands on local controversies; they invariably avoided criticism of the basic social and economic arrangements of their towns. It was only at about mid-century, a generation after Tocqueville, that news content of the town paper came to have "a significant relationship to the communities where they were printed."[109] Even then, the local news that appeared was not political. Partisan editors of the day understood state and national news as political, but local news was community news. Local items were likely to originate with subscribers themselves and to cover a wide array of personal and social topics. News reported who was ill or who had harvested their crops. The absence of attention to local political affairs may reflect that town and county governments simply didn't do much, but it also suggests that editors found political conflict violated the image of country life they sought to maintain. Narrating the local meant preserving its apolitical character.[110]

In recent years, some historians have seen the commercialization of the press that began, or accelerated, in the 1830s and developed enormously after the Civil War as a devolution from an earlier state of literate, attentive, politically engaged and informative, if vitriolic, journals.[111] But this won't do. The antebellum press had notable strengths, but in the countryside, political news was not among them; in the cities, the coverage of political affairs was advanced as much by the commercially minded upstarts as by their politically partisan, but journalistically cautious, rivals.

The Press as the Patron of Oratory

One notably important community of newspaper-reading animals was that of national political leaders in Washington. At the 8th Congress in 1801, members could receive at government expense subscriptions to three daily newspapers (or as many copies of nondailies as would equal three dailies). The thirty-four senators got ninety-five subscriptions spread among twenty-three newspapers. The largest number of subscriptions went to the *National Intelligencer,* not only the leading Republican paper but the paper providing the best record of congressional debates. Twenty-two senators subscribed to this paper, including four Federalists, while thirteen subscribed to the *Washington Federalist* (including three Republicans). Philadelphia's *Aurora* took in eighteen senatorial subscribers—all of them Republicans; its *Gazette of the United States* had four subscribers—all Federalists. What is notable is not only the partisan distribution of subscriptions but the overwhelming preponderance of nationally oriented newspapers. Only eleven of the thirty-four senators ordered any newspaper at all from their home states.[112] Private correspondence must have remained the primary means for representatives in Washington to get news from home.

Politicians used newspapers not only to read news but to make it. Newspaper reporters would refashion for them what they had said or wished they had said. Reporters took it as their responsibility to turn the rough oratory of legislators into acceptable English in a "consultative" relationship where politicians sat down with them to go over their notes and to improve upon their own views for the printed record. It was common practice for politicians to have publication of their remarks delayed until the memory of what they actually had said would not jar too sharply with the printed record.[113]

Reporting of debates increased the interest congressmen themselves took in debate. Senator William Plumer, a New Hampshire Federalist, writing to his son in 1806, held that senators paid very little attention to one another's speeches. Debate as such changed no one's mind; indeed, senators rarely listened at all. Plumer suggests that debates may have been more attended to in the House than the Senate because newspaper stenographers were more often to be found there and speeches were more often reported in the press. Generally, the House in these years received more public attention because it was popularly elected, it originated more bills, and it took roll call votes more often.[114]

But the Senate should not be neglected, especially in and after the Jacksonian period, when oratory was so highly prized as an American art form. The Senate was rarely a deliberative assembly on the floor, but more often a site for the long, formal oration. Speeches of the day were long enough to help kill two presidents—William Henry Harrison, who died from complications of exposure at his own inauguration, and Zachary Taylor, who died following the dedication ceremonies for the Washington Monument.[115] Formal oratory was a specialty of the Whigs, for whom it was an extension of evangelical didacticism.[116]

There was extraordinary faith in the power of oratory in these years. Alexander Stephens held that orators "move masses," "impress their ideas upon the world," and "control the destiny of nations."[117] In 1840, at a celebration of what Bostonians judged the four hundredth anniversary of printing with moveable type, the mayor of Boston spoke humorously of the evils of the press:

> The most flagrant of these he considered the encouragement which it gave to the manufacture of public speeches, which had now become so common that if he were asked what were the principal products of the New England states, he should answer not granite and ice, but public speeches. This was all the fault of the press; folks would not take the trouble of making addresses if it were not for the pleasure of seeing in the paper the next day that Mr. So-and-so electrified a most delighted audience with the most thrilling eloquence. Nay, such was the benevolence of the press that if any gentleman was particularly dull or stupid in his remarks, it was announced that Mr. Blank made a most sensible speech.[118]

Oratory's value could be greatly amplified by print. In 1850, William H. Seward had his maiden speech in the Senate printed, an anti-slavery address invoking a "higher law." A hundred thousand copies were distributed within weeks, with perhaps another 100,000 copies available in the verbatim reports of the speech in the press.[119] In 1856, the *New York Tribune* distributed 162,000 copies of another Seward anti-slavery address. After Lincoln delivered his famous Cooper Union speech in New York in 1860, he went to the *Tribune* office to read the speech in proof; the *Tribune's* copy of the speech was then available for other newspapers. The editor of the *Chicago Tribune*, Joseph Medill, a supporter of Lincoln, printed the speech as a pamphlet for mass distribution.[120] If the antebellum period was a golden age of American oratory, it was in no small measure because the press beat the typographical drum for it.

Politics as a Vocation

It is hard for Americans in a post–New Deal age to read nineteenth-century political history in proper perspective. By design, the national government at first had little to do. Most of its manpower was assigned to the military, the postal service, and tax collection. In the first quarter of the nineteenth century, there were more people in the federal government making laws than executing them, more members of Congress than all judges, district attorneys, marshals, and so forth combined.[121] Washington seemed remote from citizens, a poor replica of a city, known for its mud and unfinished buildings. People who served in Congress and in the executive, such as it was, had little esteem for their own positions and considerable distress at the loss of privacy they entailed. John Quincy Adams wrote that to be a politician meant to be the object of "perpetual and malignant watchfulness with which I am observed in my open day and my secret night, with the deliberate purpose of exposing me to public obloquy or public ridicule." Longtime government official William Wirt held that "every man, in a high public station, must become fire-proof and bullet-proof, in his own defense. . . . My skin is too thin for the business." Early national leaders feared the corrupting influence of office. It is difficult to imagine, one historian observes, "a community which entertained a more unflattering, disdainful, indeed abhorrent, image of itself."[122]

Not least of the self-hatred must have come from the increasing necessity of electioneering. Seeking office by openly soliciting the support of the general populace was not acceptable and, until the 1790s, barely conceivable. But in the 1790s, "the Jeffersonians revolutionized electioneering," as David Hackett Fischer puts it in his remarkable study of Federalist election practices.[123] Jeffersonians unabashedly sought out popular approval. Traditional Federalists, like Gouverneur Morris, castigated them as "brawlers, who make popularity a trade."[124] But younger Federalists were more willing to take a leaf from the Jeffersonian book. Josiah Quincy found his elders' anti-electioneering principles "merely an apology of inactivity." Federalists began after 1800 to adopt the Jeffersonian practice of mass meetings to pass resolutions and express support for candidates. In New York State, the Federalists reformed their practices, and even adopted a new name that would appeal to the populace, the Federal Republicans. Town, county, district, and state committees were organized, with delegates chosen in annual conventions. While old guard Federalists remained essential for party financing, they left electioneering to "a new generation of aggressive young conservatives, primarily printers and lawyers on the rise and on the make."[125] The length of the political season grew and even holidays far from election day became occasions for party celebration.

The Federalists made a point of Washington's birthday and both parties exploited the Fourth of July; indeed, party rivalry essentially institutionalized Independence Day, which had not been regularly observed in the 1790s, as the preeminent national holiday. The barbecue became a staple political activity, supplemented in New England by fish fries and clambakes. At these events, which parties provided free to the willing citizens, food was accompanied by oratory. The oratory tended toward personal invective, especially as the election drew near. In the South, a speaker might accuse his opponent of leading a slave rebellion; in New England, Republicans accused the Federalists of having advocated the Boston Massacre and thirsting for the blood of Republicans.

Electioneering worked more quietly, too. Parties organized town committees. Federalist committees saw to it that each voter, unless known to be a Jeffersonian, would be personally visited. They distributed party tickets house to house and provided horses and carriages to take voters to the polls. Newspapers exhorted their loyal party readers to vote. Candidates themselves took to the road with electioneering tours.

The innovations in campaigning spread and gained legitimacy. Gouverneur Morris wrote in 1809 that he went "for the first time in my life, to attend a popular meeting in my county."[126] Other Federalists, too, who just a decade before would have joined George Washington in condemning private associations, now collaborated to organize them. In 1802, Alexander Hamilton himself proposed a network to be called the Christian Constitutional Society, intent on diffusing information through newspapers and pamphlets and organizing elections. While Hamilton's plan never developed, a similar plan gained ground—the Washington Benevolent Societies, with more than two hundred established by 1816.

A suspicious view of party politics and political leadership has never disappeared from American politics. Indeed, distrust is practically enjoined in a representative democracy. If the people at large are sovereign, then anyone else holds only delegated power and anyone seeking such power is potentially a usurper. But the second generation of American citizens, born into the new republic rather than founders of it, were able to achieve something the founders could not—equanimity about organized political life. "Organize Without Delay!" urged the Whig *Cincinnati Gazette* in 1844. The Democratic organ, the *Daily Cincinnati Enquirer*, warned in 1848 that the presidential campaign would be an "arduous conflict." It then added: "The first thing in view of this is ORGANIZATION."[127] The representative figure here is Martin Van Buren. He was the first president whose whole career had been that of a politician. Along with other leaders of the so-called Albany Regency group of New York state politicians, Van Buren was of modest middle-class origins, the son of a tavernkeeper. These men were, Richard Hofstadter has written, "modern political professionals who loved the bonhomie of political gatherings, a coterie of more-or-less equals who relied for success not on the authority of a brilliant charismatic leader but on their solidarity, patience, and discipline. Their party gave them a creed, a vocation, and a congenial social world all in one."[128]

Van Buren's dedication to the life of a party professional was not without qualms. Being a career politician was in some ways for him "a doubtful and precarious identity, one which led him to admire, perhaps to envy, the courage, solidity, and decisiveness of a Wellington, the poise and flair and proud idiosyncrasy of a Randolph." Van Buren admired Andrew Jackson to the point of hero worship and praised him as "no politician."[129] One historian portrays Van Buren as the first president who had no ennobling ties of kinship or friendship with the founders, who had not lost or shed blood in the national cause, and "whose remembered past included no battlefields but the courtroom and the back room."[130]

Van Buren and his fellow Regency leaders provided in their writings and speeches in the early 1820s "a complete, articulate, quite sophisticated, quite modern defense of the political party."[131] Still, nowhere is the justification of parties ever so full-bodied that one fails to recognize it as apology against the presumption of corruption, of partiality, of interestedness. Only when the rationale shifts from the virtues of partisan allegiance to the virtues of a system of contending forces built on partisanship is there an opportunity to make the rationalization stick. This is not unlike the justification of the legal system as an adversary process—no one doubts that advocacy regularly leads attorneys astray from the path of truth and virtue, but the excuse is that both sides have the same opportunity to do so and to present their cases as best they can before a judge or jury. It may not be incidental that so many of the professional politicians of the second generation came from legal backgrounds.

In the end, Van Buren was forgotten. Father of the American political party he may be, but it is Washington, Jefferson, and Jackson who have survived as models for emulation. The ambivalence with which Americans honor their great invention, the political party, is perhaps in no better way indicated than by the obscurity into which Van Buren fell.

Anti-party feeling was never extinguished. It would revive early in the 1850s when the Know-Nothings incorporated opposition to all politicians and parties into their declared philosophy. It was part of the appeal of the Republican Party during the Civil War in its self-conscious "no-partyism," representing their cause as one of Union and patriotism.[132] It would reappear again among the genteel reformers of the 1870s and in a way that ultimately would weaken the hold of party on the American psyche. Still, the Know-Nothings of the 1850s, the Republicans of the 1860s, and the reformers of the Gilded Age never fully revived republican anti-partyism. The Gilded Age reformers would object less to parties than to their excesses. They sought a more rational politics but not necessarily a more consensual one. The legitimation of the party process was a permanent legacy and permanent element in the democratic transition even if, by the late nineteenth century, it would produce a vigorous reaction, one strong enough to color political sentiment to this day.

At mid-century, the parties the founders had struggled against were not only established but strong beyond what either Federalist or Antifederalist could ever have imagined. The parties were a fourth branch of government, responsible more than any other institution for the political education and mobilization of the voting population out of doors, and for the creation of a functioning leadership inside the legislatures and halls of Congress.

This was the "American political nation." [133] It was the democratic transition: a growing egalitarian spirit, majoritarian institutions, including the state constitutional conventions that delivered them, the proliferation of both profit and nonprofit associations in building a bustling public arena, and most of all the political parties. The party was the centerpiece of political history from Andrew Jackson to Woodrow Wilson. The party system built the highest level of citizen participation in electoral politics of any period in our history. Popular acceptance of parties replaced, or at least came to overlay, the republican fear of factions. The creation of the modern political party as a mass-based endeavor with a permanent organization that both mobilized popular participation and evoked strong mass allegiance was a boon to democratic politics. Ironically, before the end of the century it would be reviled as the chief barrier to a democracy authentically committed to the public interest.

The Public World of the Lincoln-Douglas Debates

In 1858, with the whole nation increasingly shaken by the battle over the extension of slavery to new territories, the contest in Illinois for the United States Senate received widespread attention. Stephen Douglas, the incumbent, a national leader of the Democratic Party, the author of the controversial Kansas-Nebraska Act of 1854, and a front-runner for the presidency in 1860, stood for reelection. His opponent, Abraham Lincoln, a Springfield attorney, had been a loyal member of the Whig Party who, like many others, switched to the Republican standard as the Whigs' prospects deteriorated. Lincoln's only experience in public office was one term in the U.S. Congress, but he had served loyally first the Whigs and then the Republicans and seemed the obvious choice.

Lincoln at first resolved to pursue Douglas in campaign appearances, turning up wherever Douglas had just spoken. But this was not very satisfying; Lincoln was the underdog and the crowds he drew paled in comparison to those of the famous senator. In some desperation, Lincoln then challenged Douglas to a series of debates. Douglas agreed, though whittling down their number from Lincoln's proposed fifty to just seven, and so was launched the famous verbal duels that are frequently upheld, to this day, as a high point of American deliberative politics.[1] Here was a time when people would stand outside for hours listening to detailed, erudite, complex arguments on the nation's most pressing political controversy. What kind of political culture made such an extravagant exercise in public argument possible? (And the question that regularly shadows this one: why don't we have it today?)

Two assumptions fuel the question. The first is that the debates reveal citizens on the Illinois prairie in 1858 to have been strongly interested in national political affairs, spirited and caring participants in the common public life. The second is that the debates themselves were the sort of events that responded faithfully to the people and to a bold democratic ideal of public life, that they were an exercise in rational public deliberation. Neither assumption is groundless, but neither offers a very fair-minded perspective of what the politics of 1858 were actually like. Both assumptions read twentieth-century political values back into a time when those values would not have been recognizable.

To turn to the first assumption: were the citizens who listened to Lincoln and Douglas the spirited civic participants we wish we had more of today? We don't know enough about the political views and values of the ordinary people of the mid-nineteenth century to say. What we do know does not afford a clear-cut answer. Everyone's favorite source, Tocqueville, offers a surprisingly contradictory portrait. The two volumes of Democracy in America, published in 1835 and 1840, respectively, provide two very different views. In volume one, the citizen is constantly active in public life and regularly recruited to it through elections, jury service, reading the newspapers, and joining private associations oriented to public affairs. But in the second volume, citizens are absorbed in private life; they are small shopkeepers obsessed with their own material advancement and likely to shun general ideas, philosophy, the arts, or politics itself.[2]

In volume one, elections keep society "in feverish activity." Political concerns are primary for the American: "To take a hand in the government of society and to talk about it is his most important business and, so to say, the only pleasure he knows." In America "each man is as interested in the affairs of his township, of his canton, and of the whole state as he is in his own affairs."[3] But in volume two, people "find it a tiresome inconvenience to exercise political rights which distract them from industry. When required to elect representatives, to support authority by personal service, or to discuss public business together, they find they have no time." It is hard to get people to attend to the public business: "It is very difficult to make the inhabitants of democracies listen when one is not talking about themselves." The very equality of condition that gives each person a stake in the social order as a whole also separates him from it: "When social conditions are equal, every man tends to live apart, centered in himself and forgetful of the public." There is a strong tendency for citizens "to shut themselves up more and more narrowly in the little circle of petty domestic interests. . . ." Tocqueville concludes, "I see an innumerable multitude of men, alike and equal, constantly circling around in pursuit of the petty and banal pleasures with which they glut their souls. Each one of them, withdrawn into himself, is almost unaware of the fate of the rest. Mankind, for him, consists in his children and his personal friends. As for the rest of his fellow citizens, they are near enough, but he does not notice them. He touches them but feels nothing. He exists in and for himself, and though he still may have a family, one can at least say that he has not got a fatherland."[4]

Would the real American please stand up! Which of the Tocquevilles are we to credit? This contradictory portrait, although based on travels in America some years before the full flowering of mass-based political parties and a quarter century before the great debates themselves, should give pause. Should we really posit the Lincoln-Douglas debates as a moment of unequaled glory in American democracy? Do these debates reveal an unequaled intensity of popular attention to the moral heart of politics?

The Lincoln-Douglas debates *were* a high point of nineteenth-century American political discourse and political participation. But it is important to remember four central features of them before bemoaning our failure to reproduce them in our own day:

1. No one who listened to Lincoln and Douglas speak voted for them.

No one who attended the debates for three hours on hot summer afternoons in small Illinois towns ever actually voted for Lincoln or for Douglas. The U.S. Senate, for which the two men were running, was elected by state legislatures, not directly by citizens until ratification of the Seventeenth Amendment (1913). We do not know how much local issues in the different legislative districts or personal or party loyalties to legislative candidates influenced the outcome of the Lincoln-Douglas contest itself. The mid-nineteenth century did not have sufficiently democratic electoral institutions for us ever to be very sure. They did not have the proliferation of elected offices, ballot propositions, and other signal democratizations of the political system that came in the Progressive Era.

2. Politics was entertainment.

It is not likely that the people who listened to the debates were swayed one way or another by the arguments of the debaters. The debates attracted multitudes, to be sure. In the first debate, at Ottawa, on August 21, 1858, a city with a population of about 7000, anywhere between 10,000 and 20,000 people were assembled. Think about what these numbers suggest for an outdoor gathering in the days before microphones, the breeze blowing, children shouting, clothes rustling, insects abuzz: chances are that only a minority of the audience, perhaps a small minority, could even have heard the speakers, let alone followed their arguments!

So what were the people there for? To cheer their champions to victory. And cheer, laugh, applaud, and shout out they did. Douglas's opening speech in Ottawa was interrupted over and over by cries of "Hit him again" and "Put it at him" and "That's it," and "He can't dodge you" and other enthusiastic expostulations.

This was the best show in town. Politics, as one historian observes, "still offered sparsely populated communities not only the opportunity to take sides on crucial issues but their sole access to grand entertainment as well. Politics provided high drama and spirited fun to neighborhoods devoid of activities anywhere near as engaging and exciting."[5] Compare that to the solemnity with which we conduct televised presidential debates today. The moderator in the 1988 debates cautioned the studio audience against applauding for their favorite. People may or may not have been educated at the debates in 1858; they were certainly entertained.

As the next chapter will make clear, reformers of the late nineteenth century made politics a good deal less fun and more puritanical in practice and in ideal. The late-nineteenth-century decline in campaign parades, barbecues, and brass bands came as part of a self-conscious effort to remove emotion from the political scene. Our political piety is inherited from these Gilded Age and Progressive Era reforms. It is not necessarily to be preferred to the old camp meeting–style campaigns and elections. But the reform era separates us dramatically from mid-nineteenth-century politics, so much so that comparisons are nearly meaningless.

3. *The debaters did not provide models of high-minded, issue-oriented,*
   reasoned discourse.

Lincoln and Douglas were neither as high-minded nor as reasonable in their addresses as myth supposes. In the course of the debates, Lincoln and Douglas did make highly detailed, elaborate, and in places closely reasoned arguments. They also made ad hominem attacks, raised conspiracy theories that had little basis in fact, and tried to maneuver their opponent into politically embarrassing admissions. Much of the debate time was occupied with Lincoln and Douglas "haranguing each other on purely diversionary points," and frequently the debates focused on entirely personal rather than politically substantive matters.[6]

Lincoln, for instance, in the opening debate at Ottawa, advanced the groundless argument that Douglas had conspired with former president Franklin Pierce, President James Buchanan, and Chief Justice Roger Taney to expand slavery throughout the nation. Evidence? Lincoln did not require any. "We cannot absolutely know," he admitted, that the tendencies he pointed to were "the result of preconcert. But when we see a lot of framed timbers, different portions of which we know have been gotten out at different times and places, by different workmen—Stephen, Franklin, Roger, and James for instance, and mortices exactly fitting, and all the lengthy proportions of the different pieces exactly adapted to their respective places, and not a piece too many or too few . . . in such case we find it impossible to not believe that Stephen and Franklin and Roger and James all understood one another from the beginning, and all worked upon a common plan or draft before the first lick was struck."[7]

One can certainly admire Lincoln's gift with metaphor and, as Lincoln warms to the conspiracy theme over what takes up another two pages of print, his humor. But one is entitled to wonder how many in the audience caught the subtleties of the extended legal metaphor he then employed:

> I demur to that plea—I waive all objections because it was not filed until after default was taken, and I demur to it upon the merits. What if Judge Douglas never did talk to Chief Justice Taney or the president until the decision was made? Does it follow that he could not have as perfect an understanding with them without it as with it? But I am disposed to take his denial rather as an answer in chancery, that he neither had knowledge or belief of the existence of any such conspiracy. Now, I ask you, after that is denied, if he had done so, have I not the right yet to prove it on him, and is there not more than the evidence of the two witnesses to prove it, and if it does not prove the existence of conspiracy, does it disturb the facts at all that would run to show that he had been used by the conspirators instead of being the leader of them?[8]

Almost two months later, having raised the conspiracy charge again and again, Lincoln was still at it and closed the sixth (Quincy) debate with one final thrust at his phantom conspiracy. This rhetorical approach was not original with Lincoln. Standard Republican rhetoric portrayed the South as an aristocratic "Slave Power" intent on destroying Northern liberties (linked frequently, though not by Lincoln, to the dangers posed by popery as well). Not antipathy to slavery but fears of Southern aggrandizement fueled the Republican movement, fears by no means groundless but greatly exaggerated.[9]

Douglas, meanwhile, dished out the same sort of slop that was hurled his way. Again and again he mocked Lincoln for his measured opposition to the Mexican War and his "Spot Resolutions" of 1848 that asked President James Polk to identify the exact spot on American soil where Mexico supposedly shed American blood. Douglas raised the matter, always in a jeering fashion, in five of the seven debates. And he raised also a conspiracy charge of his own about a cabal of Republicans that secretly designed to guarantee Lincoln a Senate seat.

When the Lincoln-Douglas debates were printed in the newspapers, they were edited. Only recently has a historian, Harold Holzer, thought to compare the Democratic and Republican newspapers' coverage of the debates in an effort to arrive at the best possible text of what the candidates actually said. Holzer concludes that there was a significant amount of cooperation between the Republican candidate and Republican editors, and likewise the Democratic candidate and Democratic editors in rewriting, smoothing out, elaborating, and improving the candidate's remarks for print. The newspapers apparently left the rival candidate's words untouched, so the Democratic papers give the nearest approximation of what Lincoln actually said and the Republican papers offer the best account of Douglas's remarks.[10] The result is a rather more ragged and prosaic text than earlier accounts acknowledge—although even historians who worked with less accurate texts recognized the debates to be "burdened with tiresome repetition and trivial dispute."[11]

It should be added that the nineteenth-century press did not routinely print campaign speeches. For one thing, there were no campaign speeches from presidential candidates, and they were not common for lesser offices, either. When Lincoln challenged Douglas, he had to remind the senator that stump speaking was a common habit in the frontier West.[12] As for reporting the speeches, the news coverage of the Lincoln-Douglas debates may have been the first time ever that campaign speeches were reported verbatim.[13]

The debates did provide occasional moments of clarity and stirring rhetoric. Douglas offered his views frankly: "I believe that this government was made on the white basis . . . I am in favor of confining the citizenship to white men—men of European birth and European descent, instead of conferring it upon Negroes and Indians, and other inferior races." Lincoln, in a more delicate effort to affirm the civil rights of African-Americans while denying their social equality with whites, held that between the two races there is a "physical difference" that "will probably forever forbid their living together on terms of respect, social and political equality, and inasmuch as it becomes a necessity that there must be a superiority somewhere, I, as well as Judge Douglas, am in favor of the race to which I belong having the superior position; but I hold that because of all this there is no reason at all furnished why the negro after all is not entitled to all that the Declaration of Independence holds out, which is, 'life, liberty, and the pursuit of happiness' and I hold that he is as much entitled to that as the white man." [14]

There were moments in the debate of deft argument and moral clarity, but, in truth, these were the rare sound bites amidst charge and countercharge, personal invective and name-calling. CBS News anchor Dan Rather, criticizing the Clinton-Bush debates of 1992, said, "When you read the Lincoln-Douglas debates, they jump off the page at you for the depth and substance of the argument. It's exciting, even riveting." [15] One strongly suspects Rather was reading an executive summary, not the actual transcripts. The talents of Lincoln and Douglas were squandered on defending themselves, in detail, against baseless or irrelevant charges. They struggled to insist on the consistency of their positions on slavery over time as their opponent pointed to contradictions both serious and trivial—the debates at times seem to provide a textbook example of Emerson's point about the hobgoblin of small minds. The debaters carried the melody of democracy, but the lyrics more often than not were the "doo-ron-rons" and "sh-boom sh-booms" of their day.

These were mortals, after all, indeed, politicians. Moreover, they were bringing to public discussion strong arguments on a topic that the political parties had worked desperately to keep off the agenda for several generations. The whole course of national political development from the War of 1812 to the Civil War can be seen as a set of maneuvers to keep from making a decision about slavery. Both leading parties in 1852 urged in their platforms that slavery be kept off the national agenda. Nathaniel Hawthorne, in his 1852 campaign biography of Democratic presidential contender Franklin Pierce, averred, "The two great parties of the nation appear—at least to an observer somewhat removed from both—to have nearly merged into one another; for they preserve the attitude of political antagonism rather through the effect of their old organizations, than because any great and radical principles are at present in dispute between them." [16]

The whole weight of respectable political opinion was to condemn the abolitionists as uncivilized firebrands and unreasonable men. The term "abolitionist" remained in 1858 a dirty word, and Douglas kept trying to assign it to Lincoln just as Lincoln kept trying assiduously to portray himself as a moderate rather than a "black Republican." Lincoln was as fleet-footed in running from the *a* word in 1858 as Michael Dukakis from the *l* word in 1988.

Remember, too, that Lincoln and Douglas in the debates discussed no issue other than slavery. They debated an issue that was central to American democracy. They dealt with it in a setting of relative moral clarity. It cannot be compared to, say, our muddled national debate over the Clinton health care plan. It might be more readily compared to the controversy over abortion. Twenty-five years after *Roe* v. *Wade* provided a central focus to the abortion debate, public discussion is no less sophisticated than the Lincoln-Douglas battle thirty-eight years after the Missouri Compromise gave an authoritative stamp to the question of slavery in the territories.

4. Lincoln's candidacy represented a failure of antebellum politics.

The enthusiasm Lincoln inspired was in part a revulsion with politics-as-usual. Lincoln represented a third party, one that had offered its first presidential ticket just two years before. All over the country there were complaints about the ways party bosses and "wire pullers" had hijacked the democratic process. The Know-Nothings (the American Party) emerged as a powerful national movement in the early 1850s, reviving republican rhetoric in an attack on parties, corruption, patronage, and the "hordes of political leeches that are fattening their bloated carcasses in the people's money." Know-Nothings prided themselves that they would not ask, "Will it aid the party?" but "Will it be RIGHT?" The famous anti-Catholic nativism of the Know-Nothings was in part a response to politicians' efforts to win immigrant votes. The Know-Nothings were the first to profit from the intense anti-partyism of the early 1850s, but the Republicans followed in their footsteps, sometimes cooperating to mutual advantage, supporting local Know-Nothing candidates in return for Know-Nothing support for the Republican national ticket. In the late 1850s, as their own electoral prospects faded, Know-Nothings in large numbers joined the Republican Party. So when Lincoln challenged Douglas in 1858, his success was a powerful sign of the deep failure of the second party system. What may look retrospectively like a great moment for the American political order at the time represented a profound disillusionment with leading political institutions of the day.[17]

L ike other high points of American political communication, the Lincoln-Douglas debates may seem testimony to our national virtues only in the glow of nostalgia. Just as the brilliant *Federalist* papers failed to rally a pro-ratification constitutional assembly in New York, just as President Woodrow Wilson's national whistle-stop tour to sell the League of Nations to the American public failed even as he was struck down in the midst of his campaign, just as Martin Luther King, Jr.'s 1963 speech at the Lincoln Memorial failed to propel a sluggish Congress toward a civil rights bill (what mattered, in the end, was Lyndon Johnson's skill and determination in taking up the civil rights cause), so Lincoln lost the contest to Douglas. He came to the White House two years later not because his moderate position on slavery had won widespread support but because the Democrats had splintered in three directions.

Moreover, the moral high notes that Lincoln and Douglas struck (in between the fervent declarations of racism on Douglas's part and the grenades about conspiracy that Lincoln lobbed across the platform) broke from rather than represented the dominant political mode. The anti-slavery movement overcame, after a struggle of two decades, the resistance of the political parties and the political system to confronting it. By the 1870s, the pendulum would swing back again from "ideological" to "organizational" politics.[18] In the brief, bloody interregnum, slavery was laid to rest and a set of constitutional amendments passed that would, in time, provide the basis both for new federal powers and for the constitutionalization of citizenship. The cost was enormous; the benefits equally incalculable.

Nothing I have said here is meant to deride or diminish the Lincoln-Douglas debates. They were a fine moment for American politics, in some ways an astonishing moment, where the representative of an upstart third party came face-to-face with a national leader of the dominant political party and brought squarely onto the political agenda the question of slavery, not mincing words about its immorality, nor failing to take up the delicate point of what, moral or immoral, the national government could constitutionally do to control it.

But the Lincoln-Douglas debates did not depend on greater virtues in the populace than we have today, nor do they indicate a generally higher level of public deliberation on pressing questions in that day than in ours. The debates were an explosion into a political campaign of an issue that politicians did their best to shun. There is much to learn from the Lincoln-Douglas debates about the politics of the 1850s, but there are no lessons to "apply" to our own time, certainly not in the form of a rebuke to a purportedly diminished political culture.

Chapter 4

The Second Transformation
of American Citizenship

1865–1920

Prospectus

The definition of the vote as a civic function, rather than a partisan one, is one of the unique and cardinal features of the electoral system of the United States.[1]

Americans know little, and think rarely, about our late-nineteenth-century political history. There are good reasons for this. Leading contemporary interpreters taught that this was the Gilded Age, an age of corruption—and we have believed them. No president between Lincoln and Theodore Roosevelt captured the national imagination or can be identified with any large moral mission. While we may be indebted to people of modest ambition or pragmatic aims, we are not, generations later, inspired by them. This string of hirsute presidents faded from public consciousness quickly, firecracker duds in the night sky of politics. The novelist Thomas Wolfe, whose brother Benjamin Harrison Wolfe was named for one of these forgettable figures, wrote in the 1930s of his father's political heroes—Garfield, Arthur, Harrison, Hayes—as "the four lost men." "And where was Harrison? Where was Hayes? Which had the whiskers, which the burnsides: which was which?"[2] With Reconstruction deconstructed in the 1870s and 1880s, with the cause of woman suffrage struggling outside the national spotlight, moral progress on the national level seemed stymied; while significant social and political reforms emerged by the 1890s, especially in the cities, none achieved mythic proportion.

And yet, in the past decades, revisionists in American history and political science have found reasons to treat the years from Appomattox through 1900 with sympathy and even admiration. These were the years of the highest voter turnout in our entire history. Americans of that era *enjoyed* politics. They found it simultaneously serious and entertaining, both intellectually and emotionally satisfying. Why? What did they know or what did they have that we have lost?[3]

To find out, it is necessary to return to the original interpretations of Gilded Age politics, and there is no better starting place than James Bryce's *American Commonwealth*. Bryce, in this magisterial work of 1888, sought to be the British Tocqueville, lucidly anatomizing the United States in the waning decades of the century. He did quite respectably in that ambition. *The American Commonwealth* is still lively, readable, and perceptive, but not so quotable nor as visionary as *Democracy in America*. It falls short not only because Bryce's gift, though considerable, is not as luminous as Tocqueville's; equally important, his subject matter lacks the greatness of his predecessor's.

His subject matter, after all, was late-nineteenth-century politics, which did not inspire wonder or reverence. Tocqueville wrote as the Jacksonian era was coming into its own and a significant expansion of the political world was taking shape. Bryce wrote when the new democratic politics had become well institutionalized—and not a little unsightly. He asked of the leading political parties of the day, "What are their principles, their distinctive tenets, their tendencies? Which of them is for free trade, for civil service reform, for a spirited foreign policy, for the regulation of telegraphs by legislation, for a national bankrupt law, for changes in the currency, for any other of the twenty issues which one hears discussed in the country as seriously involving its welfare?" And he answered, sadly:

> This is what a European is always asking of intelligent Republicans and intelligent Democrats. He is always asking because he never gets an answer. The replies leave him in deeper perplexity. After some months the truth begins to dawn upon him. Neither party has anything definite to say on these issues; neither party has any principles, any distinctive tenets.[4]

This is the large, uncomfortable fact of late-nineteenth-century politics to couple with the exceptional record of voter participation. Both sides of this political equation—on the one side, lively political campaigns and deeply held political loyalties; on the other, a politics light on ideas or efforts to arrive at a public good, a politics of sections, jobbery, ethnic, racial, and religious scares and slurs—must be recognized as one of the cultural contradictions of democracy. The more politics could be understood as team sport and the rivalry of social groups, the more enthusiastically people participated in the public sphere, but the less elevated the substance of politics.

The question of *who votes* cannot be separated ultimately from the question of *what voting means*. It may be impressive that, in the North, 80 percent of eligible voters typically went to the polls in presidential elections in the late nineteenth century, but if the parties to which these voters were passionately attached had as their primary concern "getting or keeping the patronage of the government," as Bryce asserts, if whatever political doctrines they might have stood for had by then vanished, and if "All has been lost except office or the hope of it," we can scarcely see this period as the zenith of American political life.[5]

The views of those who find much to admire in late-nineteenth-century politics must be reconciled with the views of those who have been repulsed. The Mugwumps of that time and the Progressives who followed them, in their disgust with the enthusiastic party politics of the

day, helped create a new model citizenship that made it both more difficult and less interesting to be a "good citizen." The Mugwumps concentrated their attacks on parties and patronage, while the Progressives
sought to tame capitalist barons as well as party chiefs and advocated
forms of direct democracy the Mugwumps would not have favored. Even
so, both generations of reformers helped transform voting from a social
to a civic act, rationalizing electoral behavior and depriving elections of
most of what made them compelling.[6] The meaning of the human act
of casting a ballot changed. Correspondingly, as I will suggest, the act of
reading a newspaper and the process of political education changed; the
discourse of citizenship and citizenship ideals was transformed. The outcome was a world in many respects more democratic, inclusive, and dedicated to public, collective goals, and, for all that, less politically
engaging. By the close of the Progressive Era, the cultural contradictions
of democracy would reach a point of mournful clarity.

Party Patronage and Civil Service Reform

"How are you goin' to interest our young men in their country if you
have no offices to give them when they work for their party?" So George
Washington Plunkitt famously asked in *Plunkitt of Tammany Hall* (1905).
Civil service reform, he held, was "the curse of the nation." Men who
worked for Tammany at election time could no longer be provided for.
"These men were full of patriotism a short time ago. They expected to be
servin' their city, but when we tell them that we can't place them, do you
think their patriotism is goin' to last?"[7]

Jobs were the heart of politics in the late nineteenth and early twentieth centuries. At the local level, this is dramatically indicated by figures for New York City. Taking the Tammany-controlled number of
public payroll jobs as a percentage of the vote totals for Tammany's mayoral candidates, the "payroll share" of the vote was 20 percent in 1897, as
high as 36 percent in 1913, and never under 20 percent until the 1920s.
Payroll jobs, of course, were not the only economic resources of an urban
political machine; machines also controlled private sector employment
through government contracts and "unofficial" patronage in firms de-

pendent on them, so these figures probably underestimate the dependence of voters on the machine.[8]

At the national level, too, government was preoccupied with "distributive" functions. A large part of governing was the distribution of offices to party loyalists. Jobs were closer to the heart of a party than issues. Some issues did divide and help define the parties. The Republicans more often supported federal programs, especially pensions for Union Army veterans and, early on, but with declining enthusiasm after Reconstruction, efforts to enforce the rights of African-Americans in the South. Democrats tended to favor individual enterprise rather than government solutions to economic and social problems. Even so, the parties were political mongrels. In the South, people of varied backgrounds and interests voted Democratic out of tradition and out of resentment at federal efforts to enforce rights for ex-slaves. In the West, Democrats were loosely anti-federal individualists, many becoming Democratic as a result of their Southern background. In the North, urban ethnic immigrants voted with the Democratic machines, but relatively poor rural voters were more likely to favor Republicans or to support quite varied political positions while still voting Democratic.[9] Key issues were often ethnocultural—natives separated from immigrants, Protestants from Catholics, temperance advocates from their opponents. The parties typically avoided issues that might evoke these vast cultural divides; platforms and speeches stressed party loyalty, personal attacks on the opposition, and empty patriotic platitudes. It was all but impossible to consistently identify the Democrats and Republicans with particular issues.[10] As national amalgamations of localized groups, the parties were ideologically incoherent congeries and coalitions.

So politics in Washington focused on handing out jobs. When Abraham Lincoln was elected president, he stated that his policy in filling offices would be "Justice to all." What that meant to him was that all factions within the Republican Party that had served the national ticket would be rewarded with federal jobs. Lincoln tried to follow this principle, even when it was sometimes painful to do so. Republicans in California, for instance, were divided into factions, each seeking control over key jobs (Collector of the Port of San Francisco, Superintendent of the Mint in San Francisco, Postmaster of San Francisco, Sub-Treasurer at San Francisco). One faction was headed by Lincoln's old Illinois friend Edward D. Baker. Baker had not only organized the Republicans in California; he had organized the party in Oregon and been elected U.S. senator from Oregon. He still wanted to control California appointments, but an anti-Baker faction led by *San Francisco Bulletin* editor James W. Simonton laid claim to these positions, too. Lincoln gave key posts to each faction.[11]

Patronage preoccupied President-elect Lincoln. One issue that perplexed him was how to reward Carl Schurz, a key Wisconsin Republican. Schurz hoped for a diplomatic post, but it was a delicate matter to find a spot for this German-born American and former German revolutionist. At the same time, Schurz was very influential with German-born voters and had to be treated well. The problem became public enough for the *New York Herald* to observe, "Next to the difficulty about Fort Sumter, the question as to what is to be done with Carl Schurz seems to bother the administration more than anything else."[12] Schurz, years later to be a leading exponent of civil service reform, at last secured the post of minister to Spain.

Overall, Lincoln removed and replaced 1195 of the 1520 officials holding presidential appointments when he came into office. Nor was he finished then, as patronage became a weapon he wielded in his contested bid for reelection. In September 1864, some anti-Lincoln employees in the New York Customhouse were dismissed; in October, anti-Lincoln workers at the Brooklyn Navy Yard were fired; in November, Lincoln carried New York by 7000 votes.[13] The president who pledged to preserve the Union had first to unify the Republican Party as a force for preservation, and he closely attended to this formidable task.

Every president from Lincoln on to the turn of the century complained of the plague of "office-seekers" who descended upon him. President James Garfield was astonished by the "inundation" he faced. "My God! What is there in this place that a man should ever want to get into it?"[14] Chester A. Arthur met with office-seekers "only" three days a week.[15] Grover Cleveland took a moment in his second inaugural address to condemn "the demoralizing madness for spoils"; he even asked people to stay away from Washington.[16] Seeking to blaze a trail some-where between full-scale party patronage and all-out civil service reform, he did not approve "swift official decapitation for partizan [sic] pur-poses." At the same time, he wrote, "I have no sympathy with the intol-erant people who, without the least appreciation of the meaning of party work and service superciliously affect to despise all those who apply for office as they would those guilty of a flagrant misdemeanor."[17]

But this was not enough of a defense of spoils for some. Journalist Frank Carpenter recorded the views of an unnamed congressman chaf-ing at Cleveland's measured use of the patronage power. The civil service idea, he said, "is the most ridiculous thing ever attempted in the domain of politics." On the civil service theory, he went on, Cleveland should have said to outgoing president Chester Arthur, "Mr. Arthur, it's true the people have chosen me to fill your place. But I believe that when a man is in office and is doing well, he should not be disturbed. Everyone says you are a good President, so I'll just go back to my law practice in Buffalo and leave you in the White House."[18]

The postmasterships around the country were a central part of the patronage system. These positions were as much party sinecures as gov-ernment posts. Postmasters served as agents for party newspapers and acted as party organizers. They distributed party literature and withheld literature of the opposite party from the mails. They displayed "disgust-ing and irritating placards" of a partisan nature in the post offices and "tauntingly" pointed them out to customers of the opposing party.[19] Postal workers raised campaign funds in their offices and continued to actively use their offices for political purposes even after Cleveland's ex-ecutive order of 1887 prohibited such activity.[20] The postal positions, which numbered 78,500 patronage slots by 1896, were especially impor-tant to the parties since they represented employment in every district in the country. The average congressman in the president's party held power over about two hundred postal service appointments; senators and other party leaders controlled the positions in districts represented by the opposing party.[21]

From the point of view of an ordinary citizen, the post office was not just an incidental part of the federal presence but, after the demobilization of the army, the only part. "No other federal activity was known," Louis Brownlow recalled of his upbringing in a small Missouri town in the 1870s, "except to those few who paid customs duties on imports or excise taxes for the manufacture of whiskey, tobacco, and matches or bought revenue stamps to validate their bank checks." [22]

In the 1870s and 1880s, the federal government gathered more than half of its total revenues from a single institution, the New York Customhouse. This institution did five times more business than the largest private corporation in the country. It was the largest federal office anywhere. No office was more central to the patronage system, and employees came to it not just from New York but from all over the country. Formally an agency of the federal government, the customhouse was practically a settlement house for Roscoe Conkling's New York Republican machine. It "symbolized the fusion of party and state." [23]

Since 1789 the customhouses in New York and elsewhere had distributed fines and forfeitures on the "moiety system" by which half of the proceeds went to the Treasury and the other half was divided among the informer, the customhouse collector, the naval officer, and the surveyor. Following a particularly egregious episode in which New York Customhouse officials defrauded the import company Phelps, Dodge, Congress passed the Anti-Moiety Act (1874). Customhouse collector and future president Chester A. Arthur's annual income promptly plunged from $56,000 to $12,000. [24]

Political parties were financed primarily by assessments they made on the salaries of those holding patronage appointments and on candidates for office who ran on the party ticket. Assessments on employee salaries were presumably "voluntary contributions"—they had to be voluntary by President Hayes's executive order of 1877 pledging enforcement of an 1876 law curtailing political assessments. But "voluntary" was a matter of interpretation. In 1880 in New York, state Republican chairman and vice presidential candidate Chester A. Arthur supervised the collection of "voluntary contributions." The state committee mailed twelve printed assessment circulars in the months before the election, reaching every postmaster, every worker in offices of the Internal Revenue Service, and every customhouse employee, not to mention federal judges, construction workers employed on the capitol building at Albany, and many others. Written by hand onto each letter was the amount of money the committee expected—routinely, 3 percent of salary. If employees did not respond favorably, they received more urgent circulars.[25] These solicitations, civil service reformer Dorman Eaton complained, were, in fact, demands couched in language "rather that of a master to a servant than in the style of one independent citizen addressing another."[26]

Not only political appointees but political candidates provided financial support to the parties. Candidates had to pay handsomely to secure a place on the party ticket. William Ivins's 1887 account of machine politics in New York City held that a candidate for alderman would ordinarily pay $15 a district for 812 districts, or $12,180. A candidate for the House or Senate would pay $25 a district, or $20,300. Candidates for judgeships would pay $10,000 each.[27]

The parties were huge enterprises. The Pennsylvania Republican organization, with some 20,000 regular workers earning wages from the party, represented more "employees" than most of the large railroads in the state.[28] In New York City, the Democracy fielded four full-time workers year-round for each of the 812 electoral districts in the 1880s. In addition, of course, election-day expenditures could be heavy. Each party in New York City had to provide two election inspectors and an election clerk for each of the 812 districts, with each man paid $7.50 a day for five days—this alone cost each party nearly $100,000. Of course, in general elections, the parties could count on tens of thousands of additional workers and the additional expense of their wages.[29]

Assessments continued as the primary means of fund-raising for the parties in the 1880s, but they began to decline thereafter. By 1892, Republican National Committee chairman James S. Clarkson called assessments an "old barbarism." He held that the party could not "honorably accept, much less assess and coerce subscriptions from clerks or officers whose salaries are all needed to support their families." He declared that he would rather try to raise $10,000 from businessmen than $1000 from officeholders.[30] But assessments came from national, state, and several local-level party organizations. At the local level, assessments were sustained through the 1890s. In Cincinnati, lower-rank Republican office-holders paid 2 to 2.5 percent of their salaries, sometimes through payroll deductions. Department heads and other higher officials made "voluntary" contributions, as did candidates for office themselves, not to mention contractors with the city.[31]

Even at the local level, however, fund-raising began to shift from modest contributions from the many to substantial contributions from the few. "There was a time in New York City," Harvard political scientist William B. Munro wrote in 1912, "when even the scrubwomen who earned their dollar a day by hard labor in the city hall yielded their toll to the party's war-chest as the price of continued employment. That day has gone by."[32] In fact, even after 1912 assessments continued in some parts of the country to be a primary means of party fund-raising.[33] Even so, the steady movement from party financing by many small assessments to a few large contributions was significant. Not only did parties become less important to citizens; citizens also became less important to the parties.

During the period of the domination of government by parties and parties by patronage, with what amounted to an extortionate party-run income tax for government workers and candidates for office, civil service reformers held the moral high ground, and they knew it. It wasn't difficult to see in the assassination of reform-minded President James Garfield in 1881—by a disappointed office-seeker, no less—a tragic sign of the moral depravity of the spoils. Civil service reform was deeply felt and intensely moralistic, and its leaders were "as evangelical (and as strenuously resisted) as any crusaders in history."[34] Civil service reformer George William Curtis declared his cause to be "the people's cause, the people's reform," and he predicted that the first administration to vigorously champion it "will acquire a glory only less than that of the salvation of a free Union."[35]

Civil service reform was an international movement. Major reforms became law in Britain in 1870, in Prussia in 1873, and in Canada in 1882.[36] The New York Civil Service Reform Association began in 1877 and quickly won a national membership. The National Civil Service Reform League organized in 1881. Both groups were active in propaganda, the New York organization in 1880–82 circulating half a million pamphlets and documents, not to mention sponsoring essay contests, petitioning Congress, and writing for the newspapers and magazines.[37] Business support for such reform was high as business nationalized and grew more dependent on the public infrastructure of the postal service and customhouses.[38]

Reform seemed ultimately irresistible. When Chester A. Arthur succeeded Garfield in 1881, even he called for civil service reform and he would ultimately be the one to sign into law the Pendleton Act of 1883, creating the Civil Service Commission to supervise competitive examinations. State civil service reform, however, was more limited than federal; only New York and Massachusetts took steps in the 1880s, followed by Illinois, Indiana, and Wisconsin in 1895. State-level reform spread more quickly thereafter while cities lagged behind.[39]

At the federal level, once civil service reform became law, reform ratcheted upward as different parties in power would each put their men in office and then reclassify the offices under the merit system to protect their own appointees from partisan dismissal by future administrations. Even one of the biggest expansions of the civil service, Theodore Roosevelt's reclassification of offices in 1908, fit this pattern. Roosevelt put all fourth-class postmasters under civil service—so long as they were north of the Ohio River and east of the Mississippi. This covered states that consistently voted Republican from 1896 on, so Roosevelt still bequeathed postal patronage to his Republican successor, William Howard Taft, wherever Republicans had yet to consolidate their control.[40] As the merit system expanded between 1883 and 1900, this system of self-serving incorporation, plus the general increase of federal employment, cushioned the patronage system. In 1883, the Pendleton Act placed 14,000 of 131,000 positions under the merit system; by 1900, 95,000 positions were merit appointments—but the total number of patronage appointments (113,000) was barely diminished.[41] The parties could accommodate civil service reform because it "imposed no present costs on them."[42]

Bipartisan endorsement of civil service reform, hypocritical and halting as it may have been, helped produce a new climate, establish a new ideal, and found a new internal constituency of bureaucrats committed more to the federal service than to party. This may have improved the efficiency of the post office and other federal agencies but at the expense of weakening the social solidarity of party organizations and the general capacity of parties to mobilize enthusiastic followings. Patronage had been the heart and soul of political communication in the party era.

It cannot be overemphasized how important patronage was to nineteenth-century parties, and how central civil service reform was as the beacon to a new political era. It may help reimagine this world of patronage to recall that Nathaniel Hawthorne was a political appointee, holding down a clerkship in the Salem Customhouse he immortalized in *The Scarlet Letter*. So was Herman Melville, an outdoor inspector for the New York Customhouse from 1866 to 1885. So was Walt Whitman, taking on in 1865 a position as copyist in the army paymaster's office in Washington.[43]

In the lingering demise of patronage, the musculature of American democracy weakened, and the flesh that made the constitutional bones move in synchrony, if only in certain directions, went slack. Maybe, as the reformers said, the job-hungry parties had begun to get in the way of truly democratic government in the public interest. At the same time, weakening the parties, structurally and psychologically, may have left the public sphere not only cleansed but bleached of the color that had made people care about it.

Campaign Practices: "What's the Matter with Champ Clark? He's All Right!!!"

The spectacular political campaigning of the nineteenth century was carried on largely out of doors, in the streets, with elaborate rituals. These included the erection of "liberty poles" up to one hundred feet high, each party seeking to raise a pole taller than the other, each pole subject to nighttime raids by rivals.[44] Parades, likewise, were competitive events. If one party produced 272 paraders, "not counting the small boys that tagged on behind" and the other only 251, "the whole town knew what it meant."[45] Music also became competitive. In Sullivan County, Indiana, both parties organized glee clubs for the 1896 campaign. The

Sullivan Republican Glee Club traveled to rallies in a huge wagon with roof, curtains, flags, a small organ behind the driver, chairs and benches for forty singers, and a string of full dinner pails to remind onlookers of McKinley's slogan. That glee club was driven by a team of merely six horses; others were pulled by as many as twenty mules.[46]

To a late-twentieth-century ear, it sounds like nothing so much as high school or college fraternity council elections, a boys-will-be-boys extravaganza. At the time the American election extravaganzas were internationally notorious. French novelist Jules Verne had his hero, Phileas Fogg, swept up in an election rally soon after setting foot in San Francisco. A brawl ensues between the partisans of the two candidates, Mr. Camerfield and Mr. Mandiboy, with canes and sticks brandished wildly. Escaping the hullaballoo, Fogg asks a porter later what all the commotion was about. The man indicates it was just an ordinary political meeting. For "the election of a general-in-chief, no doubt?" Fogg inquires. "No, sir; of a justice of the peace."[47]

Political campaigns included a wide variety of preliminary meetings. There were hundreds of assemblies, caucuses, and primary elections to arrive at a ticket of party nominees. New York City's parties alone in 1880 held seventy-two primary elections and 111 conventions before settling on their ticket for the general campaign. A thousand delegates thronged the 1877 convention of New Jersey Democrats; 18,000 Republicans traveled to Chicago for the 1880 Republican National Convention.[48] There were so many links in the pyramidal scheme between township caucuses and statewide conventions and so many opportunities to participate in the campaigns to follow that citizens could choose many routes to civic participation, and could find it often highly entertaining and sometimes remunerative. As many as 20 percent of voters in New York City may have received payment in one form or another as election day workers during Gilded Age elections. In New Haven in 1880, a city of 62,000 people, forty-two clubs and sixty-eight marching companies organized for the political campaign, with about a third of eligible voters signing club constitutions or marching in campaign processions.[49]

Reformers could legitimately doubt, however, that any of this made the ordinary citizen an effective participant in the political process.

Nominating caucuses were often sparsely attended and the frequent record of a unanimous choice on the first ballot indicates that party leaders ordinarily brooked no surprises.[50] Reform writer William Ivins doubted that it was democracy in action when voters were engaged "only as counters in a game played by professionals," and he pointedly observed that of the 1002 nominating meetings in New York City in 1884, 719 took place in or next door to saloons.[51]

Henry George, the internationally celebrated proponent of the single tax, ran for mayor of New York in 1886 in a campaign that involved hundreds of street meetings. "The usual method was to call a meeting at a street-corner, and just before the appointed hour to draw up a truck, from the 'tail' of which one speaker after another addressed the crowd that came." So many meetings of this sort were held that the campaign was dubbed the "tail-board campaign." Speakers would move from truck to truck making two to six speeches a night.[52]

Organizing a political parade was ordinarily the task of parties. When labor organizations got together to nominate Henry George for mayor, they were without the resources of political parties but they did not have to improvise. William McCabe, a journeyman printer who had organized Labor Day parades in 1882 and 1883, served as grand marshal. He laid out instructions for aides from participating organizations, and assigned meeting places to the various "divisions" of the parade from labor organizations, the George Trades Legion, and Assembly district organizations. He urged all sympathizers to "illuminate their houses, or such part of them as they may occupy" on the parade night. "This parade," he urged, "is a prelude to the final parade of labor to the polls. As we march on Saturday, so shall we vote on Tuesday. Then, brothers, show by the numbers in your parade the magnitude of this great political movement for honest city government and the emancipation of those who live by work from the thraldom of those who live by plunder. You can elect Henry George on Saturday night."[53]

Despite a rainy evening, enthusiasts estimated turnout at 30,000. Henry George himself reviewed the paraders as they passed Union Square, watching the marchers go past for two hours. There were chants of "Hi! Ho! the leeches must go!" and "George! George! Vote for

George!" George supporters emphasized that because this parade was unusual in having no uniforms and few torches, it had an earnestness that normal political processions lacked. "The enthusiasm was not manufactured; it was the spontaneous expression of a purpose."[54]

The usual spontaneity and emotionalism of campaign rallies, conventions, and other gatherings made it difficult, or should have made it difficult, for men opposing women's entrance into the political world to complain of women's emotionality. Even so, this was one of the arguments mobilized against woman suffrage, but several suffragists exploited the contradiction. Anna Howard Shaw declared: "Women are supposed to be unfit to vote because they are hysterical and emotional. . . . I had heard so much about our emotionalism that I went to the last Democratic National Convention held at Baltimore, to observe the calm repose of the male contingent." She then described the men's screaming, yelling, and singing "the 'Hown Dawg' song." They would throw their hats in the air, shouting, "What's the matter with Champ Clark?" When the hats came down, others would throw them back up, shouting, "He's all right!!!" These antics continued until five in the morning. Dripping with sarcasm, Shaw concluded: "No hysteria about it—just patriotic loyalty, splendid manly devotion to principle."[55]

The attack on party, including both civil service reform and efforts to make campaigning more instructional and less enthusiastic, was led by a group of self-styled reformers known variously as liberals, Independents, or, after their defection from the Republican Party to support Cleveland in 1884, Mugwumps. Predominantly white, Anglo-Saxon, Northeastern urban Protestant males from business and the professions, the reformers had a genteel cast and what seemed to them genteel objectives. Their most articulate spokesman, journalist E. L. Godkin, advocated ending immigration for people from southern or eastern Europe, requiring literacy and intelligence tests for voting and a "morals" test as well for blacks, naturalization laws to keep immigrants from voting, and extra votes for the wealthy. (He opposed woman suffrage on the grounds that servant girls would outvote their mistresses.)[56] Godkin firmly believed that Anglo-Saxons were the backbone of civilization.[57] Foreigners, he held, lacked "the Anglo Saxon respect for *forms* and legal traditions," a view that other reformers frequently echoed.[58] Godkin did not oppose the vote for blacks if they could pass a moral as well as an educational test. The moral test he urged only for the first decade or so after emancipation, seeking proof that people reared in slavery could earn a living at regular labor. The educational test should be the ability to read "a piece of the newspaper of the morning of election day."[59] He insisted that Americans had placed too much stock in natural rights and not enough in "the value of education, and the authority of training and culture" for government.[60]

The reformers' attack on party did not go unchallenged, nor did their anti-democratic sentiments fail to elicit a response. New York senator Roscoe Conkling told his fellow Republicans in 1874 that "parties are the best and safest means of molding the judgment of the majority into laws and giving tone to public action."[61] The *Minneapolis Tribune* jeered that the names of Mugwump leaders "are invariably parted in the middle or else spelled out in full, as for instance, Thomas Wentworth Higginson, F. Winthrop White, James Freeman Clarke." The *New York Tribune* ridiculed Mugwump self-righteousness in a poem:

> *Oh, we are the salt of the earth,*
> *and the pick of the people too;*
> *We're all of us men of worth,*
> *and vastly better than you!*[62]

The reformers did not seek to eradicate party or faction; they accepted the necessity of parties, but they criticized excesses of party control, party obstinacy, and voters' stubborn loyalties. Do not blindly follow the party, they urged. Hold the parties to their principles. Make sure that candidates are men of character, not only of party affiliation. The reformers sought an independent American voter and their views were a kind of "political Protestantism," as one of them put it.[63] Rote devotion to party came increasingly under attack:

> The majority of the people are so wedded to the traditions and customs of the past, and they worship with such partisan and idolatrous devotion at the shrine of party name, creed and leaders, that, like the Hin-

doo, they would rather be crushed beneath the wheels of the juggernaut of their fathers than to ride in the chariot of civilization that they are capable of constructing by the intelligent use of their ballots.[64]

The Mugwumps were deeply distrustful of democracy. Things began to go wrong, they figured, during the Jacksonian era when the United States began to be a "government of mere numbers."[65] They sought to limit party influence in various ways. Of course, civil service reform was their recurrent theme. But equally important were the set of organizations and media through which they sounded it. They established extra-party associations to promote education and to exert political pressure on each of their leading issues—free trade, civil service reform, tariff reform, and municipal reform.

In those years there was an explosion of national voluntary associations, many of them with explicit programs for social and political change. Farmers organized (the Grange, 1867; the Farmers' Alliance, 1874 and 1887), labor (Knights of Labor, 1869; American Federation of Labor, 1886), veterans (Grand Army of the Republic, 1866), advocates of woman's suffrage (American Woman Suffrage Association and National Woman Suffrage Association, 1869), and campaigners for other women's issues and temperance issues (General Federation of Women's Clubs, 1890; Women's Christian Temperance Union, 1874; and Anti-Saloon League, 1894). Fraternal orders grew, as did trade associations and business lobbying groups, culminating in the organization of the National Association of Manufacturers in 1895. The courts generally supported the rights of these associations to freely incorporate and to conduct their internal affairs as they saw fit. The notable exception was that the conservative judiciary restricted the freedom of unions to strike, picket, or boycott.[66]

Recent scholarship has emphasized the importance of women's groups as leading models of interest group organizing; the suggestion is that the move from party to pressure group was a kind of feminization of the political arena. It is true that women pioneered in interest groups because they were barred from direct participation in party politics, but it is equally true that men's groups were just as significant at the time. It is hard to overlook the civil service reform organizations, largely male, or the veterans' groups, exclusively so. The Grand Army of the Republic took stands and exerted pressure on civil service reform, the tariff, and other leading issues of the day, and it was enormously successful in lobbying for pensions in the 1880s and 1890s. The veterans, as one historian put it, "discovered the welfare state."[67]

The independents worked around the parties as much as through them. Their break from party helped redefine politics as an activity of individuals choosing leaders who adhere to principle rather than groups allegiant to traditional party organizations. This view influenced parties and their campaigns as parties began to accommodate the reformers' perspective with a more restrained style of campaigning. Leaders in both parties began to praise the virtues of the "educational" campaign. Increasingly, they turned to pamphlets and leaflets rather than marching companies and parades. In 1888, despite Cleveland's failure to win re-election, Democrats took pride in their emphasis on education and noted with pleasure that the "campaign supply companies" suffered financial losses. Moving from parades to pamphlets, the new educational campaigns encouraged the centralization of party organization, giving more authority to a central literary bureau, telegraphic bureau, and central department of oratory to assign speakers to rallies. The consequence for spectacular campaigning was deadly: by 1892, national and local party leaders refused to budget significant sums for parades and partisan displays.[68] By 1896, the director of the Republican Party's literary bureau, Perry Heath, claimed that the pamphlets he produced would eschew "all party epithets, all words generally used in campaign abuse" and would indeed be "so non-partisan in character that no one will be able from reading it to tell by whom it was prepared, beyond the fact that it comes from somebody interested in sound money."[69]

There were still political parades in 1900 and 1904 but they were dying fast. Glee clubs and singing fell away. So did torchlight processions.[70] Banner-raisings and pole-raisings fell off. The parties stopped hiring the brass bands that had once accompanied rallies. Partisans no longer illuminated their homes and businesses on behalf of their champions. By 1908, New York's *World* observed, "People do not take their parades so seriously now." Already, the editorial writer calmly noted, "the occasional parade was simply a curiosity, a pale reminder of an earlier time."[71]

After the caucuses, the barbecues, the parades and pole-raising, it was finally election day. Going to the polls was a male pastime, characteristically boisterous and contentious, dominated by groups or factions allegiant to one or another political warlord, organized by local party enterprise to corral less interested citizens to the polls. Violence was common. Arrests for disorderly conduct were frequent. Drawn pistols were not unusual.[72] Money changed hands all over the place. "There would not be an election in Rhode Island . . . without money," a witness told a U.S. Senate investigation in the 1870s, "any more than a funeral without a corpse."[73] Party workers were employed for financial reward as canvassers, identifying voters sympathetic to the party before election day. Parties employed heelers to coax voters to the polls on election day and ticket peddlers stationed near the polling places to distribute preprinted party tickets that voters could simply deposit, without having to mark them in any way, in the ballot box.[74] In New York City, party workers set themselves up near polling places with a cigar box of party tickets. This was known as "boxing the districts"; paying workers to distribute party tickets was a basic expense of running a campaign.[75] Parties printed as many as five tickets per voter, anticipating waste.[76] In San Francisco, ticket vendors crowded the area around the polls. A voter had to "wade through a scene of tumult and noise, with 'every other man holding in his hands big bundles of tickets.'"[77] Election day belonged to the parties; the election itself was a sort of public franchise assigned to the privately organized political parties to operate. Just as states today may contract with private firms to run, say, the state lottery or even a state prison or a public school, so the electoral machinery of democracy itself was in the nineteenth century assigned to two private voluntary organizations, the Republicans and the Democrats. Few state laws defined the conduct of elections. New Jersey law before 1887 (when the state for the first time adopted an official ballot box) did little but identify a small group of election officials, define the format of ballots, and provide polling places.[78] The parties owned politics in the nineteenth century, almost literally.

With so many citizens on the parties' election day payrolls, it was not a radical extension to see voting itself as a kind of part-time employment for the party. New Jersey voters would often be paid $1 to $3 for turning out, with as many as one fifth to one third of the electorate anticipating payment on election day. Buying votes in this way was very likely the major party campaign expense in the 1880s.[79] Vote buying was a far cry from the "treating" of colonial days. Treating was emblematic of a relationship of social deference; it followed rather than preceded the vote and it was public rather than surreptitious. In contrast, vote buying in the late nineteenth century was organized by parties, it was used to round up persons of no social standing, and it often included some haggling over price. Party agents in Newark in 1888 bargained with voters outside the polls, agreed on a price, and paid the voter in brass tokens redeemable at the back room of a saloon nearby.[80] Reformers saw this as political corruption; for practitioners, it was just a routine extension of spoils system politics. As historian John Reynolds puts it, "The pecuniary nature of the nineteenth-century's electoral system made it difficult to draw sharp distinctions as to where payment for services rendered ended and bribery began. If the parties paid for carriages to round up citizens on election day, why should a farmer carting his laborers or neighbors not expect payment? If the ticket peddlers and heelers were rewarded for their efforts, why not the voters?"[81]

There was also outright vote fraud. Terence Powderly, who headed the Knights of Labor from 1879 to 1893, recalled his dismay when, in 1876, as chair of a Luzerne County (Pennsylvania) Greenback-Labor club of some three hundred members, he learned that only three votes were credited to the Greenback-Labor candidate for president. What happened to the other votes? An election board member explained to Powderly that he had neglected to provide a Greenback-Labor counter to sit on the election board. The board simply credited as many votes to the Democrats as might be necessary in a "naturally Democratic" district and did not like to see these other "wasted" ballots counted as the voters had intended.

People bought and sold votes in Ohio; Indiana politicians paid up to $15 a vote in 1888. Election officials falsified returns in Michigan and Indiana.[82] Yet it is difficult to validate the perennial complaints of sore losers. The winners, after all, were reluctant to publicize their methods. When Chester A. Arthur himself commented on his successful 1880 campaign at a Union League Club dinner just before assuming office as vice president, he said, "I don't think we had better go into the minute secrets of the campaign, so far as I know them, because I see the reporters are present, who are taking it all down . . . I will simply say that everybody showed a great deal of interest in the occasion, and distributed tracts and political documents all through the country. . . . If it were not for the reporters I would tell you the truth, because I know you are intimate friends and devoted adherents to the Republican Party."[83]

At a time when presidential elections turned on the votes of a single state (often, New York or Indiana) and when the parties in those contested states were evenly matched, fraud may well have decided national elections. Yet contemporary exclamations about corruption no doubt exaggerated actual practices. A study of a notoriously corrupt Jersey City election of 1889 found that there were 1500 bogus ballots, not the 10,000 contemporaries claimed. This means that 5.5 percent of the total vote can be charged to fraud, inflating turnout only from 72 to 74 percent and making no difference in who was elected to office.[84]

The language of voting reveals a great deal about the process. Party agents handed "slip tickets" to voters as they arrived at the polling place, and they could follow the voter from that moment until he deposited the ballot in the ballot box. If the voter wanted to substitute some other name for the "straight ticket" provided by the party, he "scratched" out the name and wrote in the name of his alternative. Some agents supplied gummed slips—"pasters" or "stickers"—to paste over the printed name of the party favorite. James Bryce observed that since the number of candidates was often great and the political knowledge of the average citizen ordinarily small, voters who might want to "scratch" or "paste" had "really no data for doing so, and, especially in large cities, vote the party ticket in despair."[85]

Different parties used different-sized tickets; the act of voting was thoroughly public.[86] Anyone could tell whom you voted for. Some "vest-pocket" voters might hide their ballot in a coat pocket, but this was rarely done: "Voting was, for most citizens, an opportunity to stand up and be counted among the ranks of their fellow partisans."[87]

Voting in the countryside—and America was still predominantly rural—meant taking at least half a day off from work to get into town, meet with friends, and take care of business, including the business of voting. Election day was an event, not so much because of issues or candidates for their own sake but because this was "among the few days during the year when nearly everyone gathered in the nearest village."[88]

When the polls closed the election ritual was not quite over. There was still the counting of the votes. In New York City, the vote count was compiled first at the newspapers and election night was like no other in a metropolitan newspaper. The reporters had a major task at hand—the election figures, recalled New York editor Julian Ralph, "come in driblets and atoms, and must be put together as the Florentines make their mosaics." Since election results would first be known at the newspapers, crowds gathered outside their offices. The crowd "begins with a lot of little knots of men—one in front of the *Press*, another in front of the *Times*, the others in front of the buildings of the *Sun*, the *World*, the *Tribune*, and the rest. As these knots swell they join one another and blockade Park Row, and lap over into the City Hall Park—an enormous, patient, cheering, and yelling multitude. . . ."[89]

Then it was over, but for the post-election paying off of election bets, the speeches of congratulation and recrimination, the crows of a meaningful mandate for party policies from the victors, and the cries of fraud from the defeated.

The shift in political campaign style in the late nineteenth century responded to but also helped create a new meaning for politics. As parties invested less in rallying their own loyal followers and moved toward persuading uncommitted voters or "floaters," there came to be an incentive for policy-oriented political entrepreneurship. If party loyalty could be sustained by little more than Fourth of July rhetoric, tradition, the promise of jobs, and social pressure on election day, party victories in the new era would have to rely on something different—a program that promised policies more than jobs.

It is not that parties from 1870 to 1900 stood for nothing at all, but it is not easy to find consistency in their stands. The tariff issue over which parties regularly waged their campaigns was a patchwork of local protectionist rate schedules. When Democratic candidate Winfield S. Hancock in 1880 declared it a "local" issue, he was certainly right, but a generally protectionist Republican Party and a generally free-trade Democracy made rhetorical hay out of what was not much more than special-interest politics on both sides. Similarly, in the 1880s and 1890s, when the currency question divided the parties, the symbolic weight of the issue (silver as the people's money, gold as the businessman's rock of security) provided a party rallying cry more than an ideologically coherent account of conflicting principles or interests.[90]

Campaigns were less the result of a division over issues than the efficient cause that generated issues in the first place. As parties moved from parades to pamphlets in campaigning, they were necessarily forced to articulate their own identities more precisely and consistently in terms of issues and principles. At the same time, as state-level public expenditures increased on education, care for the criminal and insane, health, and economic regulatory activities, there were more matters on which parties might take a stand rather than recycle abstract rhetorical gestures.[91] With political campaigning turned educational and with a growing role of government in economic life, issues came to the forefront of political battles.

Reform of campaign practice was one of a family of reforms and social changes that altered political culture profoundly. Other reforms, especially in the years after 1900, attacked parties either in the name of popular democracy or in the name of science and efficiency. In the former category, there was the popular primary that replaced the party caucus for nominations. Between 1900 and 1920 state after state required primaries; by 1917 all but five states had some kind of direct primary, and this included thirty-two states with mandatory direct primaries for all state offices. Presidential primaries were adopted by twenty-six states by 1916, further weakening party control over candidacy. The Seventeenth Amendment mandated the direct election of senators by popular vote and thereby, along with the party primaries, broke the link of the senator to the state party.[92] The initiative, referendum, and recall brought a novel form of direct democracy to the states, especially in the West where they were most widely adopted.

On the side of anti-party reforms in the name of "science," municipal reforms reduced the number of elected municipal officials, diluted the power of city councils in relation to the mayor, and weakened the political process in relation to administrative councils and officers in the conduct of city government. City commission systems of government began in Galveston in 1901 and by 1920 were in use in almost five hundred cities.[93] Legislative research bureaus, the active development of government statistical work, and the promotion of political science among municipal reformers emphasized the need for and possibility of applying "intelligence" and "business methods" to political life. This went hand in hand with the expansion of state authority and the growing complexity of political administration, particularly in the cities. When the cities began to be responsible not only for taxation and street cleaning but also for expanded educational systems, public parks, the regulation or even the ownership of utilities in public transportation, electricity, water supply, street illumination, and waste disposal, the rhetorical boast that city government was and should be a "business" and should be treated "scientifically" had an authoritative ring that it could not have had a generation before.

The social change of these decades pushed government into a more activist mode, especially the legislature (the courts had been interventionist for some time on economic matters). The Interstate Commerce Commission in 1887 "marked the entry of Congress into the full-fledged use of its positive authority." The Sherman Act of 1890 was not particularly effective anti-trust legislation but it did acknowledge the law's "affirmative obligation" to protect free competition in the economy. Like the ICC, it expressed a broad federal "moral and political responsibility" for maintaining a free market economy. As a national society became more integrated and more dependent on infrastructural communication and transportation services, the place of government became correspondingly more central—both nationally, in regulating railroads and at least gesturing toward control of other corporations and trusts, and municipally, in regulating mechanical power. What one historian calls "the constant, felt presence of a more organized way of life" permitted a new receptivity to government action.[94]

Amidst all these reforms and social changes, one innovation is often neglected that, from the viewpoint of what citizens learned of politics from their contact with the political system, was of great importance: the adoption of the Australian ballot. This new voting procedure swept the country from 1888 to 1896 with almost no opposition. It helped author a new relationship of the state to the parties and perfectly symbolized an ideal of the independent citizen that has dominated the American political imagination ever since.

Election Day and the Ballot

The American people have . . . been given an ark, in which to deposit the most sacred things known to man, namely, the ballots of free men; and we should see to it that only those authorized to do so by law be permitted to approach this ark, and that every person attempting to lay unclean hands upon it be overtaken by the wrath of a free people, which should be as destructive as the lightnings of Jehovah.[95]

A secret ballot had been part of the Chartist program for political reform in England in the 1840s, championed by political radicals and some liberals. John Stuart Mill, among others, opposed it, arguing that the franchise was a duty, not a right, to be exercised publicly and in accord with the voter's conscientious opinion of the public good; he objected to turning the vote from a privilege or trust to a personal right.

This is worth consideration. Mill acknowledged that in times past, when voters were strongly influenced by employers or landlords, the case for a secret ballot was strong. But where social progress no longer made the working class subservient to the middle class, or the middle class to the higher classes, the greater danger was that voters would consult only their own and not the public's interest. Secrecy would exacerbate this by instructing voters symbolically that the vote was their personal property. Open, public voting, Mill contended, would be better. "Even the bare fact of having to give an account of their conduct, is a powerful inducement to adhere to conduct of which at least some decent account can be given."[96]

Mill's assessment that undue influence of employers and landlords was largely a thing of the past was premature, certainly for America. Union leader Terence Powderly reported that he began his political career because of his sense of outrage at the danger faced by a "man who had a family depending on him" if he accepted a ticket from a peddler for a party his boss did not support. Powderly fought for the secret ballot.[97] While Mugwump reformers were strong in support of ballot reform, so was labor. Henry George and his followers strongly supported the Australian ballot. In 1883, George called it "the greatest single reform" required for cleaning up American politics.[98] Just days after his good showing (but his defeat, nonetheless) in the New York mayoral campaign of 1886, he urged that people of all parties join in support of it. "You cannot bribe a man who gets no ticket from you; you cannot intimidate him when you cannot tell how he is going to vote. All this thing of printing ballots and peddling tickets is done away with. That is a reform we ought to have."[99] The United Labor Party, formed around George's mayoral candidacy, was the first national party to endorse ballot reform.[100]

While there was considerable labor and populist support, the first effective, statewide Australian-ballot law came in Massachusetts in 1888 under the leadership of a classic Mugwump, Richard Henry Dana III.[101] By the end of 1889, nine states had followed suit. By 1892, thirty states had adopted ballot reform, and by 1896, thirty-nine states had. Generally, this meant that a ballot printed at public expense and distributed by election officers at the polls ("exclusive" or "official" ballot) listed the names of all duly nominated candidates (the "blanket ballot"). Indiana's ballot, adopted in 1889, arranged candidates in a column by party under a party emblem. The voter could simply mark the circle under the emblem to signify a vote for every candidate of that party. Supporters of the

Massachusetts law, in which candidates of different parties were grouped together according to the office they sought, objected that this encouraged "sheep-like conformity." By 1910, twenty-nine states had a "party column" ballot like Indiana, twelve the "office block" model like Massachusetts, five states had other sorts of compromise arrangements or only local laws, and two states had no Australian ballot.[102]

The novelty of the Australian ballot was not that it was printed but that it was printed by the state.[103] The state thus assumed a significant expense the parties had borne, the cost of printing the ballots and the cost of paying party workers to distribute them. This helped rally even machine politicians behind the new system.[104] Since individual voters now had to mark the ballot rather than simply deposit it, the center of political gravity moved from party to voter. Much as John Stuart Mill had feared, the new ballot transformed voting from a social and public duty to a private right. After ballot reform, voting would be enforceable less by party-directed social obligation and more by private conscience. The ballot now hailed a private individual making rational choices about policy preferences where the party-printed ticket had beckoned with the pleasures of affiliation and comradeship.

The new ballot was supported by a variety of reforms to ensure that voting would be uncoerced and unsupported by social pressures. It became illegal to pay party workers to bring voters to the polls, to provide more than a certain number of poll watchers at each polling place, and for party workers to approach within a certain number of feet of the place of voting.[105]

A change in the ballot did not create independent voters overnight. At first, scarcely any voters volunteered split tickets—only 1.2 percent of votes in Australian ballot states in 1892 and 2.9 percent in 1896. The new ballot allowed but did not induce ticket-splitting.[106] Indeed, in one respect the new system worked against it. Ticket-splitting in the 1880s had been most likely when third parties emerged and ran fusion tickets; they would distribute ballots that intermixed their candidates with those of their partner party.[107] The Australian ballot and state-prescribed requirements made it difficult for upstart parties to get on the ballot, so this kind of orchestrated ticket-splitting became more difficult. Moreover, the party-column format for the ballot—much more widely used than the office-block alternative—still made straight-ticket voting easy.

Even so, the Australian ballot posed a challenge of sheer comprehension for those unaccustomed to it. In 1896, parties in New York held "schools" for their voters to instruct them on marking the ballots. The *New York Times* devoted front-page space to a facsimile of the ballot and a full column of instructions on voting Australian style.[108] The *Los Angeles Times* did the same as late as 1928, taking up most of the front page the Sunday before the election with a feature, "How to Mark Your Ballot Next Tuesday." The paper reproduced the whole ballot—marked, of course, and advised readers to clip the page and take it to the polls with them.

This was probably a good idea on a ballot that contained twenty-one state constitutional amendments, initiatives, and referenda, twenty-one municipal propositions, and two county propositions.[109] The cognitive demands on the American voter were extraordinary. Municipal reformer and political scientist William Munro observed that the American voted in a municipal election almost annually, compared to the French citizen who voted every four years or the Prussian every six. On each ballot, the American faced more offices to vote on and more candidates per office than in a typical European election. Thanks to Progressive reforms after 1900, Americans not only elected their candidates in general elections but nominated them in primaries, unlike voters anywhere in Europe.

A reform emerged to correct reform: the short ballot. Munro backed it with enthusiasm. He cited ballots containing three hundred to four hundred names and one whopper in a New York State Assembly district listing 835 candidates. "There is something wrong with an electoral system which requires from every man a service that not one in ten thousand is willing to give." What was called the "blanket ballot" made "a hollow mockery of popular sovereignty."[110] Ballots had, indeed, grown in size. The Wisconsin state ballot in 1904 was thirty-five by twenty-four inches, the New York ballot in 1920 was nineteen by nineteen inches for presidential electors, with another seventeen- by eighteen-inch ballot for state offices, and an eight- by seven-inch ballot for constitutional amendments. The ballot in that year in Portland, Oregon, was forty by fourteen inches, including eleven state and seven municipal initiative and referendum questions, plus the listing of ninety-one candidates running for fifty-two different offices. The result, another contemporary political scientist complained, was that "the average citizen, nay the exceptional citizen, must confess that he votes blindly so far as perhaps nine tenths of the candidates and offices are concerned."[111]

Short ballot reform was the special project of New York businessman and municipal reformer Richard S. Childs. When he first voted in 1903, he was shocked to enter the polling booth and unfold his ballot: "I found to my dismay that I was hopelessly unprepared. There near the top were the four principal candidates . . . but there were fifteen other officers to be elected. . . . On these latter . . . I had no information. . . . With mortification I voted blindly for the word 'Republican' in each of the fifteen contests and thereby, of course, accepted without scrutiny the offerings of the party leaders, as they knew I would." He realized then, he later wrote, that "The long ballot is the politician's ballot; the short ballot is the people's ballot!"[112]

Childs gathered support from a variety of prominent men, most notably Woodrow Wilson, who became a great enthusiast, declaring in a 1909 speech, "I believe that the short ballot is *the key* to the whole question of the restoration of government by the people."[113] New York governor Charles Evans Hughes in 1910 urged the legislature to reduce the number of elective offices in the state: "The ends of democracy will be better attained to the extent that the attention of the voters may be focussed upon comparatively few offices, the incumbents of which can be strictly accountable for administration."[114] Both the Republican and Progressive parties endorsed the short ballot principle in 1912.[115] In this moment, the Progressive temper seemed to accept that more democracy meant less democracy, so less democracy was now necessary to gain more.

By 1912, six leading cities and more than 150 smaller municipalities had adopted short ballot reform.[116] But this did not keep the United States from having (as it still does) many more elected officials, with shorter terms, chosen at more elections than any other democracy. The passion for making government simpler ran athwart of other Progressive reforms that unquestionably made political participation more complex, from registration to the multiplication of elective rather than appointive offices, to the party primary, to the initiative, referendum, and recall. By the 1920s, all of this led at least some observers to question how realistic the premises of democracy were, at least as they had been applied, in the modern age. "The average man necessarily finds most of his energies absorbed by the process of earning a living; the average woman is largely engrossed in household cares," political scientist Robert C. Brooks observed. "With personal registration every year, and with one or two primaries or elections each year, both of the latter involving long and difficult ballots, many turn aside from politics, except perhaps when an occasional thrilling contest takes place."[117]

The Progressive Era reforms created a new kind of political performance, a new kind of political experience for the participating citizen. Nineteenth-century voting had been a performance of community with the local party integrated into communal functions. The state party and national party organizations, in contrast, did not represent a community. They were not organic expressions of anything—not economic, ethnic, or sectional—but a symbolization conjured up to suit a structured political system of national contests. In a sense, the national political party was an instrument for nationalism itself, helping to lift public attention to national issues and national identity.

Twentieth-century voting was thus free to become a performance of individualism oriented to the nation, not a performance of community directed to the locale. A nineteenth-century voter demonstrated his citizenship through loyalty to party and the local fraternity that was its most palpable manifestation. A twentieth-century voter was obliged to act out something new and untested in the political universe—citizenship by virtue of informed competence. Voting by party ticket and voting by state-supplied ballot are both acts that determine who gets elected to office. But in the former case it tends to be a matter of parties mobilizing their membership; in the latter case it is more nearly an aggregation of individual preferences. The Australian ballot indicated that a new political day and a new understanding of politics had dawned.

The mechanical voting machine offered a perfect embodiment of Progressive Era hopes for democracy. The task of counting votes automatically was just the thing to inspire Yankee ingenuity, and Thomas Edison's very first patent (1869) was for the Electrographic Vote Recorder to count votes in Congress. Voting machines for general use were introduced in the 1890s, the first one being used in Lockport, New York, in 1892. Developed further by the United States Voting Company of Jamestown, New York, more and more states began to make use of it after 1900.[118] By 1920 the use of voting machines had been approved in fourteen states.[119] In 1910, the American Voting Machine Company (which is still in existence), in a prospectus announcing an issue of capital stock, wrote of its voting machines, "They're almost human in accomplishment and mechanically infallible as to mistakes." The voting machine "is a cold piece of machinery which shows no favoritism to any candidate, or party." It would save money, do away with fraud, and preserve "the right of absolute secrecy in voting."[120] There was no question that the writer of that prospectus had a good ear for what had become the dominant strain in American political culture.

Social Change and Political Transformation

Consider the curious relationship between patronage and fire fighting. Fires were a scourge of nineteenth-century cities, their wooden buildings close together, often poorly built, with no zoning to separate industrial from residential areas. Fire fighting was handled by volunteer fire companies, but, by mid-century, complaints increased that they were inefficient and expensive to maintain. At about the same time, the horse-drawn, steam-powered pumper made bucket brigades unnecessary. Cincinnati, St. Louis, Baltimore, and Boston all instituted paid fire companies, and it seemed perfectly rational for New York to follow suit when such a reform was proposed in 1865.

But it was no accident that the reformers were Republicans. The volunteer companies were closely tied to Democratic ward organizations. For the Democrats, fire fighting was a million-dollar domain of patronage as city hall distributed equipment, firehouses, and uniforms to fire companies that doubled as party ward organizations. Those who served the party well might be beneficiaries of "bunking": they could live in a firehouse for a year at public expense. When reform triumphed and a professional fire company supplanted the volunteer bucket brigades, the change helped break apart the symbiotic structure of party, community, and neighborhood that patronage had held together.[121]

The development of municipal health, education, and welfare limited parties' social utility and their capacity to use patronage to bind voters' loyalty. The fire-fighting example is indicative. In the late nineteenth century, the communities able to sustain vital party politics and their festivals of democracy were changing rapidly. Spectacular campaigns did not vanish because a group of upper-crust reformers said they should. They receded because the character of a society that could sustain them changed. With the Civil War fading from national consciousness by the turn of the century, the martial spirit of parades and military-style clubs grew less resonant. The intimacy among different social classes that those bands, parades, and political companies had reflected was disappearing.[122] The general population did not know the local gentry.

The gentry, in truth, were no longer local. Beginning in the 1880s, affluent families moved out to the suburbs, sent their children to boarding schools, socialized at the newly organized country clubs, and vacationed at exclusive resorts. "You can do business with anyone," J. P. Morgan observed, "but only sail with a gentleman." [123] The affluent classes were not only becoming more socially distinct from the working classes but also more socially connected to one another across regions. The world of "island communities," as historian Robert Wiebe described the late nineteenth century, had never been composed of places either truly islands or idyllically communities, but a national middle class was growing as railroads, newspapers, roads, the telegraph, the mails, travel, tourism, and commerce linked people across geography. National standards came to mean something. The National Municipal League, an organization of social scientists and upper-crust reformers established in 1894, promoted uniform accounting systems across cities. Its efforts to standardize the accounting and classification of municipal expenditures, adopted by the Bureau of the Census after 1900, provided each city a view of itself in comparative perspective.[124]

Leisure became not only more commercially organized but also more socially segregated. In Providence, Rhode Island, for instance, where Protestant churches had once brought together employers and employees alike, the increasingly heterogeneous city of the late nineteenth century separated a Catholic working-class population from middle-class Protestants. In 1865, Providence did not have a single incorporated social or sports club, but by 1886 thousands of citizens belonged to the Masons, Odd Fellows, Pythians, and other lodges. Women joined tennis, cycling, and literary clubs. In antebellum Providence, temperance organizations and even the art union enrolled any white male (and often even females) who signed up, but after the Civil War the clubs and lodges adopted initiation fees, annual dues, and a culture of exclusion.[125] Elsewhere fraternal orders were surprisingly pluralist as late as the 1870s, with national organizations giving full recognition to lodges operating in languages other than English. But this changed as nativist reaction set in to southern and eastern European immigration in the 1880s.[126]

Cities grew far beyond citizens' capacity to easily imagine themselves being part of the entity. In a society interwoven by railroads and telegraph, an individual's understanding of his or her location in time and space increasingly came under the influence of the national rather than local context. For instance, as late as the 1870s, most railroads operated regionally and ran trains according to a time standard from a city or observatory in the region. Into the 1880s, few people or institutions had any use for standardizing time across regions. But then railroads nationwide adopted standard time zones, and local time quickly gave way. It was probably true, as the *New York Herald* reflected, that standard time "goes beyond the public pursuits of men and enters into their private lives as part of themselves."[127]

National markets gave rise to and were, in turn, sustained by private credit-reporting agencies and the development of new packaged goods products, easily transported and before long readily identified by distinctive names, packaging, and advertising. In the cities, the new department stores dominated retail sales and displaced the neighborhood dry goods stores. National magazines, the wire services, national professional organizations, and innovations like Bureau of the Census standardized comparative statistics on municipal expenditures and services helped bureaucrats, politicians, and reformers in one city or town learn what was happening in another.[128] Even the most remote hamlets of American society were becoming interconnected. The movement for rural free delivery in the 1890s, fully developed and incorporated into the general postal service by 1906, was what historian Daniel Boorstin has called "the least heralded and in some ways the most important communications revolution in American history."[129]

Part of the transformation of community life was engineered by the incursion of commercialized entertainments. In the mid-nineteenth century, politics attracted popular participation because it was the best entertainment in town. By the early 1900s, a political parade had major competition from vaudeville, amusement parks, professional baseball, boxing and football, an extraordinary craze for the bicycle, phonographs, and the first nickelodeons. Mass commercial entertainment, once the occasional bright spot in the calendar as the circus came to town, became available year-round.

The most devastating aspect of commercialization was that newspapers, once organs for the political parties, became more and more commercial and increasingly dared to be independent. The daily and weekly newspapers were becoming absorbed in commercially minded news gathering and less committed to advancing political parties. This transformation was not abrupt, and most newspapers continued to the end of the century to declare partisan allegiances. In some respects, partisanship even increased. In Indiana, for instance, the number of cities with two rival newspapers, each pledged to a different party, grew from eleven in 1880 to forty-six in 1910.[130] As small towns became larger and more heterogeneous, there were increasing opportunities to challenge the staid, apolitical character of the local press.

Still, it was a sign of things to come when Adolph Ochs took over the nearly moribund New York Times in 1896 with a declaration of political independence. The Times had been founded as a penny paper and quickly stood with the anti-slavery forces that helped form the Republican Party. A leading Republican standard-bearer for many years, famed for exposing Boss Tweed in 1871 and post office frauds in 1881, it joined defecting Mugwumps in 1884 to endorse the Democratic presidential candidate, Grover Cleveland. In a day when such a defection was regarded as practically treasonous, this caused the *Times* some financial pain. The paper recovered lost ground by the late 1880s, but its balance sheet took a turn for the worse with the expenses of a new building, and in 1893 the paper was sold to its editor, Charles Miller, and his business associates. This arrangement failed and the paper was again up for sale. When Ochs bought the paper, his opening statement declared, first, that he would try to be true to the "great history for right-doing" of the paper; second, that he would try to give the news "impartially"; and third, that in retaining the current editorial staff he would maintain as well the paper's commitment to certain political principles.

Only the second of these three paragraphs is quoted in the leading textbook on American journalism history.[131] It is, admittedly, a fine paragraph, setting out the paper's intention to "give the news, all the news, in concise and attractive form, in language that is parliamentary in good society, and give it as early, if not earlier, than it can be learned through any other reliable medium; to give the news impartially, without fear or favor, regardless of any party, sect or interest involved; to make of the columns of *The New York Times* a forum for the consideration of all questions of public importance, and to that end to invite intelligent discussion from all shades of opinion."

But the third paragraph also is important. There, while asserting that the paper shall be "a non-partisan newspaper," Ochs nonetheless affirms its devotion to "the cause of sound money and tariff reform, opposition to wastefulness and peculation in administering public affairs and in its advocacy of the lowest tax consistent with good government, and no more government than is absolutely necessary to protect society, maintain individual and vested rights and assure the free exercise of a sound conscience."[132] These were not trivial concerns; Ochs even took them to the street, marching, along with top editors of the paper, in the parade for the "Gold Democratic" ticket of Palmer and Buckner.[133] The paper sought to remain an "independent Democratic newspaper," in the words of its early in-house historian, an "independent conservative newspaper," in the words of more party-shy Adolph Ochs. Finding Bryan anathema, the *Times* endorsed Republican William McKinley in 1900, the Democrat Alton Parker in 1904, Republican William Howard Taft over Bryan in 1908, and Democrat Woodrow Wilson in 1912 and 1916.[134]

General histories of American journalism picture the move away from the partisan press as economically motivated; the papers supposedly sought a wider range of readers to attract increasingly important advertising dollars. In fact, the move to nonpartisanship often precipitated financial setbacks.[135] The most celebrated commercial triumphs of the day—Joseph Pulitzer's *New York World* and William Randolph Hearst's *New York Journal,* in seeking a mass urban readership, did nothing to hide their support for the Democratic Party. Pulitzer briefly served his party in the Missouri legislature. Hearst served two terms in the Congress and made a serious bid for the Democratic nomination for president in 1904.

The distinguishing feature of the new journalism, however, was not to be found in subtleties of political endorsement or political bias. In large part, what was happening was beyond the immediate control or conscious intentions of the press barons. The commercializing press was also a professionalizing press, and a new model journalism was located in the very form of the reports the paper provided. The form of newswriting began to change. The paper became less the editor's scrapbook to be shared with like-minded readers and more an organization's product. This new style can be recognized in several journalistic innovations of the day.

The most notable was the interview. The interview presumes a reader who is less a partisan than a witness, a sort of acknowledged eavesdropper, one ready to gather confidences intended for a host of similarly situated eavesdroppers. Materials in the newspaper were increasingly literary creations designed with readers in mind, rather than the reprints of official documents or transcripts of legislative debates where general readers were at best a secondary audience. But the "interview," a colloquy between a reporter and a public person, designed explicitly and exclusively for a newspaper readership, was a new form of literature. Essentially unknown before the Civil War, it spread quickly thereafter. Andrew Johnson was the first president to submit to an interview, and while the interview was widely attacked as a barbaric contrivance, its use grew relentlessly. By 1880, interviewing was a common practice and much remarked on by European visitors as a distinctively American contribution to journalism. The interview represented a new kind of deference to the audience, a new genuflection before a "public" conceived of more as consumers than as partisans.[136]

Newswriting changed even in its traditional attention to public speeches and legislative debates. Most newswriting in the mid-nineteenth century was organized chronologically. Reports on Congress appearing in New York or Chicago papers often began with a description of the weather as the reporter walked over to the Capitol. They might then describe the call to order and the chaplain's prayer and proceed chronologically through the congressional business as if transcribing the *Congressional Record*. This was standard practice, Louis Brownlow recalls, on the *Nashville Banner* at the turn of the century where legislative reporters unfailingly began their stories with notice of the chaplain's prayer.[137] After the turn of the century, reporters increasingly began with a "lead" that summarized high points of the event being reported. Reports of the president's annual message to Congress, for instance, were at mid-century strictly chronological accounts of congressional proceedings that noted the reading of the president's message in its place but made no mention of what the message said (the devoted reader could turn to a back page to read the entire speech verbatim). After 1900 the reports invariably began with a sentence or two that identified the highlights of what the president's message was about.

This new format for reporting, the "summary lead," like the interview, inserted the reporter, without benefit of party identification, between the government and the citizen. This reflected not only a newly professional self-consciousness among journalists, still only a precariously respectable occupation, but also the developing sense of politics as a managerial science rather than a partisan allegiance.

These literary innovations grew out of the daily routines and presuppositions of reporters as they became newly aware of themselves as a corporate group. Reporters in the 1880s and 1890s began to earn more money. They began to work increasingly on salary rather than "on

space"—payment for the number of column inches of print they produced. They began to gather together in city press clubs—first in New
York in 1873, and in the 1880s in Chicago, Minneapolis, Milwaukee,
Boston, St. Paul, and San Francisco. In Washington, D.C., rival clubs
were organized in 1867, 1885 (the Gridiron Club), 1891, and 1908 (the
National Press Club). By 1890, E. L. Godkin confidently wrote that
news gathering had become "a new and important calling." [138] Certainly
it was the time of the celebrity reporter, with the likes of Nellie Bly,
Henry Morton Stanley, Sylvester Scovel, and, most of all, Richard Harding Davis providing the dash and sparkle that drew attention to reporters
and attracted young men and women to the field. [139]

Journalism was increasingly differentiated from politics, to which it
had been so long connected. The intertwining of politics and press had
been most visible in Washington, where reporters lived in the same
boardinghouses frequented by politicians. Even the most prominent of
Washington reporters routinely supplemented their meager journalistic
pay with clerkships in the House or Senate. Typically newspapers paid
Washington correspondents only for the months Congress was in session
(which says something about the relative importance of the president to
the Congress in those days), so the reporters had plenty of incentive to
seek additional remuneration. Some of them, in their role as clerks,
made extra cash by selling secrets of the committees they clerked for.
Others acted as paid lobbyists. Clerkships for reporters continued to be
tolerated into the early twentieth century, but lobbying by reporters already looked unseemly. In 1879, leaders of the correspondents adopted
rules of press accreditation that barred lobbying. The rules also required
that reporters gain their primary income from sending telegraphic dispatches to daily newspapers, a measure that effectively denied accreditation to black and women reporters, nearly all of whom wrote for weeklies
and magazines and saved money by sending dispatches by mail rather
than telegraph. [140]

Journalism did not become more independent because publishers
spied the dollar sign in nonpartisanship or because reporters went
through a moral transformation, giving up their hard-drinking low life
for college degrees and ethical precepts. Journalism was not outside the

political culture looking in but a part of a world in which the deepest presuppositions of political and social life were changing. The growing organization and self-consciousness of journalists were part of what Robert Wiebe has called the "search for order" of the late nineteenth century.[141] Others have called the complex of trends by other names— professionalization, industrialization, urbanization, commercialization, or the rise of a professional-managerial class. No single or simple characterization captures all of the important changes or puts in a nutshell the movement from farm to factory, from town to city and city to suburb, from a world of natives to a world of immigrants, from a society understood in terms of regions and religions to a society that had to be reconceived more in terms of classes and ethnic groups, from a world where leisure, if not work, was organized largely by local communities to the large-scale commercialization of entertainment and the largely taken-for-granted separation of the spheres of work, home, leisure, and politics. None of this was, or is, easy to grasp, but all of it is the relevant context in which the second transformation of American citizenship took place.

The Purification of Citizenship

Progressive Era politics instructed people in a citizenship of intelligence rather than passionate intensity. Political participation became less a relationship to party than a relationship to the state, less a connection to community than to principles and issues. The voter who kept up with the news read less to bask in the glow of his party's achievements than to peruse reports on the various issues, politicians, and parties of the day— along with the sports, human interest stories, and display ads that commanded a growing proportion of the pages.

The new model of citizenship called for a voter more intelligent than loyal. It helped free people from parties, but it also provided new means to exclude some people from voting altogether. In every Southern state between 1890 and 1902, legislation requiring poll taxes and in most cases literacy tests was passed.[142] This disenfranchised nearly all blacks and a good many poor whites as well. These restrictions on the franchise, while most widespread in the South, existed elsewhere, too. Seven

Southern states instituted literacy tests between 1890 and 1908, but Connecticut had been the first state to pass a literacy requirement, in 1856, followed in 1858 by Massachusetts. Literacy tests for voting—usually specifying English literacy—became law in Wyoming in 1890, Maine 1894, California 1896, Washington and Delaware 1898, New Hampshire 1906, and Arizona 1912, followed belatedly by New York in 1922 and Oregon 1926.[143] Even where literacy was not prescribed, the Australian ballot made it practically a requirement.

Citizenship itself became a requirement for voting where, in many states, an immigrant's stated intention to become a citizen had once been sufficient. At least at some point from mid-century to the 1890s, nineteen states provided immigrants the franchise if they declared their intent to become citizens, but every one of these states repealed such provisions by the 1920s.[144] Michigan revoked the franchise for aliens in 1894 in the wake of anti-immigrant agitation following the depression of 1893–94. It did so by a constitutional amendment that voters passed overwhelmingly.[145] In 1894, Wyoming revoked alien suffrage (that it had granted only in 1890). Minnesota followed in 1896, North Dakota in 1898, Colorado in 1902, Wisconsin in 1910, Oregon in 1914; Nebraska, South Dakota, Kansas, Texas, Missouri, Indiana, and Arkansas by 1925.[146] In most states, the resulting disenfranchisement represented a very small percentage of the electorate (North Dakota and Wisconsin are exceptions), but it was a symbolically significant raising of the bar to citizenship.[147] E. L. Godkin, still holding forth at The Nation after thirty years, wrote that "there is no corner of our system in which the hastily made and ignorant foreign voter may not be found eating away the political structure, like a white ant, with a group of natives standing over him and encouraging him."[148]

The most severe limitation on immigrant rights came in legislation directed against the Chinese. Anti-Chinese agitation in California had been strong from mid-century on. In fact, it was the major factor in California's failure to ratify the Fifteenth Amendment in 1870.[149] But twelve years later national legislation followed—the Exclusion Act of 1882 not only prohibited Chinese immigration but forbade the naturalization of resident Chinese. The law was renewed in 1892 and 1902. Blacks were provided naturalization rights in the Fifteenth Amendment, but Asians not until the 1940s.

Restrictions of the franchise, then, were not the work only of Southern Democrats intent on disenfranchising blacks. Cosmopolitan reform sentiment early in the 1900s supported efforts to draw in the circle of the franchise. Reformers argued that the vote should be limited to people literate in English. William B. Munro, for instance, urged all states to adopt a literacy test: "Men can contribute to the success of free government only by using the ballot with intelligence and reasonable independence; and this they can hardly do if the ordinary avenues of information, including the newspapers, are closed to them."[150] In Maryland, a proposal to prohibit assistance to illiterate voters became law in 1901, ensuring massive black disenfranchisement in a state where 40 percent of African-Americans of voting age were illiterate. Subsequent efforts to exclude illiterates more completely failed to pass, but the same reform groups that supported regulating public utilities and passing pure food laws also favored disenfranchising blacks and took this to be a Progressive reform.[151]

The reform consensus on literacy makes it clear that the concept of universal suffrage had lost hegemony.[152] Fear of blacks in the South, of aliens and immigrants in the North, and of Asians on the West Coast endowed with legitimacy and emotional force a new rhetoric about the evils of "ignorant voting."[153] It is sobering to read, for instance, the 1941 memoirs of Josephus Daniels, editor of the *Raleigh News and Observer* and a strong Progressive Democratic backer of Woodrow Wilson, writing unrepentantly of his efforts in the 1890s to find constitutional methods to "purify" the vote—that is, to eliminate blacks as much as possible from the polling place. In this effort, Daniels traveled to Louisiana to observe the working of the Grandfather Clause at first hand. The Grandfather Clause simply required a literacy test for any citizen except those whose ancestors had been voters before 1868. Without mentioning race, this enabled illiterate whites, but not illiterate blacks, to qualify.[154]

Electoral reforms of these years, then, were by no means driven only by liberal impulses but equally by the force of what one scholar has called "ethnocultural Americanism." Many reformers wove together appeals to the rights and liberties of American citizens with tributes to the distinctive virtues of Anglo-Saxon Christianity.[155] The concept of citizenship began to change from participation by virtue of one's presence in the land to participation that rested on prequalifications: legal citizenship, literacy, the ability and interest to pay a poll tax, the ability and interest to register to vote, and—broadly defined—Americanization. The model citizen, in the reform vision, would be disciplined enough to register, educated enough to read, thinking enough to choose candidates with little or no party guidance, and docile enough to leave many matters to the experts.

All told, the new model politics increased the demands on the citizen. Those who would vote needed more information to cast a ballot than the loyal partisan of the nineteenth century. They needed to be more self-starting to go to the polls at all since doing so was increasingly detached from the rewards of a fraternal social life. There was a shift from sentiment to interest as the basis of politics and, to some degree, from parties to interest groups as their chief agents.

But just as raw, calculated interest was obliged to carry greater weight, the visible character of interest in relationship to politics receded, and at two levels. First, government services grew less connected to elected officials and more tied to administrative agencies and bureaucracies over which the voter at the polls had little control. Second, civil service reform and the decline of voting day practices that provided the ordinary citizen with monetary and social rewards for political activity also removed a manifest level of self-interest from the citizen's relation to politics. People in the nineteenth century could smell and taste the material benefits in politics; in the twentieth century, increasingly, self-interest in political life became more of an imaginative leap. Only the New Deal altered this, and then only for a time, and only by the tried-and-true method of expanding patronage, on the one hand, and the newer expedient of enlarging government social services and bureaucracies, on the other.

Conclusion: The Party System Besieged

"The best evidence of genuine popular liberty is the existence of political parties," proclaimed a campaign biography of Benjamin Harrison in

1888.[156] Not two decades later, when Vice President William Howard Taft delivered a university lecture on civic duty, he was forced on the defensive in urging party loyalty:

> I know there is a disposition on the part of the free-born American graduate from an institution of learning, full of admiration for independence of thought and a desire to maintain his independence of action, to hold himself aloof from party regularity and vote for the best men if he can find them, and thus teach the party organization that it must beware of the influence of the independent voter.

Nonetheless, Taft said, this independent-minded fellow "will after a while learn that there is much to be said in favor of party regularity if that be not carried to an extreme."[157]

When Henry Crosby Emery, professor of political economy at Yale, delivered the Page lectures in 1912 at Yale's Sheffield Scientific School, his adherence to the principle of party was even more clearly a rearguard action. He observed that men frequently say that "they always vote for the 'best man,' regardless of party." Leading thinkers argued that citizens should attend to "'measures, not men.'" Both of these counsels of independence in voting, Emery suggested, operate without attention to the fact that governmental policy is set by parties, with party leadership controlled by a relatively few men. Individuals in the Congress, he argued, matter very little; party tendencies matter very much. It would be irresponsible, he suggested, to favor the candidate of one party for president and the other party for congressional offices except under extreme circumstances; the consequence of a president and a Congress of opposite parties would be the diminution of governmental "efficiency." "I do not mean," he added, "that such splitting of the ballot is never justified. I mean it is only justified in unusual circumstances and after the most mature consideration."[158] It is not so easy, Emery acknowledged, to know just what separates Republicans and Democrats. "It is more or less true, I think, that the old parties fifteen or twenty years ago stood in the minds of the voters for little more than the question of who should get in or who should stay out." Still, for Emery, the parties were distinct, separated not by class or section but more by "fundamental differences of opinion regarding the proper powers of government and the line of government policy best adapted to securing the welfare of all."[159]

This is a backhanded defense of party allegiance. Emery, like Taft before him, in addressing college students, knew he was speaking against a presumption among them that voting for the public good "according to your conscience on such inadequate information as you may have at the moment" was enough to fulfill one's ethical duty to the public service.[160] Defenders of partisan politics after 1900 talked against the rhetorical grain.

Anti-party rhetoric was in the ascendant. You can look to 1867 and E. L. Godkin's charge that party politicians, regardless of ideological differences, "are all banded together for plunder."[161] Or you can turn to 1912 and William Allen White's retrospective accusation that "we were ruled under the party system by an aristocracy which was financed by greed, and it was the problem of democracy to break down that aristocracy."[162] Concrete political reforms and a rhetorical avalanche helped to bury traditional party loyalties. At the same time, the Democrats and Republicans grew ever stronger as nationally organized entities, recognized in law, connected to the business elite through fund-raising, tied increasingly to defined sets of public policy positions. Pressed by political reforms, driven by the newly complex needs of municipalities to build the infrastructure and social services for large urban areas, pushed by a newly independent press calling again and again for consideration of "public" rather than partisan objectives, the parties began to take policy seriously. But just as the conditions for a rational and active citizenship seemed to emerge, the citizens themselves began a retreat from political activity, voter turnout dropped precipitously, and the fate of democratic rule seemed very much in doubt.

Chapter 5

Cures for Democracy? Civil Religion, Leadership, Expertise—and More Democracy

Prospectus

The ideal of the omnicompetent, sovereign citizen is, in my opinion, . . . a false ideal. It is unattainable. The pursuit of it is misleading. The failure to achieve it has produced the current disenchantment."[1]

By the 1920s, the boisterous folk scenes of election day passed into history. Municipal reforms, civil service reform, corrupt practices acts, presidential primaries, the initiative, referendum, recall, literacy tests, and the Australian ballot sanitized politics.[2] Where it had been standard practice for parties to convey people to the polls, it was now forbidden.[3] Where party workers had distributed tickets, voters now stood in line to receive their official ballot from state-appointed officials. Where parties had mustered armies of paid election day workers, it was now illegal to do so in many states.[4] Where electioneering efforts accompanied voters right up to the ballot box, new regulations forbade electioneering close to the polling place.[5] The new politics was scientific, efficient, clean, and pure.

Reformers had tried to secure in the polling place an island of rationality amidst a rapidly changing world. In the industrial cities, electoral reform included at-large elections and city manager government to weaken the power of immigrants. In the South, reformers focused on making elections white. Purity was in the eyes of the purifiers.

None of the reforms brought assurance that the political world was under control. The sea of modern life threatened to engulf everything before it. Everywhere observers recognized a growing complexity of human affairs. They could not fathom it. They could not even name it. One of the more popular efforts was the term coined by British scholar Graham Wallas, "the Great Society."[6] Both John Dewey and Wallas's Harvard student Walter Lippmann would pick up the phrase to describe what later would be called modern industrial society or advanced capitalism. The term tried to label the complexity, density, integration, and nonlocal ties that were supplanting the small-scale communities of the nineteenth century.

Presidential candidate Woodrow Wilson offered his own image of modern times in 1912. Liberty, he said, was no longer a matter of being left alone but was instead the liberty of the machine which ran freely when all the parts "are so assembled and adjusted that friction is reduced to a minimum. . . ." In modern times, liberty means the "perfect adjustment of human interests and human activities and human energies." In this world, the best government does not govern least. Wilson conjured up Thomas Jefferson:

> . . . if Jefferson were living in our day he would see what we see: that the individual is caught in a great confused nexus of all sorts of complicated circumstances, and that to let him alone is to leave him helpless as against the obstacles with which he has to contend; and that, therefore,

law in our day must come to his assistance to see that he gets fair play; that is all, but that is much.[7]

Few followed Wilson in believing that an efficiently operating machine offers a good image of freedom.[8] Most efforts to confront the problems of democracy in his day sought less to imagine complexity than to reduce it. With great rhetorical deference to popular will, most problems were identified as "distortions" of the people's voice. The chief source of distortion remained the political party itself, but by the 1920s, with parties in retreat, independent sources of distortion could be identified in propaganda, pressure groups, and monied interests. Reforms of campaign practice sought to regulate the power of pressure groups, the influence of money, the parties' control of elections, and the reach of undiluted propaganda.

At the same time, an unsullied faith in the people also came under scrutiny. Even the people who had believed most forcefully in the new model citizen came to doubt whether that citizen existed or ever could exist. Liberal reformers, proponents of good government, enemies of the political machine, even avowed socialists arrived at a deep disquiet during or soon after World War I. Was a democratic citizenship possible?

A basis for disenchantment was the decline of voter turnout, lower in 1920 and 1924 than it had been since the 1830s (and lower than it would ever be again until 1988). Arthur M. Schlesinger and Erik M. Eriksson complained about "The Vanishing Voter" in *The New Republic* in 1924. They noted the irony that voter turnout was declining just as a more extensive and more independently exercised suffrage had been achieved: "That which had been sought as a political right was devoid of interest as a civic obligation, or even as a civic opportunity." They attributed this both to "lessening differences between the parties" and to the "increasing complexity of modern life," already a standard phrase. Ours is now a "frantic, over-organized, spectacular, urbanized, machine-driven world," they lamented.[9]

The theories of Sigmund Freud, behaviorists, crowd psychologists, and others who examined the irrationality of the human psyche offered scientific grounds to wonder whether the ideal of democracy had ever made any sense in the first place. This was a question that the prominent journalist and political essayist Walter Lippmann would take up directly in *Public Opinion* in 1922, arguing—against his own prewar optimism—that democracy could not depend on the omnicompetent citizen. He found that the citizens' capacity to clearly see and judge the world was blocked not so much by outside obstacles as by their own distortions of will and desire. The person was at last autonomous in the voting booth, but autonomy itself was now exposed as a sham. Human beings are conflicted creatures driven by desire, Freud was now teaching; and they are social creatures, the sedimentary collecting points for the deposits of social forces, as the new social psychology instructed. They were anything but rational, autonomous individuals.

Human frailties, along with the aggrandizement of special interests, loomed large as barriers to democracy because the political party no longer did. The "party era" in American politics was ending and its demise was welcomed. Each new solution to the problems of democracy was understood as an improvement not on the lost ideal of the town meeting but the practical reality of the machine. Thus city manager government was a form of rule by experts that contributed to "the elimination of spoils politics and hidden influence."[10] Business and academic leaders who sponsored early think tanks and foundations self-consciously sought to undermine the political parties.[11] To the extent that parties continued to play a role in public life, critics saw them as only further contributing to the demoralization of democracy. Walter Lippmann pointed to the parties' tendency to adopt for short-term gain any issue at all, be it "polygamy, foot binding, or voodooism." Parties were forever "attempting to distract attention from the realities of American life." The result is that "voters feel that politics is an elaborate game which has no serious and immediate consequences."[12] The political party was not as deeply buried as reformers and intellectuals imagined, but it was dead and gone in their thinking.

In a world so understood, people who took their democratic principles seriously entertained several solutions for democracy's distress. These included renewed reverence for the Constitution and American political tradition; leadership (particularly centered on the president);

expertise and the application of "science" to public affairs; scientific polling as a new and more precise means of tapping public opinion; and the revival of town-meeting democracy in small towns and neighborhood-based community gatherings.

All of these efforts at change, except the last, presumed a relatively passive public. Lippmann's gloomy portrait of the modern mass public was especially powerful, so when America's leading public philosopher, John Dewey, stepped forward to respond to it and send out a call for the renewal of a public in eclipse, it seemed a moment of potentially high drama. In the end, as we shall see, their debate failed to clarify the problems or prospects of democratic citizenship; Dewey did not escape the psychologizing of the issues that Lippmann set forth. From the other side of the New Deal and the civil rights movement, their discussion in the 1920s may look arid and abstract. Yet they raised both hopes and fears about the rightful place of expertise in democracy that have yet to be digested in either theory or practice.

Propaganda and the Assault on the Autonomous Citizen

"Some day," wrote Graham Wallas in 1908, ". . . the word 'opinion' itself may become the recognized name of the most dangerous political vice."[13] That day arrived much sooner than Wallas might have imagined. During and after World War I there was extraordinary public debate about a term that had been relatively obscure before the war: "propaganda." The debate began with the American entry into the war and the establishment of the Committee on Public Information, which was headed by muckraker George Creel and employed the likes of Walter Lippmann from the world of journalism and Edward Bernays from the new field of public relations. The debate ended, to the extent that it ended at all, with American entry into World War II and the renewed harnessing of propaganda to a national mission.

"The publicity agent is perhaps the most significant symbol of our present social life. There are individuals who resist; but, for a time at least, sentiment can be manufactured by mass methods for almost any person or cause."[14] This hyperbolic assertion by John Dewey, the nation's most renowned philosopher, indicates how deeply opinion had come to be distrusted—not out of elitist disdain for the common mind, but out of a shared unease that in the Great Society where people necessarily depend on information they cannot authenticate from everyday knowledge, the citizen's capacity for being misled is unbounded.

It was all very well to have fought the parties, the machine, and the boss with the weapons of reform, but what was to be put in their place? The reformist answer seemed to be "information," the information citizens would need to make independent judgments about their and the public's interest. But what was information? And who was providing it? Newspapers that had once served parties now seemed to supplant them. Political scientist (and president of Yale) Arthur T. Hadley said in 1914, "It is not by the personal influence which was characteristic of the old party system that nominations are now secured and the way made clear for the passage of laws. It is by the influence of the printed page, which enables the man who controls it to determine thousands of votes for good or for evil." [15]

Hadley might have had William Randolph Hearst in mind, for Hearst was the journalistic sensation of the day and not a little of a political sensation, too. Beginning his career in San Francisco, Hearst bought the *New York Journal* in 1895 to announce his national ambitions. He started the *Chicago American* in July 1900, at the urging of William Jennings Bryan, to aid Bryan's candidacy for president. The first issue contained praise for Hearst from Bryan himself, and subsequent issues railed at the Republicans with characteristic Hearstian invective. [16] Hearst made his own run for president in 1904. Failing to win his party's nomination, he remained a powerful, if often thwarted, manipulator of Democratic Party affairs. In 1912, for instance, he aided a drive to stop Wilson's march to the nomination—although ultimately to no avail. [17]

It was not just newspapers as independent molders of opinion and publishers as political manipulators that caused alarm; journalists themselves were among those scandalized by the growing influence of a new class of information-mongers—public relations specialists. There were signs of this before the war, a deluge after. Silas Bent complained in 1927 that there were five thousand publicity agents in New York and another two thousand in Washington.[18] The city editor of the *New York Herald Tribune* estimated that 60 percent of news items in the American press originated in press-agent material. Bent's own estimate was similar for one issue of the *New York Times*. Political scientist Peter Odegard, who estimated that 50 percent of news items originated in press agentry, wrote, "Many reporters today are little more than intellectual mendicants who go from one publicity agent or press bureau to another seeking 'handouts.'"[19] E. Pendleton Herring, writing his political science doctoral dissertation in 1927–28, found Washington "the happy home of propaganda and the paradise of the press agent." Not only lobbying organizations but the government itself churned out "tons of press material and manufactured news by the gross." It is hard, Herring wrote, to distinguish the work of the press agents from the work of the journalists. "It is difficult to know when news is news and when it is propaganda. But it is all publicity. . . ."[20]

As government-sponsored wartime propaganda ended, proprietary propaganda expanded. For instance, during the war Samuel Insull, Chicago's electric power baron, advised the American branch of the British propaganda office, distributed his own highly colored war information to American newspapers, and headed the Illinois State Council of Defense. After the war he established the Illinois Public Utility Information Committee, a significant force in making utilities the most prominent and controversial public relations adventurers of the decade.[21]

Of course, propaganda played its part in political campaigning. There was a sophisticated attention to what would later be known as image management. In Warren G. Harding's front porch campaign of 1920, conducted entirely from his Marion, Ohio, home until the last few weeks, Judson C. Welliver, a former *New York Sun* correspondent and after the election Harding's speechwriter, managed the candidate's news. He had help from Albert D. Lasker, the famed Chicago advertising executive and, after 1918, Republican National Committee publicity czar. Early in the campaign Harding's advisers objected that his golfing associated him with a "rich man's game." While Harding arranged to take to the links secretly in the future, Lasker, who happened also to be part-owner of the Chicago Cubs baseball team, brought the Cubs to Marion to play. Harding threw out the first three pitches as the Cubs triumphed 3–1 over the Kerrigan Tailors. Harding followed up with a speech, "Team Play," that attacked President Wilson's position on the League of Nations with egregious baseball metaphors.[22]

The Harding campaign staged one event after another to attract newspaper headlines—there was Women's Day, Colored People's Day, First Voters' Day, Foreign Voters' Day, and even Traveling Salesmen's Day in Marion. This last was an opportunity created by an editorial in Democratic rival James Cox's *Dayton Daily News* six years earlier that labeled the commercial traveler an "unmitigated bore." The Republican National Committee sponsored a Harding and Coolidge Traveling Men's League that came out in force for their day in Marion.

Lasker's contributions included developing a general campaign slogan, "Let's have done with wiggle and wobble." He got Harding to stick the phrase into a speech at the end of August, with memos to Welliver to make sure it would appear spontaneous—"merely a passing sentence that he injected, but . . . so forceful that it was spontaneously picked up." Billboards, cartoons, and other pronouncements were quickly readied to keep the phrase at the forefront of propaganda efforts.[23]

Every president in these years was attacked as a creature of or manipulator of propaganda. Harding was succeeded by Calvin Coolidge, of whom *The New Republic* complained, "No ruler in history ever had such a magnificent propaganda machine as Mr. Coolidge's and certainly it would be impossible for anyone to use it more assiduously. . . . Mr. Coolidge is our first really successful practitioner of government by publicity." [24] Walter Lippmann wrote of Coolidge's successor, Herbert Hoover, that his rise to the presidency was "planned with great care and assisted throughout by a high-powered propaganda of the very latest model. He is, in fact, the first American President whose whole public career has been presented through the machinery of modern publicity." [25] Franklin D. Roosevelt, of course, was both praised and assailed as a master showman. So were the men around him. Charles Michelson, running the propaganda arm of the Democratic National Committee in 1932, was credited with enormous power. Journalist Will Irwin, while denying that Michelson's efforts made the difference in the election, nonetheless argued that "the policy of sustained propaganda with brains behind it did turn defeat into a rout." [26] Michelson brought to electoral politics "two stock devices of the expert publicity man—constructing a background upon which to project dramatic action and warping or creating news in such manner that even hostile newspapers must needs become parties to the enterprise." [27]

The concept of a "hostile newspaper" was itself changing. As politics moved from outdoors to indoors and from the heart to the head, as campaigning shifted from mobilizing the converted to converting the immobile and independent, as the experience of politics shifted from a communal celebration to individual decision-making, so journalism moved from partisan cheerleading to professional reporting. This shift was gradual, but the direction of change was unmistakable. Journalists began to adopt the language of "objectivity" to describe the ethics of their profession. Schools of journalism multiplied and the Pulitzer Prizes, first awarded in 1917, helped cultivate a new allure for the field. Reporters and editors sought to provide value-free information, moveable from one newspaper to the next, validated by the professional judgment of other journalists rather than by the political preferences of a publisher. This new journalism took root in a political world where citizens were now expected to be rational sifters and winnowers of facts. The idea that reporters could and should be professionally detached made sense in that context. So, too, did it seem reasonable that government itself could provide neutral or nonpartisan information for citizens to consume. By the 1920s, eleven states required the publication and distribution of informational bulletins that listed ballot propositions and printed arguments for and against each question. Oregon and Montana initiated this movement in 1907, followed by Oklahoma, California, Arizona, Nebraska, Ohio, Washington, Utah, Massachusetts, and North Dakota by 1918. [28]

Information in the early twentieth century had become a commodity, marketable, moveable, and separable from value, belief, conviction, or even narrative. Buoyed by ideas of neutrality in science and efficiency in political administration, the very idea of information took on a kind of dazzle. A few complained, such as House Speaker Joe Cannon, that the separation of journalism from partisanship put a premium on entertaining news: "The cut of a Congressman's whiskers or his clothes is a better subject for a human interest story than what he says in debate."[29] But others endorsed the new emphasis on neutral information, notably the League of Women Voters.

The league, established in 1920 as the successor to the National American Woman Suffrage Association, was divided about its relationship to the political parties. At first it worked hard to encourage women to take part in party politics, but this compromised its hard-earned reputation for independence. Moreover, the rarity with which women won positions of leadership in the parties further encouraged the league to insist that women would best make their mark on public policy outside the parties.[30] Some leaders, like Lillian Feickert in New Jersey, argued that nonpartisanship took women back "to kindergarten days." It was "the indirect method" and should be forsaken, now that the vote was won; women should become "political workers." By the mid-twenties, however, the league had staked its future to nonpartisanship and an ideal of reasoned debate rather than partisan enthusiasm. As women took up the vote, they pictured themselves as exemplifying the new textbook model of the citizen—independent, informed, public-spirited and above partisanship.

Information was recognized as an agent of political reform in another domain: campaign financing. The primary source of financial corruption in politics in the late nineteenth century was taken to be the political parties' improper gathering of money. As the war on the parties gained victories, especially in civil service reform, the source of party financing shifted away from assessments on office-seekers and officeholders and toward contributions from fat cats, usually those at the head of powerful corporations. From 1896, it became a routine part of presidential campaigns for each party to charge the other with being financed by banks and corporations. By 1932, when Louise Overacker published the first important academic work on campaign financing, she acknowledged a growing concern that democracies may "inevitably become plutocracies."[31]

What was to be done? States increasingly tried to regulate either campaign contributions or campaign expenditures, but enforcement mechanisms were notoriously weak. Early federal efforts to control campaign monies had focused exclusively on prohibiting party assessments of government workers. But in 1905, President Theodore Roosevelt urged in his annual message a ban on all corporate contributions to political campaigns. In 1907, such a law passed—ironically promoted by a public scandal over corporate contributions to Roosevelt's own 1904 campaign, but the law seems never to have been taken seriously. Reform activity after the 1904 campaign also inspired a federal "publicity" bill. Modeled on state laws that required campaign contributions to be made public, the Federal Corrupt Practices Act became law in 1910. It required publication of the names of all persons or firms contributing $100 or more as well as the names of persons to whom $10 or more was paid, and the purposes of the payment. The act was amended in 1911 to set spending limits in campaigns for Congress, but there were no enforcement mechanisms. Financial corruption of elections became a perennial topic of congressional debate, a recurrent plank in the Democratic Party platform (1908, 1912, 1920, 1924, 1928, 1932) and occasionally the Republican platform (1912, 1928), and the grounds for charge and counter-charge in political campaigns.[32]

In 1918, controversy came to center on a Michigan politician, Truman Newberry, who spent $176,000 in Michigan's Republican senatorial primary (defeating Henry Ford), more than $170,000 above state and federal spending limits. Newberry and a bevy of campaign workers were indicted and convicted of campaign violations, but in 1921 the Supreme Court reversed the convictions on the grounds that the expenditures had taken place in the primary election campaign, and that federal law did not apply to primary elections. Notwithstanding, the case attracted national attention and spurred a lengthy Senate investigation. The Democrats' platform in 1924 sought "to prevent Newberryism"[33] and renewed federal campaign finance reform became law in 1925. Again, the law was weak-willed; after 1927 no one was ever prosecuted under its terms.[34]

Campaign financing was just one way among many that business reached out surreptitiously to control the political process. Lobbying was another. While lobbying was nothing new in the 1920s, there was something new in lobbying. The old lobby worked through personal bartering, bribery, and the liberal provision of social favors, including wine and women, to congressmen. The new lobby, in contrast, as E. Pendleton Herring observed at the time, established itself as the "third house of Congress," the "assistant rulers," the "invisible government." According to Herring, "These group representatives work in the open; they have nothing to hide; they know what they want; and they know how to get it. They work with precision and efficiency." [35] If they had nothing to hide, they were not exactly eager for the national spotlight. There was public criticism of the lobbying of the Anti-Saloon League and the American Legion. The Federal Trade Commission's investigation of utilities' propaganda and lobbying in the late 1920s was followed by a Senate investigation and, as early as 1929, Senator Hugo Black introduced a bill to require lobbyists to register with both the House and Senate their names, goals, and expenses. In 1935, Black initiated a controversial investigation of lobbyists, but no significant legislation to regulate lobbying activity would become law until 1946. [36]

Public relations might be accepted practice, but it was not a tolerated precept. Public relations specialists felt a need to justify their work. In a speech in 1924, John D. Rockefeller, Jr.'s own press agent, Ivy Lee, reacted to a comment by President Coolidge that attacked propaganda. "Propaganda," Coolidge had said, "seeks to present a part of the facts, to distort their relations, and to force conclusions which could not be drawn from a complete and candid survey of all the facts." Lee responded simply: "To present a complete and candid survey of all the facts concerning any subject is a human impossibility." He cited Walter Lippmann (accurately) as lending support to his view. "The effort to state an absolute fact is simply an attempt to achieve what is humanly impossible; all I can do is to give you *my interpretation of the facts*," Lee wrote. [37]

Edward Bernays was even more ardent a propagandist for propaganda. Trying to upgrade the social standing of PR, he and his wife, Doris

Fleischman, forswore the use of the term "press agent" and promoted the term "counsel on public relations" as a deservedly stately appellation for their work. The term did not catch on. Bernays found his "uphill one-man campaign for public relations" thwarted. Reviews of his *Crystallizing Public Opinion* (1923) indicate how difficult a task Bernays had set himself. The *New York Times* was sardonic: "If, with the change of name, there is to come a change in the ethics and manners of the press agent, people will be delighted to call him a public relations counsel or sweet little buttercup or anything he wishes." Public relations came to be more widely accepted in private corporations, but journalists were decidedly unimpressed. One critic, writing in the *North American Review*, complained that journalists, under the onslaught of publicity, were emerging as "a race of mere retailers of ready-made intelligence," and saw the newspaper turning "more and more to distribution, less of news than to what somebody wishes to be considered news."[38] Some journalists urged a boycott of publicity agents, to which Ivy Lee retorted: "That's as logical as my wife objecting to Macy's putting so many attractive things on their shelves."[39] Public relations became an established part of American life, but so did a distrust of it.

A fitting final chapter to the controversy over propaganda took place in the 1930s with the popularity of a revisionist theory of American entry into World War I. C. Harley Grattan's *Why We Fought* (1929), Walter Millis's best-selling Book-of-the-Month Club selection *Road to War* (1935), Charles Beard's *Devil Theory of War* (1936), C. C. Tansill's *America Goes to War* (1938), H. C. Peterson's *Propaganda for War* (1939), and Edwin Borchard and W. P. Lage's *Neutrality for the United States* (1940), among others, argued that American entry into World War I was a tragic error.[40] Some (not all) of these works held that foremost among the reasons the country fell into this error was that British propaganda hoodwinked the American public out of neutrality and into armed support for the Allied cause. Peterson argued, for instance, that the British effort "affected every phase of American life." "News, money, and political pressure each played its part and the battle itself was fought not only in London, New York, and Washington, D.C., but also in American classrooms and pulpits, factories, and offices. It was a campaign to create a pro-British attitude of mind among Americans, to get American sympathies and interests so deeply involved in the European war that it would be impossible for this country to remain neutral." [41] Peterson judged it "the most important" of the reasons America went to war.[42]

These works all mistook the New York press for the national press and the most pro-British newspapers for the New York press as a whole. They failed to note the prominence of German sources and German-originated stories in the same newspapers that relied on British sources, and they failed most of all to weigh the propaganda of words against the persuasiveness of events. Some contemporaries said as much—diplomat Charles Seymour, for instance, wrote in 1935 that Americans' anti-German bias was shaped by "the progress of war more than it was by propagandist activities." [43] But the revisionists' argument resonated in a public well acquainted with America's own domestic propaganda efforts. There was a postwar revulsion against Wilson's Committee on Public Information. Charles and Mary Beard would write in their popular *The Rise of American Civilization* of how "the entire school system of the country was easily brought into line with mechanical precision, subduing even the minds of tender children to the official thesis concerning the origins and merits of the contest." The administration's efforts were unprecedented: ". . . never before had American citizens realized how thoroughly, how irresistibly a modern government could impose its ideas upon the whole nation and, under a barrage of publicity, stifle dissent with declarations, assertions, official versions, and reiteration." The Committee on Public Information "succeeded beyond all expectations," they sadly recount, in its efforts to sell the war to the public.[44]

Too many thinkers took the existence of propaganda as proof of its efficacy. If this was an error, it was no mistake to observe that governments and corporations were acting on the assumption that they could and should manipulate the minds of citizens. Propaganda, in this respect, has an ironically democratic feature—it appears when elites feel obliged to address the public. But of course it was its manipulative intention, not its democratic context, that aroused opposition: propaganda took for granted the frailties of human reason and sought to turn them to advantage. It addressed the people as chumps, not citizens, flattering, frightening, and cajoling, whatever approach seemed most likely to succeed.

The 1920s were a time not only of disillusion but of reconstruction. Various solutions to the problem of democracy were offered. These included the promotion of a new kind of civic religiosity centered on the Constitution and American history, the elevation of expertise as a replacement for partisanship, the development of new means for tapping public opinion directly through scientific polling, new uses of public schools and other community resources as forums for face-to-face political discussion, and the endorsement of leadership, especially presidential leadership, as appropriate and necessary to a democracy. As the next sections will show, each of these responses helped to remake public life in the Great Society.

Constitutional Faith[45]

Constitutionalism between the wars "assumed a more central role in American culture than it ever had before."[46] Indeed, it acquired the trappings of a religious cult, not the least of which was the construction of a permanent home for the Supreme Court. In its early days, the Court met in the basement of the Capitol, moving in 1860 to the old Senate Chamber when the Senate moved into its new (and present) location. Only in 1929 did Congress appropriate funds for what would be known as a "temple of justice."[47] Chief Justice William Howard Taft led the campaign to win the Court its own building and Congress, approving his program in 1928, appointed him to chair the planning commission. In 1935, for the first time in the country's history, the Supreme Court settled into its own building, in which it still operates.

From the time of the founding fathers, there had been a sacred aura about the Constitution, manifest in holiday political rhetoric, but in the 1920s a burst of activity cemented that rhetoric in institutional and educational reform. A movement to make September 17 Constitution Day, begun in 1916, was by the early 1920s very successful. The American Bar Association cooperated, the National Education Association came on board, and the War Department required appropriate exercises at all military posts. By 1923, twenty-three states required instruction about the Constitution in the public schools, forty-three states by 1931. Fear of anarchism, socialism, and bolshevism, plus concern about the need to Americanize immigrants, contributed to the rapid spread of such requirements.[48] Private colleges endowed lectures on the Constitution. National oratorical contests proliferated, attracting a million participants in 1924.

It is not clear what impact this flurry of reverential activity produced, but it is plain that the appeal to the courts and the Constitution represented an effort to solve the problems of democracy. Political developments strengthened the sense that the courts and the Constitution were a brake on popular sentiment. If Roosevelt's court-packing proposal did nothing else, it identified the Supreme Court as an independent, ornery, recalcitrant defender of a constitutional tradition against even a duly elected president.

Washington, D.C., became a national icon in the 1920s and 1930s. The Lincoln Memorial was dedicated in 1922, the Jefferson Memorial in 1943. When President Franklin Roosevelt laid the foundation stone at the latter site in 1939 he emphasized particularly Jefferson's legacy in political philosophy. "He lived as we live, in the midst of a struggle between rule by the self-chosen individual or the self-appointed few, and rule by the franchise and approval of the many. He believed as we do that the average opinion of mankind is in the long run superior to the dictates of the self-chosen."[49] It was in honor of democracy that Roosevelt blessed the monument to Jefferson.

The government's own record-keeping, which had been haphazard at best, became centralized in the National Archives, established as an autonomous agency of the government in 1934. In 1920, the Constitution and the Declaration of Independence were removed from a State Department vault and in 1924 put on public display at the Library of Congress. Moviemakers filmed the documents so that they could be seen in movie houses across the country.[50] Meanwhile, in South Dakota, the redoubtable sculptor Gutzon Borglum, with the blessing of President Calvin Coolidge, was carving Washington, Jefferson, Lincoln, and

Theodore Roosevelt's visages into the side of a mountain. The face of Washington was unveiled on the Fourth of July, 1930; Jefferson was dedicated by President Roosevelt in 1936; the Lincoln unveiling came on Constitution Day, 1937; and the Roosevelt bust was dedicated in 1939 on the fiftieth anniversary of South Dakota statehood.[51] These were not monuments but shrines, part of a civic American religion. Supporters hoped Mount Rushmore would be called the "Shrine of Democracy"; Valley Forge, Jamestown, Monticello, Robert E. Lee's birthplace at Stratford Hall, and other locations were increasingly spoken of as "shrines," too.[52] Jefferson, especially, received prominent notice. The Thomas Jefferson Memorial Foundation was set up in 1923 to restore Monticello. Republicans and Democrats joined in the effort as the foundation identified its aims with America's children and collected millions of their pennies.

Leading figures of capitalist enterprise made their contributions to this civic religion. Henry Ford's Greenfield Village museum was begun in the 1920s, with its replica of an early American "street" of small shops under construction by 1931. Simultaneously, John D. Rockefeller, Jr. was buying as much real estate in Williamsburg, Virginia, as he could to realize his dream of a restored "Colonial Williamsburg." In 1933, the Raleigh Tavern was rebuilt, and with the Governor's Palace constructed in 1934, President Roosevelt came to dedicate Duke of Gloucester Street as "the most historic avenue in all America."[53]

Other indicators of national identity were perhaps more subtle but nonetheless pervasive and persuasive. One of these, certainly, was the federal income tax, authorized by constitutional amendment in 1913. Until this time citizens did not have a direct personal financial relationship to the national government; thereafter, "taxpayer" would become a synonym for citizen, even though it had not literally been so since the early 1800s.

Another economic connection to nationhood was the establishment of a uniform national currency. In the nineteenth century, not only banks but hotels, retail stores, and even brothels issued their own currencies. Standardization was initiated by the National Bank Act of 1863, but all kinds of bank-issued notes continued to circulate along with new national banknotes in the late nineteenth century. The courts finally judged the common late-nineteenth-century practice of engraving coins with sentimental phrases as "love tokens" to be a practice of "mutilation"; the national currency, in other words, began to acquire a semisacred character. In 1909, Congress at last prohibited the private production of currency.[54]

Democracy by Leaders

To many observers of the day, society had grown more complex while, in response, the press lords and special interests who manipulated public information had grown more powerful. At a time when political reforms had brought ordinary citizens into the decision-making process on more occasions (with more elective offices) and on more complex matters (initiatives and referenda), the cognitive challenge that modern democracy posed to them grew formidable. In this situation, how was government to make decisions bearing an adequate relationship to citizens' interests?

A frequently offered solution to this problem was leadership, especially presidential leadership. From the outset, this was not a very happy solution. It seemed to destroy the promise of democracy in the effort to save it, denying the capacities of common citizens to govern themselves. But it seemed increasingly inevitable as power accumulated in the presidency. Five developments contributed to this.

First, the federal government became a regulatory and redistributive state, establishing a "direct and coercive relationship" to individual citizens.[55] This includes even such traditional state and local responsibilities as law enforcement. The federal government's police powers expanded with the growth of other federal functions, and law enforcement became an integral part of the national government's immigration and border control, Bureau of Indian Affairs, alcohol tax unit, post office, Internal Revenue Service, National Park Service, and Federal Bureau of Investigation.[56] From the development of the Interstate Commerce Commission to anti-trust legislation, to the establishment of the Federal Trade Commission, the Pure Food and Drug Act, conservation legislation, the federal income tax, federal aid to vocational education, federal involvement in maternal and child health through the Sheppard-Towner Act of 1921, the long arm of the federal government was newly felt throughout the nation. It was no longer true, as one scholar said of the nineteenth century, that our chief executives were "chief of very little and executive of even less."[57]

Second, there developed in theory and in practice a president-centered rather than Congress-centered government. As the federal government grew relative to state and local governments, the power of the president grew relative to Congress inside the federal government, and a rather grandiose concept of presidential "leadership" became the governing ideology of American politics.[58] Beginning with William McKinley and Theodore Roosevelt, a presidential concentration of personal power came into being. In the nineteenth century, generally speaking, successful presidential candidates understood their elections to signify popular approval that they should hold their constitutionally defined office but not that the people at the polls had necessarily approved the particular policies or preferences they themselves may have espoused. The notion that the election represents a popular "mandate" for the president had some earlier precedents but arrived as a fully accepted assumption only with McKinley's election in 1896. The press seemed to take this for granted and McKinley explicitly called attention to the election results as "the commanding verdict of the people" upon specific policy positions, notably concerning the currency.[59] McKinley and then Roosevelt took policy initiatives more regularly than their predecessors. In 1902, for instance, Roosevelt used the majesty of his office, and not much more, to bring together the warring parties in the months-long coal strike. Although Roosevelt admitted that he had "no right or duty to intervene in this way upon legal grounds or upon any official relation that I bear to the situation," he nonetheless took the occasion to demonstrate that the president is a general trustee for the national welfare and should not stand aside from a major domestic crisis.[60]

The president's command of the legislative agenda was greatly advanced with the passage in 1921 of the Budget and Accounting Act. This act itself was a compromise—on the one hand, it represented the growing belief that an executive budget was necessary for managing government in the modern age. On the other hand, it embodied the traditional American suspicion of centralized authority and so denied the president certain controls over the budget authority, including denial of a line-item veto. (When, earlier, Congress had passed a budget act that made the budget director a congressional appointee, Wilson had vetoed the legislation.)[61] The budget act put the president at the center of the federal government's spending. While more power would accrue to the president later as Franklin Roosevelt and his successors increased the size and purview of the Office of the President, the budget act was a crucial turning point in presidential aggrandizement.

The president's growing centrality enabled him not only to bargain more effectively with the Congress but also to "go public," over the heads of the Congress to the people, in order to get his way. Presidents have increasingly employed this strategy in the television era, but its seeds were sown a century ago.[62]

This leads immediately to the third factor that brought more power to the presidency, namely, that the president became the symbolic focal point of national attention. Teddy Roosevelt's efforts especially personalized his constitutional office. That is, the president became less and less understood as the holder of a constitutionally defined and constitutionally limited executive position, and more and more conceived as a policy-maker and national leader. By 1907, William Howard Taft, Roosevelt's heir apparent, declared that he agreed with "the policies which have come to be known as the Roosevelt policies," indicating the relative novelty of identifying a president's course of action as one identified with the president personally rather than with the party he represented.[63] Roosevelt was sometimes chided for his regular reference to "my policies," but, Henry Crosby Emery told students at Yale in 1912: "The people are not offended by any talk about 'my policies' because they now expect the President to have policies." Unusually strong presidents in the past, like Jackson or Lincoln, had clearly been identified with particular policy stands, but the expectation that every president would advance a distinctive legislative agenda was new—and would be enduring, as Emery recognized: ". . . as we speak of Roosevelt policies or

Taft policies, so we will speak of a definite legislative program by the name of future Presidents."[64]

Not only did Theodore Roosevelt pursue his own policy agenda, but he took responsibility for direct and frequent communication with the general public. Clearly, he had an extraordinary appeal to a broad spectrum of Americans. But it was not Roosevelt alone and, indeed, not Roosevelt primarily who institutionalized direct communication with the general public. What Roosevelt seemed to practice out of natural exuberance, Woodrow Wilson pursued out of a theoretical insistence on the need for leadership. This was a new turn for a man who, in 1885, had written *Congressional Government*, to argue that legislatures were naturally supreme in democratic systems. As president, however, he seemed dedicated to supplanting Congress and unifying national power in himself. He now argued that Congress had accumulated far too much power and used it in a way far removed from public scrutiny. The president should not only have greater power relative to Congress but should sustain it by regular communications with the general public. Wilson was instrumental in establishing the continuing twentieth-century practice of addressing the general public in speeches rather than only the Congress in written messages. Even in addressing the Congress, Wilson had a larger audience in view, so he reestablished the practice of Washington and Adams of delivering the State of the Union address each year in person in the Congress (rather than having it read for him by a secretary).

Like Roosevelt, Wilson actively traveled in his presidential campaigns—and not in the campaigns alone. His fateful 1919 speaking tour of Western states on behalf of the League of Nations was a characteristic, not isolated, act of public communication for him. Not only in his campaigns for governor and for president, but also in efforts to overcome legislative opposition to his reform program in New Jersey in 1911 and to his program for military preparedness in 1916, he went on the road. While he was by all accounts stiff and unbending, not a backslapping politician, he felt renewed and invigorated by contact with ordinary Americans. "I am glad to get out to see the real folks, to feel the touch of their hand," he told listeners from the rear of the train in North Dakota in 1919. He wrote in *The New Freedom* that he liked to address the "common people" because he found them "quicker to take a point, quicker to understand an argument, quicker to discern a tendency and to comprehend a principle, than many a college class that I have lectured to."[65]

Presidents and presidential candidates were especially sensitive to the public mood, but in the early 1900s they were not alone in this; Progressive Era reforms brought other politicians to a new awareness of popular opinion, too. The Seventeenth Amendment mandating popular election of the U.S. Senate became law in 1913. It is no coincidence that, when Wilson nominated Louis D. Brandeis for the Supreme Court in 1916, the nomination occasioned more public debate than any before in American history. The Senate's confirmation of Brandeis proceeded when a number of senators, whose anti-Semitism made them personally opposed to Brandeis, bit their tongues and supported the nationally popular crusading attorney.[66]

A fourth factor in the presidency's new authority was that, beginning as early as Theodore Roosevelt's administration and culminating in World War II, the United States became a chief actor on the world stage. Foreign policy became an increasingly important domain of governmental activity. Since the president's statutory authority in foreign affairs is greater than in domestic matters, the enlarged importance of foreign policy also meant a growth in presidential power. To the extent that military and defense policy are at the heart of foreign policy, this development also granted the president increasing control over public information, since secrecy is tolerated in military matters where it would not be in domestic policy.

Finally, the organizational basis of political competition shifted from a party-based model to a mass-based model. The executive took power not only from the Congress but from the parties; presidential leadership came increasingly to replace party leadership in shaping legislation, setting the tone and the style of public life, and serving as a central point for popular aspirations. We will explore this point more closely in examining the New Deal at the end of this chapter.

If the president was to exercise leadership, how? The model of leadership that appealed most in the interwar years was businesslike. One can hear this in the words of Charles G. Dawes, first director of the Bureau of the Budget, when he gathered together on June 29, 1921, "the entire business administration" of the government, including the president, executive department heads, relevant members of Congress, and top clerks, chiefs, and assistant chiefs of government bureaus. President Harding introduced Dawes, who then declared:

> This is not to be a speech on my part, but a talk to you as business men, a part of the business administration to which I belong, which for the first time commences functioning under a president of a business corporation who is also the President of the United States.

Dawes insisted that the president is "the head of governmental business administration in the United States."[67] He insisted that, in a word, government is business:

> . . . the President is simply putting into effect for the first time in this country a condition which exists in any business corporation, whether it be a bank or a manufacturing corporation, or any other kind. The president of the corporation bears a responsibility for the whole institution, and he has the right to get information where he pleases and from any source in that corporation, whether it is from a washer-woman scrubbing the floor, or his first vice-president.[68]

Consistent with this view of the president as a business administrator, Herbert Hoover offered the image of the engineer-president. Hoover was praised—as late as 1930—as a distinctively expert president: "For the first time in our history we have a President who, by technical training, engineering achievement, cabinet experience, and grasp of economic fundamentals, is qualified for business leadership."[69]

The notions of the businessman or the expert as leader was certainly popular, but what many friends of business demanded from a president, and what the political system offered up, was something different, more readily understandable in the terms of Emile Durkheim, the sociologist who focused on the necessary moral solidarity of a society, than the terms of Frederick Taylor, the engineer in whose name "efficiency" became a mantra for business and government reformers. Herbert Croly observed that the "search for the great leader became a neurotic obsession." [70] For many observers, a leader must harness widespread dreams and hopes in his person. In *A Preface to Politics*, Walter Lippmann called for leaders of "creative will and insight" who would be guided not by reason but by an intuitive grasp of society's dynamic. They would present their views through a guiding and inspiring "myth." [71] Yet the desire for a leader whose strength would be in his fitness for embodying popular aspirations had ever to contend with the Progressives' continuing romance with science, efficiency, and expertise.

Democracy by Experts

The whole world is witnessing "the emergence of government by experts," political scientist Leonard D. White declared in 1927, a development he clearly approved. "It is indeed a fair question," he went on, "whether we shall not be forced to reinterpret American government as a means for utilizing the services of experts in the performances of ends democratically defined." [72] For White, clearly, experts not only served democracy but in a sense replaced it—all to the good. "American experience shows with sufficient clearness that we cannot expect to maintain standards of administrative ability in an elective office." The "best executive brains" won't tolerate "the embarrassments of a political campaign" or the uncertain tenure of political office. Making a place for expertise in government, then, helps combat "spoils politics" and "hidden influence."

White disparaged party democracy without bothering to make a case against it. Walter Lippmann in *Public Opinion* presents a careful and coherent argument to justify a place for experts in democracy. Lippmann's work remains the most important and most lasting synthesis of early-twentieth-century American thought about the public and public opinion. There is little in it that is particularly original, it should be said. Like Graham Wallas, Dewey, and the practitioners and theorists of public relations and advertising, Lippmann was deeply affected by a sense of the power and complexity of "the social" in human affairs. What *Public Opinion* provides is a convincing exposition of the conclusions of the nascent sociology and social psychology of the day—that human beings have limited attention spans; that on the rare occasions when they do turn their attention beyond their immediate, personal worlds, they are guided more by emotion, transitory circumstance, and mood than by reason; and that a vast new machinery of institutionalized persuasion was all too willing and able to exploit the situation for selfish ends.

No one made this case better than Lippmann. Moreover, Lippmann had the character to see through his assessment to its sober conclusion: that democrats would have to give up their hopes of full-bodied democracy in order to save a thin, but nonetheless worthy, version of it.

Lippmann became interested in public opinion as early as 1915 when he tried to understand why voters in New York turned down a progressive new constitution. Insiders, he argued, supported the new constitution because they got their information directly from people involved in government; the general public, however, could rely only on information in the press. The insider, then, "is not limited to gazing at the facade of public life." For Lippmann, the insiders "belong to a freemasonry of the privileged who deal with events personally and directly, not formally and at second hand." [73] During the war Lippmann became one of the insiders himself, as an intimate of the Wilson administration. In 1917, he prepared for Wilson's aide Colonel House a rough outline for a "publicity bureau," which later became the Committee on Public Information. [74] After the war Lippmann returned to a career in journalism, but also began an avocation as a critic of journalism. With Charles Merz, he published a notable essay taking apart the New York Times coverage of the Russian Revolution. He then published a more general essay on journalism, Liberty and the News, in which he placed the problem that information always comes secondhand at the center of the modern dilemma. He wrote that "the present crisis of western democracy is a crisis in journalism." [75]

Was it possible for democracy to survive when "the manufacture of consent is an unregulated private enterprise"? [76] Lippmann did not provide a very confident conclusion. He looked toward a more professional journalism, a more scientific journalism, one that would find direction in "unity of method, rather than of aim; the unity of the disciplined experiment."[77] Lippmann hoped journalism would professionalize and that journalism school might become a requirement for entry into the field. But he almost immediately thought better of this and worried that professionalism might create blindspots of its own. At least, he urged, society must recognize the dignity of journalism and invest in professional training "in which the ideal of objective testimony is cardinal." He hoped that "political observatories" could be established, private institutes and university research operations on which journalists might draw, and he proposed as well an international nonpartisan news agency.[78]

Public Opinion renews this line of argument. Lippmann articulates the problem of democracy in striking language. He observes that people no longer responded to their "environment" but to the "pseudo-environment" that, through the news media, was all they could know of the large portions of the external world that impinged on their lives. The fault lay not only in the frailties or willfulness of outside agencies of information but on the human fallibilities of us all. We fail to get accurate knowledge not only because the press fails to provide it but because we would not see it if they did. People understand the world through their own "stereotypes," a term Lippmann popularized with this book; we see the world we expect to see, the one constructed by our own stereotypes. This is perhaps the most important departure in the book: by turning to the person's internal failures of reason, not just to the external pressures, Lippmann breaks from traditional democratic theory or any theory that assumes the citizen's rationality. It was, as John Dewey recognized in his initial review of the book for *The New Republic*, "perhaps the most effective indictment of democracy as currently conceived ever penned."[79]

Lippmann, who just a few years before had placed at least some hope in a more scientific journalism, now judged journalism to be unreformable. Newspapers provided accurate news regularly and reliably only when there was a good "machinery of record" available for journalists to borrow. For example, stock market quotations, baseball scores, and similar matters could be reported accurately, but elsewhere, journalists could not be trusted to do very good work. The best remedy Lippmann could propose was to institute the "political observatories" he now renamed bureaus of intelligence. He hopes that what we now call think tanks would arise to conduct scientific studies and monitor the political world in the many ways journalists themselves were unable to, and thus serve as expert sources for journalists. Experts were experts not by virtue of higher degrees, but by virtue of a habit of mind; expertise, as Lippmann explains, was the multiplication of the number of aspects of a situation one is prepared to discover. Experts cultivate the habit of discounting their own expectations.[80] And experts were the best hope to save democracy from itself.

This conclusion did not go unchallenged. John Dewey responded in a set of lectures at Kenyon College in 1926, published in 1927 as *The Public and Its Problems*. This work has achieved a following in recent years because of its affinity with current interest in a "public sphere" and current concern about the fate of the "public intellectual." Yet it is, like so much of Dewey's writing, maddeningly circuitous and long-winded, deeply abstract in its recommendation of the concrete, and despite protestations to the contrary, utopian in its effort to recommend pragmatic social inquiry. Dewey agrees with most of Lippmann's diagnosis of the problem, but offers a very different solution. "In most circles," Dewey writes, "it is hard work to sustain conversation on a political theme; and once initiated, it is quickly dismissed with a yawn."[81] Moreover, the role Lippmann proposed for experts differed subtly, not grossly, from the role Dewey concedes. Dewey attacks the idea of rule by experts on the grounds that experts as rulers will, like any class of rulers, speak for their own private interests rather than for the public interest. When experts rule, they, too, will be an oligarchy so long as "the masses do not have the chance to inform the experts as to their needs." But "*the* problem of the public" is not to remove the experts from power but to improve communication between experts and the public. "Inquiry, indeed, is a work which devolves upon experts," Dewey acknowledges—the experts must be responsible not for "framing and executing policies" but for "discovering and making known the facts upon which the former depend." The general public does not need to have the skill to conduct social inquiry but only "the ability to judge of the bearing of the knowledge supplied by others upon common concerns."[82]

Dewey's succeeding pages argue that modern democracy can work only if it succeeds in sustaining the local, face-to-face community. Local attachments, broken and beaten down by the great impersonal forces of modern society—this, "the outstanding fact of modern life"—had to be undone. "There is no substitute," Dewey concludes "for the vitality and depth of close and direct intercourse and attachment." Dewey holds, in what he seemed to recognize was an uncharacteristic vehemence, "The local is the ultimate universal, and as near an absolute as exists."[83]

Was this an adequate answer to Lippmann? Lippmann never lost sight of his emphasis on "the outstanding fact of modern life"—that the old local community was on the ropes. Dewey's praise of the face-to-face community ran the risk of neglecting the fact that such communities were often barriers to just the kind of free social inquiry that—if there is another absolute in Dewey—he so stirringly endorsed. Dewey proclaimed again and again the centrality of *organized intelligence* and *scientific method* for political progress in the world. The liberalism he praised and sought to embody "signifies the adoption of the scientific habit of mind in application to social affairs."[84] *The Public and Its Problems* never clarified how the old-time community could practically be restored in the Great Society nor, if it could, how it could be made compatible with modernity, science, and liberalism.

Neither Lippmann nor Dewey, in articulating what role experts should play in a democracy, had much to say about the role experts were already playing. There *were* experts in politics and in areas directly bearing on public policy in the 1920s. There were increasing numbers of scholars, their quality certified by doctorates from American or European universities, who defined themselves as specialists in one or another of the social sciences, but the production of experts of this sort was still relatively new. In 1890, sociology was essentially unknown in the United States, but by 1901, 132 universities taught courses in the subject; more than three hundred did so by 1910. The change was much more than quantitative. The character of sociology was shifting rapidly, from a field of reformers oriented to popular audiences toward a field of professionals oriented to internal audiences of experts in the universities, foundations, and government.[85]

Graduate instruction in political science dated to 1880 at Columbia, but grew substantially only after 1900. The University of Wisconsin's department began in 1901, Harvard's in 1909, and there were nearly forty departments in colleges and universities by 1914.[86] The American Political Science Association was founded in 1903, and in 1908, Arthur F. Bentley published *The Process of Government*, the seminal work establishing political studies as an empirically centered field.[87] Economics had been institutionalized in the universities somewhat earlier, but in this period began to develop the quantitative tools to prove its utility to government.

By the 1920s, universities were well launched in training and certifying policy specialists whose expertise was authenticated by empirical research. These experts also won support from beyond the universities. Private foundations in 1921 provided $180,000 for research and training in the social sciences and history; by 1927, the figure was close to $8 million.[88] Beginning with the Pittsburgh survey of 1909, underwritten by the Russell Sage Foundation, a whole movement of social surveys blossomed. By 1928, there had been 2700 surveys of health, housing, schooling, wages, work hours, and other topics directly relevant to municipal, state, and federal government.[89]

Institutional sponsorship of policy expertise came also from newly created independent research institutions, oriented to public policy, employing social scientists directly, and influencing legislation. The Brookings Institution, first set up in 1916 and fully institutionalized in 1927, was an early and influential instance at the national level. Its origins lay in the federal government, on the one hand, initial impetus for it coming out of President Taft's Commission on Economy and Efficiency in 1910. On the other hand, that commission's chair, Frederick Cleveland, had directed an independent policy research institute, New York's Bureau of Municipal Research, and sought a national-level version of it.

Municipal research bureaus soon spread from New York to Baltimore, Philadelphia, and Chicago, and by 1916 to Milwaukee, Rochester, Detroit, Cleveland, Akron, Toledo, and San Francisco. These private bureaus of "efficiency" were established to watch and investigate government and to encourage business methods in government.[90] At the state level, political scientist Charles McCarthy's work in establishing the Wisconsin Legislative Research Bureau was widely noted. Reformer Frederic C. Howe, in a book meant to publicize the Wisconsin model nationally, cites the University of Wisconsin as "the state research laboratory" where graduate students in the social sciences were trained in "the exhaustive study of state problems." He proclaims that few laws were passed at one end of Madison's State Street before they had been studied thoroughly at the other end.[91]

Lippmann makes no mention of any of these bureaus in *Public Opinion*, but the political observatories he recommended in American politics were already springing up. To some extent, this happened inside the government: the Bureau of the Census became a permanent office of the federal government only in 1902, and the Bureau of Agricultural Economics consolidated policy research in agriculture in the early 1920s. Even more, it happened through independent research bureaus and associations like the National Bureau of Economic Research (1920) and the Social Science Research Council (1923) as well as the others already cited.[92] The foundations played a significant—and novel—role in this. The Russell Sage Foundation and the Rockefeller Foundation, chartered in 1907 and 1913, respectively, were explicitly dedicated to the reform of social, economic, and political conditions. The strategy for reform was study and the publicity of study results. The foundations thus placed expertise at the center of reform in what one historian has called "the paradigm of a new kind of political process—one based on policy rather than politics."[93]

By the 1920s, the idea or concept of expertise had gained a kind of dominance. Civil service reform was, of course, important in this achievement. It placed at the center of government not the idea of party but the idea of merit, established by competitive examinations, and based on the acquisition of knowledge or skills directly relevant to governmental work. In some states, the public university became a self-conscious training ground for public service.

The scientific expert became "the prototype of all administrators." Scientific management's founding genius, Frederick Taylor, wrote an essay on "Government Efficiency" (published in 1916, shortly after his death) urging that an efficiency expert be awarded a cabinet position to introduce efficiency throughout the government. Before the war, Morris L. Cooke, a follower of Taylor, became director of public works in Philadelphia and promoted in tandem "expertism" and "democracy" as his watchwords. He became a popular lecturer on municipal efficiency. His view of the relationship between experts and democracy led him to urge reducing the total number of voting decisions, saving them for "broader issues" and leaving the details of government to the experts.[94]

Expertise was a form of authority with a decidedly democratic ring to it, Dewey's trenchant criticisms notwithstanding. "Democracy not only produced the expert, it elevated him to office," Frederic Howe wrote of the successes of Progressivism in Wisconsin.[95] Arthur T. Hadley concluded a set of lectures on American politics in 1914 with the observation that democracy and expertise must be, and could be, combined. "The people as a whole must assume the double duty of voting intelligently on matters which public opinion can decide and leaving to the specialist matters which can only be decided by the specialist. . . ." Two things, he argued, are required for the success of American democracy: "popular sovereignty and efficient government." The people themselves provided the first and would have to learn to defer to experts to gain the second.[96] In a country with a broad base of public schooling and at a time when even secondary schooling had expanded, access to the ranks of experts was becoming as open as, and more "merit-based" than, access to the ranks of party workers and party elites. And that, indeed, was still the alternative—the opposite of rule by experts was not rule by the people, but rule by the parties.

In this context, then, the dialogue between Lippmann and Dewey can be understood as part of a much larger discussion. If Hoover's uninspiring administration suggested limits to the potential of expertise, the administration of Hoover's successor showed even more forcefully the limits of the Deweyan rebuttal. Whatever else Franklin Delano Roosevelt would come to represent, it was not the inviolability of the local, face-to-face community. On the contrary, Roosevelt institutionalized rule by experts on a scale previously unimagined in the country. By 1938, nearly eight thousand social scientists were employed by the federal government, including more than five thousand economists.[97] In 1939, the Executive Office of the President was created and the Bureau of the Budget moved from the Treasury Department to the EOP, making presidential leadership more central than ever.[98] The local was hopelessly overwhelmed by national and international forces of economic dislocation and war. The local ability to act in the face of national collapse was effaced. If the local was "the ultimate universal," as Dewey had called it, something very distressing was going on in the 1930s and 1940s. By World War II, an emphasis on presidential leadership was joined to Lippmann's faith in experts, and both were ensconced in Washington. Dewey's quest to reground democracy in the face-to-face community seemed out of touch. Still, the intimate connection between the small town and democracy was not easily abandoned.

Democracy Writ Small

In the twenties and thirties, there were efforts to refound democracy in face-to-face communities. If none of these efforts was quite up to imagining how they could be made to work on a national scale, they may nonetheless have provided a leavening to keep the democratic imagination alive.

This began before World War I when Mary Follett and others urged the formation of neighborhood groups and proposed making the public schools into community centers.[99] The settlement house movement had hoped to reintegrate neighborhoods around settlement houses, and, by 1910, settlement workers contributed to efforts to make the public schools social centers. In Boston, Follett organized a number of schools as recreational and social centers. In Rochester, New York, a former Presbyterian minister, Edward Ward, directed the school social center movement, using the schools as public libraries, public baths, theaters, and meeting places, adapting them to re-create in urban life "the neighborly spirit, the democracy that we knew before we came to the city."[100] Ward moved on to organize school centers throughout the state of Wisconsin, and in 1912 founded the National Community Center Association. In the same year, presidential candidates Wilson, Taft, and

Roosevelt all endorsed the school center idea. In *The New Freedom*, Wilson urged: "These buildings belong to the public. Why not insist everywhere that they be used as places of discussion, such as of old took place in the town-meetings to which everybody went and where every public officer was freely called to account?"[101] There were related efforts to use public libraries and public parks as community centers. Many reformers saw these initiatives as providing healthful substitutes for saloons, alternative centers for community life and civic and political discussion.[102]

Wilson held that the citizen who reads the newspaper and responds to it is not participating in the making of public opinion. "He cannot be said to be participating in public opinion at all until he has laid his mind alongside the minds of his neighbors and discussed with them the incidents of the day and the tendencies of the time." Getting the neighbors together would revitalize American politics. He noted, with some condescension but with a palpable sincerity, that when he spoke at Cooper Union in New York, some of the best questions came from "the least well-dressed in the audience . . . the plain fellows . . . the fellows whose muscle was daily up against the whole struggle of life." Indeed, Wilson continued, what he liked so much about the school center idea is that "there is the place where the ordinary fellow is going to get his innings, going to ask his questions, going to express his opinions, going to convince those who do not realize the vigor of America that the vigor of America pulses in the blood of every true American, and that the only place he can find the true American is in this clearing-house of absolutely democratic opinion."[103]

The idea that one would have to think small to make democracy work was boosted in the 1930s by growing institutional support for adult education programs. The Carnegie Foundation and the American Association for Adult Education helped underwrite an experiment in adult discussion groups in Des Moines. Organized by the superintendent of schools (and later U.S. commissioner of education), John Studebaker, in 1933, Des Moines ran hundreds of discussion groups on contemporary political, economic, and social issues. Studebaker explained the experiment in a familiar idiom—at its base was the growing complexity of modern society. The leading reason democracy is challenged, he wrote, is that "our common problems have become so complex that the ordinary citizen begins to despair of his ability to understand them—and more important still, of his ability to retain, and adequately discharge, responsibility for their solution."[104] Political groups were not much help. "Political meetings are generally devoted to arousing enthusiasm for a predetermined program, rather than to examining critically the issues of the day." The parties avoid issues that are genuinely nonpartisan or might alienate some groups of voters if discussed.[105]

In Des Moines, one adult in six participated in Studebaker's forums, but the grassroots character of the meetings was far from pure. Each forum was led by a paid leader to keep discussion on track. Studebaker observed, "Of incompetent thinking, uninformed opinion, and rambling talk, we already have too much. We now need expert and impartial leadership in public discussion."[106]

Studebaker hoped that forums like those in Des Moines might spread nationwide and help "make it the 'fashion' in the United States to be informed about governmental and social problems." The chief obligation of citizenship, he held, was "being informed about our common problems."[107] His wish was at least in part answered. By 1937, there were 1500 community forum projects all across the country, including a forum division of the Works Projects Administration. The Office of Education conducted demonstrations of the public forum idea in six hundred communities by 1939.[108]

If neighborhood and ward-based community groups might reconstitute a town meeting democracy in the city, there was also a new appreciation of the small town. Not in Sinclair Lewis or in Sherwood Anderson, but at least by the 1940s in an unlikely set of intellectuals, there was a sense that the small town radiated the true spirit of democracy. Former Communist Party intellectual and literary critic Granville Hicks penned a tribute to the small community where he lived, Grafton, New York. Hicks's wife joined the PTA when their daughter started school and supervised a girls' social club, the Merry Maids. This coaxed Hicks into directing a boys' social club. The Hickses' involvement in community life deepened as they assumed wartime responsibilities on the Grafton Defense Council.[109] Political theorist Carl J. Friedrich praised Hicks's *Small*

Town, especially his defense of the small community as "a practical school of democracy." Friedrich saw in Hicks's recognition that some people, known and trusted by their neighbors, carry special authority in political opinions that no radio commentator or editorial writer could match, the core of a new, unromanticized but fully positive "image of the common man."[110]

Not everyone assumed that broadcasting was antithetical to democratic participation. For urban dwellers, there were new efforts to recreate the political discussion and involvement of small-town life through the use of radio. George V. Denny, Jr. was a leading innovator in this arena. As president of New York City's League for Political Education, a civic organization dating to 1894, and its Town Hall auditorium, he created and served as moderator of *America's Town Meeting of the Air*. On this popular weekly NBC radio show, begun in 1935, prominent citizens debated vital issues of the day. Denny held that Americans had lost "much of our capacity to reason together" when the New England town meeting was abandoned as the basis of representative democracy. He held, however, that "through the miracle of radio" the nation could move back in the right direction.[111]

In 1936, Town Hall established two-way communication with Washington, D.C., where Commissioner of Education Studebaker, among others, participated in the broadcast, and with Rochester, New York, where a League of Women Voters' regular listening group aired its questions. Town Hall in New York helped establish listening groups around the country—1300 of them by the end of the 1937–38 season. The program distributed widely its town meeting bulletin, provided handbooks for discussion leaders, and offered advice on publicity, fundraising, and recruiting local speakers. Some 2400 letters a week from listeners poured into the show. Stressing always the nonpartisan virtues of public debate, town meeting advocates praised listeners not stuck in party loyalties but willing to courteously and tolerantly look at all sides of a question.[112] "I am not critical of political parties as such," Denny insisted, but he would supplement the party system with the town meeting, "this large body of nonpartisan voters who want to listen to all sides, weigh the evidence, study the issues, and cast thoughtful ballots on election day." [113] Education could inoculate American democracy from the authoritarianism overtaking Europe; education, not the parties alone nor the "virus" of pressure groups, might revitalize democracy and "bring back the town-meeting spirit." [114]

None of these efforts at building exemplary communities of political discussion went very far. It is hard to know if Denny's efforts had any lasting influence, but certainly his instinct was correct: that modern democracy would have to make use of and respond to the massiveness and complexity of society with tools of the day. A democratic order could not arise from a multiplication of isolated town meetings and urban discussion groups. But was there any way, realistically, to assemble citizen voices on a scale as large as the nation had become? George Gallup thought he could answer that question.

Democracy Through Technology

If the voter cannot grasp the details of the problems of the day because he
has not the time, the interest or the knowledge, he will not have a better
public opinion because he is asked to express his opinion more often. [115]

"What is the common man thinking?" [116] That's what George Gallup wanted to know. The poll, he believed, would be "a practical way of learning what the nation thinks." [117] Far from being a mechanism for elites to manipulate masses, the poll was a way for ordinary people to gain control—"for public opinion can be a satisfactory guide only if we can hear it and, what is equally important, if it can hear itself." [118] In this regard, it was of great importance to Gallup that his poll was underwritten by newspapers who bought his triweekly reports on "what America thinks" and made them available to eight million readers. [119]

Efforts at polling can be found as far back as the early nineteenth century. The *Harrisburg Pennsylvanian* reported results of a straw poll in Delaware on the presidential campaign in 1824. Much later, this became standard newspaper practice. The *New York Herald* polled New York voters in 1904, and joined with newspapers in Cincinnati, Chicago, and St. Louis in 1908 to sponsor street-corner election polls. The *Literary Digest* began its famous polling in 1916. Without any sense of scientific sampling, the *Digest* each presidential election year simply sent out ballots to telephone owners. Gallup, whose early experience was in the field of marketing, began polling in 1934 based on small, carefully selected samples in key districts. In 1936, the *Literary Digest* poll, based as always on ballots sent to telephone and automobile owners, outrageously underestimated Roosevelt's strength. It predicted a 57 to 43 percent victory for Landon, not the 62.5 percent landslide for Roosevelt. When Gallup predicted 56 percent for Roosevelt, the new scientific polling was in and massive sample balloting was out.[120]

Gallup was not only a pollster but a polemicist on behalf of polling and its place in democracy. It was important, in his view of polling, to recognize polling agencies as "essentially news gathering organizations." He argued against governmental regulation of polling organizations on First Amendment grounds.[121] His own American Institute of Public Opinion polling was financed by 125 daily newspapers that retained exclusive publication rights in their communities. His leading competitors were also supported by the news media: *Fortune* paid for Elmo Roper's poll, and other newspapers paid for Archibald Crossley's polling.[122]

The present institutionalization of polling in universities and in independent research organizations should not obscure their financing, past and present, by news organizations that, of course, in recent years have developed their own extensive polling services. Polling questions are still designed not to afford general knowledge of public opinion so much as to generate news. It is not a matter of any lasting scientific interest if people prefer candidate A to candidate B in "trial heats" a year before an election, but it is of *news* interest.

Gallup recognized that public opinion is not and cannot be the aggregation of separately constituted individual opinions. He judged it a "fundamental fact" that "the public consists of people clustered into social groups." As a result, the opinion surveyor "makes use of selective sampling to build up his 'miniature public.'" The trick in opinion sampling is to get different groups within the general public represented in relation to their proportions in the public.[123] Polling required intelligent understanding of social groups and social divisions, not a mechanically aggregated pointillism.

In *The Pulse of Democracy* (1940), Gallup's popular treatise on the polls and democracy, he presents polling as "a new instrument which may help to bridge the gap between the people and those who are responsible for making decisions in their name. The public-opinion polls provide a swift and efficient method by which legislators, educators, experts, and editors, as well as ordinary citizens throughout the length and breadth of the country, can have a more reliable measure of the pulse of democracy."[124] Gallup notes the dangers of pressure groups that claim to speak for the people and even the dangers of party leaders or "powerful newspapers" claiming to represent the vox populi. And the occasional election day was not enough for people to express themselves—"the right to vote, to choose between this party or that, is by itself not true democracy." True democracy "is a process of constant thought and action on the part of the citizen. It is self-educational. It calls for participation, information, the capacity to make up one's own mind." But in no way, Gallup insists, was "public opinion" to be taken as "some kind of supernatural force which will automatically operate to make democracy create the best of all possible worlds." Public opinion does not stand outside and above society: "It is not the product of an omniscient group mind, but rather a dynamic process resulting from the communication and interaction of individuals in an ever-moving society."[125]

Gallup believed polling could help democracy to work better. He never argued that politicians should slavishly follow polls, but he preached relentlessly that they should listen to the polls. The poll could put the siren calls of pressure groups in perspective. In fact, they are "almost the only present check on the growing power of pressure groups."[126] The polls could put elections in perspective since the policy implications of elections are often misinterpreted.[127] Polls help to remove power from political parties, too. They limit the power of "political bosses to pick presidential candidates 'in smoke-filled rooms.'" They do what open primaries were intended to do: put the nomination of candidates in the people's hands.[128]

Gallup made a particularly cogent critique of elections. We rarely can know from what person was elected what policies the public prefers. In 1928, he noted, "dry Southern Democrats" could not vote for Al

Smith without fear that this would be interpreted as a vote against Prohibition; wet Republicans could not support Hoover without suspecting
their votes would be taken to support Prohibition. Moreover, the divisions in legislatures do not represent the divisions in the nation; in 1936,
Gallup pointed out, Democrats controlled the Senate five to one while
the voters had supported Democrats only three to two.[129]

Gallup made his critique with the words of James Bryce very much
in mind and cited repeatedly. Indeed, he justified polling procedures by
noting Bryce's suggestion that the best way to assess public opinion is "by
moving freely about among all sorts and conditions of men and noting
how they are affected by the news or arguments brought from day to day
to their knowledge." Bryce concluded, "Talk is the best way of reaching
the truth, because in talk, one gets directly at the facts, whereas reading
gives not so much the facts, as what the writer believes, or wished to
have others believe."[130] And talk, Gallup disingenuously insisted, is just
the method of the polls—as if a paid employee asking precisely and unalterably worded questions to a random sample of citizens can be called
"talk."

For Gallup, the polls ushered in what Bryce had called the "fourth
stage of democracy." This stage could be reached, Bryce had prophesied,
"if the will of the majority of citizens were to become ascertainable at all
times."[131] Gallup ends *The Pulse of Democracy* with a tribute not to social
science but to Thomas Jefferson. Siding with Jefferson against Alexander Hamilton, Gallup pictures himself as a radical democrat, one who
trusts the common citizen.[132]

By 1948, Gallup claimed the polls had made enormous contributions to democracy. Polls informed political leaders of popular opinion
better and more swiftly than ever. They supported a faith in the common
people by showing that "the common people do make good decisions."[133]
They also centered attention on and increased interest in major issues:

> They have provided what Walter Lippmann, in his book *Public Opinion*,
> asserted was greatly needed by this democracy—a machinery for scor
> ing. By injecting the element of controversy, by showing the division of
> opinion, in fact by helping to simplify major issues by expressing them

in language understandable to the great mass of people, polls have helped to increase public interest in many national issues.[134]

Gallup directly counters Madisonian objections to the polls. The case against "government by public opinion," he retorts, "reveals suspicion not only of the public-opinion surveys, but also of the mass of the people." It is not far from the views of Mussolini and Hitler, he chides, who also argue that the stupidity and gullibility of people make them unfit to rule.[135] Has the world become so complex that only experts can properly rule? Not at all. As if he had been reading *The Public and Its Problems,* he asserts that experts can guide us only on means, not on ends.[136] "The conduct of government does not merely involve specialized knowledge. It deals primarily with human needs and human values," Gallup writes. For him, "the surest touchstone of political action is the actual experience of the mass of its citizens," and it is this to which the polls give voice.[137]

Must each citizen be well informed for polling to be responsible? Not so. "Democracy . . . requires merely that the *sum total of individual views add up to something that makes sense.*"[138] A majority "usually registers sound judgment on issues, even though a good many are ignorant and uninformed."[139] Gallup was unperturbed by the possibility that citizens responded to pollsters with "snap opinions." Even if opinions are "snap" and fleeting, the "law of averages" will even things out, and every John Smith who shifts from "yes" to "no" will be matched by a Henry Jones moving "no" to "yes." The influence of chance perturbations is slight. "Public opinion changes slowly and usually only under the impact of important events."[140]

One of those important events was no doubt the advent of polling itself. The broad acceptance of sampling methods would in time become a part of American political culture. "Numbers provide the rhetoric of our age," the demographer Nathan Keyfitz has observed. This has roots in the majoritarianism of mass democracy, the increasing reliance of governments on the generation, collection, and analysis of quantitative data of all sorts, and not least of all on the popularization of quantitative information in the work of the pollsters.[141]

If Gallup was right that the choice lies between aggregated individual opinions authenticated by scientific polling and manipulated opinion controlled by elite propaganda, special-interest pressure groups, and oligarchic parties, then the virtues of polling become evident. The trouble, easier to see today than in 1936 or 1948, is that Gallup's two alternatives both presuppose a view of opinion as virginal, preconstituted, prepolitical, presocial. This view has dominated scholarly discourse in political science and economics. But in an alternative view, opinions are deeply and essentially social, interactive, and deliberative. In fact, democracy requires that private opinions are not the point of departure for public opinion; truly public opinion does not exist until it is arrived at through discussion and in deliberative assemblies. "The public" in opinion polling is only "a data set" when it should be "a realm of action." [142] The question of democracy, in this Madisonian view, or what has recently come to be called deliberative democracy, is not how to identify authentic, presocial opinion but how to construct institutional mechanisms for arriving at public opinion. It is not enough to ascertain "raw" opinion but to develop the institutional recipes to best make the raw cooked.

Despite the merits of this critique, including its firm location in both social psychology and democratic theory, its advocates have not yet explained it convincingly to a general public. Polling, in contrast, on its own terms must be judged a monumental success. Both as a critique of other imperfect measures of "what the common man thinks" and as a positive resource for democracy, the legacy of George Gallup is great. It may be one of the enduring fruits of the nineteenth-century idea of mass democracy, however transformed and tamed.

The New Deal Synthesis: The Decentering of the Party

How new ideas and moods would shape the path of American public life would be directed by Franklin Roosevelt's pragmatism and instincts for executive authority. Roosevelt contributed his personal presence to the growing cult of democracy, making important appearances at the dedication of the Jefferson Memorial, at the dedication of Duke of Gloucester

Street in Williamsburg, and in other civic ceremonials. In his executive reorganization of 1937–39, he brought to fruition the work begun with the establishment of the Bureau of the Budget in 1921, bringing it out of the Treasury Department and directly under presidential authority, enlarging the power of the president over independent agencies, and formally organizing a White House staff for the first time.[143] He helped mightily to shift the government's center of gravity from legislature to the bureaucracy under direct presidential authority. He had anticipated this in his campaign address to the Commonwealth Club in September 1932 by declaring, "The day of enlightened administration had come." His speechwriter Adolf Berle had written, "The day of the manager has come," but this emphasized perhaps too exclusively the solution of expertise; Roosevelt, as historian Sidney Milkis argues, was just as intent on executive centralization and expansion.[144]

This is not to suggest that Roosevelt was unfriendly to the idea of expertise. Of course, like other presidents before him, he manipulated the civil service to his own advantage. Under Hoover, 80 percent of federal offices were classified under the merit system, but almost all of the many new federal agencies Roosevelt established were exempt from civil service, with the result that the total percentage of federal positions classified declined to 60 percent by 1936. (The total number of federal employees grew enormously from 1933 to 1936, from 572,000 to 824,000. This included 100,000 new civil-service-exempt positions.) At a time when polls found nearly 90 percent of Americans in favor of civil service and with the League of Women Voters engaged (from 1934 to 1936) in a massive publicity campaign on its behalf, Roosevelt was restoring patronage politics.[145] "Find the Man for the Job, Not the Job for the Man," the league urged, but FDR had other fish to fry. He increased the number of patronage positions not so much to control the Democratic Party as to achieve ideological control of the government. In the New Deal agencies, Roosevelt stressed "ideological" patronage rather than party patronage.[146] He used jobs to recruit agricultural scientists, economists, academics, and other professionals whose loyalty was to the New Deal, not the Democratic Party. Organization Democrats resented this, of course, but Roosevelt persisted.[147] When most New Deal patronage positions became part of the merit-based civil service under the Ramspeck Act of 1940 (by 1941, 95 percent of federal employees were covered by civil service), the aim was to secure permanence to an administrative service "that would be divorced from traditional partisan considerations, yet embrace the New Deal political order."[148]

The long story of federal patronage came to something of a conclusion with the Hatch Acts of 1939 and 1940. These acts significantly limited the political activity of federal employees; this included prohibiting federal employees, apart from congressmen, cabinet officers, and a few other high-ranking officials, from serving as delegates to presidential nominating conventions. The first act prohibited government employees from using office "for the purpose of interfering with an election or affecting the result thereof." The second act clarified that this applied to most nonclassified government positions as well as civil service jobs. While Roosevelt contemplated a veto of this legislation, he finally decided to sign.

Roosevelt's championing of expert-populated administrative agencies under the control of the president came at the expense of the same old bugaboo that Progressives had been fighting for more than half a century: the political party. It is often not appreciated that the famous "New Deal coalition" that revived the Democratic Party used the party as an electoral majority but not as an organizational force. As Sidney Milkis argues, "the New Deal Democratic party was organized as a party of administration that would make party politics less important in the future. Once a welfare state was formed, social and economic interests would be directly linked to it, thus diminishing the importance of a party to organize public opinion."[149] But it was the New Deal that effected this transformation at the federal level.

This was most notable in Roosevelt's efforts in 1938 to "purge" Congress of Democrats who resisted his legislative program. In the most dramatic moment in the campaign, Roosevelt, sharing a platform in Barnesville, Georgia, with Senator Walter George, attacked George's voting record and endorsed his liberal opponent in the primary. The purge failed to unseat any of the conservative Southern Democrats (and only one conservative Democrat outside the South) it targeted. At the same time, the president's efforts may have pressured other Democrats in Congress to support New Deal legislation and helped the local Democrats turn back conservative challengers in the primaries.

All of this contributed to FDR's efforts to present himself as above party labels. FDR knew that he needed to attract liberal Republicans and independents to his cause. The Democrats in 1932 were a minority party, Roosevelt only the third successful Democratic presidential candidate since before the Civil War. In Pennsylvania in 1932, Democrats were only 21 percent of registered voters, but 42 percent by 1936 as the party's registration efforts were stepped up. In California, registered Democrats were a majority for the first time in history in 1934, thanks to Upton Sinclair's registration drive in his run for governor. Roosevelt made strong appeals to recruit blacks and labor to the party, too. In 1932, 65 percent of blacks voted for Herbert Hoover; in 1936, 76 percent voted for Roosevelt. With the support of blacks and labor, the Democratic Party attained a new identity and Northern liberals came to rival and often best Southern stalwarts in the party. The conservative Jeffersonian Southerners were not reconciled to the party's new image, and seeds of discord were sown—the chief issue, of course, being race.[150]

After Roosevelt any new politics would have to invent itself without patronage. If civil service reform did not fully kill the government job machine, the unionization of public employees dealt it a final blow. Any new politics would also have to confront a problem the New Deal had only gingerly addressed: the inclusion of African-Americans, as well as other minority groups of various kinds, in the public arena. For many Americans, the possibility of blending into an undifferentiated "citizen" role, with all that that implies of civic equality, was belied and betrayed by the ways in which their local standing as stigmatized minorities stood in the way. Not polling nor expertise and, only tentatively, leadership from the president recognized the formal and informal disfranchisements of black Americans and other minorities. But in the postwar world, the struggle of blacks for inclusion in the body politic would prove the fountainhead for a new understanding of citizenship.

In the New Deal, the parties were under fire, and alternative modes of civic participation were developing both a set of practices and strong ideologies, championed by a combination of groups with a Progressive vision of the political sphere—women, university-trained experts, government officials in the classified civil service, journalists committed to nonpartisan professionalism, and an array of private foundations, research institutes, and even lobbies. This begins to suggest the growing multiplicity of actors on the political scene and efforts to define politics, all of which would wildly break loose in the rights revolution to come. As no one could have anticipated in 1922 or 1933 or even 1945, in the end the last would be first. African-Americans would launch a rebirth of democratic citizenship; still more unlikely, the institutionally last would be first, as the rights revolution would begin in the courts.

Entr'acte II

The Second Great Debate

To be public today means to be on television.[1]

A public that once snapped up pamphlets by Thomas Paine or stood for hours listening to Abraham Lincoln debate Stephen Douglas hardly exists; its span of attention shrinks as its fondness for television increases.[2]

On September 26, 1960, at 8:30 P.M. Central Standard Time, together but separately in their apartments and houses, eighty million Americans tuned in the debate between Senator John F. Kennedy, Democratic candidate for president, and Vice President Richard M. Nixon, Republican candidate.

More adults watched the television debates than would vote on election day.[3] Out of this, what one observer judged "the largest political convocation in the history of man," a modern myth would emerge about how television magnified the powers of John Kennedy (although little in that first debate indicated the wit and charm before the camera Kennedy would later demonstrate) and diminished the rhetorical advantage of Richard Nixon by exaggerating his dark, furtive look.[4]

If there is one day to pick out of a decade-long era of television's maturation, it would probably be that day in September, television's bar mitzvah, a youth announcing adulthood.[5] At the same time, the Kennedy-Nixon debate ushered in a new model of how citizenship has gone wrong. Now, it seemed, citizens judged not character, as in colonial days, and not party, as in the nineteenth century, but performance. They judged television presence. In doing so, a host of critics charged, they revealed themselves civic failures. The civic ideology we have inherited from the Progressives stands in condemnation of such "theater criticism" politics.[6] The surprisingly intimate link people feel to candidates they know—but know only through television—is discounted as dangerously false pseudo-knowledge.

Theodore White, the veteran correspondent who turned richly detailed, gossipy "inside politics" books on presidential campaigns into a small industry, shrewdly observed that before September 1960 all electoral uses of television had been partisan. Before 1960 parties or candidates bought time on the networks. For the 1960 presidential debates, in contrast, the networks offered free time and thereby anointed themselves the sponsors of the nation's most important civic exercise.[7] They had strong reason to do so, reeling as they were under the public criticism of the quiz show scandals. Sponsoring high-profile public affairs programs burnished their public image. Their initiative led in June 1960 to the decision of Congress to suspend Section 315 of the Federal Communications Act, making the Kennedy-Nixon debates possible.[8] Section 315, the "equal time" provision, required broadcasters to provide "equal time" for all of the fifteen or twenty declared candidates for president if they offered time to one, no matter how unlikely the chances of the minor party candidates.[9]

Once the networks became hosts, they saw to it that the debates were conducted on their terms. The masters of ceremony were television journalists—Howard K. Smith of CBS moderated the first debate, and a panel of television reporters asked questions of the candidates after their opening statements. (In all four Kennedy-Nixon debates, the moderators were network journalists, but the panelists included print reporters in the second and third debates. The networks insisted that only broadcast journalists serve for the first and last debates.)[10] The print media had never held such civic prominence and semi-official standing. Political figures, notably Franklin D. Roosevelt, took command of radio, but radio had never commanded political leaders as television now did.

Planners of the debates gave thought to using a well-known public figure or the president of the American Bar Association as moderator, but finally all parties agreed on a television professional.[11] This was not a presidential press conference where the president called the shots; this was a media-organized and -sponsored event in which the candidates agreed to participate. Nothing better certified the journalistic aspiration to professional neutrality; nothing is better evidence that the public, including political leaders, now accepted it. Television journalists were players in the political game as never before.

The candidates' representatives and the network representatives agreed to a *Meet the Press*–type format because they felt it would be familiar to the television audience. Both candidates' aides feared that if it was left to the candidates to question each other, they would be too polite. No one likes "the prosecuting-attorney type on television," so the candidates were happy to turn that job over to the journalists.[12] This was a moral division of labor in which the journalists would play the tough-minded heavies and willingly shoulder the dirty work.

The result was not, many critics observed, a particularly enlightening discussion of issues. Some believed television inevitably drew attention to individual combatants rather than issues. Others criticized the format for making it difficult to get deeply into the issues. On this point, critics had it backward: the absence of clear-cut issues helped decide the format. Formal debates work best with a narrow, clear-cut issue, but the candidates' representatives admitted in advance that the campaign offered no clear-cut issue.[13]

Even so, one cannot quickly write off what audiences may have learned about the candidates' and parties' positions. Survey research after the election found that Kennedy voters claimed to have learned more about the candidates and their views from the TV debates than from any other source. As many Nixon voters learned "a great deal" from the debates as from any other source.[14] Indeed, the text of the debates suggests that the candidates made serious and reasonably lucid efforts to state substantively conflicting positions.

Obviously, the debate was more than an elucidation of positions on issues. It was a collective ritual, what would later be called a media event, with millions of people at their picture-tube hearths watching the personal performance of two political leaders under stress. It was a ritual that critics feared put all its emphasis on the emotional, the nonrational, and the visual elements of performance. The experienced political journalist Samuel Lubell thought the debates tended to "elevate the significance of personality, particularly on its theatrical side." [15] Most commentary on the first debate focused on how badly Nixon looked in it, sweaty, jowly, his heavy beard giving him a sinister look despite the "Lazy Shave" powder designed to cover it. With television, it seemed, show business threatened to supplant democracy. Political scientist Clinton Rossiter, writing for the President's Commission on National Goals at the end of 1960, concluded that television was becoming "the Circus Maximus rather than the Forum of American democracy." Even the presidential debates only "scratched the surface of the democratic potentialities of this medium." Indeed, Rossiter cautioned, "the democratic dialogue is in real danger of being smothered." [16]

This point was made with devastating wit by historian Daniel Boorstin in *The Image* (1961). Boorstin found that the media revolution had produced an "age of pseudo-events." Public life was a world in which "counterfeit happenings tend to drive spontaneous happenings out of circulation." The pseudo-event invariably trumps the real event: "What happens on television will overshadow what happens off television." And nothing better illustrated this, for Boorstin, than the Kennedy-Nixon debates, which he saw (inaccurately) as the "application of the quiz show format" to a confrontation between presidential candidates. The Great Debates were "a clinical example of the pseudo-event, of how it is made, why it appeals, and of its consequences for democracy in America." He found nothing redeeming about the debates. There was no connection between "a man's ability, while standing under klieg lights, without notes, to answer in two and a half minutes a question kept secret until that moment" and the ability to be president. Television necessarily rewarded the snap answer and not the thoughtful response. The pseudo-event was especially sinister because its trivialization of reality could not even be unmasked: "Whenever we describe the lighting, the make-up, the studio setting, the rehearsals, etc., we simply arouse more interest." In the Kennedy-Nixon debates, "This greatest opportunity in American history to educate the voters by debating the large issues of the campaign failed." [17]

While political observers caviled about theatricality, show, performance, and image-making, the producers insisted that they could not have presented candidates more straightforwardly. Don Hewitt, producer of the first debate and later the mastermind behind 60 Minutes, insisted: "I realized that the most important function of my job as producer was not to be a producer, in other words, not to make a television program out of this. Just to make it possible for the people sitting at home to watch the significant event, probably the most significant event they had ever watched, and to fight the temptation to turn it into a show. I would have preferred an audience, that this debate take place in Madison Square Garden, and that we cover it as a special event, not as a television show." [18]

But a television show it was (and a television show subsequent debates have all been). This seems to automatically condemn it; nearly everyone believes television is a failed political medium. It is not a new mode for expressing citizenship but a new barrier to expression, not the speakers' corner for a new virtual community but a trivialization of the politically serious and perhaps even the leading cause of declining civic participation. [19]

Is this fair? Perhaps the performance of a candidate on television is an authentic window on his or her political soul. A good performance requires presenting a trustworthy character, with an acceptable relationship to party (stable and consistent but independent) and with knowledge of public policy. The citizen then judges the overall result, and on that September evening in 1960, people sat in their living rooms and became critics of their leaders in a new way and without the mediation of editorial writers, news photographers, or precinct captains.

Theodore White wrote the epitaph for democracy's experiment with television even as he announced its birth. Television "should have provided" a forum for issues, but the demand of television for quick answers and its incapacity to allow any dead airtime for the candidates to think invalidated it as a medium of reason. "Neither man could pause to indulge in the slow reflection and rumination, the slow questioning of alternatives before decision, that is the inner quality of leadership." As a result, "the TV debates did little to advance the reasonable discussion of issues that is the dream of unblooded political scientists. . . ."[20]

This is a cheap trick: White off-loads onto unnamed ivory tower types the perfectionist standard by which he himself judges television. Even if James Madison ran a network and hired Justice Oliver Wendell Holmes, Jr. to head the news division, television could not produce "reasonable discussion" and sophisticated citizens. It could not do much to encourage "slow reflection and rumination"—as if radio, newspapers, and the rough-and-tumble of legislative floor debate had long favored the ruminating mind! One of the great benefits of C-SPAN is that it enables Americans envious of the virtues of British politics to see the prime minister's "question period" up close. The question period is a great deal more energetic and amusing—sometimes uproarious—than the best presidential press conference, but it is even more stylized and hortatory. It is no more elevated, rational, or deliberative. It is more a scoring of points than a trading of views.

Whether the public sphere "works" is not a matter of whether television promotes rational discussion but whether the mass media and other information sources, including parties and interest groups, keep tabs on the political world. It is a matter of whether, when an issue arises, citizens have various effectual access points to governmental decision-makers. The effective operation of a public sphere depends also on whether, through the networks of talk, complaint, letters, petitions, interest groups, parties, suits, demonstrations, and picket lines, people *feel* they can and *actually* can move issues onto the public agenda.

The critics of political television notwithstanding, the Kennedy-Nixon debates were a fine moment for American public life, not the conclusive sign of its degradation. To dismiss them, it is not enough to show that they trailed off into irrelevancies about Quemoy and Matsu (islands then in dispute between Taiwan and China); the Lincoln-

Douglas debates squandered hours on phantoms, too. Demonstrating that there was an element of show business in the TV debates is easily done, but to what end? The Lincoln-Douglas debates were show biz, too, the best entertainment around. People then cheered rhetorical jabs and punches with as much fervor as in 1960 they would solemnly discuss makeup and demeanor. Can we complain that the two-and-a-half-minute statements were too short to make sound points? This, too, seems misguided: Lincoln spoke for hours in 1858 and left us no ideas or even phrases anyone knows, but in three minutes at Gettysburg he delivered the greatest American speech of all time. (Likewise, American political theorists have written volume after volume—some good, some bad, but the very best of the lot, *Federalist* No. 10, is seven pages long.)

The critique of the Kennedy-Nixon debates is itself symptomatic of a fretful political culture. No one owns politics today, not the way the gentry did in colonial days, not how the parties did in the nineteenth century. In the post-Progressive era, no one class or type of organization owns politics. The triumph of democratic sensibilities is the expectation that *everybody* owns public life. What follows from this, however, is competition and confusion that gives rise to a lingering sense of disaffection and unease in both good times and bad.

Chapter 6

Widening the Web of Citizenship in an Age of Private Citizens

Prospectus

In 1961, in a classic study of urban politics, political scientist Robert Dahl wrote that for most people politics lies at "the outer periphery of attention." Not public affairs, but "primary activities involving food, sex, love, family, work, play, shelter, comfort, friendship, social esteem, and the like" are at the center of people's interest. "Activities like these—not politics—are the primary concerns of most men and women."[1]

Nearly forty years later the distinction between primary activities and politics cannot be maintained. Every one of Dahl's "primary activities" has been politicized. Dietary guidelines have become matters for congressional debate, the Center for Science in the Public Interest has attacked the popcorn sold in movie theaters, and a well-organized social movement has put laws against tobacco use on the statute books at local, state, and federal levels. Today terms like "date rape," "marital rape," and "battered woman" are familiar. "Deadbeat dads" is a political rallying cry, a nominee to the Supreme Court has been publicly embarrassed by charges of sexual harassment, and state policy about women's decisions on abortion has fueled the most extensive populist movement of our time. The notions of representation, justice, and political participation have extended far beyond the sphere of conventional politics into "private" life.

Studying New Haven, Connecticut, in the late 1950s, Dahl unearthed the citizens of Tocqueville's volume two, not volume one, their souls absorbed to the point of obsession in private affairs, unable to stir for any matter beyond easy reach and obvious self-interest. What bears consideration is that Tocqueville discovered this self-absorbed citizen at a moment in American history that critics today look back on as a golden age of civility in cultural life and a time of active civic participation, with voter turnout at a post-1920s high, trust in leading national institutions unfailing, and civic organizations in bloom. But that is a backward glance; at the time Dahl's description was consistent with what many intellectuals pictured as "apathy" and "complacency." On television, the Cleavers and the Nelsons were happy as clams, but many leaders of opinion sensed an America adrift. The concerns were widespread enough that President Dwight D. Eisenhower appointed a commission to think about "Goals for Americans." Still in this mood, President John F. Kennedy established national standards on fitness for a people whose flabbiness was physical as well as moral and civic.

Political leaders believed Americans needed to summon virtue and vigor to stand up to the Russians in the Cold War, and they worried, in sometimes stridently masculine tones, that America had gone soft. The Cold War challenge also placed in relief a growing domestic conflict: a conflict about race. Facing it would transform not only race relations but also every corner of American life, city and suburb, home, work, and school, public and private. It would extend the reach of the national government into everyday life and magnify the place of Washington in the public's moral imagination.

There are many dimensions to this change, but its most enduring implication for the citizen's political experience has been a profound revolution in rights—a growing inclination of people and organized groups to define politics in terms of rights, a growing willingness of the federal government to enforce individuals' claims to constitutional rights, and a widening of the domain of "politics" propelled by rights-consciousness. Both the nationalization of politics and the "rights revolution" have been encouraged by, and further encouraged, the privatization of social life. This tripod of mutually reinforcing social forces—the expansion of government, the proliferation of rights, and the intensification of private social life—defines American political experience at the end of the twentieth century. It provides the framework in which a new model "rights-regarding" citizen is ascendant.

But for better or for worse? Is a rights-conscious citizenship a chastened citizenship, all too effortlessly accommodating an individualistic and privatized culture? Or is the rights-conscious citizen someone who has found inside a private-regarding world a fresh source of energy for public life? This chapter analyzes the rise of the rights-regarding citizen since World War II; the next chapter will try to assess whether this model of citizenship has redeemed American democracy, or imperiled it, or remade it on a new plane.

The Private Life of the People of Plenty

At the time John Dewey was lecturing about the public and its problems, only half of American homes had electricity; in urban areas 70 percent had electricity, on farms 4 percent. Thirty years later 99 percent of all dwellings were electrified.[2]

The integration of rural America into a national culture has been so complete that there remains little memory of how deep a divide there once was. What began with the railroads and was boosted by rural free delivery, Sears mail-order catalogs, automobiles, roads, consolidated schools, and radio was not finished until after the New Deal. The integration of rural areas into national life meant declining power for the countryside's Protestantism. William Jennings Bryan succumbed to Clarence Darrow at the Scopes "monkey" trial in 1925, the drys lost to the wets with the repeal of Prohibition in 1933, and eventually—but not until the 1960s—rural districts in state legislatures lost ground to the multi-racial, multi-ethnic urban centers.

From 1929 to 1944 the number of children under fourteen declined 1.5 million but, rebounding after the war, grew by twenty million by 1960. During this "baby boom," people bought cars, houses, and washing machines, invested in schools, and created new markets in toys, children's books, and leisure activities, making up for the lost time of the Depression and war years. The economy grew during this period in spectacular fashion. From 1947 through 1973 real median family income (in 1984 dollars) rose from $14,100 to $28,200. After 1973 real wages stagnated and even declined (down to a median family income of $26,433 in 1984).[3] Even so, the period of boom was dramatic, the subsequent decline was muffled. There was, in fact, from 1973 to 1984 a continued *increase* in real consumer expenditure per capita—not because of a growing economy but because of a growing proportion of the population in the paid labor force, a slowing birthrate, and an increase in consumer debt.[4]

One thing abundance bought was privacy. The number of persons sixty-five and over grew from thirteen million to twenty million between 1950 and 1970, but the number of them living in their children's households declined from 2.8 million to 2.3 million. Six in ten unmarried adults lived alone by 1970, compared to three in ten in 1950.[5] Sociologists saw all of this as a mixed blessing. With affluence came not only privacy but the curtailed utility of sociability as well. "Each family," as one sociologist put it, "has its own vacuum cleaner, its own set of pots and pans, its own transport, supply of water, heat, etc. Thus the necessity for social interaction, the necessity to share, is no longer a driving force in communities of abundance."[6] In postwar America, and in different ways in all modern industrial societies, abundance and privacy amplified the tendency in metropolitan life to create strongly differentiated territories—work, shopping, entertainment, and household each with its own zone, linked by public transportation, private automobiles, and telephones. The worlds of work, home, shopping, and leisure do not overlap, and one does not casually see or regularly engage with the same people in different spheres.

The townsperson is connected socially, politically, and economically to the town. Metropolitan man or woman, in contrast, lives a divided life, socially connected to a neighborhood or church, politically linked to a city or incorporated suburb, economically tied to a workplace as much as an hour's drive from home, and as a consumer oriented to the metropolitan area as a whole. Compared to the Swedes or the British, Americans have more contact with their neighbors, participate much more in church activities, work more hours in the day (with relatively frequent moonlighting), and participate in community affairs about as often.[7] In some ways, then, Americans remain more civic-minded and neighborly than many other national groups. Even so, the spatial privatization of life is more extreme in America than elsewhere. Americans are much more likely than others to own their own homes and to lavish great sums of time and money improving them. Sociologist David Popenoe observes that people tend to want more space, not less, more privacy, not less, and "where space is relatively abundant, and public and economic limits are weak, as in the United States, community spatial patterns are very much the product, for the most part unintended, of millions of such private spatial choices."[8]

For the most part—but not entirely—unintended. Government has not been an innocent bystander. "One of the ways in which the welfare state promotes happiness," writes the social democratic thinker Michael Walzer, "is by encouraging people to stay home."[9] In the 1950s and 1960s, the Federal Housing Administration was more likely to guarantee mortgages for homeowners in secure rather than "unstable" neighborhoods. This subsidized the growing suburbs. So did federal highway programs and taxes on gasoline that are far lower than in most industrialized nations. The high degree of local self-government in the United States also spurred suburban development and central city impoverishment. Much more than in Europe, local governing units control their own public services and determine their own zoning ordinances. They also raise their own revenues, primarily through property taxes. As wealthy citizens have moved out to the suburbs, the core cities have lost their tax base and suffered a rise in the proportion of residents who pay little into the city's coffers but demand much of its social services.[10]

Suburbs stand right next to television as a modern phenomenon about which almost no one has anything favorable to say. Sociologist David Riesman's critique was as evocative as any in his 1958 essay, "The Suburban Sadness." The suburbanites evinced "a pervasive low-keyed unpleasure." Moving to the suburbs for control and security, he observed, they seemed nonetheless to have lost the very control over their lives that they sought.[11] For all of that, the privatization suburbs exemplified has rightly been called "one of the landmark achievements of Western civilization."[12] Having a private life is "what the rich people of the world have always sought and usually had."[13] Now it is a perquisite of middle-class life and, beyond the middle class, it is available to large masses of people, free to mix with the people they choose rather than the ones they happen to live next to, able to attach themselves to subcultures without incurring the withering disapproval of a local majority.

But is the result an impoverished public life?

The Rights Revolution, I: Leading Toward *Brown*

On September 30, 1935, Frank Palko smashed the window of a music shop and ran off with a radio. Stopped by two Bridgeport, Connecticut, police officers, he shot and killed them both. The state sought a first-degree murder conviction, but Palko was found guilty of second-degree murder. The prosecutors, believing that the judge had made significant errors in the trial, appealed and won a retrial. In the second trial Palko was convicted of first-degree murder and sentenced to death.

Was this not double jeopardy, prohibited by the Fifth Amendment's declaration that no person shall be "subject for the same offence to be twice put in jeopardy of life or limb"? Palko's attorneys appealed Palko's second conviction on this basis, but the Fifth Amendment constrained the powers of the federal government, not the state governments. In

1833, the Supreme Court had explicitly declared that the Bill of Rights did not apply to state laws. Not until the passage of the Fourteenth Amendment after the Civil War did the Constitution acquire language that could justify using the Bill of Rights to invalidate state legislation. Even so, after Reconstruction, the Court rarely invoked the Fourteenth Amendment to strike down state laws.

In the *Palko* case, in an opinion by Justice Benjamin Cardozo, Palko's argument was rebuffed and he subsequently went to the electric chair. It could be of no consolation to Palko, then, but in losing his battle, he won a war. Cardozo held that the Fourteenth Amendment did not automatically incorporate the Bill of Rights as applying to state laws. But he also held that *some* of the liberties guaranteed in the Bill of Rights (though not the prohibition against double jeopardy) were so fundamental to our concept of "ordered liberty" and were so closely tied to "fundamental principles of liberty and justice which lie at the base of all our civil and political institutions" that they are necessarily applicable to the states. Cardozo singled out "freedom of thought, and speech" and the concept of "due process." [14] With these words Justice Cardozo helped make the Fourteenth Amendment the cornerstone of a new constitutional order.

Palko v. *Connecticut* was an important early step in a Supreme Court revolution that constructed a "second Bill of Rights" by making most of the original Bill of Rights enforceable against state laws. A few months after *Palko*, the Court handed down its decision in *United States* v. *Carolene Products*. In this otherwise obscure case, Justice Harlan Fiske Stone inserted a startling footnote in his majority opinion. Justice Stone affirmed that the Court would normally defer to state legislatures and the Congress so long as there seemed to be some rational basis for the legislature's actions. But then Justice Stone identified in "Footnote Four," as legal scholars refer to it, three situations in which the Court would not routinely defer to the legislatures or the Congress.

First, the Court would not presume constitutionality when a law on its face seemed to violate a specific constitutional protection, including those of the Bill of Rights. Second, the Court would not defer to legislatures when the law in question impinged on "the political process itself" and therefore might limit the capacity of the people to overturn bad laws. So restrictions on the right to vote, the free activity of political organizations, or the exercise of freedom of speech or assembly would be examined closely. Third, laws directed at particular religious, national, or racial minorities or that might have stemmed from prejudice against "discrete and insular minorities" and could limit the operation of the political processes normally expected to protect minorities also would be examined with careful scrutiny.[15] All three clauses gave notice to the states and the Congress that the judiciary was watching and would not routinely defer to them when the liberty of individuals as guaranteed in the Bill of Rights was at stake.

Of the three *Carolene Products* footnote clauses, the last was the most original. The founders had sought to protect minorities from majority tyranny, but what they meant by "minority" in their relatively homogeneous society (a society made all the more homogeneous by their presumption that Native Americans and African slaves stood outside it) was a temporary political or ideological minority, not an enduring minority defined by race, religion, or national origin. Only with the *Carolene Products* footnote did these ascribed minorities become "a special object of judicial protection." [16] Probably reflective of social science thought that was coming to see "minorities" so defined as having certain social and psychological features in common, and certainly responsive to Hitler's rising threat in Europe, the *Carolene Products* footnote was the first significant legal landmark to recognize and define minorities in terms of the civil rights owed them.

In 1944, in a bitter twist, the thinking in *Carolene Products* was advanced in *Korematsu v. United States*. In this case the Court again deferred to another branch of government, this time the executive branch and the military order to detain Japanese-Americans on the West Coast. Justice Hugo Black, speaking for the majority, accepted the government's argument that in this instance military necessity justified the classification of persons by race or national origin, but he added that this was a very rare exception: "All legal restrictions which curtail the civil rights of a single racial group are immediately suspect. That is not to say that all such restrictions are unconstitutional. It is to say that courts must subject them to the most rigid scrutiny. Pressing public necessity may sometimes justify the existence of such restrictions; racial antagonism never can."[17] The decision in *Korematsu* in effect endorsed the racist premises of the military order that created the West Coast internment camps and deprived Japanese-Americans of their political and civil rights. Even so, Justice Black's opinion reemphasized the Court's new concern to protect individual citizens from the racial prejudices of their neighbors enacted into law.

These cases established a new beachhead for judicial activism concerning civil and political liberties. From the early twentieth century until 1937, the Court had repeatedly struck down state laws that restricted "freedom of contract." The Constitution says nothing about "freedom of contract," but the Court read its understanding of the limited role of government and laissez-faire economics into the Constitution. So, again and again, state laws limiting work hours or establishing minimum wages or otherwise seeking to even up the bargaining power of workers and employers were found unconstitutional. This happened with such regularity that Franklin Roosevelt, seeing his New Deal programs falling under the axe of the Court, devised his "court-packing" plan. But in the Court's 1937 term, with Roosevelt ready to submit to Congress his plan to add new (pro–New Deal) justices to the Court, Justice Owen Roberts turned around and provided the fifth vote to sustain New Deal legislation. This "switch in time that saved nine" closed out one long era in Court history as the justices, including new Roosevelt appointees such as Felix Frankfurter, articulated a philosophy of judicial restraint.

The legacy of *Palko*, *Carolene Products*, and *Korematsu*, however, is that restraint would be selective. There would be not restraint but close scrutiny when it came to governmental intrusion on individual liberties. This was stated most eloquently by Justice Robert Jackson's majority opinion in a 1943 case upholding the right of Jehovah's Witnesses to refuse to salute the flag (because such a pledge of loyalty violated their religious convictions): "The very purpose of the Bill of Rights was to withdraw certain subjects from the vicissitudes of political controversy, to place them beyond the reach of majorities and officials and to establish them as legal principles to be applied by the courts."[18]

The Court, in a word, would use Hamiltonian principles of government (the relatively autonomous power of a Court appointed for life and far removed from the changing will or whim of the populace) to achieve Jeffersonian ends (the protection of individual liberties from the tyrannies of state power). The intellectual grounds for the Warren Court were laid.

The Warren Court of 1953 to 1969 put rights on the national agenda as never before. Beginning with its unanimous decision in *Brown v. Board of Education of Topeka* (1954) that found racial segregation in schools unconstitutional, the Court launched "a revolution made by judges."[19] Sharply advancing a view of democracy as one in which individuals can effectively claim rights against the state, the Warren Court became a leading agent and symbol of social and political change. By 1969, it completed the work of nationalizing the Bill of Rights that the Supreme Court of 1937 had begun.

In doing so, the Court made many legal theorists uneasy. It seemed to enshrine a new "substantive due process," the legal rationale for the much reviled economic interventionism of the early twentieth century. Most leading law professors were political liberals, however, and if they quibbled about the Warren Court's reasoning, they still applauded its substantive conclusions. Law and social progress seemed inextricably united.[20] It would not be long, however, before anxiety spread across the political spectrum that the courts were biting off more than they could chew, taking on a "greater responsibility for making public policy" in the United States than in any other democracy in the world.[21]

Between 1850 and 1935 the Supreme Court heard a total of sixteen cases concerning discrimination on the basis of race, religion, national origin, or sex, and in only nine of these cases did the person claiming to have been discriminated against prevail. From 1936 to 1945 the Court heard seventeen more cases, and the party alleging discrimination won twelve times. From 1946 to 1964 the Court passed on 106 discrimination cases, favoring those alleging discrimination ninety times.[22] To count things up in a somewhat different way, in 1935 the Court considered questions of civil liberties or civil rights in two of 160 opinions; in 1989 it was sixty-six of 132.[23] The Supreme Court and American constitutionalism in general shifted from an emphasis in the nineteenth century on "powers," concerned with the relative jurisdiction and authority of the state and federal governments, to an emphasis on rights and the obligations of government and law to the claims of individuals.[24]

The lesson here for citizenship can now be spelled out: until 1937 citizens could seek to influence the state or to be served by the state through their legislative representatives (and, to a lesser degree, through their own participation on juries, in government jobs as recipients of patronage, in the militias, or in the armed services). But the courts as makers of policy were not on the map of citizenship. One went to court to resolve a dispute with a neighbor, not to challenge governmental authority. In the nineteenth century, the courtroom was rarely a focal point of popular protest, political theory, or social reform. Now, a new avenue of national citizen power and a new model for political action emerged.

The new model citizenship added the courtroom to the voting booth as a locus of civic participation. It did not arrive at this by acts of the judiciary alone. It was pushed by voluntary political associations that turned to litigation as a politically effective lever. To be sure, a more rights-conscious Supreme Court after 1937 helped encourage the development of these groups or their turn to legal strategies. The National Association for the Advancement of Colored People, founded in 1909, only began its Legal Defense and Educational Fund in 1939, thereby providing full-time staff for litigation and enabling donors to make tax-deductible contributions.[25] The American Bar Association established its Committee on the Bill of Rights in 1938, and the American Jewish Congress its Commission on Law and Social Action in 1945.[26] Political movements and political organizations that, in the past, had only legislative points of access to political power now found that the judicial system offered an alternative route to their goals. As early as 1949 a Yale Law Journal article referred to these groups as "Private Attorneys-General."[27]

The NAACP and the American Civil Liberties Union have been the leading private associations in spearheading the expansion of rights. The NAACP, founded as a biracial organization committed to protesting the persecution of African-Americans, was, at first, relatively impotent. In the 1912 election, the Democratic, Republican, or Progressive platform did not breathe a word about civil rights—nor did the programs of the socialist parties, for that matter. The nearly total exclusion of blacks from voting in the South made it easy for the political system to turn its back on them. In the three-way race in 1912, it appeared that opinion leaders in the black community might have some political leverage, and W. E. B. Du Bois endorsed Woodrow Wilson on the basis of promises Wilson extended to African-American leaders. But the Wilson administration engineered the segregation of employment in the federal government itself. The political frustrations of the black community did not begin to change at all until the mid-1930s. In Franklin Roosevelt's first term, the power of the South in the Congress, coupled with the overriding priority of economic recovery, led Roosevelt to turn aside the advice of aides like Harold Ickes, who was committed to the cause of African-Americans. Ickes, a former president of the Chicago NAACP serving as Roosevelt's secretary of the interior, took action on his own: he desegregated cafeterias and rest rooms in the Interior Department. In the Public Works Administration, also under his supervision, he insisted on nondiscriminatory hiring.[28]

In his second term, Roosevelt began to move on civil rights. The change was in part sponsored by Eleanor Roosevelt, who worked closely with leaders of black organizations and self-consciously sought to be their voice in the president's ear. Mrs. Roosevelt publicly supported efforts to abolish the poll tax and advocated a federal anti-lynching law. This empowered New Dealers close to her to insist on equal treatment in the agencies under their control. The president appointed an African-American, William Hastie, to a federal judgeship for the first time in American history. His new attorney general, Frank Murphy, replacing the first term's Homer Cummings, created a Civil Rights Division of the Department of Justice and promised it would pursue "the aggressive protection of fundamental rights inherent in a free people." A set of African-American advisers came to be known as "the Black Cabinet," a phenomenon unprecedented in national politics. This group included both New Deal appointees—there were forty-five blacks in cabinet and New Deal agency appointments by 1935, and also leaders of major civil rights groups like the NAACP and the Urban League. By 1936, this group began meeting weekly to coordinate civil rights strategy. By 1937, Roosevelt pointedly supported Claude Pepper's successful effort to repeal the poll tax in Florida and again in 1938 spoke decisively against the poll tax as "contrary to fundamental democracy." [29]

In 1932, prominent black editors and other community leaders had urged blacks to relinquish their Civil War–based allegiance to the Republican Party. Relatively few did so, and most black voters cast ballots for Hoover, but the tide was turning. Especially in the North, the number of black voters grew, thanks to continuing migration from the South, strong registration drives, and unusually high turnouts of black registered voters. Even in the South, at least in urban areas, the hopefulness the New Deal engendered helped spawn new black political organizations and successful efforts at voter registration. In 1936, both parties—for the first time ever—directed strong appeals to black voters, but the Democrats' appeal was backed by more significant actions than Republicans could point to, and 76 percent of black voters turned to Roosevelt. [30] The politics as well as the legal doctrine that would make the civil rights movement possible was emerging.

The Rights Revolution, II: From Montgomery

It is now a familiar story: Rosa Parks had worked all day at her job as a tailor's assistant in the Montgomery Fair department store in Montgomery, Alabama. Her neck and shoulder were sore when she left work. She went across the street to the drugstore to buy a heating pad. She didn't find one but bought a few other things before going to her bus stop. The buses were crowded that evening, and the only seat she found was an aisle seat in the row just behind the seats reserved for whites only. As more people got on at the next few stops, blacks moved to the rear and stood. When a white man was left standing after all seats in the first rows were occupied, the bus driver called out to Mrs. Parks and the other blacks in her row to relinquish their seats. The practice was that the whole row would have to be emptied of blacks before a white would sit. At first no one moved. Then the driver repeated himself. The others moved, but not Mrs. Parks. "Look, woman," the driver said to her, "I told you I wanted the seat. Are you going to stand up?"

"No," she said.

"If you don't stand up, I'm going to have you arrested." She told him to go right ahead. He got off the bus, went to a phone, and called the police. Soon thereafter, Mrs. Parks was apprehended and taken to the city jail. It was December 1, 1955, and although no one knew it, the decisive phase of the civil rights movement had just begun.

Mrs. Parks later said, "I had not thought about it and I had taken no previous resolution until it happened, and then I simply decided that I would not get up. I was tired, but I was usually tired at the end of the day, and I was not feeling well, but then there had been many days when I had not felt well. I had felt for a long time, that if I was ever told to get up so a white person could sit, that I would refuse to do so."

Another passenger on the bus told a friend of hers what had happened. That friend called E. D. Nixon, past president of the Montgomery NAACP. When Nixon could not learn from the police what had happened, he called Clifford Durr, a prominent liberal white attorney. Durr got the information and, together with Nixon, posted bond for Mrs. Parks.

This was not an impromptu alliance. Mrs. Parks, Nixon, Clifford Durr, and his wife, Virginia, had worked together before. Mrs. Parks had been active in the NAACP since 1943 and had worked with Nixon in voter registration. Nixon knew the Durrs through their shared political interests. Clifford Durr had been a prominent New Dealer in Washington, serving as a Federal Communications commissioner, while Virginia Durr was a dogged activist in liberal causes, including serving as vice chairman of the National Committee to Abolish the Poll Tax in the 1940s. Mrs. Durr had asked Nixon at one point if he could recommend a good seamstress; he recommended Rosa Parks, who frequently visited the Durrs' home beginning in 1953 or 1954. As they drove to the jail to post bond, Nixon and Clifford Durr discussed the possibility of Mrs. Parks becoming a test case. They had been seeking a test case but in the recent past had rejected several possibilities because they did not have full faith in the character of the person arrested under the segregation laws. They knew Mrs. Parks's strong character and they had seen a new self-confidence in her since they had helped her to attend a two-week interracial conference that summer at the Highlander Folk School.[31]

Rosa Parks's courageous defiance of the segregation laws was neither isolated nor spontaneous. Opportunity, in this case, knocked at the door of one well prepared to take advantage of it. Decades of struggle and of the nurturing of associations and friendships dedicated to the cause lay behind it. Ironically, some of this was made possible by segregation itself, which facilitated the development of black institutions and helped build ties among blacks across differences of education and class.

The church provided the central institution of the black community and the early civil rights movement. It offered a rich culture of song, oratory, prayer, ceremony, and ideology that could easily be understood as encouraging of liberation. In the church-sponsored movement, legal and political struggles became a moral crusade: ". . . that's what got people marching," recalled Methodist minister Joseph Lowery, a leader in the Southern Christian Leadership Conference. "It opened up people's eyes for the first time to how ugly and immoral segregation was. . . ."[32]

The church not only had a broad community following but in its ministers a leadership economically independent of the white community. It also had a physical presence fit for large meetings. There was a mass meeting daily at one or another participating church in Montgomery during the boycott. Here courage, enthusiasm, and energy were renewed every day. The mass meeting was "the pulse and lifeline of the movement—its information center; the occasion for inspiration, rejuvenation, and commitment by means of rousing sermons and unifying black spirituals; the opportunity for planning and strategy sessions; and the financial center."[33] This last was important: The churches were the center for financing civil rights. The NAACP had been financed largely in the churches and many of its leaders were ministers. NAACP chapters met in churches, often the only available places for its meetings. The church basis of the SCLC gave it important access to funds.

Segregation, then, helped solidify the institutions and networks that would turn it on its head. A second irony is that the white power structure's attack on the NAACP helped the movement, too. The attacks began in the early 1950s and reached a crescendo in 1956 when Louisiana, Alabama, and Texas all secured injunctions stopping NAACP operations in their states. Laws specifically designed to curtail NAACP activities were enacted in Florida, South Carolina, and Virginia. The NAACP successfully fought the injunctions in Louisiana and Texas, but in Alabama the NAACP was forced to shut down. In 1955, there were 129,000 NAACP members in the South, but only 80,000 by 1957. Two hundred twenty-six branches in the South closed completely.[34] In breaking the hegemony of the NAACP, the segregationist South forced civil rights activists to try new, nonlegalistic tactics. Protest was deprofessionalized. Repression helped shift the movement's center of gravity from the courtroom and its motions to the churches and mass organizing.[35]

The mass movement that began in Montgomery led to dramatic changes in American race relations, including political equality for blacks enforced by federal law as well as significant initiatives toward equal treatment in education, housing, public transportation and accommodations, and public and private employment. But the success of the movement was more than this, as the young Martin Luther King, Jr. declared in 1956 when he took the Supreme Court's decision that Montgomery's bus segregation was unconstitutional to signal an end to the bus boycott. He told a mass meeting that this is "not a victory merely for 50,000 Negroes in Montgomery. That's too small. It's not a victory merely for sixteen million Negroes over the United States. . . . It will be a victory for justice and a victory for good will and a victory for the forces of light."[36] King may have imagined, but few others did, just how far-reaching a transformation Montgomery had begun.

Civil Rights Reverberating

The civil rights movement provided a model and inspiration for a wide array of new social movements and political organizations. This bold example, even for those who did not participate in it, galvanized a new egalitarianism in American culture at large. Its radiating influence made litigation a tool of social change, it secured direct action and nonviolent demonstrations as weapons of protest, and it fixed a rights-centered citizenship at the center of American civic aspiration. Each of these points deserves attention.

Litigation. First, the emphasis in the civil rights struggle on the courtroom and on the Constitution as an ally for social change brought an intensified attention to strategies of litigation. Even organizations like the American Civil Liberties Union that had long employed litigation now gave it renewed attention. The ACLU financed its legal activities by the volunteer services of its member lawyers, membership dues, and occasional philanthropic donations, but not until the 1960s did it establish a tax-deductible litigation arm. Aryeh Neier, appointed executive director in 1970, aggressively sought foundation support for specifically identified projects on prisoners' rights, mental health patients' rights, military justice, and other causes. A new generation of litigating liberals emerged, stimulated also, in part, by the organizing brio of Ralph Nader. Nader established the Center for the Study of Responsive Law in 1967 and soon thereafter the Public Interest Research Group and a network of other public interest groups.

Public interest law emerged in the 1960s, grew in the 1970s, and despite losing some ground in the Reagan years, is now well institutionalized. Before 1969 there were only twenty-three public interest law centers that employed fewer than fifty full-time attorneys. By 1975 this grew to 108 centers with 600 attorneys and by 1984 to 158 groups with 906 lawyers. Different groups focused on minorities, poverty, women, children, prisoners, the disabled, gays and lesbians, workers, civil rights generally, environmental issues, consumers, and others.[37] Most public interest law firms were so dedicated to liberal causes that the term "public interest" was at first closely identified with liberal interests. Conservative litigating organizations date to the early twentieth century, but a new set of such organizations emerged in the 1970s as a response to liberal successes in the courts.[38]

What happened outside the government was reinforced and promoted by the creation of federally funded legal services. The War on Poverty established legal services for the poor in the mid-1960s. The civil rights movement was again the inspiration, giving prominence to "the model of volunteer lawyer as social reformer."[39] Office of Economic Opportunity legal services, therefore, unlike most legal aid, focused on "law reform" as much as on serving clients one by one, and lawyers in legal services brought over a hundred cases to the Supreme Court in the program's first decade.[40] OEO lawyers not only initiated suits against hospitals that sought to reduce medical services to the poor, against landlords using eviction in ways prohibited by law, and against private companies seeking to defraud the poor, but also against government agencies, especially those responsible for providing welfare benefits. This work led to landmark cases that expanded citizens' rights to welfare and to fair hearings and due process inside the welfare bureaucracy.[41]

All of this contributed to and emerged from the egalitarian spirit of the day. The hundreds of "community action" agencies established through the Office of Economic Opportunity involved the poor people they served as decision-making participants. As the law declared, programs were to be run with "maximum feasible participation of the residents of the areas and the members of the groups served." The rule of thumb was that at least one third of the people on the policy-making bodies of community action agencies should come from the low-income groups the agencies assisted. Despite the practical failures of many of these programs, they initiated a notable conceptual change in defining powerlessness as one of the causes of poverty itself.[42] The community action groups specifically and the 1960s ethos of participation generally also encouraged innovations like civilian review boards for the police, powerful organized tenant groups in housing policy, community control of public schools, and the creation of neighborhood-based "little city halls" to bring citizens in closer touch with city government.[43]

Protest. Second, the civil rights movement helped inspire a new generation of young activists trained in and willing to use direct action methods. The role of the civil rights movement is avowed in the "Port Huron Statement," the founding document of Students for a Democratic Society in 1962. This statement identified its authors as "people of this generation, bred in at least modest comfort, housed now in universities, looking uncomfortably to the world we inherit." Their complacency, they write, was broken by events "too troubling to dismiss," the first of them being "the permeating and victimizing fact of human degradation, symbolized by the Southern struggle against racial bigotry." This was what "compelled most of us from silence to activism."[44] The students, who in the next several years would spearhead the antiwar movement and support a wide range of "liberation" movements in the 1960s and 1970s, found their original inspiration in civil rights. Many student leaders gained their formative political experience in the South. This made the New Left a significant departure from any prior expression of American populism; even in the 1930s the Left's efforts to take "the Negro problem" into consideration rarely took inspiration from black political efforts themselves.[45]

The student-spawned movements took less inspiration from the NAACP's courtroom strategies than from the mass demonstrations and civil disobedience of Montgomery, Selma, Albany, and Greenwood, the Freedom Rides, and the citizenship schools. Students risked and sometimes suffered prison sentences for refusing to register for the military draft, picketed military recruiters on campus, organized mass demonstrations to shut down college ROTC units, blockaded military recruiting stations, and gathered with other antiwar activists in the hundreds of thousands in New York, Washington, San Francisco, and elsewhere at political rallies. Democracy, the civil rights movement had taught, was to be found and to be made in the streets.

Rights. Third, the legacy of the civil rights movement was the widening of the reach of the idea of citizenship itself and the growing acceptance that citizenship is guaranteed by the federal government. Because the civil rights movement and subsequent social protests framed their objectives as demands for rights, they not only appealed to federal power for help but also lobbied to make the federal government more powerful. "Rights talk," political scientist Hugh Heclo has observed, "not only invited, it virtually compelled the nationalization of public policy."[46] This was especially so because the civil rights movement demonstrated with terrifying clarity that the Southern states failed to preserve, or even care about, individual rights.

The chief exception to a rights-based politics that saw Washington as a friend was the antiwar movement. Here the power of the federal government was enemy, not ally. It was very uncomfortable for activists to acknowledge that the government they looked to for domestic justice was responsible for a foreign policy they judged unwise, illegal, and immoral. Lyndon Johnson embodied all these contradictions, both courageous savior and tragic blunderer, and therefore the most difficult of all postwar presidents to assess.

The nationalization of public policy that rights-based social movements promoted had already been advanced by the New Deal, by the mobilization for World War II, and by the consolidation of the industrial-military complex in the Cold War. What the civil rights–inspired movements of the sixties added was that federalization became not just a by-product of national mobilization but also a normative end.[47] The Supreme Court underlined this change in its rapid move from a focus on the proper distribution of powers between federal and state governments to a new concentration on individual rights guaranteed by Washington.

Again, the Court was not alone in this. The entire logic of the civil rights movement enjoined federal controls and the use of national power to circumvent local control, and here the Congress and the executive also had a hand. Take the debates over the Civil Rights Act of 1957. President Eisenhower, reluctant to push on school desegregation, nonetheless felt committed to voting rights. He backed legislation to enfranchise black citizens in the South. His bill ran into trouble, however. It provided that federal judges could jail for contempt any individuals who disobeyed federal civil rights injunctions. Southern opponents objected that this jeopardized the right to trial by jury. They argued that blacks' right to vote could not be advanced without threatening whites' right to a jury trial. Liberals quickly pointed out the obvious: juries in the South were generally selected from lists of registered voters, and since registered voters were almost exclusively white, a Southern jury would never convict an official cited for contempt of civil rights law.

President Eisenhower, defending his position, quoted Chief Justice William Howard Taft's remark that putting a jury trial between a court order and its enforcement welcomed anarchy. The administration held firm, but in the Senate, liberals felt they had to compromise. Labor, after all, had long been wary of the federal injunction power, and while the

American Federation of Labor supported the bill as originally proposed, John L. Lewis of the United Mine Workers came out for a jury-trial amendment. In the end, a compromise provided jury trials if the official who violated a civil rights injunction risked more than forty-five days in jail and a fine of more than $300.[48]

The story of the 1957 Civil Rights Act indicates that the power of the federal judiciary did not grow by itself; congressional and presidential initiatives were necessary to endorse and encourage it. Legislation like the Voting Rights Act of 1965 and many of the important environmental laws of the 1960s and 1970s authorized private suits for the enforcement of federal regulations. Congress has also increasingly encouraged judicial review of federal administrative agencies. More legislation, from the increasingly activist Congress of the 1960s, provided more occasions for interpretation. Even in later years, when the Supreme Court moved toward narrow or cautious readings of the Constitution, expansive readings of *statutes*, rather than the Constitution, have often been upheld.[49]

The courts have been far from alone in promoting court-based solutions to political problems. Only in law school hyperbole or in neoconservative rhetoric is the Supreme Court a lone ranger of the rights revolution. The interaction of rights litigation by voluntary organizations, the changing receptiveness of the courts to such litigation, the innovations of the civil rights movement in the 1950s and the movements it inspired thereafter, the increasingly rapid national and international transmission of egalitarian norms all contributed. So did federalism itself. With multiple points of power and multiple gates to decisions, even as political power gravitated to Washington, authority in Washington was fragmented and fractured. Without presidential leadership and without a coherent and responsible governing party, individuals and organizations influenced lower federal courts and congressional subcommittees to recognize new rights and initiate policy change. Such activities gained political support in Washington and popular support beyond because they could be mobilized in the effort to face down the world historical threat of Soviet communism. Just as federal aid to education could be adopted because science served the international battle against communism, so civil rights could be championed because mistreatment of blacks made for powerful communist propaganda.[50]

A demand for rights stimulated the growth of federal power; federal power stimulated the growing demand for rights. Consider the case of women's rights. Women came to claim their "rights" in part because a federal agency, the Department of Labor's Women's Bureau, provided an organizing tool. Federal legislation (Title VII of the Civil Rights Act of 1964) established a statutory rationale, and federal intransigence (the failure of the Equal Employment Opportunity Commission to enforce Title VII) offered grounds for indignation. What happened, in short, was this: more by accident than by intention, the Civil Rights Act of 1964 banned employment discrimination on the basis of gender as well as race. Representative Howard Smith, a powerful Virginia Democrat, introduced an amendment barring gender discrimination, hoping that so ludicrous a proposal would sink the whole measure.[51]

Although treated in the Congress with considerable amusement, Smith's amendment passed and became law, despite the absence of an organized women's movement. In 1966, the Equal Employment Opportunity Commission, charged with enforcing Title VII, issued guidelines that, among other things, allowed sex-segregated job advertising ("men wanted" and "women wanted" columns) but not race-segregated ads. The EEOC's refusal to take sex discrimination as seriously as racial discrimination aroused resentment among some key Washington figures, including several women who served on the President's Commission on the Status of Women. Meanwhile, Betty Friedan, author of *The Feminine Mystique* (1963), had attracted a national following and came to know the "feminist underground" in Washington as she began work toward a book on sex discrimination law. An EEOC commissioner, Richard Graham, urged her to organize a civil rights organization for women; so did Sonia Pressman, an EEOC staff attorney. This came to a boil at a Washington convention of the state commissions on the status of women. Friedan and others were angered by the ineffectual response of EEOC and the Women's Bureau to their objections to EEOC enforcement guidelines, so they resolved to organize a group whose demands would be taken seriously. On a paper napkin, Friedan wrote down the name, National Organization for Women, and the flagship organization of the modern women's movement was born.[52] Federal initiatives, then, preceded a mass women's movement and provided the legislation and network of communication that initially made it possible.

Welfare mothers came to claim rights in the 1960s, also out of federal support. Women who received Aid to Families with Dependent Children (AFDC), the primary welfare program originally established by the Social Security Act of 1935, began meeting in the 1960s. They came together through the Community Action Programs, the Great Society anti-poverty initiative that had mandated "maximum feasible participation" of members of the communities served. Their discussions were the seedbed of political activity for welfare recipients that led to the National Welfare Rights Organization. The welfare mothers provided the local resources and womanpower when George Wiley, a civil rights activist and in 1966 founder of the Poverty/Rights Action Center in Washington, created the national organization.[53]

Born to an old Rhode Island African-American family, his father the editor of a black newspaper, Wiley went to the University of Rhode Island and then Cornell for a Ph.D. in chemistry. While successfully making his mark in chemistry as a teacher (first at Berkeley, then at Syracuse) and scholar, he became increasingly drawn into campus politics in the early 1960s at Syracuse. This led him finally, in 1965, to leave the academic world and take a full-time position as the second-in-command at CORE (the Congress of Racial Equality). But as tensions between blacks and whites in civil rights organizations mounted, Wiley, committed to the idea of interracial organizing, left CORE to organize the poor. Guided by ideas that activist social scientists Richard Cloward and Frances Fox Piven were advancing, he insisted that there were too few people, not too many, on welfare. He wanted the welfare rolls to grow and he saw poor people's connection to the welfare office as a site for organizing. "For millions—particularly people who can't work, the aged or female heads of households," he declared, "just encouraging them to assert their rights is a very attractive thing." He believed that people eligible for welfare could be a great source for political organizing: "The potential here is enormous for getting the people involved in demanding rights as human beings from a system that doesn't treat them as human beings."[54]

Wiley was right, though less in his conviction that the welfare office might offer a location for organizing than in his view that there were not enough people on welfare. Millions of people in 1965 were by social and economic circumstances fully qualified for welfare but did not receive it. Many did not know to apply for aid, others applied but were turned down by state officials who, often deliberately, misinterpreted the rules, and still others got a foot in the welfare door but were not provided all the assistance for which they qualified, and then were denied due process when they complained. As late as 1967, only 42 percent of people eligible for welfare received it; participation rates rose to 64 percent by 1970 and 87 percent by 1973.[55]

Federal provision of social welfare had not received comprehensive legislative enactment until the Social Security Act of 1935. The national government made substantial contributions to social welfare earlier, especially in the provision of pensions to veterans of the Union Army after the Civil War and in the early 1900s in social welfare subsidies for women's and children's health.[56] But specific outlays for specific purposes are different from general provisions taken to be a matter of right. The latter, traceable to the New Deal, finally came into its own in the 1960s when Aid to Families with Dependent Children expanded and Medicaid legislation made AFDC families eligible for medical services. Because of litigation, some of it initiated by government lawyers as part of the War on Poverty programs, rigid state rules about AFDC eligibility were struck down. Federal bureaucrats in the Johnson administration worked aggressively to deliver welfare benefits more effectively; a "social-welfare constituency" of bureaucrats, social workers, and social scientists pressed the changes.[57] Between 1960 and 1970 the number of AFDC recipients more than doubled, from 3.1 million to 7.4 million.[58] In the span of a decade from the early sixties to the early seventies, the percentage of the population judged "poor" by government standards dropped from 21 to 11 percent. (This figure would rise again in the 1980s, up to 14.5 percent by 1992.) The creation of Medicare (for the elderly), Medicaid (for the poor), the full development of the food stamp program, the passage of Supplemental Security Income (SSI) for the aged, blind, and disabled (1972), and the indexing of SSI and social security payments to the Consumer Price Index (1972) so that benefits would keep pace with inflation all contributed to reducing poverty and to making federal social welfare a massive enterprise and a much larger share of the federal budget.

And this was just the beginning.

The Silent New Deal and the Widening Web of Citizenship, 1964–1975

The civil rights movement opened the door to a widening web of both constitutionally guaranteed citizen rights and statutory acts based on an expanded understanding of citizens' entitlements, state obligations, and the character of due process. This affected not only the civil and political rights of African-Americans but, as I have suggested, the rights of women and of the poor and, increasingly, of minority groups of all sorts as well.

In popular thinking about the sixties, there is a tendency to settle on images—of students burning draft cards, young women burning bras (though this may never have happened), be-ins in San Francisco, body bags returning from Vietnam, the Watts riot, the police clubbing demonstrators outside the Democratic National Convention in Chicago, and the assassinations of Kennedy, King, and Kennedy. The visual record of the sixties draws our attention to revolution in the streets.

There *was* revolution in the streets and it made a big difference. But there was also a second revolution, harder to picture, at least as profound and enduring in its influence: a revolution in the Congress, and the most energetic period of legislative activity since 1933–35. It significantly extended the reach of federal regulatory powers, spurring a federalization of national consciousness and a striking expansion of the arenas that could be authentically understood as "political"—that is, as having a relationship to things that government does or might be asked to do.

The legislative efforts that made this transformation possible are too often taken piece by piece, and we fail to recognize how bold and multi-faceted a change was under way. It has been called an "unsung" legislative revolution; I think it might justifiably be called the silent New Deal.[59] In the course of a decade, the federal government put more regulatory laws on the books than it had in the country's entire prior history.[60] In schools and in universities, in families, in the professions, in private places of employment, in human relations with the environment, and not least of all in political institutions themselves, including the political parties, the rights revolution brought federal power and national norms of equality to bear on local practices. In each of these domains, the outreach of the constitutional order spread ideals of equality, due process, and rights.

Schools. In the schools, there has been a visible legalization of human relations. Affirming the right of students to wear armbands as expressions of political (antiwar) protest, the Supreme Court declared in 1969 that students do not "shed their constitutional rights . . . at the schoolhouse gate." Stated as a simple truism, this was actually a sharp departure from prevailing doctrine that had granted teachers and school boards considerable power over individual students.[61] Subsequent legislative enactments like the Education for All Handicapped Children Act (1975) had great influence on the legalization of public school procedures. A handicapped rights movement gained momentum in the late 1960s and took to litigation to achieve its ends. Winning a key court victory in Pennsylvania in 1972, advocates for the mentally retarded brought their clients under constitutional protection.[62] In the movement for children's rights, student rights, and handicapped rights, organizations (like the Children's Defense Fund and the California Rural Legal Assistance Foundation) that had participated in civil rights and poverty law litigation played key roles and helped make the rights-orientation seem inevitable.

The Workplace. In workplaces, the emergence of formal personnel practices along with the expansion of norms of anti-discrimination has been a revolution. Over the past half century, large private firms have institutionalized formal personnel departments that take responsibility for establishing affirmative action policies mandated by federal rules and grievance procedures made necessary by unionization and collective bargaining agreements. As personnel administration has become increasingly professionalized, personnel relations specialists have disseminated norms of a legal culture of due process in the private sector.[63]

States began to pass laws prohibiting discrimination on the basis of race, creed, or color in 1945. The first equal employment opportunity law in the United States was New York's, in 1945. This was the first comprehensive and enforceable statute in the country's history to prohibit racial, religious, and ethnic job discrimination.[64] When the Congress passed the Civil Rights Act of 1964, including Title VII's banning of job discrimination, 61 percent of representatives in Congress came from states with their own equal employment opportunity legislation.[65] Until 1964 private employers could hire whomever they chose without any kind of interference from the federal government. Title VII of the Civil Rights Act of 1964 changed that.[66] On the federal level, other employee rights were provided by statute in the Equal Pay Act (1963), the Age Discrimination in Employment Act (1967), the Mine Safety Act (1969), the Occupational Safety and Health Act (1970), the Rehabilitation Act (1973), and the Employee Retirement Income Security Act (1974), as well as, much later, the Americans with Disabilities Act (1990) and the Family Leave Act (1993).[67]

Before the Wagner Act (1935) sanctioned collective bargaining and galvanized the labor movement, a nonunionized worker (and that meant the vast majority of workers) could be dismissed with no notice, no due process, and no recourse. Since 1945, even nonunionized workers have been generally protected by the legacy of both collective bargaining and statutory rights at both state and federal levels. They are also supported by a wider culture of rights and the emergence of what the leading authority on the subject calls "enterprise rights," rights that companies voluntarily extend to workers, often written up in an employee handbook. Although enterprise rights were not enforced by state courts until the mid-1980s, they now have substantial legal backing; even without the law behind them, competition among companies for the best workers and efforts to forestall unionization have been incentives, at least for large firms, to develop these rights.[68]

Also governing the workplace are laws prohibiting sexual harassment. Based on Title VII of the Civil Rights Act of 1964, workers (usually women) by the late 1970s were bringing successful suits against supervisors who retaliated against them if they refused sexual advances. By 1986, workplace behavior that created a "hostile environment" was judged to be sexual harassment, even if retaliation, demotion, or firing was not at issue.[69]

The application of governmental regulation to the workplace came at an unprecedented pace. One scholar observes that the federal government established one administrative agency to regulate business (the Food and Drug Administration) between 1900 and 1964 and ten agencies between 1964 and 1977. Where five federal consumer health and safety laws were passed in the Progressive Era (1902–14) and eleven in the New Deal, sixty-two became law between 1964 and 1979, and they were generally broader in their coverage across industries than earlier legislation.[70]

Higher Education. In universities, students in the 1960s proclaimed that their basic constitutional rights, especially a right to free speech, could not be abrogated by college administrators. In what would become the powder keg of the student movement, students at the University of California, Berkeley tested the rules limiting political speakers on campus. In the 1940s and 1950s, the university administration had the authority to approve or reject any speakers that official student groups wanted to bring to campus. (The UCLA administration even cleared prospective speakers with the FBI in the worst days of the anti-communist panic of the early 1950s.) At Berkeley in 1952, a policy of political neutrality on campus was strict enough to force presidential candidate Adlai Stevenson off campus to speak. But increasingly the distinction between the world off campus and the self-consciously insular university domain began to blur. At Berkeley, there were seven political speakers on campus in 1954–55, thirty-seven in 1959–60, sixty-eight in 1962–63, and 188 in 1964–65, the year the Free Speech Movement turned the campus upside down.

In that preface to a student movement that by 1968 would shatter the isolation of college campuses and widen the divisions in the Democratic Party over Vietnam, the position of the university as a sheltered enclave was challenged. The Berkeley faculty voted to end all administration regulations on the content of speech on campus. Increasingly there was a consensus among faculty and students—though not within the administration—that students should be free to hear or speak of politics as they chose and that they should be guaranteed "due process" in the promulgation and enforcement of whatever rules the university might employ to regulate on-campus speech.[71]

The Home. A rights-oriented politics has called attention to the rights of individuals even inside a family unit. The civil rights movement and especially the women's movement drew attention to violence inside the family—child abuse, incest, and wife-beating. In the case of child abuse, radiologists began in the 1940s to recognize a pattern of broken bones and bruises in children that only parental violence seemed able to explain. But the medical community was unwilling to acknowledge the prevalence of parental styles so remote from the domestic ideal until the early 1960s. Then the invention of the phrase "battered-child syndrome" medicalized the phenomenon sufficiently to let it enter into and organize a public discussion that the mass media, the state legislatures, and the Congress kept alive. Between 1963 and 1967 every state passed laws that required physicians to report cases of child abuse. As one thing led to another, reporting requirements pressured the states to enact expanded child protection services.[72]

Or take the case of the law concerning marital rape. Since the seventeenth century British and American courts recognized a marital exemption to criminal statutes governing rape. This changed in the 1970s. Nebraska in 1976, Oregon in 1977, and New Jersey in 1979 ended the marital rape exemption completely, and by 1990 every state made at least some provision for prosecuting marital rape.[73]

Before the 1960s there was essentially no state support for victims of child abuse, spouse abuse, or rape. But in 1973, following federally funded medical research that identified and publicized child abuse, and following federally supported assistance for the passage of state laws requiring physicians to report suspected child abuse, Congress enacted the Child Abuse Prevention and Treatment Act, which financed child-abuse service programs. Meanwhile, spurred by the women's movement, rape crisis centers had sprung up around the country, and, by the mid-1970s, their advocates sought federal support. Over President Gerald Ford's veto, the Congress established the National Center for the Prevention and Control of Rape at the National Institute of Mental Health, providing a new source of funding for rape-victim and rape-prevention services.[74]

There should be no mistake here: the mobilization of law on behalf of subjugated persons in the home has been rapid and far-reaching. One case study of Hilo, Hawaii, found the courts there issued seven temporary restraining orders to prevent abusive spouses from contact with their spouse between 1971 and 1978. In the year 1990 alone, there were 338 temporary restraining orders. There was new law, new police behavior about when to make an arrest in cases of domestic violence, new judicial sensitivity to the issue of battered women, and new state-funded counseling resources for both men and women. Much more than legal doctrine had changed—the whole criminal justice system was in transformation, and so was the consciousness of women who were coming to see that they had marital rights.[75]

One of the most far-reaching legal changes came in the easing of divorce law and the changing rules of child custody and alimony. New York led the way in 1966, liberalizing the legally acceptable grounds for divorce and altering a statute that had not changed since Alexander Hamilton wrote it in 1787. More dramatically, California in 1970 passed the first no-fault divorce law. Taking courage from New York and from a 1966 report of the Archbishop of Canterbury that indicated a markedly more conciliatory attitude of the Catholic Church toward divorce, California legislators transformed divorce law with surprisingly little fanfare or controversy. By 1974, forty-five states had no-fault laws. The new divorce laws developed independently of the emerging women's movement but certainly contributed to both a growing understanding of marriage as a relationship between equals and to increasing acceptance of state intrusion in the family. Under the new laws, the courts played a larger role than before in setting rules by which the divorced partners could relate to each other and to their children.[76]

The Professions. In essentially every professional organization in the 1960s and 1970s, there were strong efforts to reduce the gap between expert authority and client competence. Just when individuals seemed severed from their social moorings as never before, there emerged a newly self-conscious public-regardingness and community-minded reform spirit in one profession after another. In medicine, there was a new emphasis on preventive health care and community clinics; in law, new interest in legal aid and a shift in styles of legal work to share decision-making with clients; in journalism, investigative reporting and a variety of other innovations emerged in critique of bureaucratized practices; in social work, there was new interest in treating families and even communities, rather than individuals. Although each professional group has its own history and its own special circumstances, obviously the general atmosphere that the civil rights movement inaugurated also contributed to reform. Sometimes the connections were very concrete, as in the case of patients' rights in medical care. From the mid-1950s the courts oversaw a significant broadening of a patient's right to "informed consent" about medical procedures a physician intended to perform on them. In medical schools, there was a sharp increase in interest in medical ethics and in teaching about the ethics, policy, and politics of medicine. In 1969, a private-hospital accrediting organization issued a new statement of policy. Various consumer groups, led by the National Welfare Rights Organization, asked that the group redraft its statement with more attention to patients. To help matters along, the NWRO drafted a statement listing twenty-six patients' "rights." Here, out of an organization that arose during the War on Poverty, founded by a civil rights activist, the "patients' rights movement" was born. By 1972, the American Hospital Association adopted "A Patient's Bill of Rights" and "rights" had become "a new kid on the block in medical ethics."[77]

Environmental Protection. The Clean Air Acts of 1963, 1967, and 1970 and Clean Water Acts of 1965, 1970, and 1972 put the federal government more substantially in the role of protecting the environment than ever before. Before 1963 the federal government had enacted only seven laws regulating toxic substances (going back to the Food and Drug Act of 1906), but by 1975 had added fourteen more, including the Motor Vehicle Air Pollution Control Act (1964), the Solid Waste Disposal Act (1965), the Occupational Safety and Health Act (1970), the Consumer Product Safety Act (1972), and the Hazardous

Materials Transportation Act (1975). Most of these interventions escaped deregulation in the 1980s.

These laws, along with the establishment of the Environmental Protection Agency in 1970, organized a substantial federal obligation toward the environment. A new ecological consciousness became part of the government's mission, not only protecting the public health from immediate threats but protecting plant and animal populations whose long-term survival might be of importance to the health of future generations. In the protection of endangered species, for instance, federal laws as far back as 1894 (banning the hunting of buffalo in Yellowstone National Park) sought to protect particular species that had won popular favor, but the Endangered Species Acts of 1966, 1969, and 1973 and the Marine Mammal Protection Act of 1972 gave the federal government for the first time responsibility for the general protection of all species. These regulations remain contentious, to be sure, but even after the anti-regulatory efforts of the Reagan administration, they remain, as does a general understanding that the federal government is entrusted with the protection of the nation's biological heritage.[78]

The Political Process. Political institutions themselves were transformed by the aggressive new ideal of citizenship. The federal courts began to pay close attention to the conduct of elections. Where the Supreme Court had declared primary elections a private matter, in the *Newberry* case of 1921, the Court reversed itself in the "white primary" cases, finding in *United States v. Classic* (1941) and *Smith v. Allwright* (1944) that elections that barred African-Americans from participating, both primary and general, both state and federal, were unconstitutional. In the early 1960s, the Court decided a series of cases (*Baker v. Carr* in 1962; *Gray v. Sanders*, 1963; *Wesberry v. Sanders*, 1963; and *Reynolds v. Sims*, 1964) that struck down state congressional and legislative district apportionments because they had created a vast overrepresentation of rural areas relative to the cities. These decisions precipitated a "reapportionment revolution" that for the first time enforced a principle of "one person, one vote" and reorganized representation throughout the country. The amicus brief by U.S. Solicitor General Archibald Cox in *Baker v. Carr* made explicit the analogy between laws and policies that barred blacks from voting and practices that effectively denied full representation to urban residents.[79]

In municipal elections, like many in the West and Southwest where minority populations were relatively small and "reform" governments had made it difficult for them to gain power, the civil rights movement brought more ethnic diversity in slates for office and in the appointment of minorities to public office, and in some cities led politicians for the first time to curry favor with minority voters. Cities run since early in the century by citywide elections moved to a district system that provided better representation for minorities—for instance, Albuquerque, Dallas, San Antonio, and San Jose in the 1970s; Phoenix and San Diego in the 1980s.[80]

Also heir to the civil rights movement was the internal reform of the presidential nominating system in the Democratic Party. Between the fateful Democratic convention of 1968 and its next convention in 1972, the nominating system was reformed to encourage the growth of popular primaries for nominating candidates, to weaken the hold of party insiders over the nominating process, to centralize the control of the national party organization over state party practices, and altogether to effect the most stunning internal reform in the party since the days of Andrew Jackson.[81] This transformation, which in the end guaranteed substantial representation of blacks, women, and young people among the convention delegates, was heir to the general egalitarian spirit of the day, but it was also, quite specifically, the brainchild of Geoff Cowan, a young lawyer with experience in the civil rights movement, who designed the original Commission on the Selection of Presidential Nominees, staffed it with other lawyers whose political experience came out of civil rights and poverty law, and through Harold Ickes, Jr., a friend from the civil rights movement, secured its funding. Cowan, at the time the Connecticut director of Senator Eugene McCarthy's presidential campaign, was directly inspired by civil rights activist Fannie Lou Hamer and the efforts of the Mississippi Freedom Democratic Party to be seated as the legitimate representatives of their state at the Democratic Party's national convention in Atlantic City. "I would never have thought of the convention's power to enforce fairness and democracy had it not been for the events in Atlantic City in 1964," Cowan said.[82]

At the same time, the operation of legislatures themselves was democratized. The rule of deference was very powerful in the U.S. Congress into the 1950s and early 1960s and, of course, is still far from extinguished. But the 1960s saw major procedural reforms in the Congress and a revolt against the seniority system and the power of committee chairmen. Subcommittees proliferated, decentralizing authority and providing multiple new points of access for various constituencies, including minority groups.[83] The members of Congress became more co-equal, each member grew more dependent on his or her own entrepreneurial endeavors and less dependent on currying favor with senior colleagues, and increasingly even freshmen legislators could make speeches on the floor and propose significant policy initiatives.[84]

What happened in practically every sphere of American life enacted, under the concept of rights, what political philosopher George Kateb has said happens under the concept of "citizen":

> ... the mere status of citizen in which one is eligible to run for office and to vote in the contested elections for office is a continuous incitement to claim the status of citizen—or something analogous—in all nonpolitical relations of life. Indeed, the incitement is to politicize the nonpolitical relations of life and thus to democratize them.[85]

This is a precise definition of the political side of the sixties and of the legacy of the civil rights movement for American society. The civil rights movement sprang the concept of "rights" from its confinement in dusty documents and in brave, but isolated, courtroom dramas. Individuals spurred by it carried the gospel of rights from one field of human endeavor to another, transporting rights across the cultural border of public and private. They would also cross the political borders of nation-states and insist that "human rights" internationally act as a limit on state sovereignty. Rights and rights-consciousness have become the continuous incitements to citizenship in our time.

In the end, two questions about the era of the rights-bearing citizen must be confronted. First, in an age of the individualization of citizenship, who owns politics? Who organizes political life? With points of access to the state multiplying and with a growing array of means available to individuals for reaching them, how is the political field organized and controlled? Who contends for power? It is not plausible to think that one individual, backed by nothing more than his or her consciousness of rights, is as likely to take effective political action as the next person. But what is plausible? In the next sections, we will take a closer look at three possible answers to the question of political ownership in the present: political parties, interest groups, and the media.

Second, have rights gone too far? Does an emphasis on rights distort political discourse, political values, and political action in a way that weakens the life of the community or the possibilities of a truly public-minded citizenship? Does it place in the shadows any and all legitimate political questions—like the distribution of economic resources and benefits—that do not readily translate into the language of rights? We will take up this question in the final sections of the chapter.

Who Owns Politics? I. Parties and Interest Groups

Who owns politics? Who controls what counts as political experience?

These are easy questions for the eighteenth century: social elites owned politics. They are relatively easy for the nineteenth century, too: for the most part, political parties owned politics and defined what counted as political experience. But in the post–Progressive Era the questions are vexing. Big business? Political leaders? Experts? Pollsters? All have made strong bids to wrest control from the political parties. So, too, have the news media, especially television. All of these institutions have had some success in accumulating power. But a century of political reforms and political contention notwithstanding, the party remains a powerful claimant for defining political life.

In many respects, the parties are weaker than ever. They command strong political loyalties from fewer and fewer people, and they mobilize fewer people in active political campaigns. In 1952, 75 percent of Americans identified with a party; in 1992, 61 percent. They split their tickets with increasing frequency; between 1952 and 1992 the proportion of the electorate who voted for a presidential candidate from one party and a

House candidate from the other rose from 12 to 36 percent. In 1952, half the citizens felt "positive" about one party and "negative" about the other, and only 13 percent felt "neutral." By 1992, the "positive/negative" group was down to 34 percent and the "neutral" group more than doubled to 32 percent.[86] With declining partisan fervor, candidates neglect party labels as they appeal for voter support, and campaign advertising in the past generation has only in the exceptional case emphasized (or even mentioned) party affiliation. A British scholar observed that what most struck him about the 1992 presidential election was the absence of two words: "One is 'Democrat' and the other is 'Republican.'"[87] The news media increasingly mention candidates rather than parties in both headlines and stories, both indexing and promoting the decline of party in American political culture.[88] The shift from newspapers to television as the central source of political information for most Americans accelerates this trend because it is a move from institutions still associated with parties, at least on the editorial page, to nonpartisan institutions with neither traditions nor continuing practices of party affiliation or party endorsement.

The continuing decline of party spirit has many causes, including:

1. *The declining economic significance of parties*

If you can get what you want privately, why seek it through a party? As a growing share of the population became economically more secure, their need for jobs and favors from a political machine declined and politics, as political scientist Walter Dean Burnham observed, came to have "the character of an item of luxury consumption in competition with other such items, an indoor sport involving a host of discrete players rather than the teams of old."[89] This is not to say that pork barrel legislation is a thing of the past, but fewer people need the rewards that patronage can offer. Either they are employed or supported by someone who is employed or they receive aid through federal programs of social security and Aid to Families with Dependent Children. In such a world, the demand for the charitable services of city machines has shrunk.

Urban political machines remained effective in many cities into the 1950s, but their power was fading. State and city government employees began to unionize and to professionalize. Hiring was increasingly based on "merit," and arbitrary firing was increasingly prevented by government employee unions.[90] As late as the 1960s, the governor of Pennsylvania controlled 40,000 patronage positions; by 1988, it was only 2000. Civil service reform, coupled with the unionization of government employees, eroded federal patronage, too. In 1993, with some three million federal civilian employees, only a few thousand were political appointments.[91] The heart of the patronage system seems gone forever.[92]

2. Westernization

The American population has gradually moved westward. The eleven states of the West and Southwest (Arizona, California, Colorado, Idaho, Montana, Nevada, New Mexico, Oregon, Utah, Washington, and Wyoming) accounted for 13 percent of the votes in the electoral college for elections governed by the census of 1940 (71 out of 531), 20 percent by the election of 1992 (112 out of 538). California alone more than doubled its delegation in that period, from 25 electoral votes to 54. With this population shift, there has been a Westernization of American politics, a growing influence nationally of the political culture of the West, the regional political culture least attached to parties.

Many of the most far-reaching anti-party reforms of the Progressive Era took place first or most fully in the West. City manager forms of government and citywide rather than ward-based electoral systems advanced most in the West.[93] The initiative also originated in the West and, in the entire history of initiatives from 1898 to 1979, five Western states are among the leading six states in numbers of initiatives proposed (along with prairie state North Dakota), and make up by themselves more than half of the national total.[94] Woman's suffrage became state law first in the West, and the foothold gained there helped advance the cause nationally. Suffragists themselves attributed this in part to the absence of the drag of European immigration. The prominent New York reformer Florence Kelley, speaking in California in 1915 (where woman's suffrage was already law), held, "There is nothing the matter with our men in the State of New York. Our trouble is with the steerage. They inundate our shores year after year. We slowly assimilate and convert; but each year there is the same work to do over—the same battle with ignorance and foreign ideas of freedom and the 'place of woman.'"[95]

Because most Western states were at first territories governed by appointed federal officials rather than by their own elected executives, their parties were weakly institutionalized. The president, not locally elected leaders, controlled territorial patronage. There was more incentive in the West than elsewhere to remain flexible, less incentive to stick loyally to one party or the other. Moreover, to the extent that the party politics of the nineteenth century was ethnocultural politics, closely connected to ethnic loyalties and animosities, the relative absence of enmity between native-born and immigrant whites in the West or between Protestants and Catholics also weakened party ties. Weakly institutionalized parties encouraged candidates for office to stand on their own and, when elected to office, to operate as independent entrepreneurs rather than party loyalists.[96]

3. The fiscal state and the Cold War consensus

Parties require issues, but issues became less available after 1945. As the Cold War emerged, so did a bipartisan consensus on foreign policy. Just as foreign policy was becoming a more vital part of American policy, it was removed—not fully, of course, but in large measure—from partisan struggle.

Some economic issues were also removed from the partisan battlefields. The fiscal policy of government became more important but less controlled by Congress or parties in the Congress. Control over the federal budget shifted increasingly to the executive, and more and more spending was automatically enacted by transfer payments to individuals through social security, unemployment compensation, and other programs outside the ordinary budgetary process.

Economic growth, like defense of the Free World, was supported by a bipartisan consensus. As sociologist Gianfranco Poggi observes, the idea of economic growth gained "an overwhelming grip on the public imagination" throughout the Western world in the postwar period.[97] Likewise, Keynesian economic planning and budgeting offered a fundamental groundwork for policy-makers of various political persuasions, at least until the late 1970s. As macroeconomic management became a more central task of the state and more dependent on technical expertise beyond partisan politics, citizens could rightly recognize parties as less relevant to governance. When, in the late 1970s and the 1980s, "supply-side" economics challenged the Keynesian consensus, partisanship in the Congress, though not in the populace at large, took on a new vitality.[98]

4. Internal political reforms

Parties have lost control of nominations since the 1960s. As indicated, the Democratic Party's left failed to capture the presidential nomination in 1968 but gained control of the process of institutional reform. The new rules strongly encouraged delegate selection by primaries rather than party conventions, and the number of Democratic primaries grew from fifteen in 1968, selecting 40 percent of delegates, to thirty in 1976, selecting 76 percent.[99] As states hastened to accommodate the new rules, the Democratic Party reforms affected the Republican Party, too, and party professionals lost power.

5. The rise of interest group alternatives

Since the 1960s, as more and more interest groups organized more intensive lobbying activity and centered it increasingly in permanent Washington headquarters, interest groups found they could reach government decision-makers directly rather than operating through or alongside party structures.

Private associations today are odd birds, often neither private nor associational. Their "privacy" has been compromised not only by federal civil rights legislation but perhaps even more by their dependence on government financing. By 1981, the federal government spent an estimated $46 billion in support of nonprofit institutions, a sum that amounts to 38 percent of the revenues of those organizations.[100] Today most private social service agencies receive half or more of their funding from federal, state, or local government. Funds come either through contractual arrangements with private organizations that provide social services to clients or through direct payments to individuals, especially in programs like Medicaid, with which people purchase medical or social services.[101]

Private associations today are often no more associational than they are private; frequently they have a paper membership that supports with annual dues a professional, policy-making staff. There has been a movement from the participatory to the professional and representative form of voluntary organizations. This extends even to social movements. "Movement" is a term that connotes spontaneity and grassroots participation, but increasingly sociologists speak of "social movement organizations," the professionalization of citizen activism, and the establishment of a permanent, professional world that builds grassroots activity.

The political parties are threatened as the number of interest groups has mushroomed, with more and more of them operating offices in Washington, D.C., and representing themselves directly to Congress and federal agencies.[102] Many organizations that keep an eye on Washington seek financial and moral support from ordinary citizens. Since many of them focus on a narrow set of concerns or even on a single issue, and often a single issue of enormous emotional weight, they compete with the parties for citizens' dollars, time, and passion. To take just one important example, there are at least a hundred national anti-abortion organizations today, some of them with membership upwards of a quarter of a million people, others staffing hundreds of counseling centers around the country. This is quite apart from broad-based Christian groups on the political right that include abortion among their primary concerns.[103] Another example: In 1991, 180 separate organizations collaborated in forming the National Breast Cancer Coalition, seeking to take control from "politicians and physicians and scientists" over research and policy on breast cancer. They succeeded in their very first year in winning a 50 percent increase in federal spending on breast cancer research.[104]

Little love has been wasted on interest groups in either popular thought or political science. George Washington's distrust of self-created societies remains with us, even if it has had to compete with a Tocquevillian appreciation of how Americans organize themselves to solve social problems. In the past two decades, at the very moment that groups established to represent general or public interests have gained new prominence, especially in environmental policy and civil rights, popular political discourse has lumped all groups together, including these, under the epithet "special interests." Just as the capacity to form broad-based, public-spirited, and rights-oriented institutions grew significantly, economists and political scientists grew enamored of a theory of social action that explained why such institutions were almost impossible to build.[105] At the same time, sociologists have drawn attention to civil society—all those myriad associations between the state and the household; they have emphasized the vital importance of the local, the face-to-face, and the many sites in which public conversations can take place. These, in the American idiom, are inherently good while the professionalized, staffed, nationalized, computerized operation of the thousands of associations that get typed as special interests are always bad. These two images of civic life have yet to be reconciled in American political and social thought.

In the face of all these challenges to parties, the parties have adapted rather than disappeared. Like so many other private associations, they have adjusted to a new state-centered regime, and are now directed by large Washington offices with professional employees and mailing lists for fund-raising. They have declined as associations or causes with which individual citizens identify, but their professionally staffed national organizations have grown wealthier and more powerful.

The parties did not even have permanent national headquarters until the Republicans established one in 1918 and the Democrats in 1929.[106] The national organizations became significant actors in state and local campaigning only in the 1970s with the new legal limitations on campaign financing and new means for raising funds with the aid of zip codes and computerized mailing lists. William Brock, then chairman of the Republican National Committee, led the RNC to expand its activities in unprecedented ways, including taking on campaign training sessions for 10,000 Republican activists and directing financial support to favored candidates in local primaries.[107]

The Democrats played catch-up to the "Brock revolution," copying its techniques as best as their more limited financial resources would allow. Both parties came to rely on computer technology, professional political operatives, and national coordination rather than local volunteers. Today national party organizations are "financially secure, institutionally stable, and highly influential in election campaigns and in their relations with state and local party committees." [108] This is a world away from participatory nineteenth-century parties. Parties today are a kind of umbrella pressure group with one unique and indispensable feature: they nominate candidates for office. They thereby still control the framework of political life—in the last instance, but they compete with many other groups for authority in Washington, for a presence in the news, and for a place in the hearts of citizens.

Who Owns Politics? II. The Case of the Media

In 1952, in the first full television presence at a national political party convention, television journalists dutifully covered the opening ceremony—the presentation of the colors, the Pledge of Allegiance, the national anthem, the invocation, and the welcoming speeches. None of this actually interested the journalists, nor did they expect it to interest audiences. To them, as CBS news director Sig Mickelson later recalled, this was all merely "ceremonial." Television reporters wanted to get behind the ceremony to the decisions behind the scenes. "We at CBS," Mickelson remembers, "had decided months earlier that we would approach the conventions as a very large and complex news story." [109]

To treat the conventions "as . . . news" meant that any elements of the convention that could be predicted could not be held in high esteem. Only elements of novelty or surprise merited coverage. "It became increasingly clear during the opening session that not much news was being made on the rostrum," Mickelson writes. So CBS interrupted the proceedings to report action on the convention floor or in the hotels surrounding the convention. Mickelson's conclusion is important: "The expectation of the leaders of the parties had been that television would be much more attentive to the formal program on the rostrum. Instead, a precedent was being set in which television executives made the decisions." [110] The hierarchy of values was clear: "breaking news" would trump "the ceremony in progress."

Television, usually thought of as the perfect technology of spectacle, ironically operates with an ideology that resists spectacle. No flag-waving, no parades, just the news. Television coverage of the conventions thus emphasized whatever was most recent, least predictable, and thereby rich in "information." Television journalists never imagined the possibility that they and their TV audience were invited guests, watching the business meeting cum revival meeting of a fundamental, if not cherished, political association. Nor did it occur to them that the conventions' ritual events themselves spoke volumes as symbolic representations of party bargaining, efforts at inclusion and exclusion of factions and ideas, attempts to honor the old or debut the new. None of this mattered. What mattered was news, and, practically speaking, that reduced the convention to choosing candidates and to conflicts among party factions.

Then how are the media to cover conventions when candidate selection is decided in advance? Why cover the 1956 Republican convention at all? Why cover most of the conventions since the upturn in delegation selection through primaries in the 1960s? When news maestro Ted Koppel departed the 1996 Republican convention in a huff, complaining that it offered no news, he only carried to completion a logic that had been operating more and more visibly since 1952.[111]

The sorest test of that logic came at the Democratic convention in Chicago in 1968. There the bloody clash of antiwar demonstrators and the Chicago police outside the convention hall pushed the actual nomination of Hubert Humphrey into the television shadows. Humphrey's name was put in nomination by Mayor Joseph Alioto of San Francisco. Then Carl Stokes, the black mayor of Cleveland, rose to second the nomination and visually reinforce Humphrey's longtime commitment to civil rights. But as he began to speak, NBC had completed the editing of its film on the battle raging outside, and replaced Stokes with violent conflict. Humphrey's campaign staff was aghast, but the networks "operating on a consensual standard of newsworthiness and under direct and fierce competition to get their version of the most newsworthy events on the screen first" acted professionally and as if there was no real choice.[112]

What is the difference between treating politics as politics and treating politics as news? If politics is to be treated as news, then conflict will count more than harmony, violent conflict more than civil dispute, change more than stasis. The actions of identifiable leaders will be emphasized over the initiatives of the unknown, and if mass movements loom too large to ignore, the news media will seek to identify and celebrate leaders within them.[113] Despite this attention to individual leaders, there will also be a tendency to frame politics within the ideological presuppositions of Progressivism.[114] That is, politics will be understood as mass democracy—what goes through people's minds in the voting booth, rather than with the division of powers among institutions, subgroups, or associations in the polity. Television contributes to an emphasis on the national government over state and local government, on the president over the Congress, and a unified "agenda" rather than separate party, regional, or other agenda. All of this helps to further discredit partisanship in American politics.

By the 1972 election, television was the central forum of American national politics and everyone knew it. The New York Times that year assigned a reporter to cover the campaign by watching it on TV—only then would he know what the campaign looked like to the ordinary citizen.[115] The role of the national press corps, both print and television, was also symbolically identified in that year when Rolling Stone writer Timothy Crouse covered not the campaign but the journalists covering the campaign.[116] Today network audience share is in decline and the Big Three networks provide less access to a mass audience than they once did, but the structure of today's public forum is inextricably linked with them. They have developed a remarkable position of authority in presenting politics to the American people.

As early as 1936, CBS chairman William Paley refused airtime to the Republicans to respond to President Roosevelt's State of the Union message. Paley argued that he could not "surrender into the keeping of others the exercise of editorial judgment and responsibility."[117] The networks themselves from that day on have amassed extraordinary power to determine the ground rules for the public sphere. Think about the range of decision points that can arise—and have arisen. Imagine that President Smith wants airtime to speak on an important issue to the American public. The networks must determine whether President Smith's speech is a "presidential" speech or a "campaign" speech. If it is a campaign speech, then the Section 315 "equal time" rule is invoked and the opposition candidate merits reply time. On October 31, 1956, for instance, President Eisenhower spoke by television to the nation concerning the Suez crisis. Democratic candidate Adlai Stevenson requested rebuttal time, but one day before the election the Federal Communications Commission ruled that a presidential speech concerning an international crisis stood outside the "equal time" provision.[118]

If President Smith's address passes muster as a presidential speech and broadcasters find the topic of the speech sufficiently important to qualify for free airtime, which network or networks will air the speech? Will all three leading networks (plus PBS, CNN, and C-SPAN) provide time? Or will it be sufficient for a single network to take responsibility?

Independent of that decision, when will the speech be aired? Will it be in prime time when the largest audience is available? How will that be negotiated between the president's representatives and the networks? Will the opposition party be granted an opportunity to respond? Will the networks select respondents themselves from known opponents of the president's policies or use their own journalists to answer the speech as political analysts rather than political partisans? During the Vietnam War the networks turned to "instant analysis" where network journalists appeared on air after a presidential address to critically assess the president's remarks.[119]

Other questions have also arisen. Why, for instance, should the opposition party have access to television time only to react to presidential initiatives? In 1970, with controversy over the Vietnam War in full flower, Yale University law students filed a complaint with the FCC against stations WTIC-TV in Hartford and WCBS-TV in New York, arguing that they had violated the "fairness doctrine" by failing to provide time for views contrary to the president's while the president appeared on the air time and again in prime-time foreign policy addresses. A group called Business Executives Move for Vietnam Peace filed a similar complaint against all three leading networks. Fourteen U.S. senators similarly complained.

These initiatives won some sympathy from CBS president Frank Stanton, who held that the power of the president "has become so great, and his right to address the nation virtually at his own terms so accepted that some balance must be provided to overcome what could become a monolithic voice on public affairs." He offered the opposition a chance to provide its views on television several times a year and agreed to accept paid spots from political parties for fund-raising purposes. But the very first time the Democrats took up this offer, making use of twenty-five minutes of free time on the program that CBS called "The Loyal Opposition," the Republican Party asked for reply time and the FCC sided with the Republicans. CBS held that this was a reply to a reply whose impact was "to vitiate the series" Stanton had intended. It was never revived.[120]

At about the same time Senator J. William Fulbright introduced a bill to provide televised appearances for members of Congress to discuss "issues of public importance." Like Stanton, and at a time when the president was prosecuting an undeclared and unpopular war in Vietnam, Fulbright objected to the inflated powers of the presidency. But the networks opposed his initiative, and no one was more forceful in doing so than the very same Frank Stanton. The networks did not want control over who would appear on television to pass from themselves to the Congress, and the Fulbright proposal died.[121]

The networks' primary criterion for deciding when and whether to broadcast presidential or opposition speeches has been "newsworthiness." This gives a great advantage to the president who, as ABC executive vice president Richard Wald put it, "always makes news."[122] Even so, during the years since 1974 networks turned down requests for airtime at least eight times—once each for Ford and Carter, four times for Reagan, and twice for Clinton in his first term.[123]

Private commercial organizations, then, on their own authority determine how, when, and whether the lawmaking branches of government will appear on the television screen. This pertains especially to the occasional formal addresses of presidents and congressional leaders to the public. In everyday news, there is a different division of labor, with an ongoing negotiation between journalists and officials. A war of technical and strategic sophistication has escalated, with broadcast news taking new initiatives to independently define political reality and political leaders and political candidates taking new initiatives to control political reality themselves in the face of television professionalism and, judo-like, through its very capacities.

Van Gordon Sauter, president of CBS News in the 1980s, urged his staff to seek memorable "moments" in news—which is exactly what the growing cadre of TV-oriented political consultants liked to serve up.[124] In 1968, "photo opportunity" was an ironic neologism; with the Reagan-Carter campaign of 1980, it became part of everyday political discourse.[125]

The television "sound bite" is the amount of time the camera stays on one scene or speaker before shifting to a journalist's interpolation, another speaker, or another part of the same speaker's speech. The length of the average sound bite in television news has shrunk rapidly over the past two decades. This has often been taken as an index of the decline of American political discourse, but that is not a necessary conclusion. In campaign coverage, the shorter sound bites enable journalists to organize stories more carefully to illuminate political issues rather than political bombast.[126] What the shorter sound bite does inescapably reveal is that TV journalists have become aggressively interventionist in controlling political storytelling.

It is easy to exaggerate television's authority, and there is now a long line of media critics who do exactly that. In the late 1960s and early 1970s, it was widely claimed and widely believed that television's vivid portrayal of carnage in Vietnam turned Americans against the war—even though, it is now clear, the public began to lose faith in the war as early as 1967 while television news coverage was still upbeat about the war and shielded viewers from direct photographic evidence of American casualties into 1968. In the 1980s, commentators claimed and believed that Ronald Reagan's mastery of the television medium propelled him into the national spotlight, sustained his inordinate popularity with the general public, and thus helped convert his right-wing, anti-government agenda into stunning congressional victories. In fact, Reagan's early legislative successes came while public approval of his presidency was lower than that for any other president since organized polling began; even public approval of his "personality," though high, was no higher than for his predecessors. Whatever Reagan's magic was, he exercised it more on the Congress than on the general public.[127]

If television is less powerful than people believe, newspapers retain more authority than people often realize. Newspapers are no longer the primary source of news for most people *directly*, but they remain the primary source indirectly because they supply news to television. Television news, even the national network news programs, are parasites of print. Rarely does a broadcast journalist pick up a story that newspapers and newsmagazines are not already on top of. Television confirms, anoints, and dramatizes news, and when it covers events live, it witnesses news. But it rarely finds news. That remains almost entirely the task of print.

Television's claim on political space is only a second-order claim—to define not what politics should be but who should control access to its discussion. So the concern of media critics that the news media "set the agenda" of politics is valid only in the obvious sense that the media organizations in the final analysis get to say what is on the evening news or what story will make page one. But it is difficult to know how much power this gives journalists relative to interest groups, parties, corporations, and government officials in declaring what questions the nation shall debate.

Television executives and broadcast journalists do not own American politics any more than the parties or the interest groups. Least of all do they own politics on those rare occasions when television is the citizens' primary point of access to political life—in live coverage of congressional hearings or presidential speeches or candidate debates. On these occasions, television vividly displays a world of power, one that the media can observe and transmit but cannot control.

Is There Too Much Talk of Rights?

Rights have been a powerful lever of social change, but tools have a way of taking their users in unanticipated directions. In the past decade, critics have increasingly worried that an emphasis on rights has had some alarming consequences for democratic politics.

Law professor Mary Ann Glendon has been particularly eloquent in criticizing rights-talk for reducing political discourse to the matter of adjudicating individual rights. For her, the "strident rights rhetoric that currently dominates American political discourse" is disastrous. A rights-centered political discourse is "anemic." It is "vacuous, hard-edged, and inflexible." It is "shallow." It is "careless." It has created a language not truly about human dignity but about "insistent, unending desires." It legitimates individual and group egoism and emphasizes at every turn the individual, self-gratification over self-discipline, the economic over the moral, the short term over the long term, the personal over the social. Glendon does not suggest that we act poorly because we talk poorly, but she does urge that we think poorly because our language is impoverished and that we need to find a language, to paraphrase Jimmy Carter, as good as the people.[128]

For Glendon, the contemporary preoccupation with rights can be blamed on "many bright, ambitious public lawyers of the 1960s" whose views of politics focused narrowly on the judiciary as "the first line of defense against all injustice." She portrays these lawyers and other activists as immature, impatient, and perhaps narcissistic in seeking in politics total, uncompromising victory—the sort one might come up with in a judicial decision but never in the give-and-take of legislative work. Activists chose "litigation that could yield total victory" over "long hours at political organizing, where the most one can hope to gain is, typically, a compromise." Federal courts, activist attorneys, and the academic gallery that cheered them on and transmitted a zeal for rights to a younger generation created an environment in which dozens of groups came to "articulate their concerns in terms of rights"—women, defenders of abused children, mental patients, people with disabilities, gays and lesbians, consumers injured by product defects, and many others.[129]

Glendon is one of a number of critics who contend that a rights-based politics is anti-democratic in removing political controversy from the legislatures to the courts; hyper-individualistic in legitimating views of the private individual as more important than the public community; and distressingly bureaucratic in replacing informal and personal (if invariably paternalistic) relations in schools and workplaces with due process hearings and adversary procedures. A corollary is that rights-based citizenship makes our politics far too dependent on lawyers. Critics point out that the United States has more lawyers per capita than other nations and that the ratio of lawyers to population has grown sharply in the past two decades.[130] The increasing familiarity of lawyer jokes is no accident.

Rights-consciousness incurs real social costs. And there is no denying that the individualist rights tradition imposes limits on the political imagination. When Robert Bellah and his colleagues referred to the vocabulary of autonomous and self-reliant individuals as "the first language of American moral life," they were correct, and they offered a useful reminder that most Americans also have fluency, would they but recognize it, in various "second languages" of communal and religious life.[131] In everyday practice, no man or woman is an island, facing others alone while brandishing the Bill of Rights in one hand and a "Don't Tread on Me" flag in the other. Instead, people have sentimental attachments to families, to tightly or loosely bound communities defined by a church, neighborhood, enduring professional or commercial tie, town or city or alma mater. What we do not have is an articulate political philosophy to counterpose these commitments to social and moral communities against the claims of individual rights.

It is not enough to end there, however, with a restatement of the conflict between individual rights on the one hand and a solidary community life on the other, between liberalism and communitarianism. This kind of dichotomy caricatures the world that rights-consciousness builds. Of course, rights-consciousness is quite able to caricature itself, and many of the darts from communitarian critics strike home when they direct attention to the public language that turns every slight into an invasion of rights and every disappointment into a cry of victimization. Glendon is particularly astute in pointing out that rights-talk has become practically universal since World War II and that it is not rights or rights-language in general to which she objects but only its American idiom. She would have Americans learn from the Canadians and Germans to speak of individual rights in a way that also gives credit to social responsibilities. Without denying that Americans might pick up some pointers from abroad, it is still important to affirm that American rights-talk at its sometimes uncivil best promotes a strong self-assertion that is distinguishable from the wailing self-pity that is now its widely circulating counterfeit. In the best—and most widely reverberating—instances, the assertion of individual rights does more to build community than to tear it apart. Think of Rosa Parks before presuming that the assertion of rights cuts against the grain of community. Of course, the civil rights movement did challenge the "community" of the South but did so by demonstrating that that community's premise was one of inequality and inhumanity.

People do not always see the connection between "my" rights and "yours," or between "mine" and "ours," or between my rights and my responsibilities, but those connections can be made. Contemporary social movements may emerge as much from a "personalist" politics as from more traditional solidary communities.[132] Individuals can grow mindful of communities that they make as well as communities from which they come. Scarcely a day passes without the media bringing news of another individual who crafts a social issue from a personal grievance and builds a community from a sense of a right denied.

In my own city of San Diego, Azim Khamisa, a Persian-Indian immigrant whose son was murdered delivering pizza, joined with the African-American grandfather of the incarcerated murderer to establish a foundation in his son's name dedicated to the prevention of youth violence.[133] And there is Donna Frye, also of San Diego, who runs a surfing equipment store. When her husband kept getting sick after surfing near their home, she sprang into action, organized a group called Surfers Tired of Pollution that successfully embarrassed a local congressman in his vote to weaken the Clean Water Act, led the effort to pass a state law that requires weekly testing of bacteria at popular swimming and surfing beaches, and works to teach beach area businesses to assist beachgoers in reporting symptoms of illness they think connected to their recreational use of the ocean.[134] These are two instances among thousands. The rights-bearing citizen can and often does carry a rights-based social imagination.

There is even a growing tendency to mark this in the way legislation is named—not after legislative sponsors but after the people whose tragic experience prompted the bill. One example is the Brady Bill, a federal gun control measure named for President Reagan's press secretary James Brady, who was paralyzed by a bullet in the 1981 attempted assassination of the president, and Brady's wife, Sarah, who lobbied for the law for many years. Many states passed Megan's laws to protect citizens from sex offenders released from prison after one convicted offender molested and murdered Megan Kanka in suburban New Jersey in 1994.[135]

Are these only fairy tales of democracy to pacify critics and to prevent more far-reaching movements for change? Politicians and the media are drawn to these stories in part because they legitimate the world-as-it-is and momentarily veil formidable structures of power and psychologies of intransigence. Still, if these are mythologies, they are mythologies of the real; they tell of real people taking decisive actions, often against great odds, to genuinely change lives.

The rights-conscious world that the sixties revolution began to build on the model of the civil rights movement transformed political life. It did so by appealing to common American traditions of equality and liberty, in many cases from the point of view of the people who had been left out of the founders' compact. This must be kept in view as people struggle with some of the problems that have accompanied an orientation to rights. The problems are real. There is an institutional problem when the courts are burdened with too many cases to handle, including too many cases that turn on scientific and technical questions judges are not competent to evaluate, as often happens when industries or environmental groups sue the Environmental Protection Agency.[136] If the United States intends to keep regulating economy and society through the courts, it needs also to provide the courts with resources to do the job effectively.

A frequent result of a rights-oriented politics is to call forth additional governmental regulation or judicial intrusion in areas of life the state once left alone. A quest for liberty has often produced a growing governmental presence, and invariably a growing disaffection with government, as citizens deal with everything from minor inefficiencies to major abuses.[137] There has been a reaction against the rights-oriented expansion of government, from the movement against school busing for racial balance in the 1970s to the anti-abortion movement spurred by the

Supreme Court's decision in *Roe* v. *Wade*, to the current efforts to roll back or end programs of affirmative action. One result of the expansion of rights in the 1970s has been the empowerment of Republicans who could take advantage of and encourage discontent with the regime of rights.

A rights-orientation, along with a growing cultural reluctance to defer to authority of any sort under any circumstances, burdens institutional capacities. Without the emphasis on rights, they might be just as seriously burdened, but in some other direction, with the shoe pinching in some other spots. Would American society be better off if it did not recognize the rights of African-Americans, women, the physically disabled, the learning disabled, employees in the workplace, students in the university, patients in the hospital, and battered women in the home? Critics of rights-talk do not say so. They seem to be saying that we would be better off if we held rights in check; if our political culture did not so readily encourage people to think of themselves as victims; if our political discourse more forcefully directed people to their responsibilities as well as their rights. With this, one can certainly agree, but broadsides against rights-talk do not seem a promising method for getting from here to there.

At Century's End

A funny thing happened on the way to the twenty-first century: communism collapsed. What began in nineteenth-century Europe as a dream of a revolution for social equality came to a climax of political terror and mass murder in the Stalinist Soviet Union and finished in a whimper of corruption, inefficiency, and demoralization in 1991.

The fall of the Soviet Union was galvanized by the remarkable "velvet revolution" in eastern Europe in the 1980s. That liberation was made possible by the nurturing of "civil society," at first little more than discreet gatherings of people in coffeehouses or in private homes to talk politics. With little opportunity to speak freely in public, private gatherings took on a vitality, and depended on a courage, that many in the West could barely conceive (although NAACP members in the South in the 1940s and 1950s knew very well what it means to nurture civil society inside a repressive regime).

The events in eastern Europe attracted considerable interest in the United States where, independently, there was a growing concern that liberalism had gone too far, that individualism had run rampant, that democracy could be saved in the end not by institutions and procedural rules but only by the revival of virtue in the citizenry.

But do the social foundations of virtue exist? Has the rise of rights-based liberalism in America established a democratic home but failed to educate anyone fit to inhabit it? Is the effort to realize the sovereignty of the people awash in contradictions—the more people become self-actualizing individuals, the more likely they are to rend the social fabric; the more decisions they take on in elections, referenda, and direct participation in decision-making, the less adequate they are to the myriad choices they are asked to make; the more Americans vest social welfare provision in the federal government, the more private structures of self-help atrophy; the more the protection of rights is vested in the judiciary, the less citizens engage in the discussion and persuasion and democratic give-and-take of the legislative process?

My own sense is that the rise of the rights-regarding citizen has done more to enhance democracy than to endanger it. If the practice of American liberalism today is deeply flawed, this is not because it has a long record of failure but because American political leadership has long stepped around it. A full-bodied expression of liberal ideals has emerged only since 1965. Its continuing faults may run deep, but they may also have much to do with our inexperience in working through what it means to run a country conceived in liberty and dedicated to the proposition that all of us are created equal.

Rights are not necessarily opposed to community, although sometimes there is stark confrontation. Often, however, rights redefine the character of community. As I shall argue in the final chapter, a rights-regarding citizenship now stands alongside the informed citizen, but it does not substitute for the ideal of the informed citizen. We live in a new complexity, not a transformed simplicity. Therein lies the great temptation to grasp at a reductive formula, but also the difficult opportunity to work with our multiple resources.

Conclusion

A Gathering of Citizens

Citizenship in the United States has not disappeared. It has not even declined. It has, inevitably, changed.

Past models of citizenship have not vanished as newer models became ascendant. The legacy of a colonial citizenship built on social hierarchy survives in the deference old families command and the traditions of public service they sometimes nurture. It endures in the trust people place in individuals who have a visible record of public service, personal integrity, charitable giving, and mentorship and sponsorship of younger leaders. It persists in the framework of our government in the ways that the constitutional machinery sifts raw opinion through deliberative legislative processes.

Similarly, the nineteenth-century citizenship of mass political participation carries on into our own day. Political parties, popular social movements, the social honor that citizens of every rank accrue for active participation in their communities, and the widespread obeisance in political rhetoric to public opinion, "the people," and majority rule all testify to the permanent contribution of mass democracy to modern politics. As for the Progressive Era ideal of the informed citizen, it, too, exerts enormous influence. It is the lamp held aloft by journalists committed to their profession, it directs civic education in and out of the schools, and it still dominates public understanding of civic obligation at election time. Even as rights-consciousness places the courtroom alongside the polling place in the practice of public life, and opens the political like a Pandora's box to cover a vastly expanded range of meanings, earlier visions of politics and citizenship survive and even prosper.

The successive coats that laminate our political ideals and practices have transformed citizenship profoundly. The United States has come from an era dominated by gentlemen to one dominated by parties, to one in which many groups and interests not only compete for political power but also contend with one another to define what powers are political. With such dramatic changes in who is free to participate in politics, what means are available for political participation, and what domains of human endeavor fall within the political, it would be remarkable if one could quickly sum up the changing quality of civic life as rise or fall. But many critics over the past two decades have made a case that the American story is, at least in the past half century, one of decline; civic life has collapsed. "By almost all the available evidence, we are witnessing a widespread turning away from public life," wrote the political philosopher Hanna Pitkin in 1981.[1] "Public life is disappearing," the editors of Harper's declared in 1990, and many heartily agreed.[2] Evidence is everywhere: the decline of parties; the fiscal impoverishment of cities strangled by suburbs; the dwindling of newspaper readership; disappearing trust in government and nearly all other major institutions; shrinking voter turnout; citizens' paltry knowledge of national and international affairs; the lack of substance in political campaigns; the decline of conversation and the informal gathering places where it is said to have flourished; the fear of street crime that keeps people behind their locked doors; the spread of scandal as a political issue—and more.[3] The general point, it seems, has scarcely to be argued; the only question is what to do about it.

Yet intellectuals have complained that "we no longer have citizens" at least since 1750, when Jean-Jacques Rousseau penned those words in Geneva.[4] Pick your appropriate quotation from Tocqueville in 1840, E. L. Godkin in the 1890s, Walter Lippmann in the 1920s, or political scientists and sociologists in the 1950s and you will find the theme sounded again.[5] In 1979, President Jimmy Carter worried out loud about moral and civic decline in his "malaise" speech; in 1985, a concern with American moral decline was vividly renewed as sociologist Robert Bellah and his colleagues, in their widely discussed *Habits of the Heart*, criticized the ways liberal individualism had narrowed the American political imagination.[6] Energetic discussion in American history, political science, and law in the 1970s and 1980s looked to eighteenth-century "civic republicanism" as a superior alternative to liberalism or socialism for our own day.[7]

All the social criticism of privatized citizens and the various solutions offered to renew or reawaken their public involvement took a new turn and gained new substance with the recent writings of Robert Putnam. In 1993, Putnam, a Harvard political scientist, published a study of Italian democracy that argues, on the basis of considerable historical evidence, that the parts of Italy that best nurture local political democracy are distinguished not by economic standing or class cohesion or other likely variables but by long-standing traditions of active voluntary associations. The number of choral societies, soccer teams, and bird-watching clubs in a region in the late nineteenth century turned out to be the best predictor of the late-twentieth-century success of the region in self-government.[8] Tocqueville was alive and well and dining on pasta.

This work gained broader attention when Putnam published a brief but clever and provocative paper that tried to make a related case for the United States. This essay, "Bowling Alone," like the Italian study, focused on the importance to democracy of "social capital." What sustains viable democratic politics is the underlying strength of social bonds that people can draw on to propel them into and sustain them in civic affairs. Voluntary organizational involvement, from bowling leagues to the PTA, are the signs of community health. They provide the social resources and the civic training that citizens need to make democracy tick. Putnam shows that membership in organizations from the League of Women Voters to the Red Cross to business clubs like the Rotary, Lions, Elks, and Jaycees have fallen off dramatically in the past twenty-five years. The "Bowling Alone" title refers to the fact that the number of people who go bowling has remained constant over twenty-five years but the number enrolled in bowling leagues has declined sharply—in other words, people bowl, as ever, but they do not do so as part of organized social life.[9] (It was not long before a wry critic pointed to the extraordinary growth of soccer participation in the same period and titled his article "Kicking in Groups.")[10]

As always, the most decisive index of decline is voter turnout. People who became eligible to vote in 1968 or later have had turnout rates sharply lower than those who came to voting age between the 1930s and 1964. In 1972, post–New Deal generation citizens with less than a high school education had a turnout rate of 41 percent, whereas 62 percent of New Deal generation citizens with the same level of education voted. With a high school degree, 83 percent of the New Deal generation voted, 55 percent of the post–New Deal. With some college, the figures were 88 percent and 79 percent, respectively. By 1992, the disparity between the generations in voter turnout remained huge, except for those with some college.[11]

Other measures present a somewhat more complicated picture. For instance, where Putnam reported PTA membership down from twelve million in 1964 to five million in 1982, the Roper Center for Public Opinion Research found that in 1969 only 16 percent of people surveyed had ever attended a school board meeting, whereas 39 percent did so in 1995.[12] Charitable financial contributions from those who itemize their returns declined from 1960 to 1980, but there was also a self-reported increase in volunteer activities from 1965 to 1981.[13] Putnam himself discovered that an error in calculation had led him to overestimate the decline in the number of organizations people belong to.[14]

Even so, a lot of substantial civic organizations have clearly lost members. Putnam's data, drawn from the best national surveys that have repeated the same questions to the general public every few years, is simply more thorough than any alternatives anyone else has provided. His data can be supplemented with still other evidence that points in the same direction. Alexander Astin and his colleagues at UCLA have gathered data annually in a national survey of college freshmen from 1966 to the present. In 1966, 58 percent of college men and women held "keeping up to date with political affairs" an essential or important objective, but only 33 percent of men and 27 percent of women made the same affirmation by 1996. Attitudes toward service rather than toward politics showed more modest change, but in the same downward direction: in 1966, 59 percent of the men judged it essential or important to "help others who are in difficulty," sliding very slowly to 53 percent in 1996, while for women the slippage was from 80 percent (the single most important objective for women in that year) to 70 percent (in second place, behind "be well off financially" at 72 percent).[15]

It may be that Putnam has not counted all that should be counted. Does the survey data in which people report how many organizations they belong to truly reflect the social capital he seeks to measure? For instance, what about the millions of people who go to commercial health clubs, often making friends there and developing an informal group life? Should this activity be counted as contributing to social capital? In an earlier generation, after all, some of the kinds of people who now go to the commercial fitness center probably joined the Y or the Elks for no purpose but to use their gyms and steam rooms. Today they would be unlikely to list the family fitness center as an organization they belong to; yesterday they would have listed the Y. The market has expanded in useful ways and serves needs that associational life once catered to. Other kinds of organizational life, from soccer leagues (that no adults, after all, would identify as organizations they belong to—it is their children who belong) to neighborhood watch meetings or block associations (that no adults would be likely to list as full-fledged associations or organizations of which they are members) have taken up some of the slack of associational life.

Assume that the problems of measuring organizational involvement could be resolved and that the results show a decline in significant individual engagement in associational activity. This seems to me plausible, indeed, likely. The burden of proof at this point in the debate rests with Putnam's critics, not with Putnam. However, even if Putnam's data holds up, it would still be premature to infer from it a decline in civic participation. The reason, as the last chapter suggested, is that civic participation now takes place everywhere. It exists in the microprocesses of social life. In the cultural shift from the informed citizen model of the Progressive

Era to the rights-regarding citizen of the present day, a dimension of citizenship has come to color everything. Whatever the measures on social capital may finally show, it will still be the case that individual political activity in the past quarter century has actually risen.[16] It could scarcely be otherwise when the idea of citizenship has colonized so many of the territories of private life that once were beyond its jurisdiction.

Citizens still exercise citizenship as they stand in line at their polling places, but now they exercise citizenship in many other locations. They have political ties not only to elected public officials in legislatures but also to attorneys in courtrooms and organized interest groups that represent them to administrative agencies. Moreover, they are citizens in their homes, schools, and places of employment.[17] Women and minorities self-consciously do politics just by turning up, so long as they turn up in positions of authority and responsibility in institutions where women and minorities were once rarely seen. They do politics when they walk into a room, anyone's moral equals, and expect to be treated accordingly. The gay and lesbian couples in Hawaii in 1991 or in Vermont in 1997 are political when they try to be legally married (and, of course, so are their opponents in Congress and the twenty-five states that have passed laws to bar recognition of such marriages).[18] Others do politics when they wear a "Thank You For Not Smoking" button or when they teach their children to read nutritional labeling at the supermarket or when they join in class action suits against producers of silicone breast implants, Dalkon shields, or asbestos insulation.

The changes that have made the personal political have been profound, arguably more so than the slackening of voter turnout, the decline in PTA membership, the decreasing willingness of college freshmen to affirm political obligations and political convictions, or television's incursion into living rooms and bedrooms. What also has invaded the household is talk—talk between husband and wife as equals, political talk between husband and wife, political talk even between parents and children, no doubt often prompted by the television news or even the outrageous TV magazine or talk shows. And the language of this talk is a public language that, within it, bears the seeds of rights-consciousness and its premises of moral equality. There is evidence of this in, for instance, the ways that even women who claim no allegiance to feminism and no interest in politics have come to use terms like "male chauvinist" in their everyday language.[19] There is evidence of it also in the ways that ordinary Americans from all walks of life address their congressional representatives in letters—which they do, as it happens, with more frequency than ever before.[20]

It is hard to fully credit the 1990s rhetoric of decline when it is so easy to recall almost the same language from the 1950s. I remember, from my own growing-up, David Riesman's *The Lonely Crowd* on my parents' bookshelf along with William Whyte's *Organization Man* and Sloan Wilson's novel *The Man in the Gray Flannel Suit*, and other popular statements that condemned American conformity, complacency, and mediocrity. The pursuit of private material gain was widely condemned. I remember listening to the rabbi at my synagogue in Milwaukee attack my elders for failing to participate in community and religious life. He called his congregants "cardiac Jews" because they were Jewish "in their hearts" but not in their participation in the life of the Jewish community.

Much of the alarm at the time was pegged to the Cold War and the need to stand up to the forces of evil in the world. Americans not only lacked community, it was said, they lacked courage. They were without role models, heroes, and wisdom. What they did not lack was trust in major institutions. In retrospect, they had far too much of it. They trusted a Cold War government that tested radioactive fallout on unwitting citizens, welfare bureaucrats who told the poor they were not eligible for benefits they were qualified for, registrars of voters who denied the franchise to blacks in the South who could not explain complex clauses of the Constitution, doctors who kept from patients the knowledge they were dying or concealed the risks of elective surgery, teachers who told parents their children could not learn because they were retarded (when they were not) or because their skin was not white. Perhaps they even trusted too much in marriage and the family, with a higher percentage of the population marrying than ever before, and at younger ages, and with more children spaced more closely together, reversing a long-term decline in fertility. Divorce rates declined, too, bucking a historical trend upward.[21] Could the nuclear family satisfy all the demands made of it?

A society cannot long endure without basic social trust, nor can a democracy survive without well-organized and well-institutionalized distrust. Because of distrust, we have a Bill of Rights; because of distrust, we have checks and balances; because of distrust, we are enjoined as citizens to be watchful.

Reviewing the broad contours of the 1950s should breed skepticism about contemporary exclamations of moral degradation. What sense are we to make of today's critique when examined alongside the lamentations from the 1950s about the apathetic Americans, the suburbanites David Riesman characterized as "seldom informed, rarely angry, and only spasmodically partisan" or the citizens C. Wright Mills judged politically "inactionary" and "out of it"?[22] These thinkers wrote at exactly the moment when the World War II generation that Putnam has called the "long civic generation" was in command, social capital was supposedly at its height, and the television virus had not yet spread. The rhetoric of decline should send up a red flag; for the socially concerned intellectual, it is as much an off-the-rack rhetoric as is a rhetoric of progress for the ebullient technocrat.

How could we know if citizenship and community are in decline? What kinds of measures might we look to, recognizing, of course, that the question is far too general to admit of any simple index?

The most familiar measure has been voter turnout—the percentage of citizens eligible to vote who do so has declined in the past generation. This is a relevant measure, indeed, in part because voting is an act not only of citizen participation but also of general faith in the political system. Voting is an instrumental act to elect one candidate and not another, but it is also a mass ritual, and failure to engage in it suggests declining fervor for the religion of democracy. A decline in turnout is, on its face, a worrisome sign. On the other hand, high voter turnout is not necessarily a sign of civic health. An analyst would have to examine not only what percentage of the eligible electorate vote but also who is eligible to vote (the number doubled with woman's suffrage in 1920 and rose again after the Civil Rights Acts of 1964 and 1965 were passed and enforced) and what the act of voting means. The turnout decline since the

1960s is scarcely conclusive in itself. The high turnout figures of the nineteenth century, as I have argued, do not reveal that the civic health of America's party period was glowing; neither do recent low turnout figures indicate fatal illness.

A second measure would be people's expressed trust in government and other leading social institutions. Here, too, there has been a substantial decline; people are much less likely in the 1990s than in the 1960s to tell pollsters they "trust in" the president, the Congress, the medical profession, the military, the Supreme Court, business, unions, universities, or the news media.[23] Still, as I have suggested, there can be too much trust as well as too little, and the baseline measures of trust from the 1950s and early 1960s surely reflected a moment of unusual consensus in American life held together by Cold War paranoia, middle-class complacency, postwar affluence, and the continuing denial of a voice in public life to women and minorities. Some of the skepticism about major institutions today is amply warranted. Skepticism can be healthy. Some of today's skepticism is in a grand old American tradition that distrusts all politics and politicians. Then again, some of it seems to express a deeper alienation or aimlessness, especially among the young. But in the crude measures we have, there is no distinguishing a healthy inclination to question authority from a depressed withdrawal in which it is impossible to place faith in anyone or anything.

A third plausible measure of civic health would be the stock of social capital as measured by people's membership in and connection to social groups in which they can and do participate. As Putnam has argued well, this is an important measure. Still, it is difficult to know how to weigh it against the growth of individual choice, which is its flip side. Let me offer an example. The Roman Catholic Church in America has long been a powerful institution in community-building, especially among the urban, immigrant working-class Catholics who for a century were the core of its membership. The Catholic parish was disciplined by the priest who had enormous power in prescribing norms of behavior for everyday life. His authority was exercised through a dense network of youth groups, fraternal organizations, parish sports teams, choirs, women's clubs, and, of course, parochial schools and the church itself. More than for Protestants or Jews, Catholic adherence to church was also involvement in a neighborhood. Into the 1950s, rental listings for homes and apartments in cities like Philadelphia and Chicago were categorized *by parish*.[24] In the 1960s, the Catholic Church, like the rest of America, experienced profound changes, but more so. Pope John XXIII called the Second Vatican Council together in 1962, the first such council since 1870. The report of Vatican II, issued in 1965, declared that the church should adapt itself to modernity, dissent within the church could be tolerated, religious freedom should be prized, and the liturgy should be revised to make it more comprehensible to parishioners and more participatory. The Mass in Latin was now in English, the priest who had faced the wall and prayed silently now led the congregation in prayer; the once silent congregation now sang hymns, shook hands, and stood rather than knelt.

Vatican II was an authoritative statement that questioned authority. It had far-reaching consequences. The traditional deference of the laity to the clergy in the conduct of the church declined. As Catholics, both laity and clergy, participated actively in the civil rights movement, lay parishioners, nuns, and seminarians all were "imbued with new notions of 'rights'" and explicitly compared their lack of power or their ghettoization within the church to the condition of blacks in American society.[25] When Vatican II was followed in 1968 by *Humanae vitae*, Pope Paul VI's encyclical that reaffirmed the prohibition on birth control, millions of Catholics were at least confused, and many of them felt betrayed, by a church they had believed was modernizing. Both clergy and laity protested, some by leaving the church or their vocations. There were 181,000 women in religious orders in 1966 and 127,000 by 1980, and the downward trend was the same for men. Even for those who remained, clerical leadership changed as lay leaders came to take a larger and larger role in church governance.[26] The church became increasingly pluralistic: "There is no longer one way to do theology, to worship at Mass, to confess sin, or to pray. There are various ways of being Catholic, and people are choosing the style that best suits them."[27] As Catholics moved to the suburbs, the link between parish, church, ethnicity, and personal identity did not break down, but it did to a degree break apart. Suburban Catholics are not Protestants and retain, as Andrew Greeley has argued, a distinctive Catholic "imagination," but the locus of authority about what it is to be Catholic has gravitated further from the church and closer to the household than a generation ago.[28]

Was the old way better? Did the authoritarian structure that held together a parish community provide a stronger basis for self-fulfillment and a rich public life than the new structure that offered the individual more choice, autonomy, and power? The Catholic Church is, of course, only one example of the kind of institution that built social capital in the old days, and it is obviously an example of a particularly rigid and hierarchical cast. Yet it is one of the fundamental constituents of twentieth-century American society, the strength of its community life a major source of the strength of urban machine politics, the Democratic Party, and the union movement. Its broad influence seems much more important in this context than its atypicality, and its transformation reveals starkly that the trade-off between community and individualism is also a trade-off between hierarchy and egalitarianism, between authoritarian codes and democratic ones, between unitary, rigid ways of living and pluralistic ones, between imposition and individual choice. There are costs to the decline of traditional authority in the church, patriarchal family, party machine, and settled elites of community life. The costs are grounds for regret, nostalgia, and a variety of imaginative efforts at renewal, but few people find them grounds for turning back.

Voting, social trust, and social membership are the three most familiar measures of civic health, and the three most familiar bases on which it is argued that the present has slipped from a more desirable past. Other measures might be given consideration, too. A fourth measure is the quality of public discourse. Critics look at daytime talk shows, or listen to Howard Stern or Rush Limbaugh, or read pornography or scurrilous political gossip on the Internet, or feel assaulted by the public use of words that a generation ago could be heard only in locker rooms and not on television, or observe the reduction of political speeches to catchphrases that might win the attention of broadcast journalists committed to ever shorter sound bites. Can this be judged anything but degradation?

I do not have an answer here, but on this measure, too, there is another side of the story. The greater openness and rawness of public talk that produced raunchy talk shows also produced *All in the Family*,

Maude, and *Ellen* in entertainment and programs like *60 Minutes* in television news. All of these programs share with their more disparaged and tasteless cousins a frank and aggressive style, a quest for transgression, and a pushing of the limits of conventional civility. Meanwhile, a serious argument can be made that ordinary Americans have better access to solid news reporting and analysis today than they did in 1960 or 1965. Journalists are less complacent in general; more individual journalists have become expert and ambitious contributors to public dialogue with magazine essays, long newspaper pieces, and nonfiction books; our leading newspapers reach many more people than ever through national editions and their own wire services (notably the *New York Times, Washington Post,* and *Los Angeles Times*); national network news is more sophisticated than a generation ago even if local television news is increasingly a moral desert; and in some major cities and regions there are today exponents of the best journalism the country has produced where none existed in 1960—I think of Chicago, Washington, D.C., and Los Angeles.[29]

A fifth measure: how great is the disparity between rich and poor? Related to this: is there an economic bottom below which society by private and public efforts will not allow people to fall? Prosperity as such is no measure of civic life, nor is it apparent what level of economic inequality might endanger the public good. But there is a quality of care for the poor, lacking which a society has clearly failed. The United States remains a reluctant welfare state, never fully committed to seeing economic equality or even a baseline minimum economic subsistence as an obligation of the state. Even so, a smaller percentage of the population lives in poverty today than in 1960, although the percentage was higher in 1990 than in 1980.[30]

One must consider quality as well as quantity in the disparity between rich and poor. It is important to know not only how great is the gap between those at the top and those at the bottom but how hopeless the world appears from the bottom. Do economic and social inequalities take on a castelike form? How well can one predict the economic or social life-chances of an infant from the economic status, skin color, age, and marital status of his or her mother? If these predictions are becoming easier, then on this measure public life is getting worse.

Sixth, is the capacity of the least advantaged groups in society to make their voices heard in the political process increasing or decreasing? And what of less advantaged groups, say, blue-collar workers? If the power of unions is declining, as certainly it is, and if the Democratic Party is correspondingly less responsive to working-class concerns, has a large segment of the population lost its clearest access to political power?

Finally, is the reach of state-guaranteed rights increasing or decreasing? If it is increasing, then public life is improving in that public responsibility is growing and the range of human actions in which publicly accountable language is brought to bear is enlarging. Of course, state-guaranteed rights increase only because people believe that state or private power has violated the fundamental autonomy of individuals—the government has quartered its soldiers in your house without permission, the police have searched your house or person without a warrant, your school board has expelled you from school because your religious beliefs forbid you to salute the flag, your husband beats you, your employer threatens you for refusing sexual favors, your public transportation has not accommodated your wheelchair. If none of these things ever happened, then there would be no requirement of state-protected rights. But the existence of state-protected rights is a force for keeping these violations from happening or, at least, for calling people to account when they do. By this measure, it can scarcely be doubted that public life has improved in the past generation.

Public life can be measured by the inclusiveness of public deliberations. The more people among the total population who are eligible to shoulder the burden of public decision-making and who are equipped to do so, the better the public life of a society. By this measure, certainly, the United States after 1920 has a better public life than at any earlier time, and the United States after 1965 has a better public life than at any earlier time. To the extent that certain senseless discriminations, apart from limitations on voting, are struck down—for instance, discrimination in employment or housing on the basis of sexual orientation—this also helps to fully empower citizens to speak and participate. By this measure, American society is better since *Romer* v. *Evans* (1995) struck down Colorado's anti-homosexual state constitutional amendment than it was before. To the extent that the poor and the oppressed whose voices have commonly been excluded from public deliberation today at least have institutionalized surrogates in public interest associations, law firms, foundations, and other organizations, there is progress rather than decline.

How is American public life doing today on these seven measures? Voter turnout offers troubling evidence of decline. Polling that indicates a lessening of trust in major institutions is a much more equivocal measure of civic health. We do not know what it means. How does the answer people give to an abstract question about their level of trust relate to actual behavioral indices of trust—compliance with the Internal Revenue Service or willingness to defer to the authority of a medical doctor, a government bureaucrat, a school administrator, or a court order? Nor do we know what the optimal level of trust would be. Surely it would be deeply troubling if 100 percent of the people placed "a great deal" of faith in the president, the Congress, big business, labor, medicine, universities, or the media. But is 75 percent the right level? Or 50 percent? Or 25 percent?

I do not think that trust, so far as polls are able to measure it, is an intelligible indicator of anything. What then, about social capital? Is declining membership in important civic organizations a clear sign of declining social health? I think a reasonable observer must be agnostic on this one. The decline in organizational solidarity is truly a loss, but it is also the flip side of a rise in individual freedom, which is truly a gain. Assessments of the state of public discourse must likewise reckon with its double-edged character. On the down side, public talk has clearly grown more harsh, more crude, and more uncivil over the past several decades. On the up side, however, public discourse is more honest and more inclusive of a wide range of persons and topics that the late, lamented "civility" excluded. These two measures seem to have an inherently paradoxical quality; the very social changes that give good reason for regret also give good reason for satisfaction.

As for the disparity between the most and least advantaged citizens, a straight-line trend seems hard to find. This measure seems to be very sensitive to party politics, so a society that grew more kind and just in the 1960s and 1970s became notably less so in the Reagan eighties, and only under President Bill Clinton has it begun to inch back toward decency.

Regarding the measures of political inclusion and protection for individual rights, Americans are unquestionably better off in the past quarter century than at any prior moment in our history. There are ups and downs here, too, but the 1960s and 1970s saw the emergence of a consensus that, though assaulted and even shaken, has not surrendered the field. It is, on the contrary, our new foundation.

By my count, then, there is a clear decline on one measure, clear progress on two others, a mixed verdict on three, and a judgment that one measure (trust) is thus far too faulty a concept to use. To summarize all of this as amounting to a decline in civic well-being is, to put it kindly, premature.

Of course, this is no more than a provisional thought-experiment, not a definitive assessment of the state of the nation. We do not truly know how to measure change on these seven dimensions, nor do we know how to weigh one dimension against another.

The historical analysis I have undertaken here cannot settle the matter, but it can help to more adequately assess our present state and to improve upon it. For instance, it calls attention to the multiply layered resources for citizenship available today that are rarely viewed in the whole. In popular political discourse, there is too literal an appeal to Progressive ideals of the informed citizen and too rarely an appreciation of the rights-regarding citizen. When a leading college textbook in American history cannot in its more than nine hundred pages find space to mention the *Carolene Products* footnote (or the *Palko* case or the *Korematsu* case), it seems clear that the vital significance of the rights-regarding model of citizenship is not yet integrated into American collective self-understanding or civic education.[31] When we dismiss the vast social legislation of 1965–75 as a failure because the Great Society programs did not end poverty, we badly fail to recognize our own times. Voices on the right decry Great Society initiatives because they want so desperately to prove the ideological claim that government only makes things worse; voices on the left are dismissive because their preoccupation with the elimination of economic inequality makes them strangely blind to political and social advances in human dignity.

To acknowledge that a sense of rights is now part of the political bloodstream, seeping into the capillaries of social life, is not yet to affirm that a rights-conscious citizenship is adequate to our world. I do hold that prior models of citizenship do not suffice for the tasks of the present and that the political dialogues and practices they engendered were marked by a pathetically low regard for minority rights and a miserly vision of what human differences could be tolerated, appreciated, and even cherished. But this is not to suggest that rights-regarding citizenship is in itself a solution. Does it guide people to (1) commit themselves to dialogue and deliberation with fellow citizens recognized as moral and political equals (2) while keeping minority rights in mind and (3) holding in view not only themselves but their posterity, while also (4) demanding of themselves, in everyday circumstances, ordinary but not heroic efforts at information-gathering and civic participation? Can a rights-conscious citizenship build institutions that allow people to be citizens without forcing them to be saints? Can it encourage people to be citizens even as they normally maintain a primary devotion to private tasks? Or, instead, does it reduce citizenship to a what's-in-it-for-me relationship to public life? Does it provide new tools and new access primarily for the people whose wealth and position gave them a disproportionately large say in governing in the first place?

A rights-regarding citizenship does not "answer" democracy's discontents, but it is a necessary part of any answer. Moreover, it automatically implies respect for the rights of others and the willingness to engage in public dispute according to public norms and a public language. We have to recognize that the claiming of rights, though it should not be the end of a citizen's political consciousness, is an invaluable beginning to it. It deserves to be nurtured, not condemned. We need to teach ourselves and our children more, not less, about rights.

But each of the historical eras of citizenship practice is yet a resource if we can understand how that citizenship practice functions and how it might function in our own time. Take, for instance, the model of the informed citizen. It still holds a cherished place in our array of political values, as I think it should, but it requires some modification. A stale mugwumpery does not face up to what we know of human cognition or what we have so far failed to figure out about the relationship of popular knowledge and expertise in a democracy. I would propose that the obligation of citizens to know enough to participate intelligently in governmental affairs be understood as a monitorial obligation. Citizens can be monitorial rather than informed. Monitorial citizens scan (rather than read) the informational environment in a way so that they may be alerted on a very wide variety of issues for a very wide variety of ends and may be mobilized around those issues in a large variety of ways. They may learn that a product they own has been recalled; that a drought will make produce more expensive in a few weeks (and they might want to buy that lettuce or those blueberries now while they still have a chance); that the road they normally drive home on is tied up with traffic and they should take an alternate route; that an earthquake has made it impossible to contact friends in Los Angeles directly so they should stay tuned for further information; that right-wing militia are far more numerous and serious than they had thought so the context in which they understand the dangers or possibilities in current politics has to be altered. When they hear that on one coast President Clinton is defending affirmative action policies while on the other California voters have put an end to affirmative action in their state, some citizens may be led to read more on the subject, write on the subject, or talk to their friends. But even for the vast majority who do no more than scan the headlines, they are thereby greatly informed about an important turn in the climate of popular opinion. Print journalists regularly criticize broadcast media for being only a headline service, but a headline service is what, in the first instance, citizens require. ("The redcoats are coming!" said Paul Revere as he rode through every Middlesex village and farm, apparently not embarrassed by the brevity of his sound bite.)[32]

Walter Lippmann was right: if democracy requires omnicompetence and omniscience from its citizens, it is a lost cause. There must be some distribution across people and across issues of the cognitive demands of self-government. Consider an analogy: it is fun to go camping and to be able to take care of one's every need for a few days in the mountains. But in everyday life most people are glad to turn on the stove rather than rub two sticks together and to buy a packaged chicken at the supermarket rather than trap a rabbit in the woods. We rely on the farms, milk processors, and government inspectors to see that milk is pasteurized, we do not do it ourselves; we trust in the metropolitan water supply to purify water, not our own chemicals. Why, then, in public life, do we expect people to be political backpackers?

People may find pleasure in knowing the ropes of political information just as they may enjoy developing wilderness survival skills. There can be pleasure in this, there can be social advantage, one can gain in social esteem by knowing more than others in the same circles, and this can even lead people to seek power or political office. But most people will not be so inclined. How, then, if we are not to be full-time political backpackers, can anything like a democracy exist?

The idea of the monitorial citizen offers one possible answer. Monitorial citizens tend to be defensive rather than proactive. They are perhaps better informed than citizens of the past in that, somewhere in their heads, they have more bits of information, but there is no assurance that they know at all what to do with what they know. They have no more virtue than citizens of the past—but not less, either.

The monitorial citizen engages in environmental surveillance more than information-gathering. Picture parents watching small children at the community pool. They are not gathering information; they are keeping an eye on the scene. They look inactive, but they are poised for action if action is required. The monitorial citizen is not an absentee citizen but watchful, even while he or she is doing something else. Citizenship during a particular political season may be for many people much less intense than in the era of parties, but citizenship now is a year-round and day-long activity, as it was only rarely in the past.

How much of the obligation to be knowledgeable about politics can people relinquish without doing violence to their democratic souls? There is surely some line of willful ignorance that, once crossed, crosses out democracy itself. There should be more attention, not less, in our schools and in our homes to explaining the rights and responsibilities of citizenship. The teaching of democracy and the modeling of democracy should never stop. At the same time, we should have in view plausible aims that integrate citizenry competence with specialized expert resources. We cannot be and should not be political backpackers. Over the past century and a half Americans have delegated fire fighting in our cities to professionals rather than relying on volunteers, although it remains important that everyone understand basic fire safety, perhaps keep a fire extinguisher at home or in the car, maintain smoke detectors in the house, and know how to dial 9-1-1. We have subcontracted much of childhood education to public schools and expert teachers rather than to ourselves as parents. Parents still help with the homework, "enrich" their children's education with efforts of their own, and know how to assist or intervene in the school system when necessary. We have divided medical care among hospitals and physicians on the one hand, and households on the other, where our shelves are stocked with diet books, women's magazines, Dr. Spock, and an array of over-the-counter medicines.

We have arrived, in short, at a division of labor between expertise and self-help that gives credit to both. We do this in politics, too, but without having found a place in either popular rhetoric or democratic theory for the use of specialized knowledge. That quest for a language of public life that reconciles democracy and expertise merits renewed attention. No such language arose from the Lippmann-Dewey debate of the 1920s; the matter remains entirely unresolved in political thought today.

Political theorists are eloquent about public life, the role of public intellectuals, the necessity of a public sphere, and the virtues of the common good, but there is a time also to think further on private life, on the pains of personal loss that continue in the best of societies or on the joys of appreciating a sunset, humming a tune, or listening to the quiet breathing of a sleeping child that can endure in all but the worst. These moments hold their own with, or displace, the political. A good society would accommodate this and a good citizen would know it. The good society would also work to provide, on the basis of the moral and social equality of its members, access to a satisfying private life for all.

There can be an intense thrill to political life. Some people have never felt more whole than in the midst of political combat or in the sweet pleasure of political camaraderie. They have felt a powerful, heightened sense of connection to their time and their humanity. In these same moments, however, individuals are deeply vulnerable to situations and passions that they cannot control. These are moments of great opportunity but also genuine danger. Sometimes it is necessary to take great risks, but in the long run, a desirable civic life is one where people can participate at acceptable levels of risk. When, without jeopardizing life, liberty, or conscience, and without subjugating or demeaning private life, people can speak freely, deliberate collectively, and work together in hope, political democracy will have achieved its aspirations.

Obviously, the United States is not there yet. It will not get there in a social world riven by racial and ethnic antagonisms, by the absurd inequalities of wealth that in recent years have grown even wider, by the limited horizon that face the children of the poor, and by the insecurity that confines and confuses even the children of the middle class. Our society is beset by unsolved problems and a political system that too often today, as in the past, is unprepared even to acknowledge them. But we have the resources, including the human resources, to rethink those problems and remake the political world.

Is the glass of citizenship, of political democracy, of membership in a moral community of equals entitled to the rights and responsibilities of self-government half empty or half full? If this is a question about a three centuries' stretch of history or even a half century's expanse, and not an attitude survey on the politics of the moment, then the answer is easy. For women, wage laborers, racial, ethnic, sexual preference, or religious minorities, the poor, and the elderly, progress toward genuine inclusion in the past half century has been extraordinary. A significant part of that progress came in the 1960s and 1970s, far-reaching and unsettling enough that society is still reacting and adjusting to the changes wrought in those years.

Progress or decline is not the real question. All that is required to criticize the present state of affairs is to know that some serious injustices persist, that some remediable conditions that limit human possibility lie before us, and that resources for reconstituting ourselves can be found. Injustices and exclusions remain, especially in the bifurcation of society into the relatively comfortable and the abjectly poor. We do not need to beat ourselves with the stick of the past. We cannot enact now the founders' politics of assent or the nineteenth century's politics of affiliation, nor should we want to. We will not recover our heritage by hiding behind it, nor will we relinquish it by facing the present as honestly as we can.

Notes

Introduction: Election Day

1. Robert Fishman, *Bourgeois Utopias* (New York: Basic Books, 1987), p. 17, speaks of technoburbs; Rob Kling, Spencer Olin, and Mark Poster, eds., *Postsuburban California* (Berkeley: University of California Press, 1991), discuss postsuburbs; and Joel Garreau, *Edge City* (New York: Doubleday, 1991), writes on edge cities.

2. My emphasis in discussing "citizenship" is on the idea of the good citizen—what the character and civic practices are of a person who admirably carries out the responsibilities of citizenship. The more familiar study of citizenship centers either on legal definitions of inclusion and exclusion or, following T. H. Marshall, the history of citizen entitlements guaranteed by the state. Both of these topics are relevant to this study and will enter into it. But my preoccupation is with understanding how individuals come to participate in political life, how they arrive at an understanding of political questions, and how they think about what obligations their citizenship entails.

3. Walt Whitman, "Election Day, November, 1884," in *Walt Whitman: Complete Poetry and Collected Prose* (New York: Library of America, 1982), p. 620.

Chapter 1: Colonial Origins of American Political Practice: 1690–1787

1. J. G. A. Pocock, "The Classical Theory of Deference," *American Historical Review* 81 (1976): 516.

2. Charles E. Clark, *The Public Prints* (New York: Oxford University Press, 1994), p. 72. Clark makes the case that the article on the Iroquois was the offensive one.

3. The *locus classicus* for a discussion of the "public sphere" is Jurgen Habermas, *The Structural Transformation of the Public Sphere* (Cambridge: MIT Press, 1989). The best secondary source is Craig Calhoun, ed., *Habermas and the Pub-*

lic Sphere (Cambridge: MIT Press, 1992), with Calhoun's wonderfully lucid, critical introduction. I have made my own contributions to the industry of Habermas criticism in the Calhoun volume and in "The 'Public Sphere' and Its Problems: Bringing the State (Back) In," *Notre Dame Journal of Law, Ethics, and Public Policy* 8(1994): 529–46.

4. For a rich discussion of this in England, see Mark Kishlansky, *Parliamentary Selection* (Cambridge: Cambridge University Press, 1986).

5. Robert J. Dinkin, *Voting in Provincial America* (Westport, CT: Greenwood, 1977), p. 7.

6. Ian K. Steele, *The English Atlantic, 1675–1740* (New York: Oxford University Press, 1986), pp. 121–22.

7. Michael Kammen, *Deputyes and Libertyes: The Origins of Representative Government in Colonial America* (New York: Knopf, 1969), p. 57.

8. Gary Nash, *The Urban Crucible* (Cambridge: Harvard University Press, 1979), p. 55.

9. David S. Lovejoy, *The Glorious Revolution in America* (New York: Harper & Row, 1972), p. 348.

10. T. H. Breen, *Puritans and Adventurers* (New York: Oxford University Press, 1980), pp. 83–84.

11. John Murrin, "A Roof Without Walls: The Dilemma of American National Identity," in Richard Beeman, Stephen Botein, and Edward C. Carter II, eds., *Beyond Confederation* (Chapel Hill: University of North Carolina Press, 1987), p. 338.

12. Jack P. Greene, "The Growth of Political Stability: An Interpretation of Political Development in the Anglo-American Colonies, 1660–1760," in John Parker and Carol Urness, eds., *The American Revolution: A Heritage of Change* (Minneapolis: Associates of the James Ford Bell Library, 1975), p. 27.

13. John G. Kolp, "The Dynamics of Electoral Competition in Pre-Revolutionary Virginia," *William and Mary Quarterly*, 3rd series, 49 (1992): 670.

14. Nash, *The Urban Crucible*, underlines the role of economic disturbance on political involvement. See pp. 84–85, 156–57, 264–65.

15. Kenneth A. Lockridge, *A New England Town: The First Hundred Years* (New York: Norton, 1970), p. xi. See also Michael Zuckerman, *Peaceable Kingdoms: New England Towns in the Eighteenth Century* (New York: Alfred A. Knopf, 1972), p. 3. On the New England town myth among Progressive Era intellectuals, see Jean B. Quandt, *From the Small Town to the Great Community* (New Brunswick, NJ: Rutgers University Press, 1970), pp. 5–10.

16. Richard L. McCormick, *The Party Period and Public Policy* (New York: Oxford University Press, 1986), pp. 228–59.

17. See Lockridge, *A New England Town*, pp. 38–56; also Kenneth Lockridge and Alan Kreider, "The Evolution of Massachusetts Town Government, 1640 to 1740," *William and Mary Quarterly* 23 (1966): 549–74.

18. Bruce C. Daniels, *The Connecticut Town* (Middletown, CT: Wesleyan University Press, 1979), pp. 68, 74–75, 105, 130, 132–34. The quotation concerning Rhode Island is on p. 75.

19. David Hackett Fischer estimates that turnout normally ranged from 10 to 30 percent of adult males, a figure close enough to Mansbridge's if we assume that

roughly half of adult males held enough property to qualify for the franchise. See David Hackett Fischer, *Albion's Seed: Four British Folkways in America* (New York: Oxford University Press, 1989), p. 198.

20. Jane Mansbridge, *Beyond Adversary Democracy* (New York: Basic Books, 1980), p. 131.

21. Dinkin, *Voting in Provincial America*, pp. 146, 173.

22. Daniels, *The Connecticut Town*, p. 131.

23. Mansbridge, *Beyond Adversary Democracy*, p. 132.

24. James A. Henretta, "The Morphology of New England Society in the Colonial Period," *Journal of Interdisciplinary History* 2 (1971): 394. See also Robert Zemsky, *Merchants, Farmers, and River Gods: An Essay on Eighteenth-Century American Politics* (Boston: Gambit, 1971), p. 69.

25. Lockridge, *A New England Town*, p. 128.

26. Lockridge and Kreider, "The Evolution of Massachusetts Town Government," and Lockridge, *A New England Town*, pp. 119–38.

27. Daniels, *The Connecticut Town*, pp. 67, 80, 90.

28. Stephen Foster, *Their Solitary Way: The Puritan Social Ethic in the First Century of Settlement in New England* (New Haven: Yale University Press, 1971), p. 157. See also Michael Zuckerman, "The Social Context of Democracy in Massachusetts," *William and Mary Quarterly*, 3rd series, 25 (1968): 538–39.

29. Fischer, *Albion's Seed*, pp. 199–205.

30. Patricia U. Bonomi, "The Middle Colonies: Embryo of the New Political Order," in Alden T. Vaughan and George A. Billias, eds., *Perspectives on Early American History: Essays in Honor of Richard B. Morris* (New York: Harper & Row, 1973), pp. 63–92. The *Gazette* (March 11–18, 1734) is cited on p. 87.

31. Gordon Wood, *The Radicalism of the American Revolution* (New York: Knopf, 1992), pp. 42, 63; Rhys Isaac, *The Transformation of Virginia, 1740–1790* (Chapel Hill: University of North Carolina Press, 1982), p. 131, and Nash, *The Urban Crucible*, p. 8.

32. Nash, *The Urban Crucible*, p. 31.

33. Zemsky, *Merchants, Farmers, and River Gods*, pp. 239–41.

34. Kolp, "The Dynamics of Electoral Competition," p. 670.

35. Ibid., p. 670.

36. Charles S. Sydnor, *Gentlemen Freeholders* (Chapel Hill: University of North Carolina Press, 1952), p. 77.

37. Ibid., pp. 61–62.

38. David W. Conroy, *In Public Houses* (Chapel Hill: University of North Carolina Press, 1995), pp. 12–20, and John O. and Margaret T. Peters, *Virginia's Historic Courthouses* (Charlottesville: University Press of Virginia, 1995), pp. 5–26.

39. Sydnor, *Gentlemen Freeholders*, pp. 60, 68–70, 124.

40. Ibid., pp. 51–54.

41. Isaac, *The Transformation of Virginia*, pp. 113–14.

42. On this double-edged quality of representation in the period, see Edmund S. Morgan, *Inventing the People* (New York: Norton, 1988), pp. 175–76, 178, 197–98.

43. Daniels, *The Connecticut Town*, pp. 86, 134. See also Conroy, *In Public Houses*, p. 208.

44. Bruce C. Daniels, ed., "Introduction," *Power and Status: Officeholding in Colonial America* (Middletown, CT: Wesleyan University Press, 1986), pp. 3–13.

45. Bernard Bailyn, *The Origins of American Politics* (New York: Knopf, 1968), p. 88.

46. Chilton Williamson, *American Suffrage: From Property to Democracy, 1760–1860* (Princeton: Princeton University Press, 1960), p. 41.

47. Baron de Montesquieu, *The Spirit of the Laws*, vol. 1, book 2 (New York: Hafner, 1966), p. 12.

48. Patricia U. Bonomi, *A Factious People: Politics and Society in Colonial New York* (New York: Columbia University Press, 1971), p. 7.

49. This may be traced to the particular regional cultures within England from which settlers came. New England settlers especially came from parts of the south and east of England notable for their independence and also for the influence of Dutch customs upon them. East Anglia had a history of political rebellion, was a strong center of resistance to Charles I, and was a center for dissenting sects as well. See Fischer, *Albion's Seed*, pp. 44–47.

50. Cited in James Henretta, *The Evolution of American Society, 1700–1815* (Lexington, MA: Heath, 1973), p. 102.

51. Gordon Wood, *The Creation of the American Republic, 1776–1787* (Chapel Hill: University of North Carolina Press, 1969). See also Francis N. Thorpe, *A Constitutional History of the American People, 1776–1850*, vol. 1 (New York: Harper, 1898), pp. 80–82, on the solutions to this problem in the early state constitutions, where the lower house of state legislatures was generally apportioned on the basis of population, the upper house on the basis of property.

52. Mary Patterson Clarke, *Parliamentary Privilege in the American Colonies* (New York: Da Capo, 1971), pp. 227, 229. Originally published 1943.

53. This is the use of the term in the English Bill of Rights of 1689 and in the state constitutions of Maryland, Massachusetts, New Hampshire, Vermont, and the Articles of Confederation. Vermont also uses the phrase with respect to citizens' rights, as did Pennsylvania's constitutions, both of 1776 and 1790. See the valuable compilation, Thurston Greene, *The Language of the Constitution* (Westport, CT: Greenwood, 1991), pp. 801–803.

54. Wood, *The Radicalism of the American Revolution*, pp. 96, 98.

55. Richard L. Bushman, *King and People in Provincial Massachusetts* (Chapel Hill: University of North Carolina Press, 1985), pp. 92–93. See also Howard Nenner, "Liberty, Law, and Property: The Constitution in Retrospect from 1689," in J. R. Jones, ed., *Liberty Secured? Britain Before and After 1688* (Stanford: Stanford University Press, 1988), pp. 88–121.

56. Cited in Edmund S. Morgan, *American Slavery—American Freedom: The Ordeal of Colonial Virginia* (New York: Norton, 1975), p. 372.

57. Pauline Maier, *From Resistance to Revolution* (New York: Norton, 1972, 1991), p. 210; Morgan, *Inventing the People*, p. 244.

58. Murrin, "Roof Without Walls," p. 340.

59. Pauline Maier, "Coming to Terms with Samuel Adams," *American Historical Review* 81 (1976): 21.

60. Jack N. Rakove, *The Beginnings of National Politics* (New York: Knopf, 1979), p. 10.

61. Jack P. Greene, "The Role of the Lower Houses of Assembly in Eighteenth-Century Politics," *Journal of Southern History* 27 (1961): 451–74.
62. Henretta, *The Evolution of American Society*, p. 110.
63. Kenneth Colegrove, "New England Town Mandates," *Publications of the Colonial Society of Massachusetts* 21 (Boston: Colonial Society of Massachusetts, 1920): 421–23. We do not know how frequently instruction was provided, only that it happened and was legitimate, although Robert Zemsky suggests that in Massachusetts "many, if not most, representatives seldom allowed their constituency's preferences to influence their legislative behavior." Zemsky, *Merchants, Farmers, and River Gods*, p. 248.
64. J. R. Pole, *The Gift of Government* (Athens: University of Georgia Press, 1983), p. 109.
65. Ibid., p. 141.
66. John Phillip Reid, *The Concept of Representation in the Age of the American Revolution* (Chicago: University of Chicago Press, 1989), p. 83. See also Bailyn, *The Origins of American Politics*, p. 85.
67. Conroy, *In Public Houses*, p. 207. The pamphlet was *A Letter to the Freeholders and Other Inhabitants of the Massachusetts-Bay* and the critical letter appeared on April 30, 1739, in the *Boston Gazette*.
68. Quoted in Sydnor, *Gentlemen Freeholders*, p. 36. Thomas Jefferson suggested in a letter (to William Wirt, Aug. 5, 1815) that the point of the property qualification was not to disqualify the poor but to limit the power of the rich by disfranchising their tenants and servants who would be entirely dependent on them. Cited in Sydnor, *Gentlemen Freeholders*, p. 123.
69. Thomas Jefferson, *Notes on the State of Virginia*, in Adrienne Koch and William Peden, eds., *The Life and Selected Writings of Thomas Jefferson* (New York: Modern Library, 1944), p. 280.
70. See Drew McCoy, *The Elusive Republic* (Chapel Hill: University of North Carolina Press, 1980), pp. 5–47.
71. Williamson, *American Suffrage*, pp. 12–15.
72. See Stephanie McCurry, "The Two Faces of Republicanism: Gender and Proslavery Politics in Antebellum South Carolina," *Journal of American History* 78 (1992): 1263.
73. Williamson, *American Suffrage*, pp. 12–16.
74. Richard R. Beeman, "Deference, Republicanism, and the Emergence of Popular Politics in Eighteenth-Century America," *William and Mary Quarterly*, 3rd series, 49 (1992): 419.
75. Robert Brown concludes for eighteenth-century Massachusetts that it was a "middle-class society" in economic terms, with property easily acquired and with a large share of the population making a living as property-owning farmers. Brown's work began a historiographic debate on the subject. The current consensus seems to be that Brown overemphasizes the democratic character of colonial life. See Robert E. Brown, *Middle-Class Democracy and the Revolution in Massachusetts, 1691–1780* (New York: Russell and Russell, 1955), p. 401.
76. See Bonomi, *A Factious People*, p. 7.
77. See Michael Kammen, *People of Paradox* (New York: Vintage, 1972), p. 40.

78. Raymond C. Bailey, *Popular Influence Upon Public Policy* (Westport, CT: Greenwood, 1979), p. 64. These figures must be interpreted with caution since petitions were often "acts of ventriloquism" initiated by elites, even by legislators themselves. See Morgan, *Inventing the People*, p. 230.

79. See Bailyn, *The Origins of American Politics*, pp. 26, 101–104; Jack P. Greene, *Pursuits of Happiness: The Social Development of Early Modern British Colonies and the Formation of American Culture* (Chapel Hill: University of North Carolina Press, 1988), p. 200; Jack P. Greene, "The Growth of Political Stability," pp. 28–29; Wood, *The Radicalism of the American Revolution*, p. 82; Alan Taylor, *William Cooper's Town* (New York: Knopf, 1995), pp. 206–207; Reid, *The Concept of Representation*, pp. 29–30.

80. Morgan, *American Slavery—American Freedom*, p. 208.

81. Wood, *The Radicalism of the American Revolution*, pp. 85–86.

82. Zemsky, *Merchants, Farmers, and River Gods*, p. 59.

83. Catherine Albanese, *Sons of the Fathers* (Philadelphia: Temple University Press, 1976), p. 11.

84. Barry Alan Shain makes this point about the centrality of religious communication in *The Myth of American Individualism* (Princeton: Princeton University Press, 1994), p. 216. See also Richard D. Brown, *Knowledge Is Power* (New York: Oxford University Press, 1989), p. 79, on the central role of the ministry as a source of information until the early national period.

85. There is a small academic industry that tries to sort out what medium of communication mattered most in this period—heaven knows why. In the colonial resistance, claims Michael Warner, "writing was the dominant mode of the political." Michael Warner, *The Letters of the Republic* (Cambridge: Harvard University Press, 1990), p. 67. In early national America, the written word was "supreme," according to Keith Baker, pointing to the primacy of the Constitution. Baker finds the written word gaining "supremacy" in France by 1794 or 1799. See Keith Michael Baker, *Inventing the French Revolution* (Cambridge: Cambridge University Press, 1990), p. 8. Others insist that print culture and oral culture supplemented rather than competed with each other. See Clark, *The Public Prints*, p. 169. Rhys Isaac, for instance, emphasizes the blurred boundaries between oral, dramatistic, and written culture. See *The Transformation of Virginia, 1740–1790*, p. 122. Elsewhere, however, he feels impelled to write of the "domination of print," but only for a period he did not study—the world after 1776. (Rhys Isaac, "Dramatizing the Ideology of Revolution: Popular Mobilization in Virginia, 1774 to 1776," *William and Mary Quarterly* 33 [1976]: 385.) I don't see the point. The claim that print was more important than oral modes of politics or oral modes more important than print are both unintelligible, not least of all because politics took place in a medium neither "oral" nor "printed" but dramatized. Elections, for instance, as rituals for the reaffirmation of solidary hierarchical communities, were not oral, written, or printed. They were dramatized, a collective ceremony, a case of what Isaac terms "dramatized ideology." In the years leading up to the Revolution, beginning with the Stamp Act rebellion, the "Liberty Tree" became a central symbol for dramatized ideology. Particular

trees in different towns became Liberty Trees, the place for the hanging of effigies, for meetings and demonstrations. Some of these events were spontaneous but others, in the next years, became annual commemorative events as in Boston, where August 14, the day when the stamp distributors resigned, received annual recognition. Many colonies commemorated March 18, the day of the repeal of the Stamp Act. See Arthur M. Schlesinger, *Prelude to Independence: The Newspaper War on Britain, 1764–1776* (New York: Knopf, 1958), p. 29, and Albanese, *Sons of the Fathers*, pp. 59–63.

86. Benjamin Franklin, *The Autobiography and Other Writings*, ed. Kenneth Silverman (New York: Penguin, 1986), pp. 13–17, 26, 30.

87. Ibid., p. 20.

88. Ibid., pp. 106–107.

89. Ibid., p. 69.

90. Franklin, "Apology for Printers," 1731, in J. A. Leo LeMay, *Benjamin Franklin: Writings* (New York: Library of America, 1989), pp. 172–73. Stephen Botein refers to the "Apology for Printers" as "the best known and most sustained colonial argument for an impartial press." This takes the piece far too seriously. It is written in a jocular fashion, is self-contradictory, and is very nearly self-mocking. See Stephen Botein, "Printers and the American Revolution," in Bernard Bailyn and John Hench, eds., *The Press and the American Revolution* (Worcester, MA: American Antiquarian Society, 1980), p. 20.

91. Franklin, *Autobiography*, p. 107. Charles Clark finds that printers' acceptance or rejection of potentially controversial writing had to do with several factors. There was a general openness, at least in principle, to controversy, for fear of being accused of partisanship. But this apparent openness was limited by adherence to norms of polite society and, especially, to a reluctance to publish works that might be defamatory of individuals. But there was no well-articulated, let alone shared, journalistic ethic in this period. See Clark, *The Public Prints*, pp. 208–209.

92. Franklin, *Autobiography*, pp. 90–91.

93. Charles Clark, "'Metropolis' and 'Province' in Eighteenth-Century Press Relations: The Case of Boston," *Journal of Newspaper and Periodical History* 5 (1989): 5. Also, Clark, *The Public Prints*, pp. 96–97.

94. The advertisement is reprinted, along with the full run of the *Pennsylvania Gazette*, in a facsimile edition, *The Pennsylvania Gazette 1728–1789* (Philadelphia: Microsurance, 1968).

95. See Botein, "Printers and the American Revolution," p. 17.

96. See Stanley N. Katz, ed., "Introduction," to James Alexander, *A Brief Narrative of the Case and Trial of John Peter Zenger* (Cambridge: Harvard University Press, 1963), p. 2. I follow Katz's very useful narrative of the Zenger case throughout.

97. Charles E. Clark and Charles Wetherell, "The Measure of Maturity: The *Pennsylvania Gazette*, 1728–1765," *William and Mary Quarterly*, 3rd series, 46 (1989): 292–93, and Clark, *The Public Prints*, pp. 216, 221. The remaining news items were 9.1 percent concerning the West Indies and Latin America, and .8 percent on Asia, Africa, and the Middle East.

98. Alison G. Olson, "Eighteenth-Century Colonial Legislatures and Their Constituents," *Journal of American History* 79 (1992): 564, and Anna Janney DeArmond, *Andrew Bradford: Colonial Journalist* (Newark: University of Delaware Press, 1949), pp. 10–11.

99. See Zemsky, *Merchants, Farmers, and River Gods*, pp. 240–42, and Colegrove, "New England Town Mandates," p. 432.

100. Gary Nash, "The Transformation of Urban Politics, 1700–1765," *Journal of American History* 60 (1973): 616, 618. Nash's study overemphasizes the increase in political activity by looking only at the leading urban areas, not at rural lands where more than 90 percent of the population lived. Virginia, where the great minds of the revolutionary period were being nurtured, experienced no notable upturn in political activity from 1700 to 1765; indeed, there actually was a decline in the number of competitive elections. See Kolp, "The Dynamics of Electoral Competition," pp. 652–74.

101. I differ here from Stephen Botein's provocative claim that the printers "acted in such a way as to retard the development of a public forum where conflicts could be fully and continuously articulated." See Stephen Botein, "'Meer Mechanics' and an Open Press: The Business and Political Strategies of Colonial American Printers," *Perspectives in American History* 9 (1975): 199, and Botein, "Printers and the American Revolution," p. 22.

102. Wood, *The Radicalism of the American Revolution*, p. 77.

103. Michael Kraus, *Intercolonial Aspects of American Culture on the Eve of the Revolution* (New York: Columbia University Press, 1928), pp. 91–105. Even lesser families tended to have multiple influences and interconnections. William Goddard learned the printing trade as apprentice to James Parker in New Haven beginning in 1755. Parker had apprenticed with William Bradford in New York; a silent partner in Parker's printing establishment from 1742 on was Benjamin Franklin. Parker, in fact, bought the printing equipment in New Haven from Franklin. He became public printer in New York in 1743, succeeding his mentor Bradford, and he served under Franklin as comptroller-general of the colonial post office in the 1750s. Goddard, his apprenticeship with Parker complete, opened a print shop in Providence and became proprietor of Providence's first newspaper in 1762. His sister, Mary Katherine, also worked in the print shop and his mother, Sarah, ran it on her own after William left to seek better opportunities elsewhere. In 1768, Goddard became printer for the *Pennsylvania Chronicle*, taking it over with help from William Franklin, Benjamin Franklin's son. Meanwhile, he also began the *Maryland Journal* in 1773, the first newspaper in Baltimore, early in 1774 turning it over to Mary Katherine. See Ward L. Miner, *William Goddard, Newspaperman* (Durham, NC: Duke University Press, 1962), pp. 13–14, 20, 66, 70–71, 140, 145.

104. Conroy, *In Public Houses*, pp. 179–80, 236–40.

105. Nash, *The Urban Crucible*, p. 202.

106. Sally F. Griffith, "'Order, Discipline, and a Few Cannon': Benjamin Franklin, the Association, and the Rhetoric and Practice of Boosterism," *Pennsylvania Magazine of History and Biography* 106 (1992): 140–41. See also Warner, *The Letters of the Republic*, p. 38.

107. Warner, *The Letters of the Republic*, pp. xi–xii, 38–42. Warner's emphasis on

the affinity between print and republican thought is provocative, but it does little to account for variability (in some nations print and republicanism advanced hand in hand, in other places print and autocracy have managed a centuries-long alliance), timing (there was printing in British North America from the 1630s on, but little printing of political controversy until the mid-1700s), and the particular dynamics by which print actually assisted republican thought and practices. Warner sees a "reciprocal determination" between print and republican politics, but this may have been less the logic of affinity he implies and more a dialectic of irony, as suggested by Nash, "The Transformation of Urban Politics, 1700–1765," pp. 605–32. Political participation in elections emerged when elites out of office sought to enlarge the circle of support to get back into office, but this suggests opportunism, not principled belief in the practice of public reason. The irony of electoral change was that a strategy designed for victory in intra-elite struggles became an element in social change that would in time threaten elite control altogether. The irony of print is that a mechanism as often as not intended to serve the ends of social control through instruction became a means of popular empowerment. Elections in this period, of course, never lost their Janus-faced qualities as both rituals of legitimation and agencies of participation. Print never lost its two-sided character, as both weapon of control and as incitement to universal reason.

108. Cited in Clark, *Public Prints*, p. 24.
109. Cited in Carl Kaestle, "The Public Reaction to John Dickinson's 'Farmer's Letters,'" *Proceedings of the American Antiquarian Society* 78 (Worcester, MA: American Antiquarian Society, 1969): 334.
110. Ibid., p. 325.
111. Richard John, "Communications and Information Processing," *Encyclopedia of American Social History*, vol. 3 (New York: Scribner's, 1993), p. 2353.
112. Kaestle, "The Public Reaction," p. 344.
113. Ibid., p. 337.
114. "Reluctant partisans" is Stephen Botein's phrase in "Printers and the American Revolution," p. 32.
115. G. Thomas Tanselle, "Some Statistics on American Printing, 1764–1783," in Bailyn and Hench, eds., *The Press and the American Revolution*, p. 348.
116. Patricia U. Bonomi, *Under the Cope of Heaven* (New York: Oxford University Press, 1986), pp. 203–208.
117. Kraus, *Intercolonial Aspects of American Culture*, pp. 212–15.
118. Pauline Maier, *The Old Revolutionaries* (New York, Knopf, 1980), p. 72.
119. Cited in Miner, *William Goddard, Newspaperman*, pp. 121–22.
120. Ibid., pp. 126–27.
121. Tanselle, "Some Statistics on American Printing," p. 351.
122. Thomas Paine, *Common Sense* (London: Pelican, 1976), p. 120.
123. Cited in Eric Foner, *Tom Paine and Revolutionary America* (New York: Oxford University Press, 1976), p. 83. See also John Keane, *Tom Paine: A Political Life* (Boston: Little, Brown, 1995), pp. 110–14.
124. Cited in Foner, *Tom Paine and Revolutionary America*, p. 79.
125. Ibid., p. 99.

126. Fletcher Green, *Constitutional Development in the South Atlantic States, 1776–1860* (Chapel Hill: University of North Carolina Press, 1930), pp. 84–88. North Carolina had a taxpaying requirement to vote for the lower house but a fifty-acre freehold requirement for the upper house. Maryland and North Carolina required larger estates for upper-house members (but Virginia and South Carolina did not). Terms of office were longer for the upper house than the lower house in Maryland, Virginia, and South Carolina. These regulations were part of the constitutions approved in South Carolina, Virginia, North Carolina, and Maryland in 1776.

127. Bushman, *King and People in Provincial Massachusetts*, p. 53.

128. Maier, *From Resistance to Revolution*, p. 21.

129. Daniel N. Hoffman, *Governmental Secrecy and the Founding Fathers* (Westport, CT: Greenwood, 1981), p. 14.

130. Wood, *The Creation of the American Republic*, pp. 166–67. James Burgh's *Political Disquisitions* was published in Philadelphia in 1775 and was a central source for Antifederalists. In it he wrote, "Where annual elections end, slavery begins." See Jackson Turner Main, *The Anti-Federalists* (Chapel Hill: University of North Carolina Press, 1961), p. 12.

131. Williamson, *American Suffrage*, pp. 117–37.

132. Ibid., pp. 121–22.

Chapter 2: The Constitutional Moment: 1787–1801

1. Cited in Daniel N. Hoffman, *Governmental Secrecy and the Founding Fathers* (Westport, CT: Greenwood, 1981), p. 22.

2. Quoted in ibid., p. 21.

3. James Madison, *Notes of Debates in the Federal Convention of 1787* (New York: W. W. Norton, 1987), p. 64.

4. Ibid., p. 483.

5. Ibid., p. 106.

6. Ibid., p. 197.

7. Ibid., pp. 322–23.

8. Ibid., p. 369.

9. Ibid., p. 306.

10. Ibid., p. 39.

11. Ibid., p. 308.

12. Ibid., p. 235.

13. Ibid., p. 107.

14. Journal, May 29, 1787, cited in Max Farrand, ed., *The Records of the Federal Convention of 1787*, vol. 3 (New Haven: Yale University Press, 1911), p. 15.

15. George Mason to George Mason, Jr., letter of May 27, 1787, in ibid., vol. 3, p. 28. James Madison to Thomas Jefferson, June 6, 1787, in ibid., vol. 3, p. 35.

16. Wilbur Samuel Howell, ed., *Jefferson's Parliamentary Writings* (Princeton: Princeton University Press, 1988), p. 357.

17. Emile Durkheim, *The Division of Labor in Society* (New York: Free Press, 1933), pp. 206–19.

18. On the anti-party sentiment of eighteenth-century Anglo-American political thought, see Richard Hofstadter, *The Idea of a Party System* (Berkeley: University of California Press, 1972), pp. 1–39.

19. James Roger Sharp, *American Politics in the Early Republic* (New Haven: Yale University Press, 1993), p. 86.

20. Eugene Perry Link, *Democratic-Republican Societies, 1790–1800* (New York: Columbia University Press, 1942; Octagon, 1965), p. 114.

21. Ibid., p. 116.

22. Quoted in Sharp, *American Politics in the Early Republic*, p. 85.

23. "At a Meeting of the Democratic Society," New York, 1794, Broadside Collection, American Antiquarian Society, Worcester, MA.

24. Richard Pares, *King George III and the Politicians* (Oxford: Clarendon, 1953), p. 52. See, generally, pp. 50–53. In France, too, political associations were deeply distrusted. Political associations and public meetings were banned in 1791. Under Napoleon, similar restrictions were codified and persisted through the nineteenth century, requiring governmental authorization for any meetings or gatherings of more than twenty people. See Jeremy Popkin, "Claiming Public Space: Press Banquets and Press Trials in the July Monarchy," paper presented at the 1996 meeting of the Western Society for French History, Charlotte, NC.

25. Stanley Elkins and Eric McKitrick, *The Age of Federalism* (New York: Oxford University Press, 1993), p. 476.

26. See German Republican Society, "Resolutions Adopted on the Resistance of Citizens in Western Pennsylvania, July 29, 1794," and Democratic Society of Pennsylvania, "Minutes, July 31, 1794," in Philip S. Foner, ed., *The Democratic-Republican Societies, 1790–1800: A Documentary Sourcebook of Constitutions, Declarations, Addresses, Resolutions, and Toasts* (Westport, CT: Greenwood, 1976), pp. 59, 88.

27. James Kirby Martin, "Introduction: The Whiskey Rebellion Redivivus," gives a brief summary of the Whiskey Rebellion, which I follow here, in Steven R. Boyd, ed., *The Whiskey Rebellion: Past and Present Perspectives* (Westport, CT: Greenwood, 1985), pp. 2–7, along with James Roger Sharp, "The Whiskey Rebellion and the Question of Representation," in Boyd, pp. 119–33.

28. Thomas P. Slaughter, *The Whiskey Rebellion* (New York: Oxford University Press, 1986), p. 43, and Mary K. Bonsteel Tachau, "A New Look at the Whiskey Rebellion," in Boyd, ed., *The Whiskey Rebellion*, p. 97.

29. See Sharp, "The Whiskey Rebellion and the Question of Representation," in Boyd, p. 125.

30. Letter to Burges Ball, Sept. 25, 1794, in John Rhodehamel, ed., *George Washington: Writings* (New York: Library of America, 1997), p. 885.

31. Letter to Edmund Randolph, Oct. 16, 1794, in ibid., p. 887.

32. Cabot, 1795, cited in Hofstadter, *The Idea of a Party System*, p. 95.

33. Cited in Foner, *Democratic-Republican Societies*, p. 32.

34. *Philadelphia Gazette and Universal Daily Advertiser*, Dec. 29, 1794, in ibid., p. 62.

35. Minutes, Oct. 9, 1794, in ibid., p. 96.

36. To Madison, Dec. 28, 1794, Robert A. Rutland, ed., *The Papers of James Madison*, vol. 15 (Charlottesville: University Press of Virginia, 1985), pp. 426–29.

37. See a discussion of this point in Hofstadter, *The Idea of a Party System*, p. 50. A valuable, brief account of the Whiskey Rebellion and its aftermath is Elkins and McKitrick, *The Age of Federalism*, pp. 474–88.

38. Washington to Madison, May 20, 1792, and Madison to Washington, June 20, 1792, in Robert A. Rutland, ed., *The Papers of James Madison*, vol. 14 (Charlottesville: University Press of Virginia, 1983), pp. 310–12, 319–24.

39. Rhodehamel, ed., *George Washington: Writings*, p. 969.

40. Pauline Maier, *The Old Revolutionaries*, (New York: Knopf, 1980), p. 30. She quotes from Adams's letter to Noah Webster, April 30, 1784.

41. Cited in Hofstadter, *The Idea of a Party System*, p. 28.

42. Ronald Formisano, *The Transformation of Political Culture* (New York: Oxford University Press, 1984), p. 109.

43. Cited in Hofstadter, *The Idea of a Party System*, p. 123.

44. Noble E. Cunningham, Jr., *The Jeffersonian Republicans* (Chapel Hill: University of North Carolina Press, 1957), p. 97.

45. Ibid., p. 106.

46. *American Mercury* (Hartford, CT), Sept. 11, 1800, cited in ibid., p. 206.

47. Stephen Botein, "Printers and the American Revolution," in Bernard Bailyn and John Hench, eds., *The Press and the American Revolution* (Worcester, MA: American Antiquarian Society, 1980), p. 41.

48. *Federal Gazette* (Philadelphia), Dec. 6, 1791, cited in David P. Nord, "Readership as Citizenship in Late-Eighteenth-Century Philadelphia," in J. Worth Estes and Billy G. Smith, eds., *A Melancholy Sense of Devastation* (Canton, MA: Science History Publications, 1997), p. 23.

49. In remarks in Congress, Dec. 28, 1791, quoted in Richard B. Kielbowicz, *News in the Mail* (Westport, CT: Greenwood, 1989), p. 233.

50. Richard R. John, *Spreading the News* (Cambridge: Harvard University Press, 1995), p. 37.

51. John Nerone, *The Culture of the Press in the Early Republic: Cincinnati, 1793–1848* (New York: Garland, 1989), p. 67, gives figures for Cincinnati papers—more than a third for 1815, 1825, and 1835, somewhat less for 1795, 1805, and 1845.

52. Kielbowicz, *News in the Mail*, p. 234; John, *Spreading the News*, pp. 36–37.

53. John Steele, Jan. 15, 1792, in Noble E. Cunningham, Jr., ed., *Circular Letters of Congressmen to Their Constituents, 1789–1829*, vol. 1 (Chapel Hill: University of North Carolina Press, 1978), p. 99. The postal law was revised in 1794 to enable newspapers to circulate through the mails anywhere in their own state of publication at the lower, one-penny rate. Thus the post office would carry newspapers at a loss—indeed, prominent Republicans (but not only Republicans) favored no postage at all. Washington's Postmaster General Timothy Pickering suggested in 1794 that the post office carry the newspapers with no postage. Jefferson in 1801 would ask for the abolition of all postage on newspapers. Although these proposals for postage-free newspaper mailing never passed, the early federal subsidy of the press was still of great importance.

54. John, *Spreading the News*, pp. 37–39.

55. Feb. 8, 1799, in David B. Mattern, ed., *The Papers of James Madison*, vol. 17 (Charlottesville: University Press of Virginia, 1991), p. 229. See also Madison to Jefferson, April 5, 1798 (p. 107) and Jan. 25, 1799 (pp. 220–21).

56. James Madison, Jr. to James Madison, Sr., in Rutland, ed., *The Papers of James Madison*, vol. 14, pp. 106–107 (Nov. 13, 1791), 226 (Feb. 9, 1792), 293 (April 27, 1792), and 455 (March 1, 1793).

57. Madison to James Monroe, June 1, 1801, and to Wilson Nicholas, July 10, 1801, in Robert J. Brugger, ed., *The Papers of James Madison* (Secretary of State Series), vol. 1 (Charlottesville: University Press of Virginia, 1986), pp. 245, 393.

58. Cunningham, *The Jeffersonian Republicans*, p. 15, citing a letter of Jefferson to George Washington, Sept. 9, 1792.

59. James Sullivan to George Tacher, Aug. 1, 1790, Chamberlain Collection, Boston Public Library. Cited in Cunningham, ed., *Circular Letters of Congressmen to Their Constituents, 1789–1829*, p. xxviii.

60. Cunningham, *The Jeffersonian Republicans*, pp. 13–14.

61. Michael Lienesch, "Thomas Jefferson and the American Democratic Experience," in Peter Onuf, ed., *Jeffersonian Legacies* (Charlottesville: University Press of Virginia, 1993), p. 319.

62. Noble E. Cunningham, Jr., *In Pursuit of Reason: The Life of Thomas Jefferson* (Baton Rouge: Louisiana State University Press, 1987), pp. 169–71.

63. Lienesch, "Thomas Jefferson and the American Democratic Experience," p. 329. Even later, as vice president in the Adams administration, Jefferson stirred the newspaper pot. He promoted James Carey's *Recorder* and Benjamin Franklin Bache's *Aurora* in his correspondence. "If these newspapers fall," he warned Madison, "republicanism will be entirely brow beaten." April 26, 1798, cited in Jeffery Smith, *Franklin and Bache* (New York: Oxford University Press, 1990), pp. 151–52.

64. *Federalist* No. 49 in Alexander Hamilton, John Jay, and James Madison, *The Federalist Papers* (London: Penguin, 1987), pp. 313–14.

65. Washington to Edmund Randolph, Aug. 26, 1792, in Rhodehamel, ed., *George Washington: Writings*, p. 821.

66. Elkins and McKitrick, *The Age of Federalism*, p. 497.

67. Smith, *Franklin and Bache*, p. 139.

68. Elizabeth G. McPherson, "The Southern States and the Reporting of Senate Debates, 1789–1802," *Journal of Southern History* 12 (1946): 228–32, 239, 241.

69. Lawrence Cremin, *American Education: The Colonial Experience, 1607–1783* (New York: Harper & Row, 1970), p. 192.

70. "A Bill for the More General Diffusion of Knowledge," (1778), in Julian P. Boyd, ed., *The Papers of Thomas Jefferson*, vol. 2 (Princeton: Princeton University Press, 1950), pp. 526–27.

71. Thomas L. Pangle, *The Ennobling of Democracy* (Baltimore: Johns Hopkins University Press, 1992), p. 173.

72. Leonard W. Levy, *The Emergence of a Free Press* (New York: Oxford University Press, 1985).

73. Richard Buel, Jr., "Freedom of the Press in Revolutionary America: The Evolution of Libertarianism, 1760–1820," in Bailyn and Hench, eds., *The Press and the American Revolution*, p. 81.

74. Quoted in ibid., p. 85.

75. *Columbian Centinel*, Oct. 5, 1798, quoted in *Albany Centinel*, Oct. 12, 1798. Cited in James Morton Smith, *Freedom's Fetters: The Alien and Sedition Laws and American Civil Liberties* (Ithaca, NY: Cornell University Press, 1956), p. 178.

76. Ibid., pp. 177–85.

77. Donald K. Stewart estimates Federalist papers outnumbered Republican ones by ninety-two to thirty-four in 1796 and outnumbered Republican papers again by about two to one in 1800. See Donald K. Stewart, *The Opposition Press of the Federalist Period* (Albany: State University of New York Press, 1969), pp. 622–24.

78. J. R. Pole, *The Gift of Government* (Athens: University of Georgia Press, 1983), p. 138.

79. Culver Smith, *The Press, Politics, and Patronage* (Athens: University of Georgia Press, 1977), pp. 39–41, 45.

80. Adrienne Koch and William Peden, eds., *The Life and Selected Writings of Thomas Jefferson* (New York: Modern Library, 1944), pp. 411–12 (letter to Colonel Edward Carrington, Jan. 16, 1787) and 581–82 (letter to John Norvell, June 11, 1807).

81. Jackson Turner Main, *The Anti-Federalists* (Chapel Hill: University of North Carolina Press, 1961), pp. 209, 250–51. On the tribulations of New York's sole Antifederalist outlet, Thomas Greenleaf's *New-York Journal*, see John Nerone, *Violence Against the Press* (New York: Oxford University Press, 1994), pp. 60–63.

82. See Thomas S. Engerman, Edward J. Erler, and Thomas B. Hofeller, eds., *The Federalist Concordance* (Chicago: University of Chicago Press, 1988), p. 351.

83. See the following section on "representation" for more discussion of the founders' views on overcoming the problem of distance.

84. Gordon Wood, "The Democratization of the American Mind," in Robert Horwitz, ed., *The Moral Foundations of the Republic* (Charlottesville: University Press of Virginia, 1986), p. 130.

85. *Pennsylvania Gazette*, July 9, 1788, in Merrill Jensen and Robert A. Becker, eds., *The Documentary History of the First Federal Elections, 1788–1790*, vol. 1 (Madison: University of Wisconsin Press, 1976), p. 242.

86. Cunningham, *The Jeffersonian Republicans*, pp. 34, 35, 44.

87. Alan Taylor, "'The Art of Hook & Snivey': Political Culture in Upstate New York During the 1790s," *Journal of American History* 79 (1993): 1382.

88. Broadside, Albany, New York, 1799, on display at the Museum of American Political Life, University of Hartford, West Hartford, CT.

89. Taylor, "'Hook & Snivey,'" p. 1392.

90. Cunningham, *The Jeffersonian Republicans*, pp. 190–91.

91. Elkanah Watson, *Men and Times of the Revolution*, ed. Winslow C. Watson (New York: Dana, 1857), pp. 301–302.

92. Alan Taylor, *William Cooper's Town* (New York: Knopf, 1995), p. 174. Taylor's account of this election, pp. 170–98, gives a vivid portrait of contemporary electoral behavior.

93. *Federal Post* (Trenton, New Jersey), Nov. 18, 1788, in Gordon DenBoer, Lucy Trumbull Brown, and Charles D. Hagermann, eds., *The Documentary History of the First Federal Elections, 1788–1790*, vol. 3 (Madison: University of Wisconsin Press, 1986), p. 62.

94. Fischer, *The Revolution of American Conservatism*, p. 94.

95. Cunningham, *In Pursuit of Reason*, pp. 221–23.

96. Cited in David Hackett Fischer, *The Revolution of American Conservatism* (New York: Harper and Row, 1965), p. 95.

97. Letter to Theodore Sedgwick, April 7, 1800, cited in Cunningham, *The Jeffersonian Republicans*, p. 187.

98. Jeffrey Abramson, *We, the Jury* (New York: Basic Books, 1994), pp. 25–29, 36.

99. "Cornelius," 1788, in Herbert J. Storing, ed., *The Complete Anti-Federalist*, vol. 14 (Chicago: University of Chicago Press, 1981), p. 141, cited in Rosemarie Zagarri, *The Politics of Size: Representation in the United States, 1776–1850* (Ithaca, NY: Cornell University Press, 1987), p. 19.

100. Zagarri, *The Politics of Size*, p. 9.

101. Ibid., p. 21.

102. Cited in ibid., p. 88.

103. J. R. Pole, *Political Representation in England and the Origins of the American Republic* (London: Macmillan, 1966), p. 280.

104. "A Farmer," *Complete Anti-Federalist* III: 184, and "Federal Farmer," *Complete Anti-Federalist* II: 268, cited in Zagarri, *The Politics of Size*.

105. Oct. 12, 1787, p. 35, in J. R. Pole, ed., *The American Constitution: For and Against* (New York: Hill & Wang, 1987), p. 35.

106. "Brutus," Nov. 15, 1787, in *The Debate on the Constitution*, vol. 1 (New York: Library of America, 1993), p. 320. Pole, *The American Constitution*, p. 46.

107. See Bernard Bailyn, ed., *Pamphlets of the American Revolution*, vol. I, *1750–1765* (Cambridge: Harvard University Press, 1965), pp. 92–99.

108. Donald S. Lutz, "The Theory of Consent in the Early State Constitutions," in Daniel J. Elazar, ed., *Republicanism, Representation, and Consent: Views of the Founding Era* (New Brunswick, NJ: Transaction Books, 1979), pp. 11–42.

109. *Federalist* No. 10. See also Isaac Kramnick, "Editor's Introduction," in Hamilton, Jay, and Madison, *The Federalist Papers*, pp. 41–43.

110. *Massachusetts Centinel*, Nov. 1, 1788, cited in Jensen and Becker, eds., *Documentary History*, p. 469.

111. "Real Farmer," in *Hampshire Chronicle*, Oct. 22, 1788, cited in ibid., p. 469. Pennsylvania switched to representation by district after the 1792 election. See Cunningham, *The Jeffersonian Republicans*, p. 111.

112. Jensen and Becker, eds., *Documentary History*, p. 282.

113. *Pennsylvania Gazette*, July 30, 1788, cited in ibid., p. 246.

114. Oct. 8, 1778, cited in ibid., p. 303.

115. Quoted in Elkins and McKitrick, *The Age of Federalism*, p. 75.

116. Jefferson to Madison, Sept. 6, 1789, in James Morton Smith, ed., *The Republic of Letters: The Correspondence Between Thomas Jefferson and James Madison, 1776–1826*, vol. 1 (New York: Norton, 1995), p. 634.

117. James Madison to Edmund Randolph, Jan. 10, 1788, in Robert A. Rutland et al., eds., *The Papers of James Madison*, vol. 10 (Chicago: University of Chicago Press, 1977), pp. 355–56.

Chapter 3: The Democratic Transition in American Political Life: 1801–1865

1. "Such are republican governments which it is the glory of America to have invented, and her unrivalled happiness to possess." "The Spirit of Governments," from *The National Gazette*, Feb. 20, 1792, in Gaillard Hunt, ed., *The Writings of James Madison*, vol. 6 (New York: Putnam's, 1906), p. 94.
2. Thomas Perkins Abernethy, *From Frontier to Plantation in Tennessee: A Study in Frontier Democracy* (Memphis: Memphis State College Press, 1955), p. 352.
3. Jefferson to Spencer Roane, Sept. 6, 1819, cited in Noble E. Cunningham, Jr., *In Pursuit of Reason: The Life of Thomas Jefferson* (Baton Rouge: Louisiana State University Press, 1987), p. 237.
4. Joyce Appleby, *Capitalism and a New Social Order* (New York: New York University Press, 1984).
5. David Hackett Fischer, *Growing Old in America* (New York: Oxford University Press, 1977), pp. 77–112. See also Steven Mintz and Susan Kellogg, *Domestic Revolutions: A Social History of American Family Life* (New York: Free Press, 1988), pp. 43–65.
6. E. Jennifer Monaghan, *A Common Heritage: Noah Webster's Blue-Back Speller* (Hamden, CT: Archon, 1983), p. 205.
7. Kenneth Cmiel, *Democratic Eloquence* (New York: Morrow, 1990).
8. Cited in Merle Curti, *The Social Ideas of American Educators* (Paterson, NJ: Littlefield, Adams, 1961), p. 112. Originally published 1935.
9. From Mann's "Report for 1845" as secretary of the board of education in Massachusetts, cited in Rush Welter, *Popular Education and Democratic Thought in America* (New York: Columbia University Press, 1962), p. 98.
10. Curti, *The Social Ideas of American Educators*, p. 135.
11. Richard D. Brown, *The Strength of a People: The Idea of an Informed Citizenry in America, 1650–1870* (Chapel Hill: University of North Carolina Press, 1996), p. 120.
12. Nathan Hatch, *The Democratization of American Christianity* (New Haven: Yale University Press, 1989), pp. 4, 10, 35.
13. For a detailed account of these matters in Virginia, Maryland, North Carolina, South Carolina, and Georgia, see Fletcher Green, *Constitutional Development in the South Atlantic States, 1776–1800* (Chapel Hill: University of North Carolina Press, 1930).
14. Robin Einhorn, *Property Rules: Political Economy in Chicago, 1833–1872* (Chicago: University of Chicago Press, 1991).
15. Merrill D. Peterson, ed., *Democracy, Liberty, and Property: The State Constitutional Conventions of the 1820's* (Indianapolis: Bobbs-Merrill, 1966), p. xv.
16. See ibid., pp. 3–17, for a summary of the convention's work.
17. Daniel Webster, in ibid., pp. 94–95, 101.
18. Non-Freeholders of the City of Richmond in ibid., pp. 377–86.
19. Donald H. Cole, *Martin Van Buren and the American Political System* (Princeton: Princeton University Press, 1984), pp. 79–80.
20. Richard P. McCormick, *The Second American Party System* (Chapel Hill: University of North Carolina Press, 1966), p. 29.

21. Lawrence L. Martin, "American County Government: An Historical Perspective," in David R. Berman, ed., *County Governments in an Era of Change* (Westport, CT: Greenwood, 1993), pp. 6–7.

22. Mary Kupiec Cayton, *Emerson's Emergence* (Chapel Hill: University of North Carolina Press, 1989), pp. 35–36.

23. Alexis de Tocqueville, *Democracy in America*, tr. George Lawrence (Garden City, NY: Doubleday Anchor, 1969), p. 513.

24. Ibid., p. 517.

25. John S. Gilkeson, Jr., *Middle-Class Providence, 1820–1940* (Princeton: Princeton University Press, 1986), pp. 28, 31–32, and Ian R. Tyrrell, *Sobering Up* (Westport, CT: Greenwood, 1979), pp. 65–67.

26. Richard John, "Taking Sabbatarianism Seriously: The Postal System, the Sabbath, and the Transformation of American Political Culture," *Journal of the Early Republic* 10 (1990): 517–67. See also Richard John, *Spreading the News* (Cambridge: Harvard University Press, 1995), pp. 169–205.

27. Gilkeson, *Middle-Class Providence*, p. 28.

28. Daniel Walker Howe, *The Political Culture of the American Whigs* (Chicago: University of Chicago Press, 1979), p. 55.

29. John, "Taking Sabbatarianism Seriously," pp. 541–42.

30. Howard B. Rock, *Artisans of the New Republic* (New York: New York University Press, 1979), pp. 128–33.

31. Ibid., pp. 277–79.

32. Tocqueville, *Democracy in America*, p. 193.

33. Ibid., p. 524.

34. Ibid., p. 522.

35. Hatch, *The Democratization of American Christianity*, p. 199.

36. Tocqueville, *Democracy in America*, p. 194.

37. Clifford S. Griffin, *Their Brothers' Keepers: Moral Stewardship in the United States, 1800–1865* (New Brunswick, NJ: Rutgers University Press, 1960), p. 25.

38. Horace Mann to Calvin Pennell, May 23, 1837, quoted in Jonathan Messerli, *Horace Mann: A Biography* (New York: Knopf, 1972), pp. 231–32.

39. See Griffin, *Their Brothers' Keepers*, pp. 177–97.

40. Quoted in ibid., p. 58.

41. Ibid., p. 121.

42. Ibid., p. 122.

43. Jack S. Blocker, Jr., *American Temperance Movements* (Boston: Twayne, 1989), pp. 11, 12, 14.

44. Peter Dobkin Hall, "A Historical Overview of the Private Nonprofit Sector," in Walter W. Powell, ed., *The Nonprofit Sector: A Research Handbook* (New Haven: Yale University Press, 1987), pp. 3–26, especially pp. 6–8.

45. Leonard L. Richards, *The Life and Times of Congressman John Quincy Adams* (New York: Oxford University Press, 1986), p. 94. The discussion that follows relies primarily on Richards, pp. 115–31, 176–78. See also Edward Magdol, "A Window on the Abolitionist Constituency: Antislavery Petitions, 1836–1839," in Alan M. Kraut, ed., *Crusaders and Compromisers* (Westport, CT: Green-

wood, 1983), pp. 45–70, and William Lee Miller, *Arguing About Slavery* (New York: Knopf, 1996), for a full and engaging discussion of the gag rule controversy. The size of the petition campaign was formidable. Edward Magdol counts two million signatures on anti-slavery petitions in 1838–39. The average number of signatures per petition grew from thirty-two in 1836–37 to 107 in 1839–40. See Magdol, p. 46. There were 412,000 petitions in 1837–38 on abolitionist questions, including 182,000 opposing annexation of Texas and 130,000 calling for abolition in the District of Columbia (Magdol, p. 51). It is important that petitioning was an avenue of political expression open to many who were excluded from voting; women were prominent among signers of petitions. See Edward Magdol, *The Antislavery Rank and File* (Westport, CT: Greenwood, 1986), pp. 55–56.

46. Richards, *The Life and Times of Congressman John Quincy Adams*, p. 95.
47. Cited in Miller, *Arguing About Slavery*, p. 94.
48. See Dorothy Ganfield Fowler, *Unmailable: Congress and the Post Office* (Athens: University of Georgia Press, 1977), pp. 26–36.
49. Calvin Colton, cited in Donna Lee Dickerson, *The Course of Tolerance: Freedom of the Press in Nineteenth-Century America* (Westport, CT: Greenwood, 1990), p. 106. See, in general, pp. 81–113.
50. Richards, *Life and Times of Congressman John Quincy Adams*, p. 120. On petitioning in Anglo-American political thought, see Edmund S. Morgan, *Inventing the People* (New York: Norton, 1988), pp. 223–33.
51. Griffin, *Their Brothers' Keepers*, p. 128.
52. Adams is cited in Miller, *Arguing About Slavery*, pp. 263–68.
53. Whether the gag rule can be defended is a question political theorist Stephen Holmes has recently revived. If you believe that the nation had to end slavery to fulfill itself as a liberal democracy, then efforts to keep slavery off the national agenda are to be condemned. If, on the other hand, you believe that the minimal requirement of a liberal democracy is that it prevent citizens from killing one another over political questions, then efforts to keep irreconcilable differences from preoccupying the political stage and moral extremists from monopolizing debate may be applauded. American politics failed in the Civil War; the dilemma is that preventing the war would not have been a success if it meant the perpetuation of slavery, only a different kind of failure. The nation required a refounding, and it was refounded through a trial of blood. No theory rises to the occasion of this awful fact.

Holmes takes the position that liberal democracies often operate best not only by encouraging public debate and discussion but also by tabling some forms of discussion that would be destined to cause rancor. He cites the separation of church and state as a prime example of a decision in the Constitution to keep a powerful and divisive topic off the political stage. But this is not quite the same thing as a gag rule. The First Amendment does not say that religion is not open to discussion and debate; it says that government may not give state sanction to one religion over others or to religions in general, as the Court has come to interpret it, over none at all. Now, of course, effectively that limits the amount of time legislatures are going to spend talking religion, but it does not in any way prevent the press, voluntary associations, or even a representative on the floor of Congress from dealing with the subject or petitioning the government concerning it. The gag rule on slavery was different. It insisted that the Congress avert its eyes from legitimate expressions of popular opinion. The gag rule did not prevent division but expanded and exacerbated the controversy. See Stephen Holmes, *Passions and Constraint* (Chicago: University of Chicago Press, 1995), pp. 202–35.

54. Maria Weston Chapman of the Boston Female Anti-Slavery Society, cited in Lori D. Ginzberg, *Women and the Work of Benevolence* (New Haven: Yale University Press, 1990), p. 80.

55. John Quincy Adams, speech delivered in 1838, cited in ibid., p. 93.

56. Cited in ibid., p. 94.

57. Carol Gilligan, *In a Different Voice* (Cambridge: Harvard University Press, 1982).

58. John, *Spreading the News*, p. 185.

59. I draw here on a well-developed literature on the nature and functions of parties. See, among others, Leon Epstein, *Political Parties in the American Mold* (Madison: University of Wisconsin Press, 1986); Frank J. Sorauf, "Political Parties and Political Analysis," in William Nisbet Chambers and Walter Dean Burnham, eds., *The American Party Systems* (New York: Oxford University Press, 1975); and William Nisbet Chambers, "Party Development and the American Mainstream," in Chambers and Burnham, pp. 3–32.

60. Ronald P. Formisano reviews the conflicting viewpoints and argues strongly that the Federalists and Republicans were not full-fledged parties. See Ronald P. Formisano, "Federalists and Republicans: Parties, Yes—System, No," in Paul Kleppner et al., *The Evolution of American Electoral Systems* (Westport, CT: Greenwood, 1981), pp. 33–76. The discussion of parties as "explicit ends in themselves" is on p. 66. It is at least fairly well settled that the ideological groupings of the 1790s were something less than parties. Noel Cunningham insists that the election of 1800 was a party election, that Jefferson in office was a party leader, and that congressional votes divided as much along party lines as anything else. But Ronald Formisano counters that if there were parties, there was no party system; and Lee Benson argues that if there were party associations and factions, there was still no mass electorate involved in and organized by party organizations. See Noel Cunningham, "Presidential Leadership, Political Parties, and the Congressional Caucus, 1800–1824," in Patricia Bonomi, James MacGregor Burns, and Austin Ranney, eds., *The American Constitutional System Under Strong and Weak Parties* (New York: Praeger, 1981), pp. 1–20, and "Discussion," pp. 23, 24.

61. Jefferson to Madison, Dec. 17, 1796, cited in J.C.A. Stagg, ed., *The Papers of James Madison* vol. 16 (Charlottesville: University Press of Virginia, 1989), pp. 431–32.

62. Richard Hofstadter, *The Idea of a Party System* (Berkeley: University of California Press, 1972).

63. Paul Goodman, "The First American Party System," in Chambers and Burnham, eds., *The American Party Systems*, p. 57. William Nisbet Chambers de-

fines a party system as "a pattern of interaction in which two or more political parties compete for office or power in government and for the support of the electorate, and must therefore take one another into account in their behavior in government and in election contests." See Chambers, "Party Development and the American Mainstream," in Chambers and Burnham, p. 6.

64. Goodman, ibid., p. 87.

65. Adrienne Koch and William Peden, eds., *The Life and Selected Writings of Thomas Jefferson* (New York: Modern Library, 1944), p. 322. First inaugural address, March 4, 1801, and letter cited in Hofstadter, *The Idea of a Party System*, p. 182.

66. Richard P. McCormick, *The Presidential Game: The Origins of American Presidential Politics* (New York: Oxford University Press, 1982), pp. 81–82.

67. See Ronald P. Formisano's discussion of the "Politics of the Revolutionary Center" in *The Transformation of Political Culture: Massachusetts Parties, 1790s–1840s* (New York: Oxford University Press, 1983).

68. Daniel P. Jordan, *Political Leadership in Jefferson's Virginia* (Charlottesville: University Press of Virginia, 1983), p. 99, observes the continuation of deferential and personal politics in Virginia through 1825. So does William G. Shade, *Democratizing the Old Dominion: Virginia and the Second Party System, 1824–1861* (Charlottesville: University Press of Virginia, 1996), pp. 165–66.

69. Formisano, *The Transformation of Political Culture*, p. 17.

70. Michael Wallace, "Changing Concepts of Party in the United States: New York, 1815–1828," in Lance Banning, ed., *After the Constitution: Party Conflict in the New Republic* (Belmont, CA: Wadsworth, 1989), p. 465. On the conditions for political party development, see Chambers, "Party Development and the American Mainstream," pp. 9–10.

71. This discussion is informed by Epstein, *Political Parties in the American Mold*. On the "presidential party," see Epstein, pp. 84, 205.

72. McCormick, *The Presidential Game*, pp. 194–96.

73. Ibid., p. 124.

74. Ibid., pp. 177–79, 199.

75. Ellen Carol DuBois, *Feminism and Suffrage* (Ithaca, NY: Cornell University Press, 1978), pp. 23, 29, 35.

76. Edward Dicey, in Herbert Mitgang, ed., *Spectator of America* (Chicago: Quadrangle, 1971), p. 29.

77. Thomas Hamilton, *Men and Manners in America*, vol. 2 (Edinburgh: Blackwood, 1833), p. 74.

78. John Nerone, *The Culture of the Press in the Early Republic: Cincinnati, 1793–1848* (New York: Garland, 1989), p. 57.

79. Noble E. Cunningham, Jr., ed., *Circular Letters of Congressmen to Their Constituents, 1789–1829*, vol. 1 (Chapel Hill: University of North Carolina Press, 1978), p. xxv.

80. April 22, 1816, in ibid., vol. 2, p. 973.

81. Jan. 22, 1794, in ibid., vol. 1, p. 17.

82. March 24, 1794, in ibid., vol. 1, p. 20.

83. May 20, 1824, in ibid., vol. 3, pp. 1211–12.

84. William J. Gilmore, *Reading Becomes a Necessity of Life* (Knoxville: University of Tennessee Press, 1989), p. 194.

85. Ibid., pp. 112, 348–49.

86. Ibid., p. 357.

87. David Jaffee, "The Village Enlightenment in New England, 1760–1820," *William and Mary Quarterly*, 3rd series, 47 (1990): 327, 339, 344, 345.

88. Gilmore, *Reading Becomes a Necessity*, pp. 349–53, 19.

89. Nerone, *The Culture of the Press in the Early Republic*, p. 66.

90. Culver H. Smith, *The Press, Politics, and Patronage: The American Government's Use of Newspapers, 1789–1876* (Athens: University of Georgia Press, 1977), p. 90.

91. Harry J. Carman and Reinhard Luthin, *Lincoln and the Patronage* (Gloucester, MA: Peter Smith, 1964), pp. 119–21. Originally published 1943.

92. Ibid., p. 121.

93. Ibid., pp. 122–28. See also pp. 70–74.

94. Tocqueville, *Democracy in America*, p. 517. In his notebooks, Tocqueville's concern seems to have been with the license of the press. He did not inquire of his informants how the press might be made more useful to democracy, but he did ask and pursued the question, "What is your view on the way to diminish the power of journalism?" Alexis de Tocqueville, *Journey to America*, ed. J. P. Mayer, tr. George Lawrence (Garden City, NY: Doubleday, 1971), p. 30.

95. Tocqueville, *Democracy in America*, p. 180.

96. As usual, Tocqueville says many different things and finds some considerable virtue in the strengths as well as weaknesses of U.S. journalism. The press "lays bare the secret shifts of politics, forcing public figures in turn to appear before the tribunal of opinion." It "makes political life circulate in every corner," and though newspapers individually are powerless, the press collectively is "nonetheless the first of powers" after the people themselves. Ibid., p. 186.

97. *The Weekly Advocate*, Jan. 7, 1837.

98. *The Colored American*, March 4, 1837.

99. David Nord, "Tocqueville, Garrison and the Perfection of Journalism," *Journalism History* 13 (1986): 56–63.

100. *New York Herald*, Nov. 21, 1837.

101. Tocqueville, *Democracy in America*, p. 519.

102. David Paul Russo, "The Origins of Local News in the U.S. Country Press, 1840s–1870s," *Journalism Monographs* 65 (February 1980): 2; Gerald Baldasty, *The Commercialization of News in the Nineteenth Century* (Madison: University of Wisconsin Press, 1992), p. 179, note 80; Jordan, *Political Leadership in Jefferson's Virginia*, p. 149.

103. Nerone, *Culture of the Press in the Early Republic*, p. 57. Nerone extensively sampled two newspapers a year for six years from 1795 to 1845. Cincinnati news as a percentage of all news was 16 percent in 1795, 8 percent in 1805, 9 percent in 1815, 18 percent in 1825, 16 percent in 1835, and 19 percent in 1845.

104. Richard B. Kielbowicz, *News in the Mail* (Westport, CT: Greenwood, 1989), p. 63.

105. Stuart Blumin, *The Urban Threshold* (Chicago: University of Chicago Press, 1976), pp. 126–49.

106. On the grand hotel in the country town, see Daniel Boorstin, *The Americans: The National Experience* (New York: Random House, 1965), p. 141.

107. Sally Foreman Griffith, *Home Town News: William Allen White and the Emporia Gazette* (New York: Oxford University Press, 1989), p. 14.

108. Jerome A. Watrous, ed., *Memoirs of Milwaukee County*, vol. 1 (Madison: Western Historical Association, 1909), pp. 431–32.

109. Russo, "Origins of Local News," p. 35.

110. Ibid., pp. 19–20. See also Paula Baker, "The Culture of Politics in the Late Nineteenth Century: Community and Political Behavior in Rural New York," *Journal of Social History* 18 (1984): 170.

111. See, for instance, Baldasty, *The Commercialization of News in the Nineteenth Century*.

112. Noble E. Cunningham, Jr., *The Process of Government Under Jefferson* (Princeton: Princeton University Press, 1978), pp. 258–59.

113. Thomas C. Leonard, *The Power of the Press* (New York: Oxford University Press, 1986), pp. 77–81.

114. Cunningham, *The Process of Government*, pp. 259, 268–70.

115. Howe, *The Political Culture of the American Whigs*, p. 26.

116. Ibid., pp. 215–16.

117. Cited in ibid., p. 240.

118. *New-York Commercial Advertiser*, June 26, 1840, p. 2.

119. Howe, *The Political Culture of the American Whigs*, pp. 204–205.

120. Reinhard H. Luthin, *The First Lincoln Campaign* (Gloucester, MA: Peter Smith, 1964), pp. 28, 81. Originally published 1944.

121. James Sterling Young, *The Washington Community, 1800–1828* (New York: Columbia University Press, 1966), pp. 28–31.

122. Ibid., pp. 51, 52, 57.

123. David Hackett Fischer, *The Revolution of American Conservatism* (New York: Harper & Row, 1965), p. 93.

124. Morris to R. R. Livingston, 1805, in ibid., p. 96.

125. Alan Taylor, *William Cooper's Town* (New York: Knopf, 1995), p. 358. Taylor focuses here on changes in electoral practices in Otsego County, New York, 1808–1809.

126. Cited in Fischer, *The Revolution of American Conservatism*, p. 100.

127. Cited in Nerone, *The Culture of the Press in the Early Republic*, pp. 168, 171.

128. Hofstadter, *The Idea of a Party System*, p. 242.

129. Van Buren, *Autobiography*, cited in Marvin Meyers, *The Jacksonian Persuasion* (New York: Vintage, 1957), p. 147.

130. Ibid., p. 149.

131. Hofstadter, *The Idea of a Party System*, p. 252.

132. See Paul Kleppner, *The Third Electoral System, 1853–1892* (Chapel Hill: University of North Carolina Press, 1979), pp. 80–82.

133. Joel H. Silbey, *The American Political Nation, 1838–1893* (Stanford: Stanford University Press, 1991).

Entr'acte I: The Public World of the Lincoln-Douglas Debates

1. David Zarefsky, *Lincoln, Douglas and Slavery* (Chicago: University of Chicago Press, 1990), p. 49.
2. Abraham S. Eisenstadt, ed., "Introduction" to *Reconsidering Tocqueville's "Democracy in America"* (New Brunswick, NJ: Rutgers University Press, 1988), p. 19, raises as a fundamental issue the task of explaining these "variant portraits of democracy." For a stimulating analysis of the differences between Tocqueville's two volumes, see Seymour Drescher, "More Than America: Comparison and Synthesis in *Democracy in America*," in Eisenstadt, pp. 77–93.
3. Alexis de Tocqueville, *Democracy in America* (Garden City, NY: Doubleday Anchor, 1969), pp. 202, 243, 236.
4. Ibid., pp. 540, 642, 639, 645, 692.
5. Harold Holzer, *The Lincoln-Douglas Debates* (New York: HarperCollins, 1993) p. 5.
6. Ibid., p. 22.
7. Ibid., p. 67.
8. Ibid., p. 69.
9. William E. Gienapp, *The Origins of the Republican Party, 1852–1856* (New York: Oxford University Press, 1987), pp. 360–67. William W. Freehling gives some credence, but not much, to the notion of a Slavepower Conspiracy. See *The Road to Disunion* (New York: Oxford University Press, 1990), p. 558, and *The Reintegration of American History: Slavery and the Civil War* (New York: Oxford University Press, 1994), pp. 158–75.
10. Holzer, *The Lincoln-Douglas Debates*, p. 9.
11. Don Fehrenbacher, *Prelude to Greatness: Lincoln in the 1850's* (Stanford: Stanford University Press, 1962), p. 104. Holzer, p. 9.
12. Zarefsky, *Lincoln, Douglas, and Slavery*, pp. 49–50.
13. Ibid., p. 54.
14. Holzer, *The Lincoln-Douglas Debates*, pp. 54, 63.
15. Richard L. Berke, "Debating the Debates: John Q. Defeats Reporters," *New York Times*, Oct. 21, 1992, A-13.
16. Nathaniel Hawthorne, *Life of Franklin Pierce* (Boston: Ticknor, Reed, and Fields, 1852), p. 137.
17. Michael F. Holt, *Political Parties and American Political Development* (Baton Rouge: Louisiana State University Press, 1992), pp. 265–90 and Tyler Anbinder, *Nativism and Slavery: The Northern Know Nothings and the Politics of the 1850s* (New York: Oxford University Press, 1992), pp. 47–48, 122–26. Quotations are from Know-Nothing newspapers in 1855 cited in Anbinder, p. 123.
18. Morton Keller, *Affairs of State* (Cambridge: Harvard University Press, 1977), p. 259.

Chapter 4: The Second Transformation of American Citizenship: 1865–1920

1. John F. Reynolds, *Testing Democracy: Electoral Behavior and Progressive Reform in New Jersey, 1880–1920* (Chapel Hill: University of North Carolina Press, 1988), p. 173.

2. Thomas Wolfe, *From Death to Morning* (New York: Scribner's, 1935), p. 121.

3. For works that seek in the late nineteenth century sources of inspiration for the apparently dispirited political culture of the 1980s, see Jean H. Baker, *Affairs of Party* (Ithaca, NY: Cornell University Press, 1983), p. 9, and Michael McGerr, *The Decline of Popular Politics* (New York: Oxford University Press, 1986), p. vii. See also Mark Lawrence Kornbluh, *From Participatory to Administrative Politics: A Social, History of American Political Behavior, 1880–1918,* Ph.D. diss., Johns Hopkins University (Ann Arbor, MI: UMI Dissertation Information Service, 1987), and Robert Wiebe, *Self-Rule* (Chicago: University of Chicago Press, 1995).

4. James Bryce, *The American Commonwealth,* vol. 2 (Chicago: Charles H. Sergel, 1891), p. 20.

5. Ibid., p. 20. Of course, Bryce has his limitations as an observer and critic. His perspective on America was borrowed from the Mugwumps. Indeed, Bryce explained later that he would have liked to dedicate his book to E. L. Godkin, but chose not to even mention this preeminent reformer in the acknowledgments to the first edition for fear he would be dismissed as Godkin's mouthpiece. To Godkin he wrote that "if I had said what I owed to you in the Preface, you being the head and front of the Mugwumps and Reformers, those who are attacked in the book . . . would at once have said, 'this is an utterance of the Mugwumps; the Mugwumps have put up an Englishman to say this and that'. . . ." See James Bryce to E. L. Godkin, Jan. 24, 1889, Godkin Papers, Houghton Library, Harvard. Quoted in William M. Armstrong, *E. L. Godkin: A Biography* (Albany: State University of New York Press, 1978), p. 95. See also Paula Baker, "The Culture of Politics in the Late Nineteenth Century: Community and Political Behavior in Rural New York," *Journal of Social History,* 18 (1984): 181, where she writes, "Party politics in this period may be considered only marginally political, in the sense that it lacked a direct connection with government or policies. The fragmented nature of party alignments, their roots in local animosities, and their reflection of voters' values rather than issue positions all suggest that politics may indeed have been nearly as empty of policy considerations as James Bryce claimed it was." For similar judgments, see Richard L. McCormick, *The Party Period and Public Policy* (New York: Oxford University Press, 1986), pp. 4–5; Richard Hofstadter, *The American Political Tradition* (New York: Knopf, 1948), p. 169; Martin Shefter, *Political Parties and the State* (Princeton: Princeton University Press, 1994), p. 72; and Theda Skocpol, *Protecting Soldiers and Mothers* (Cambridge: Harvard University Press, 1992), p. 72.

6. I borrow language here from Reynolds, *Testing Democracy,* pp. 172–73.

7. William L. Riordon, *Honest Graft: The World of George Washington Plunkitt* (St. James, NY: Brandywine, 1993; reprint of *Plunkitt of Tammany Hall,* [New York: Dutton, 1905), p. 63. The same point is made by an Illinois politician writing to President Ulysses S. Grant. See Dorothy Ganfield Fowler, *The Cabinet Politician: The Postmasters General, 1829–1909* (New York: AMS Press, 1967), p. 149. Originally published 1943.

8. Steven P. Erie, *Rainbow's End: Irish-Americans and the Dilemmas of Urban Machine Politics, 1840–1985* (Berkeley: University of California Press, 1988), pp. 98, 61.

9. H. Wayne Morgan, *From Hayes to McKinley* (Syracuse: Syracuse University Press, 1969), pp. 267–68.

10. Robert D. Marcus, *Grand Old Party* (New York: Oxford University Press, 1971), p. 9.

11. Harry J. Carman and Reinhard H. Luthin, *Lincoln and the Patronage* (Gloucester, MA: Peter Smith, 1964), pp. 61, 68–70. Originally published 1943.

12. *New York Herald*, March 19, 1861, cited in ibid., p. 82.

13. Ibid., pp. 297–98.

14. Morgan, *From Hayes to McKinley*, p. 128. For another complaint from Garfield, see Morton Keller, *Affairs of State: Public Life in Late Nineteenth Century America* (Cambridge: Harvard University Press, 1977), p. 298. Nor had it been any better for Garfield as a senator when he estimated that a third of his time was devoted to appointments. Cited in Dorman B. Eaton, "A Report Concerning the Effects of the Spoils System and Civil Service Reform," 46th Congress, House of Representatives Ex. Doc. No. 94, 1881, p. 16.

15. Thomas Reeves, *Gentleman Boss: The Life of Chester Alan Arthur* (New York: Knopf, 1975), p. 293.

16. Morgan, *From Hayes to McKinley*, p. 446.

17. Grover Cleveland, *Presidential Problems* (New York: The Century, 1904), p. 39.

18. Frank G. Carpenter, *Carp's Washington* (New York: McGraw-Hill, 1960), p. 122. This volume was edited by Frances Carpenter from Frank Carpenter's newspaper writings for the *Cleveland Leader* and the American Press Association.

19. Cleveland, *Presidential Problems*, pp. 42–43.

20. Stephen Skowronek, *Building a New American State* (Cambridge: Cambridge University Press, 1982), p. 77.

21. Ibid., p. 72.

22. Louis Brownlow, *A Passion for Politics* (Chicago: University of Chicago Press, 1955), p. 5.

23. See Reeves, *Gentleman Boss*, pp. 62–63. The quotation is from Skowronek, *Building a New American State*, p. 61.

24. Reeves, *Gentleman Boss*, pp. 59, 82–84.

25. Ibid. See also Fowler, *The Cabinet Politician*, p. 160.

26. Eaton, "A Report Concerning the Effects of the Spoils System and Civil Service Reform," p. 44.

27. William M. Ivins, *Machine Politics and Money in Elections in New York City* (New York: Arno, 1970), p. 57. Originally published 1887.

28. C. K. Yearley, *The Money Machines: The Breakdown and Reform of Governmental and Party Finance in the North, 1860–1920* (Albany: State University of New York Press, 1970), p. 102.

29. Ibid., p. 105. See also Louise Overacker, *Money in Elections* (New York: Macmillan, 1932), pp. 36–37.

30. Marcus, *Grand Old Party*, p. 179.

31. Zane L. Miller, *Boss Cox's Cincinnati* (New York: Oxford University Press, 1968), p. 164.

32. William B. Munro, *The Government of American Cities* (New York: Macmillan, 1912), p. 288.

33. Yearley, in *Money Machines*, p. 265, cites convincing evidence from Michigan.
34. Edmund Morris, *The Rise of Theodore Roosevelt* (New York: Ballantine, 1979), p. 398.
35. Curtis, writing in 1871, cited in Paul P. Van Riper, *History of the United States Civil Service* (Evanston, IL: Row, Peterson, 1958), p. 82.
36. Skowronek, *Building a New American State*, p. 47.
37. Van Riper, *History of the United States Civil Service*, p. 78.
38. Skowronek, *Building a New American State*, p. 51.
39. Munro, *The Government of American Cities*, pp. 17, 21.
40. Skowronek, *Building a New American State*, p. 179. Skowronek emphasizes another side of this, however—that Roosevelt was particularly committed to an executive-centered civil administration and that this act significantly advanced this cause.
41. Ibid., p. 69. A large part of the growth was in post offices; there were 27,000 post offices in 1869, 77,000 by 1901. Leonard D. White, *The Republican Era: 1869-1901* (New York: Macmillan, 1958), p. 259.
42. Shefter, *Political Parties and the State*, p. 75.
43. On Melville, see Leon Howard, *Herman Melville: A Biography* (Berkeley: University of California Press, 1951), p. 282. On Whitman, David S. Reynolds, *Walt Whitman's America* (New York: Knopf, 1995), p. 412. As late as 1972 there is evidence that patronage politics stimulates voter turnout. In that year, in states with relatively high rates of patronage, government workers voted 9 percent more than similarly educated workers outside government; the difference between these groups in nonpatronage states was only 3 to 4 percent. See J. Morgan Kousser, "Suffrage," *Encyclopedia of American Political History*, vol. 3 (New York: Scribner's, 1984).
44. Will H. Hays, *The Memoirs of Will H. Hays* (Garden City, NY: Doubleday, 1955), p. 39. Hays was chairman of the Republican National Committee in the 1920s and later gained fame as director of Hollywood's Hays Office. The term "spectacular politics" has a specific meaning as developed in Michael McGerr's important account of changing styles of politics from 1865 to 1920, a shift from what he calls "spectacular" to "educational" to "advertised" politics. See his *The Decline of Popular Politics*, pp. 12–41.
45. "The Passing of the Parade" (editorial), *New York World*, Nov. 2, 1908, p. 6.
46. Hays, *Memoirs*, p. 39.
47. Jules Verne, *Around the World in 80 Days* (New York: Heritage Press, 1962), p. 180.
48. Keller, *Affairs of State*, p. 240.
49. Ivins, *Machine Politics and Money in Elections in New York City*, p. 77; McGerr, *The Decline of Popular Politics*, p. 26.
50. Reynolds, *Testing Democracy*, p. 20.
51. Ivins, *Machine Politics and Money in Elections in New York City*, pp. 15, 20–21.
52. Louis F. Post and Fred C. Leubuscher, *Henry George's 1886 Campaign* (Westport, CT: Hyperion, 1976), p. 105. Originally published 1887.
53. Ibid., p. 152.
54. Ibid., p. 154.

55. Quoted in Aileen S. Kraditor, *The Ideas of the Woman Suffrage Movement, 1890–1920* (New York: Norton, 1981), p. 109. On the masculine culture of Gilded Age politics, see Keller, *Affairs of State*, pp. 247–49.

56. Armstrong, *E. L. Godkin*, p. 99. Godkin vacillated on blacks; see Allan P. Grimes, *The Political Liberalism of the New York Nation* (Chapel Hill: University of North Carolina Press, 1953), pp. 5–12.

57. Armstrong, *E. L. Godkin*, pp. 120–23.

58. Letter to Charles Eliot Norton, March 10, 1864, in William Armstrong, ed., *The Gilded Age Letters of E. L. Godkin* (Albany: State University of New York Press, 1974), p. 13.

59. Letter to Charles Eliot Norton, April 13, 1865, in Armstrong, ed., *Gilded Age Letters*, p. 28.

60. Armstrong, *E. L. Godkin*, p. 74.

61. Cited in Joel H. Silbey, *The American Political Nation, 1838–1893* (Stanford: Stanford University Press, 1991), p. 215.

62. *Minneapolis Tribune*, Oct. 11, 1884, and *New York Tribune*, July 11, 1884, cited in Morgan, *From Hayes to McKinley*, p. 211.

63. McGerr, *The Decline of Popular Politics*, p. 56. The quotation is from R. R. Bowker.

64. J. H. Randall, "The Political Catechism and Greenback Songbook," 1880, quoted in Silbey, *The American Political Nation*, p. 215.

65. E. L. Godkin, "The Government of Our Great Cities," *The Nation*, Oct. 18, 1866, p. 312, cited in Armstrong, *E. L. Godkin*, p. 123.

66. James Willard Hurst, *Law and the Conditions of Freedom in the Nineteenth-Century United States* (Madison: University of Wisconsin Press, 1956), pp. 85–87.

67. Walker Evan Davies, *Patriotism on Parade* (Cambridge: Harvard University Press, 1955), pp. 139, 208, 281, 348. Theda Skocpol's more recent work confirms Davies's insight, arguing that both veterans' groups and women's groups made demands on the government that created the early formation of an American welfare state. See *Protecting Soldiers and Mothers*. On the special role of women's groups as a model of interest group politics, see Michael McGerr, "Political Style and Women's Power, 1830–1930," *Journal of American History* 77 (1990): 864–85.

68. McGerr, *The Decline of Popular Politics*, pp. 86, 151.

69. Ibid., pp. 90, 141.

70. See, for instance, Josephus Daniels, *Editor in Politics* (Chapel Hill: University of North Carolina Press, 1941), pp. 174–75.

71. "The Passing of the Parade," *New York World*, Nov. 2, 1908, p. 6.

72. Philip J. Ethington, *The Public City: The Political Construction of Urban Life in San Francisco, 1850–1900* (Cambridge: Cambridge University Press, 1994), p. 75.

73. John S. Gilkeson, Jr., *Middle-Class Providence, 1820–1940* (Princeton: Princeton University Press, 1986), p. 181.

74. Terence Powderly recalls that in Pennsylvania there was a separate slip for each office that could be folded to show the name of the office and not of the candidate; this scarcely provided secrecy, for the different parties used different

types and qualities of paper. But I have not found other references to a system like this one. Terence V. Powderly, *The Path I Trod*, ed. Harry J. Carman, Henry C. David, and Paul N. Guthrie (New York: AMS Press, 1968), pp. 70, 174. Originally published 1940.

75. Post and Leubuscher, *Henry George's 1886 Campaign*, p. 155.

76. Powderly, *The Path I Trod*, p. 70, discussing voting in Luzerne County, Pennsylvania, in the 1870s.

77. *Alta*, Nov. 7, 1860, cited in Ethington, *The Public City*, p. 74.

78. Reynolds, *Testing Democracy*, p. 47.

79. Ibid., p. 54.

80. Ibid., p. 54.

81. Ibid., p. 61.

82. Marcus, *Grand Old Party*, pp. 13–14; Richard Jensen, *The Winning of the Midwest* (Chicago: University of Chicago Press, 1971), pp. 38–41. See also Keller, *Affairs of State*, pp. 242–43, 524–25.

83. Feb. 11, 1881, quoted in Reeves, *Gentleman Boss*, p. 215.

84. John F. Reynolds, "A Symbiotic Relationship: Vote Fraud and Electoral Reform in the Gilded Age," *Social Science History* 17 (1993): 243, 246. On vote fraud, see also Overacker, *Money in Elections*, pp. 33–34. Paul Kleppner argues that the outcries of corruption are not only poorly documented but clearly intended to cover practices that we might not think of as corruption at all. The lamentations of Mugwumps must be taken with a grain of salt, since they distrusted universal suffrage and party politics as inherently corrupt for bringing to the voting booth people ill equipped by background and training (Negroes, immigrants, and working people generally) to vote. See Paul Kleppner, *Continuity and Change in Electoral Politics, 1893–1928* (Westport, CT: Greenwood, 1987), pp. 168–70.

85. Bryce, *The American Commonwealth*, vol. 2, p. 137.

86. Many sources report that different parties used different colors of paper for their tickets. This may be so, although in examining about a hundred tickets from the 1830s through the 1880s at the Museum of American Political Life (West Hartford, CT), I found every one was on white paper. Almost all were printed in black, a few in red or blue. Most of the tickets had party symbols printed at the top of the ticket that would have made different tickets readily identifiable and also made literacy largely irrelevant as a qualification for voting.

87. Reynolds, *Testing Democracy*, p. 36.

88. Paula Baker, "The Culture of Politics in the Late Nineteenth Century: Community and Political Behavior in Rural New York," *Journal of Social History* 18 (1984): 180. Baker's "half a day" estimate comes from her reading of diaries.

89. Julian Ralph, *The Making of a Journalist* (New York: Harper and Brothers, 1903), pp. 148, 159.

90. See Keller, *Affairs of State*, pp. 376–85.

91. Yearley, *The Money Machines*, p. 260.

92. Kornbluh, *From Participatory to Administrative Politics*, p. 313. See David J. Rothman, *Politics and Power* (Cambridge: Harvard University Press, 1966), pp. 243–67.

93. Kornbluh, *From Participatory to Administrative Politics*, p. 314. See Melvin Holli, "Urban Reform in the Progressive Era," in Lewis L. Gould, ed., *The Progressive Era* (Syracuse: Syracuse University Press, 1974), pp. 133-52.

94. Hurst, *Law and the Conditions of Freedom*, pp. 49, 72-73, 92.

95. John P. Altgeld, "Protecting the Ballot Box—The Australian Plan," in *Live Questions* (New York: Humboldt, 1890), p. 57.

96. John Stuart Mill, "Consideration on Representative Government," in *Three Essays* (Oxford: Oxford University Press, 1975), p. 309. Originally published 1861.

97. Powderly, *The Path I Trod*, p. 174.

98. Henry George, "Money in Elections," *North American Review* 136 (March 1883): 201-11. See also L. E. Fredman, *The Australian Ballot* (East Lansing: Michigan State University Press, 1968), p. 32. See Henry George, "Bribery in Elections," *Overland Monthly* 7 (December 1871): 497-504.

99. Speech at Cooper Union, Nov. 6, 1886, cited in Post and Leubuscher, *Henry George's 1886 Campaign*, pp. 172-73.

100. Walter Dean Burnham, "Communications," *American Political Science Review* 65 (1971): 1149-52.

101. Fredman, *The Australian Ballot*, p. 36.

102. Ibid., p. 48.

103. Most of the state constitutions of the revolutionary period prescribed paper ballots. Kentucky maintained oral voting as late as 1892, but this was the exception. Oregon abandoned viva voce in 1872, Arkansas in 1868, Virginia 1867, and Missouri 1863; of other states, only Illinois and Texas had ever used viva voce and they gave it up in the 1840s. Paul Bourke and Donald Debats, "Individuals and Aggregates: A Note on Historical Data and Assumptions," *Social Science History* 4 (1980): 231.

104. David Thelen, *The New Citizenship: Origins of Progressivism in Wisconsin, 1885-1900* (Columbia: University of Missouri Press, 1972), pp. 27-28.

105. Earl R. Sikes, *State and Federal Corrupt-Practices Legislation* (Durham, NC: Duke University Press, 1928), pp. 24-26, 41.

106. Walter Dean Burnham, "Communications," pp. 1149-52. See also Kornbluh, *From Participatory to Administrative Politics*, pp. 119-21.

107. Kornbluh, *From Participatory to Administrative Politics*, p. 119.

108. *New York Times*, Nov. 1, 1896 and Nov. 2, 1896.

109. John Randolph Haynes Collection, Box 39, UCLA Special Collections.

110. Munro, *The Government of American Cities*, pp. 145-46.

111. Robert C. Brooks, *Political Parties and Electoral Problems* (New York: Harper, 1923), p. 428.

112. Richard S. Childs, *Civic Victories: The Story of an Unfinished Revolution* (New York: Harper, 1952), pp. 11, 22, cited in John Porter East, *Council-Manager Government* (Chapel Hill: University of North Carolina Press, 1965), p. 44.

113. Ibid., p. 48. See also Bernard Hirschhorn, *Democracy Reformed: Richard Spencer Childs and His Fight for Better Government* (Westport, CT: Greenwood, 1997).

114. Quoted in Elihu Root, *Addresses on Government and Citizenship*, Robert Bacon and James Brown Scott, eds. (Freeport, NY: Books for Libraries Press, 1969), p. 192. Originally published 1916.

115. Ibid., p. 193.
116. National Short Ballot Organization, Digest of Short Ballot Charters (1912) counting cities with short ballots adopted as of May 15, 1912. John Randolph Haynes Collection, Box 5, UCLA Special Collections.
117. Brooks, *Political Parties and Electoral Problems*, p. 429.
118. Voting Machine Service Center, Inc., Gerry, NY. On Edison, see Thomas A. Edison, *The Papers of Thomas A. Edison*, vol. 1 (Baltimore: Johns Hopkins University Press, 1989), pp. 52, 84–85.
119. Brooks, *Political Parties and Electoral Problems*, p. 406.
120. "Voting Machines" Box, Museum of American Political Life, West Hartford, CT. Voting machines "afford the greatest safeguard for honesty in elections now available," wrote the chief clerk of Chicago's Board of Election Commission. Isaac N. Powell, "Voting Machines in Use," *Technical World Magazine*, n.d., pp. 710–12. The date is some time after 1904 when Chicago adopted the voting machine. John Randolph Haynes Collection, Box 5, UCLA Special Collections.
121. James C. Mohr, *The Radical Republicans and Reform in New York During Reconstruction* (Ithaca, NY: Cornell University Press, 1973), pp. 25–34. In New York City, the $1.6 million street cleaning budget (in 1864) was also all patronage money—in contracts, kickbacks, and sanitation department jobs. Republican-sponsored reform in this arena was again sensible both for public health and for Republican efforts to weaken the Democrats. See Mohr, p. 63. Volunteer fire companies were not connected to parties early in the 1800s. See Stephen F. Ginsberg, *The History of Fire Protection in New York City, 1800–1842*, Ph.D. diss., New York University (Ann Arbor, MI: University Microfilms, 1968). For a brief general account of developments in urban fire protection, see Jon C. Teaford, *The Unheralded Triumph: City Government in America, 1870–1900* (Baltimore: Johns Hopkins University Press, 1984), pp. 162–66, 240–45.
122. McGerr, *The Decline of Popular Politics*, p. 147.
123. E. Digby Baltzell, *The American Protestant Establishment* (New York: Vintage, 1964), p. 119.
124. Kenneth Fox, *Better City Government: Innovation in American Urban Politics, 1850–1937* (Philadelphia: Temple University Press, 1977), pp. 63–89.
125. Gilkeson, *Middle-Class Providence*, pp. 134–37, 164.
126. Mary Ann Clawson, *Constructing Brotherhood: Class, Gender, and Fraternalism* (Princeton: Princeton University Press, 1989), p. 131.
127. *New York Herald*, Nov. 19, 1883, cited in Michael O'Malley, *Keeping Watch: A History of American Time* (New York: Viking Penguin, 1990), p. 145. See generally pp. 99–144.
128. On municipal statistics, see Fox, *Better City Government*, pp. 63–89.
129. Daniel Boorstin, *The Americans: The Democratic Experience* (New York: Random House, 1973), p. 132.
130. Charles S. Hyneman, C. Richard Hofstetter, and Patrick F. O'Connor, *Voting in Indiana* (Bloomington: Indiana University Press, 1979), p. 2.
131. Michael Emery and Edwin Emery, *The Press and America*, 6th ed. (Englewood Cliffs, NJ: Prentice-Hall, 1988), p. 274.

132. Elmer Davis, *History of The New York Times, 1851–1921* (New York: The New York Times, 1921), pp. 194–95. On business losses in 1884, see p. 156.

133. Ibid., p. 218.

134. Ibid., pp. 248–55; on the *Times's* politics as "independent Democratic," p. 248; Ochs's "Introduction" to the Davis book, p. ix; for "independent conservative newspaper," p. ix.

135. Elliot King, "Ungagged Partisanship: The Political Values of the Public Press, 1835–1920," Ph.D. diss., University of California, San Diego, Department of Sociology, 1992, pp. 396–98, 467–68.

136. Michael Schudson, *The Power of News* (Cambridge: Harvard University Press, 1995), pp. 72–93.

137. Brownlow, *A Passion for Politics*, p. 234. On the emergence of the summary lead, see Schudson, pp. 53–71.

138. E. L. Godkin, "Newspapers Here and Abroad," *North American Review* 150 (February 1890), p. 198.

139. On the rise of reporting as an occupation, see Michael Schudson, *Discovering the News* (New York: Basic Books, 1978), pp. 61–87.

140. Donald A. Ritchie, *Press Gallery: Congress and the Washington Correspondents* (Cambridge: Harvard University Press, 1991), pp. 109, 121, 151.

141. Robert Wiebe, *The Search for Order* (New York: Hill & Wang, 1967).

142. J. Morgan Kousser, *The Shaping of Southern Politics* (New Haven: Yale University Press, 1974), p. 239.

143. Ibid., p. 239, and Kornbluh, *From Participatory to Administrative Politics*, p. 324.

144. Kornbluh, *From Participatory to Administrative Politics*, pp. 251, 320.

145. Melvin G. Holli, *Reform in Detroit: Hazen S. Pingree and Urban Politics* (New York: Oxford University Press, 1969), p. 67.

146. Kornbluh, *From Participatory to Administrative Politics*, pp. 251, 320.

147. Kleppner, *Continuity and Change in Electoral Politics*, p. 166.

148. "The Harm of Immigration," *The Nation*, Jan. 19, 1893, p. 43, cited in Armstrong, *E. L. Godkin*, p. 122.

149. William Gillette, *The Right to Vote: Politics and the Passage of the Fifteenth Amendment* (Baltimore: Johns Hopkins University Press, 1965), pp. 153–56.

150. Munro, *The Government of American Cities*, p. 120. See also Holli, *Reform in Detroit*, p. 174.

151. James B. Crooks, *Politics and Progress: The Rise of Urban Progressivism in Baltimore, 1895 to 1911* (Baton Rouge: Louisiana State University Press, 1968), pp. 70–71.

152. See Kleppner, *Continuity and Change in Electoral Politics*, p. 170. The evidence on this point gathered in Kousser, *The Shaping of Southern Politics*, pp. 47–62, and not confined to the South, is particularly persuasive.

153. See Kousser, *The Shaping of Southern Politics*, pp. 52–53, 56–57.

154. Daniels, *Editor in Politics*, pp. 374–81.

155. Rogers M. Smith, "'The American Creed' and American Identity: Limits of Liberal Citizenship in the United States," *Western Political Quarterly* 41 (1988): 225–51.

156. Lew Wallace, *Life of Gen. Ben Harrison* (Hartford, CT: S.S. Scranton, 1888), p. 247.

157. William Howard Taft, *Four Aspects of Civic Duty* (New York: Scribner's, 1906), pp. 21–22.

158. Henry Crosby Emery, *Politicians, Party and People* (New Haven: Yale University Press, 1913), pp. 61–62, 82.

159. Ibid., pp. 144, 40.

160. Ibid., p. 8.

161. April 23, 1867, in Armstrong, ed., *Gilded Age Letters*, p. 105.

162. William Allen White, *The Old Order Changeth* (New York: Macmillan, 1912), p. 39.

Chapter 5: Cures for Democracy? Civil Religion, Leadership, Expertise— and More Democracy

1. Walter Lippmann, *The Phantom Public* (New York: Harcourt, Brace, 1925), p. 39.

2. Purification is a term contemporaries used as they assailed "dirty" politics. I do not know when politics was first called dirty, but it was certainly common terminology in the Progressive Era. For instance, the campaign law Tennessee passed in 1890 was the "Act to preserve the purity of elections." See *Burson v. Freeman* 504 U.S. 191 (1992). See also John Fiske, *Civil Government in the United States* (Boston: Houghton Mifflin, 1891), in which Fiske recommends the "purification" of city government (p. 135) and frequently writes of "dirty" politics.

3. Earl R. Sikes, *State and Federal Corrupt-Practices Legislation* (Durham, NC: Duke University Press, 1928), p. 24. Sikes lists legislation against providing conveyance on election day in thirteen states.

4. Louise Overacker, *Money in Elections* (New York: Macmillan, 1932), p. 306.

5. See the concurring opinion of Antonin Scalia in *Burson v. Freeman* at 214–15. Scalia finds thirty-four states had banned political speech near the polling place (usually within a hundred feet) by 1900. In Alabama, a 1940 statute went so far as to prohibit any electioneering at all on election day; state courts interpreted that to prohibit even newspaper editorials on election day. The U.S. Supreme Court declared this provision of the Alabama Code unconstitutional in *Mills v. Alabama* 384 U.S. 214 (1965).

6. Graham Wallas, *The Great Society* (Lincoln: University of Nebraska Press 1967). Originally published 1914.

7. Woodrow Wilson, *The New Freedom* (New York: Doubleday, Page, 1913), pp. 281–83.

8. Interestingly, Graham Wallas himself begins his book with a quotation from Woodrow Wilson. In the human past, Wilson declares, people related to one another "as individuals" while, today, "the everyday relationships of men are largely with great impersonal concerns, with organizations, not with other individual men." See Wilson, *The New Freedom*, pp. 6–7, and Wallas, *The Great Society*, p. 3. For Wilson, this is "nothing short of a new social age," and Wallas clearly agrees. A series of inventions, he writes, brought on the transcendence of "old limits to the creation of mechanical force, the carriage of men and goods, and communication by written and spoken words. One effect of this

transformation is a general change of social scale." What people were seeking was the idea of society itself as a relatively integrated entity, and one exerting force far beyond the capacity of individuals or governments to control or, even, understand. It is no wonder that the discipline of sociology should have become institutionalized in these years.

9. Arthur M. Schlesinger and Eric M. Eriksson, "The Vanishing Voter," *The New Republic* 40 (Oct. 15, 1924): 162, 165, 166. Walter Lippmann endorses their concerns in *The Phantom Public*, p. 17: "The students used to write books about voting. They are now beginning to write books about nonvoting," he opines. Lippmann points to the important study of Chicago elections by Charles E. Merriam and Harold F. Gosnell, *Non-Voting: Causes and Methods of Control* (Chicago: University of Chicago Press, 1924).

10. Leonard White, *The City Manager* (Chicago: University of Chicago Press, 1927), p. 297.

11. The creation of the Brookings Institution, for instance, writes its historian, was part of "a grand political strategy to limit partisan influence in government by depoliticizing public policy." Donald T. Critchlow, *The Brookings Institution, 1916–1952: Expertise and the Public Interest in a Democratic Society* (De Kalb, IL: Northern Illinois University Press, 1985), p. 9.

12. Walter Lippmann, "The Causes of Political Indifference To-Day," in *Men of Destiny* (New York: Macmillan, 1928), pp. 18, 20, 34.

13. Graham Wallas, *Human Nature in Politics* (Lincoln: University of Nebraska Press, 1962), p. 211. Originally published 1908.

14. John Dewey, *Individualism Old and New* (New York: Minton, Balch, 1930), p. 43. See also John Dewey, "Propaganda," in *Character and Events*, vol. 2 (New York: Octagon, 1970), pp. 517–21. Originally published as "The New Paternalism" in *The New Republic*, Dec. 21, 1918.

15. Arthur T. Hadley, *Undercurrents in American Politics* (New Haven: Yale University Press, 1915), pp. 152–53.

16. James Allen Myatt, *William Randolph Hearst and the Progressive Era, 1900–1912*, Ph.D. diss., University of Florida (Ann Arbor, MI: University Microfilms, 1960), pp. 9–10.

17. See Evans Johnson, *Oscar W. Underwood* (Baton Rouge: Louisiana State University Press, 1980), p. 172.

18. Silas Bent, *Ballyhoo* (New York: Boni and Liveright, 1927), p. 122.

19. Peter Odegard, *The American Public Mind* (New York: Columbia University Press, 1930), p. 132.

20. E. Pendleton Herring, *Group Representation Before Congress* (New York: Russell and Russell, 1929), pp. 16–17.

21. See Ernest Gruening, *The Public Pays* (New York: Vanguard, 1931).

22. "Harding Demands Team Government," *New York Times*, Sept. 3, 1920, p. 3. The *New York Times* editorialized ("Stooping to Conquer," Sept. 4, 1920, p. 8) critically on Harding's baseball oratory.

23. See Randolph C. Downes, *The Rise of Warren Gamaliel Harding* (Columbus: Ohio State University Press, 1970), pp. 472–74, 484, 490–92, and John Gunther, *Taken at the Flood* (New York: Harper, 1960), pp. 99–113.

24. "Government by Publicity," *The New Republic* 48 (Sept. 22, 1926): 111.

25. Walter Lippmann, "The Peculiar Weakness of Mr. Hoover," *Harper's* 161 (June 1930): 1.

26. Will Irwin, *Propaganda and the News* (New York: Whittlesey House, 1936), p. 302.

27. Ibid., p. 301.

28. Robert C. Brooks, *Political Parties and Electoral Problems* (New York: Harper, 1923), pp. 473–76.

29. L. White Busbey, *Uncle Joe Cannon* (New York: Holt, 1927), p. 295.

30. Louise M. Young, *In the Public Interest: The League of Women Voters, 1920–1970* (Westport, CT: Greenwood, 1989), pp. 93–95; Felice D. Gordon, *After Winning: The New Jersey Suffragists, 1910–1947*, Ph.D. diss., Rutgers University (Ann Arbor, MI: University Microfilms, 1982).

31. Overacker, *Money in Elections*, p. vii. She borrowed this language from Oswald Spengler's popular *The Decline of the West*, 2 vols. (New York: Knopf, 1926 and 1928). Spengler argues that "the freedom of public opinion involves the preparation of public opinion, which costs money; and the freedom of the press brings with it the question of possession of the press, which again is a matter of money; and with the franchise comes electioneering, in which he who pays the piper calls the tune." See Overacker, p. 381.

32. A useful account of this legislation is Spencer Ervin, *Henry Ford vs. Truman H. Newberry* (New York: Richard R. Smith, 1935), pp. 309–25. Ervin defends Newberry's actions as not violating laws that limit, in his view, candidate contributions but not political committee contributions. His work is also introduced by political scientist William B. Munro, who observes (p. x) that though we complain that not enough voters go to the polls we simultaneously "place hindrances in the way of those campaign activities which would be most effective in bringing them there. The way to bring out the vote is to bring out the issues. The way to bring out the issues is to use the channels of publicity, which of course cannot be done without spending money." The national party platforms are reprinted in George T. Kurian, ed., *Encyclopedia of the Republican Party/Encyclopedia of the Democratic Party*, 4 vols. (Armonk, NY: Sharpe, 1997).

33. Kurian, *Encyclopedia of the Democratic Party* 4: 520.

34. Further campaign finance law was enacted in 1940 and, with respect to labor unions, 1948, but no law had much practical effect on campaign contributions, expenditures, or the public reporting of them until the campaign reform acts of 1971 and 1974. Robert E. Mutch, *Campaigns, Congress, and Courts: The Making of Federal Campaign Finance Law* (New York: Praeger, 1988), p. 27. This is the best history of the subject available, but it is unsatisfying in no small measure for the reason Mutch indicates: there is no reliable data on campaign financing before the Federal Election Campaign Act of 1971 mandated public disclosure and provided a public agency to maintain the data and penalties for failure to report.

35. Herring, *Group Representation Before Congress*, p. 41. See the same distinction in David S. Barry, *Forty Years in Washington* (Boston: Little, Brown, 1924), p. 130.

36. Virginia Van Der Veer Hamilton, *Hugo Black: The Alabama Years* (Baton Rouge: Louisiana State University Press, 1972), pp. 245–59; Karl Schriftgiesser, *The Lobbyists* (Boston: Little, Brown, 1951), pp. 48–87.

37. Emphasis in original. The lectures in *Publicity* were delivered to the American Association of Teachers of Journalism and the Advertising Club of New York and were promptly anthologized in an academic text: W. Brooke Graves, *Readings in Public Opinion* (New York: Appleton, 1928).

38. The article is from 1921, cited in Richard S. Tedlow, *Keeping the Corporate Image: Public Relations and Business, 1900–1950* (Greenwich, CT: JAI Press, 1979), p. 176.

39. Cited in Graves, *Readings in Public Opinion*, p. 581.

40. C. Hartley Grattan, *Why We Fought* (New York: Vanguard, 1929), is a sober, even-tempered indictment. Grattan devotes a ninety-page chapter to "propaganda" that judges British propagandists to have "had little to do beyond confirming and elaborating prejudices already pretty firmly set in the American mind" (p. 38).

   Charles Beard's *The Devil Theory of War* (New York: Vanguard, 1936; Greenwood, 1969) sought to prevent American entanglement in a next European war by asking how the nation was drawn into the First World War. Its point of departure was the Nye munitions committee investigation in January and February 1936 (p. 11). This investigation "ought to put on their everlasting guard all people who want to be intelligent" by disclosing how little Americans knew in 1914–18 of how American policy was actually determined (p. 12).

41. H. C. Peterson, *Propaganda for War: The Campaign Against American Neutrality, 1914–1917* (Norman: University of Oklahoma Press, 1939), p. 4.

42. Ibid., p. 326.

43. Charles Seymour, *American Neutrality, 1914–1917* (New Haven: Yale University Press, 1935; Archon, 1967), p. 148. My critique of the revisionists follows the persuasive work of Kevin O'Keefe, *A Thousand Deadlines: The New York City Press and American Neutrality, 1914–1917* (The Hague: Martinus Nijhoff, 1972).

44. Charles and Mary Beard, *The Rise of American Civilization* (New York: Macmillan, 1930), p. 640. Concern over propaganda in schoolbooks prompted a great deal of controversy and state-level investigations. See Bessie Louise Pierce, *Public Opinion and the Teaching of History in the United States* (New York: Knopf, 1926).

45. I borrow the term from Sanford Levinson, *Constitutional Faith* (Princeton: Princeton University Press, 1988).

46. Michael Kammen, *A Machine That Would Go of Itself* (New York: Knopf, 1986), p. 219.

47. Ibid., pp. 266–69.

48. Ibid., p. 232.

49. "President's Jefferson Talk," *New York Times*, Nov. 16, 1939, p. 16.

50. Kammen, *A Machine That Would Go of Itself*, p. 487.

51. June Culp Zeitner and Lincoln Borglum, *Borglum's Unfinished Dream* (Aberdeen, SD: North Plains Press, 1976), pp. 47, 71, 73, 76.

52. Michael Kammen, *Mystic Chords of Memory* (New York: Knopf, 1991), p. 486, and Merrill D. Peterson, *The Jefferson Image in the American Mind* (New York: Oxford University Press, 1960), pp. 384–87.

53. Kammen, *Mystic Chords of Memory*, pp. 361–62.

54. Viviana A. Zelizer, *The Social Meaning of Money* (New York: Basic Books, 1994), pp. 13–17.

55. Theodore J. Lowi, *The Personal President* (Ithaca, NY: Cornell University Press, 1985), p. 46.

56. See Arthur C. Millspaugh, *Crime Control by the National Government* (Washington, DC: Brookings Institution, 1937).

57. Lowi, *The Personal President*, p. 40.

58. See especially Jeffrey K. Tulis, *The Rhetorical Presidency* (Princeton: Princeton University Press, 1987).

59. Richard J. Ellis and Stephen Kirk, "Presidential Mandates in the Nineteenth Century: Conceptual Change and Institutional Development," *Studies in American Political Development* 9 (1995): 175–76.

60. Lewis Gould, *The Presidency of Theodore Roosevelt* (Lawrence: University Press of Kansas, 1991), pp. 66–69.

61. Barry D. Karl, *Executive Reorganization and Reform in the New Deal* (Cambridge: Harvard University Press, 1963), p. 189. For a history of the role of the president in the federal budget, see Louis Fisher, *Presidential Spending Power* (Princeton: Princeton University Press, 1975).

62. Samuel Kernell, *Going Public* (Washington, DC: CQ Press, 1986).

63. Gould, *The Presidency of Theodore Roosevelt*, p. 272.

64. Henry Crosby Emery, *Politician, Party and People* (New Haven: Yale University Press, 1913), p. 143.

65. Woodrow Wilson, "Address from Rear Platform, Mandan, No. Dak. September 10, 1919," in Albert Shaw, ed., *The Messages and Papers of Woodrow Wilson*, vol. 2 (New York: Review of Reviews, 1924), p. 866; Wilson, *The New Freedom*, p. 85; and John Milton Cooper, Jr., "Fool's Errand or Finest Hour? Woodrow Wilson's Speaking Tour in September 1919," in John Milton Cooper, Jr. and Charles E. Neu, eds., *The Wilson Era: Essays in Honor of Arthur S. Link* (Arlington Heights, IL: Harlan Davidson, 1991), p. 200. See also John Milton Cooper, Jr., *The Warrior and the Priest* (Cambridge: Harvard University Press, 1983), pp. 176–77, 298–99.

66. John Maltese, *The Selling of Supreme Court Nominees* (Baltimore: Johns Hopkins University Press, 1995), p. 51.

67. Charles G. Dawes, *The First Year of the Budget of the United States* (New York: Harper & Bros., 1923), p. 7.

68. Ibid., p. 9.

69. William Trufant Foster and Waddill Catchings, "Mr. Hoover's Road to Prosperity," *Review of Reviews*, January 1930, cited in Arthur M. Schlesinger, Jr., *The Crisis of the Old Order, 1919–1933* (Boston: Houghton Mifflin, 1957), p. 155.

70. Charles Forcey, *Crossroads of Liberalism: Croly, Weyl, Lippmann, and the Progressive Era, 1900–1925* (New York: Oxford University Press, 1961), p. 41.

71. Walter Lippmann, *A Preface to Politics* (New York: M. Kennerley, 1913).

72. White, *The City Manager*, p. 295.

73. Walter Lippmann, "Insiders and Outsiders," *The New Republic* 5 (Nov. 13, 1915): p. 35. Lippmann returns to the insider/outsider distinction in *The Phantom Public*: "The fundamental difference which matters is that between insiders and outsiders. . . . Only the insider can make decisions, not because he is inherently a better man but because he is so placed that he can understand and can act. The outsider is necessarily ignorant, usually irrelevant and often meddlesome, because he is trying to navigate the ship from dry land" (p. 150).

74. Michael Stockstill, "Walter Lippmann and His Rise to Fame, 1889–1945," Ph.D. diss., Mississippi State University, 1970, p. 152.

75. Walter Lippmann, *Liberty and the News* (New York: Harcourt Brace & Hone, 1920), p. 5.

76. Ibid., p. 5.

77. Ibid., p. 67.

78. Ibid., pp. 81–82.

79. John Dewey, "Public Opinion," *The New Republic* 30 (May 3, 1922): 286.

80. Walter Lippmann, *Public Opinion* (New York: Macmillan, 1922), p. 76.

81. John Dewey, *The Public and Its Problems* (New York: Henry Holt, 1927), p. 139.

82. Ibid., pp. 207, 208, 209.

83. Ibid., pp. 98, 213, 215. Dewey had announced his claim for the local some years before when he wrote, "We are discovering that the locality is the only universal." This appeared in *The Dial*, June 1920, and is reprinted as "Americanism and Localism," in John Dewey, *Characters and Events*, vol. 2, pp. 537–42.

84. John Dewey, "Justice Holmes and the Liberal Mind," *The New Republic* 53 (1929): 210–12; reprinted in Dewey, *Characters and Events*, vol. 1, pp. 100–101.

85. See William Buxton and Stephen P. Turner, "From Education to Expertise: Sociology as a 'Profession,'" in Terence C. Halliday and Morris Janowitz, eds., *Sociology and Its Publics* (Chicago: University of Chicago Press, 1992), pp. 374–407.

86. Edward A. Purcell, Jr., *The Crisis of Democratic Theory* (Lexington: University Press of Kentucky, 1973), p. 16.

87. Ibid., p. 17.

88. Ibid., p. 28.

89. Ibid., p. 32.

90. Critchlow, *The Brookings Institution, 1916–1952*, p. 28. See also Guy Alchon, *The Invisible Hand of Planning: Capitalism, Social Science, and the State in the 1920s* (Princeton: Princeton University Press, 1985), and Samuel Haber, *Efficiency and Uplift* (Chicago: University of Chicago Press, 1964), pp. 108–16. Critchlow's list of early research bureaus omits Baltimore; on Baltimore, see James B. Crooks, *Politics and Progress: The Rise of Urban Progressivism in Baltimore, 1895–1911* (Baton Rouge: Louisiana State University Press, 1968), pp. 101–102.

91. Frederic C. Howe, *Wisconsin: An Experiment in Democracy* (New York: Scribner's, 1912), p. 42.

92. See Gene M. Lyons, *The Uneasy Partnership: Social Science and the Federal Government in the Twentieth Century* (New York: Russell Sage Foundation, 1969).

93. Peter Dobkin Hall, *Inventing the Nonprofit Sector* (Baltimore: Johns Hopkins University Press, 1992), p. 48. Just beyond the time of the Lippmann-Dewey discussion, an expert would be elected to the presidency and would use the office to further institutionalize the importance of social science in public policy. Herbert Hoover was not the first "expert" to be president—Woodrow Wilson probably was that—but he was the first whose expertise was held up as a chief qualification for office and, apart from military leaders, the first whose leadership experience had been in exclusively appointive positions, and, in this century, the last. The experiment of the bureaucrat president would not be repeated—a fact worth considering by those who fear that rule by the experts has overtaken us.

94. Haber, *Efficiency and Uplift*, pp. 108–10.

95. Howe, *Wisconsin*, p. 190.

96. Hadley, *Undercurrents in American Politics*, pp. 176–77.

97. James Allen Smith, *The Idea Brokers: Think Tanks and the Rise of the New Policy Elite* (New York: Free Press, 1991), p. 79.

98. Larry Berman, *The Office of Management and Budget and the Presidency, 1921–1979* (Princeton: Princeton University Press, 1979), p. 13.

99. Frederic C. Howe, *The Modern City and Its Problems* (New York: Scribner's, 1915; College Park, MD: McGrath, 1969), pp. 311–15; Mary P. Follett, *The New State* (New York: Longmans, Green, 1918; Gloucester, MA: Peter Smith, 1965).

100. Quoted in Allen F. Davis, *Spearheads for Reform: The Social Settlements and the Progressive Movement, 1890–1914* (New York: Oxford University Press, 1967), p. 80. See generally pp. 76–83 on the settlement houses and the school social centers movement.

101. Wilson, *The New Freedom*, p. 96.

102. Raymond Calkins, *Substitutes for the Saloon*, 2nd ed. (New York: Arno, 1971), p. 54. Originally published 1901.

103. Wilson, *The New Freedom*, pp. 99, 101.

104. John W. Studebaker, *The American Way: Democracy at Work in the Des Moines Forums* (New York: McGraw-Hill, 1935), p. 14.

105. Ibid., pp. 25–26.

106. Ibid., pp. 45–46.

107. Ibid., p. 132.

108. William Graebner, *The Engineering of Consent* (Madison: University of Wisconsin Press, 1987), pp. 101–102.

109. See Granville Hicks, *Small Town* (New York: Macmillan, 1946), and Leah Levenson and Jerry Natterstad, *Granville Hicks: The Intellectual in Mass Society* (Philadelphia: Temple University Press, 1993), pp. 139–46.

110. Carl J. Friedrich, *The New Image of the Common Man* (Boston: Beacon Press, 1950), pp. 346–47. Originally published in 1942 as *The New Belief in the Common Man*.

111. George V. Denny, Jr., "Public Opinion and Citizen Action," in *Citizenship in Action* (Bulletin of New York State Council of School Superintendents) No. 18 (March 1941): 3. In John Randolph Haynes Collection, UCLA Special Collections.

112. Roland Marchand, "Radio and the Restoration of Participatory Democracy: America's 'Town Meeting of the Air,'" manuscript, pp. 10, 11, 31.

113. George V. Denny, Jr., "Bring Back the Town Meeting!" in Warren C. Seyfert, ed., *Capitalizing Intelligence: Eight Essays on Adult Education* (Cambridge: Harvard Graduate School of Education, 1937), pp. 115–16.

114. Ibid., pp. 124–25. On the *Town Meeting of the Air,* see also Harry A. Overstreet and Bonaro W. Overstreet, *Town Meeting Comes to Town* (New York: Harper & Brothers, 1938).

115. Lippmann, *The Phantom Public,* p. 37.

116. George Gallup and Saul Forbes Rae, *The Pulse of Democracy: The Public-Opinion Poll and How It Works* (New York: Simon & Schuster, 1940), p. v.

117. Ibid., p. 5.

118. Ibid., p. 14.

119. Ibid., p. 118.

120. Ibid., pp. 221–27.

121. George Gallup, *A Guide to Public Opinion Polls* (Princeton: Princeton University Press, 1948), p. 98.

122. Ibid., p. 107.

123. Gallup and Rae, *The Pulse of Democracy,* pp. 63–64.

124. Ibid., p. 14.

125. Ibid., pp. 11–15.

126. Gallup, *A Guide to Public Opinion Polls,* p. xi.

127. Ibid., p. xii. See also George Gallup, *The Sophisticated Poll Watcher's Guide* (Princeton: Princeton Opinion Press, 1972), pp. 18–19.

128. Gallup, *A Guide to Public Opinion Polls,* p. xi.

129. Gallup and Rae, *The Pulse of Democracy,* p. 20.

130. Ibid., p. 31.

131. Cited in ibid., p. 125.

132. Ibid., pp. 283–85.

133. Gallup, *A Guide to Public Opinion Polls,* pp. ix–x.

134. Ibid., p. x.

135. Gallup and Rae, *The Pulse of Democracy,* p. 259.

136. Ibid., p. 264.

137. Ibid., pp. 287–89.

138. Gallup, *A Guide to Public Opinion Polls,* p. 85.

139. Ibid., p. 85.

140. Ibid., p. 91.

141. Nathan Keyfitz, "The Social and Political Context of Population Forecasting," in William Alonso and Paul Starr, eds., *The Politics of Numbers* (New York: Russell Sage Foundation, 1987), p. 235. See in the same volume, Paul Starr, "The Sociology of Official Statistics," pp. 7–58.

142. John Durham Peters, "Historical Tensions in the Concept of Public Opinion," in Theodore L. Glasser and Charles T. Salmon, eds., *Public Opinion and the*

Communication of Consent (New York: Guilford, 1995), p. 20. Other thoughtful critics of polling include Herbert Blumer, "Public Opinion and Public Opinion Polling," *American Sociological Review* 13 (1948): 242–49; Pierre Bourdieu, "Public Opinion Does Not Exist," in Armand Mattelart and Seth Siegelaub, eds., *Communication and Class Struggle* (New York: International General, 1979), pp. 124–30; Benjamin Ginsberg, *The Captive Public: How Mass Opinion Promotes State Power* (New York: Basic Books, 1986); Susan Herbst, *Numbered Voices: How Opinion Polling Has Shaped American Politics* (Chicago: University of Chicago Press, 1993); and James W. Carey, "The Press, Public Opinion, and Public Discourse," in Glasser and Salmon, eds., *Public Opinion and the Communication of Consent*, pp. 373–402.

143. Sidney M. Milkis, *The President and the Parties* (New York: Oxford University Press, 1993), pp. 127–28.

144. Ibid., pp. 41–42; Sean J. Savage, *Roosevelt: The Party Leader, 1932–1945* (Lexington: University Press of Kentucky, 1991), pp. 20–23.

145. Paul P. Van Riper, *History of the United States Civil Service* (Evanston, IL: Row, Peterson, 1958), p. 334.

146. Ibid., p. 324.

147. Savage, *Roosevelt: The Party Leader*, pp. 24–25.

148. Milkis, *The President and the Parties*, p. 116. See also pp. 55, 57, 115, 133, and Van Riper, *History of the United States Civil Service*, pp. 338–47.

149. Milkis, *The President and the Parties*, p. 103. Mary Follett had seen it happening at the state level a quarter century before: "As politics comes to mean state employment bureaus, sickness and accident insurance, mothers' pensions, Tammany is being shorn of much of its power." Follett, *The New State*, p. 223.

150. Savage, *Roosevelt: The Party Leader*, pp. 41–47, 110, 146–48.

Entr'acte II: The Second Great Debate

1. Newton N. Minow, John Bartlow Martin, and Lee M. Mitchell, *Presidential Television* (New York: Basic Books, 1973), p. 125.

2. Russell Jacoby, *The Last Intellectuals: American Culture in the Age of Academe* (New York: Basic Books, 1987), p. 6.

3. Exact number of viewers is not well established. The most comprehensive review of the research literature estimates seventy million adults and ten to fifteen million younger people watched the first debate (compared to the sixty-eight million who voted in November). See Elihu Katz and Jacob J. Feldman, "The Debates in the Light of Research: A Survey of Surveys," in Sidney Kraus, ed., *The Great Debates* (Bloomington: Indiana University Press, 1962), p. 190.

4. The "convocation" quotation is from Theodore White, *The Making of the President 1960* (New York: Atheneum, 1961), p. 279, one of the most powerful carriers of the myth. For a critique of works that overstress the effects of the visual in the Kennedy-Nixon debates, see Michael Schudson, *The Power of News* (Cambridge: Harvard University Press, 1995), pp. 113–23.

5. Not that everyone agrees on when (or if) political television reached maturity. Michael Oreskes, covering television for the *New York Times* in the 1988 cam-

paign, held that "television has come of age in this Presidential election. No longer is the tube some dark, new force distorting the process through which voters select their Presidents. In the new electronic democracy, television *is* the force that shapes the process through which voters select their Presidents." Oreskes added that Walter Mondale's complaint that he lost in 1984 because he was bad on television "is not likely to be heard again from a candidate for national office." Of course, it was heard again, from Michael Dukakis, two months later. See Michael Oreskes, "Talking Heads: Weighing Imagery in a Campaign Made for Television," *New York Times*, Oct. 2, 1988, 4:1.

6. See Kiku Adatto, *Picture Perfect* (New York: Basic Books, 1993), for the development of the notion that the news media have turned to a "theater criticism" approach to political coverage.

7. White, *The Making of the President 1960*, p. 282.

8. See ibid., pp. 281–82.

9. Sig Mickelson, *From Whistle Stop to Sound Bite* (New York: Praeger, 1989), pp. 66–67. The law was amended only in 1976, establishing new rules for the second—and subsequent—presidential debates, including that independent organizations rather than the television networks themselves would have to organize the debates. See Mickelson, pp. 130–34.

10. Herbert A. Seltz and Richard D. Yoakam, "Production Diary of the Debates," in Kraus, ed., *The Great Debates*, p. 79.

11. Ibid., p. 78.

12. Ibid., p. 79, and Douglass Cater, "Notes from Backstage," in Kraus, ed., *The Great Debates*, p. 129. Cater, a journalist for *The Reporter* magazine, was a panelist in the third debate.

13. Seltz and Yoakam, "Production Diary of the Debates," p. 77.

14. Katz and Feldman, "The Debates in the Light of Research," p. 203.

15. Samuel Lubell, "Personalities vs. Issues," in Kraus, ed., *The Great Debates*, p. 152.

16. Clinton Rossiter, "The Democratic Process," in President's Commission on National Goals, *Goals for Americans* (New York: The American Assembly, 1960), p. 72.

17. Daniel J. Boorstin, *The Image* (New York: Atheneum, 1961), pp. 41–44.

18. Quoted in Seltz and Yoakam, "Production Diary of the Debates," p. 86. As for "image-making," it seems to me that what Jonathan Schell proposed two decades ago still makes sense—that atomic weapons and the Cold War fostered a world of image-making more than anything else. See Jonathan Schell, *The Time of Illusion* (New York: Knopf, 1976). In 1960, the presidential candidates debated the level of American "prestige" in the world. In the second debate, Vice President Nixon urged that we "launch an offensive for the minds and hearts and souls of men. It must be economic; it must be technological; above all it must be ideological." Even so, he averred, "at the present time Communist prestige in the world is at an all-time low and American prestige is at an all-time high." See Kraus, ed., *The Great Debates*, p. 376.

19. Robert Putnam, "The Strange Disappearance of Civic America," *American Prospect* 24 (Winter 1996): 34–49.

20. White, *Making of the President 1960*, pp. 292–93.

Chapter 6: Widening the Web of Citizenship in an Age of Private Citizens

1. Robert Dahl, *Who Governs?* (New Haven: Yale University Press, 1961), p. 279.
2. U.S. Bureau of the Census, *Historical Statistics of the United States, Colonial Times to 1957* (Washington, DC: Government Printing Office, 1960), p. 510 (S 70-80).
3. Frank Levy, *Dollars and Dreams: The Changing American Income Distribution* (New York: Russell Sage Foundation, 1987), p. 17.
4. Ibid., p. 69.
5. Ibid., p. 154.
6. Richard Sennett, *The Uses of Disorder* (New York: Knopf, 1970), p. 48.
7. David Popenoe, *Private Pleasure, Public Plight* (New Brunswick, NJ: Transaction Books, 1985), p. 83. The latest figures on church attendance show Americans to attend church far more often than people in most other developed nations. The World Values Survey of 1995–97 found 44 percent of Americans attend church weekly, 27 percent of the British, 21 percent of the French, and 4 percent of the Swedes. Richard Morin, "Keeping the Faith," *Washington Post National Weekly Edition*, Jan. 12, 1998, p. 37.
8. Popenoe, p. 118.
9. Michael Walzer, *Radical Principles* (New York: Basic Books, 1980), p. 29.
10. Derek Bok, *The State of the Nation* (Cambridge: Harvard University Press, 1996), pp. 107–108.
11. David Riesman, "The Suburban Sadness," in William M. Dobriner, ed., *The Suburban Community* (New York: Putnam, 1958), p. 377.
12. Popenoe, *Private Pleasure, Public Plight*, pp. 122–23.
13. Ibid.
14. *Palko v. Connecticut* 302 U.S. 319 (1937). Cardozo quoted the phrase about "fundamental principles of liberty and justice . . . at the base . . ." from Justice Willis Van Devanter's majority opinion in *Hebert v. Louisiana* 272 U.S. 312 (1926). On the Palko case, see Richard C. Cortner, *The Supreme Court and the Second Bill of Rights* (Madison: University of Wisconsin Press, 1981), pp. 126–32.
15. *United States v. Carolene Products* 304 U.S. 144 (1938).
16. Robert M. Cover, "The Origin of Judicial Activism in the Protection of Minorities," *Yale Law Journal* 91 (1982): 1294. See also Louis Lusky, "Minority Rights and the Public Interest," *Yale Law Journal* 52 (1942): 1–41. Lusky discusses the *Carolene Products* footnote, attributing great importance to it (pp. 19–26) but failing to mention that he himself was Justice Stone's clerk at the time and had a hand in writing it. On Lusky's role and Stone's in authoring the footnote, see Alpheus Thomas Mason, *Harlan Fiske Stone: Pillar of the Law* (New York: Viking, 1956), pp. 512–15.
17. *Korematsu v. United States*, 323 U.S. 214 (1944).
18. *West Virginia State Board of Education v. Barnette*, 319 U.S. 624 (1943).
19. Anthony Lewis, "Earl Warren," in Richard H. Sayler, Barry B. Boyer, and Robert E. Gooding, Jr., eds., *The Warren Court: A Critical Analysis* (New York: Chelsea House, 1969), p. 1. See also Laura Kalman, *The Strange Career of Legal*

Liberalism (New Haven: Yale University Press, 1996), p. 43, for a catalog of other estimates of the revolutionary character of the Warren Court.

20. See Kalman, *The Strange Career of Legal Liberalism*, p. 54.

21. Donald L. Horowitz, *The Courts and Social Policy* (Washington, DC: Brookings Institution, 1977), p. 3.

22. Paul Burstein, *Discrimination, Jobs, and Politics* (Chicago: University of Chicago Press, 1985), p. 17.

23. William E. Leuchtenburg, *The Supreme Court Reborn* (New York: Oxford University Press, 1935), p. 235.

24. Morton Keller, "Powers and Rights: Two Centuries of American Constitutionalism," in David Thelen, ed., *The Constitution and American Life* (Ithaca, NY: Cornell University Press, 1988), pp. 15–34.

25. Stephen L. Wasby, "How Planned Is 'Planned Litigation'?" *American Bar Foundation Research Journal* 5 (1984): 98.

26. Samuel Walker, *In Defense of American Liberties: A History of the ACLU* (New York: Oxford University Press, 1990), p. 111.

27. Norman Redlich, "Private Attorneys-General: Group Action in the Fight for Civil Liberties," *Yale Law Journal* 58 (1949): 574–98.

28. Harvard Sitkoff, *A New Deal for Blacks* (New York: Oxford University Press, 1978), pp. 9–20, 51, 66–67, and Hugh Davis Graham, *The Civil Rights Era* (New York: Oxford University Press, 1990), p. 9.

29. Sitkoff, *A New Deal For Blacks*, pp. 77–79, 134. On the issue of the poll tax, by 1942 the Civil War was legislatively reenacted. In the House, a bill abolishing the poll tax was approved 254–84 with only four Southerners in favor and only six Democrats outside the South opposed. A filibuster killed the bill in the Senate, where every Northern Democrat favored the bill and every Southern Democrat except Claude Pepper opposed it. See p. 136.

30. Ibid., pp. 89–95, 99. All of this is entirely overlooked in Jill Quadagno, *The Color of Welfare* (New York: Oxford University Press, 1994), in a vigorous effort to show that the New Deal "left intact—indeed reinforced—the rigid color line" (p. 24). Quadagno shows how New Deal social welfare programs, dependent on Southern votes in Congress, generally minimized African-American participation, but she underestimates the importance of political changes, including the integration of black voters into the Democratic Party.

31. This narrative follows the detailed account in David J. Garrow, *Bearing the Cross: Martin Luther King, Jr., and the Southern Christian Leadership Conference* (New York: Morrow, 1986), pp. 11–16. See also the interviews in Howell Raines, *My Soul Is Rested* (New York: Penguin, 1977), with E. D. Nixon (pp. 37–39, 43–51) and Rosa Parks (pp. 40–42). See also Hollinger F. Barnard, ed., *Outside the Magic Circle: The Autobiography of Virginia Foster Durr* (Birmingham: University of Alabama Press, 1985), pp. 278–83.

32. Raines, *My Soul Is Rested*, p. 70.

33. Aldon Morris, *The Origins of the Civil Rights Movement* (New York: Free Press, 1984), p. 23. This quotation refers to the role of the black church in social protest in Baton Rouge, Louisiana, in 1953. Morris takes this to be the same model Montgomery developed in 1955.

34. Ibid., pp. 31, 33.

35. Ibid., p. 35.

36. Martin Luther King, Jr., "Address to Montgomery Improvement Association Mass Meeting," Holt Street Baptist Church, Nov. 14, 1956, in Clayborne Carson, ed., *The Papers of Martin Luther King, Jr.*, vol. 3 (Berkeley: University of California Press, 1997), p. 428.

37. Nan Aron, *Liberty and Justice for All: Public Interest Law in the 1980s and Beyond* (Boulder, CO: Westview, 1989), pp. 27, 34–35. See also Lee Epstein, Tracey E. George, and Joseph F. Kobylka, *Public Interest Law: An Annotated Bibliography and Research Guide* (New York: Garland, 1992).

38. Lee Epstein, *Conservatives in Court* (Knoxville: University of Tennessee Press, 1985), pp. 119–33.

39. Ellen Jane Hollingsworth, "Ten Years of Legal Services for the Poor," in Robert H. Haveman, ed., *A Decade of Federal Antipoverty Programs* (New York: Academic Press, 1977), p. 293.

40. Earl Johnson, Jr., "Discussions," in ibid., p. 315.

41. Robert D. Plotnick and Felicity Skidmore, *Progress Against Poverty* (New York: Academic Press, 1975), pp. 17–18. See also R. Shep Melnick, *Between the Lines: Interpreting Welfare Rights* (Washington, DC: The Brookings Institution, 1994), p. 43. The key case was *Goldberg v. Kelly* 397 U.S. 254 (1970). See also James T. Patterson, *America's Struggle Against Poverty, 1900–1994* (Cambridge: Harvard University Press, 1994).

42. Michael B. Katz, *In the Shadow of the Poorhouse: A Social History of Welfare in America* (New York: Basic Books, 1996), pp. 267–69.

43. Paul E. Peterson and J. David Greenstone, "Racial Change and Citizen Participation: The Mobilization of Low-Income Communities Through Community Action," in Haveman, ed., *A Decade of Federal Antipoverty Programs*, pp. 241, 257, 271.

44. "The Port Huron Statement," June 11–15, 1962, in James Miller, *"Democracy Is in the Streets"* (New York: Simon & Schuster, 1987), p. 329.

45. Michael Kazin, *The Populist Persuasion* (New York: Basic Books, 1995), p. 199.

46. Hugh Heclo, "The Sixties' False Dawn: Awakenings, Movements, and Postmodern Policy-Making," in Brian Balogh, ed., *Integrating the Sixties* (University Park: Pennsylvania State University Press, 1996), p. 51.

47. See Martha Derthick, "Crossing Thresholds: Federalism in the 1960s," in ibid., pp. 64–80.

48. Steven F. Lawson, *Black Ballots: Voting Rights in the South, 1944–1969* (New York: Columbia University Press, 1976), pp. 165–202.

49. Melnick, *Between the Lines*, pp. 23–24, 34, 39–40, 255.

50. John David Skrentny, *The Ironies of Affirmative Action* (Chicago: University of Chicago Press, 1996), p. 107.

51. Bruce J. Dierenfield, *Keeper of the Rules: Congressman Howard W. Smith of Virginia* (Charlottesville: University Press of Virginia, 1987), pp. 194–96. Smith clearly hoped to torpedo the civil rights bill, but his advocacy of women's rights was apparently sincere. See Graham, *The Civil Rights Era*, pp. 134–39.

52. Cynthia Harrison, *On Account of Sex: The Politics of Women's Issues, 1945–1968* (Berkeley: University of California Press, 1988), pp. 176–97. See also Betty Friedan, *It Changed My Life* (New York: Random House, 1976), pp. 75–86.

53. Martha F. Davis, "Welfare Rights and Women's Rights in the 1960s," in Balogh, ed., *Integrating the Sixties*, pp. 146–49.

54. Nick Kotz and Mary Lynn Kotz, *A Passion for Equality: George A. Wiley and the Movement* (New York: Norton, 1977), p. 198.

55. Steven M. Teles, *Whose Welfare? AFDC and Elite Politics* (Lawrence: University Press of Kansas, 1996), p. 20. Patterson, *America's Struggle Against Poverty*, p. 179, cites a rise from a third of those eligible applying for welfare in 1960 to 90 percent in 1971.

56. Theda Skocpol, *Protecting Soldiers and Mothers* (Cambridge: Harvard University Press, 1992), and Kriste Lindenmeyer, *"A Right to Childhood": The U.S. Children's Bureau and Child Welfare, 1912–46* (Urbana: University of Illinois Press, 1997).

57. Kirsten A. Gronbjerg, *Mass Society and the Extension of Welfare: 1960–1970* (Chicago: University of Chicago Press, 1977), p. 158.

58. Patterson, *America's Struggle Against Poverty*, p. 197.

59. James T. Patterson uses the phrase "unsung revolution." Ibid., p. 155.

60. R. Shep Melnick, *Regulation and the Courts: The Case of the Clean Air Act* (Washington, DC: Brookings Institution, 1983), p. 5.

61. Lawrence M. Friedman, "The Rise and Fall of Student Rights," in David L. Kirp and Donald N. Jensen, eds., *School Days, Rule Days* (Philadelphia: Falmer, 1986), p. 241. Despite the title of the essay, Friedman argues (p. 252) that the judicialization and legalization of school policy is "probably an irreversible process."

62. David Neal and David L. Kirp, "The Allure of Legalization Reconsidered," in ibid., p. 347.

63. See Frank R. Dobbin et al., "The Expansion of Due Process in Organizations," in Lynne G. Zucker, ed., *Institutional Patterns and Organizations* (Cambridge, MA: Ballinger, 1988), pp. 71–100, especially pp. 86–87. Note that in the 1920s and 1930s nonunion firms as well as unionizing firms began to formalize personnel practices; as Dobbin et al. note (pp. 74–75), both union organizing and firm efforts to forestall union organizing led to similar results.

64. Arthur E. Bonfield, "The Origin and Development of American Fair Employment Legislation," *Iowa Law Review* 52 (1967): 1071; Graham, *The Civil Rights Era*, pp. 19–21.

65. Burstein, *Discrimination, Jobs, and Politics*, pp. 21, 64. This is part of Burstein's argument that it was a broad change in public opinion, not the specific dramatic events of the civil rights movement, that brought about civil rights legislation.

66. Lance Liebman, "Immigration Status and American Law: The Several Versions of Antidiscrimination Doctrine," in Donald L. Horowitz and Gerard Noiriel, eds., *Immigrants in Two Democracies: French and American Experiences* (New York: New York University Press, 1992), p. 369.

67. Richard Edwards, *Rights at Work* (Washington, DC: Brookings Institution, 1993), p. 108.

68. Ibid., pp. 17-19, 35-36, 157, 163, 165.

69. Anja Chan, *Women and Sexual Harassment* (New York: Haworth, 1994), pp. 3-7.

70. David Vogel, "The 'New' Social Regulation in Historical and Comparative Perspective," in Thomas K. McCraw, ed., *Regulation in Perspective* (Cambridge: Harvard University Press, 1981), pp. 161-62.

71. C. Michael Otten, *University Authority and the Student: The Berkeley Experience* (Berkeley: University of California Press, 1970), pp. 145-46, 164, 179-87.

72. Barbara J. Nelson, *Making an Issue of Child Abuse* (Chicago: University of Chicago Press, 1984). See also Linda Gordon, *Heroes of Their Own Lives: The Politics and History of Family Violence, Boston 1880-1960* (New York: Viking, 1988), pp. 24-25.

73. Rebecca M. Ryan, "The Sex Right: A Legal History of the Marital Rape Exemption," *Law and Social Inquiry* 20 (1995): 941-1004; Diana E.H. Russell, *Rape in Marriage*, rev. ed. (Bloomington: Indiana University Press, 1990); and Raquel Kennedy Bergen, *Wife Rape* (Thousand Oaks, CA: Sage, 1996).

74. Steven Rathgeb Smith, "Federal Funding, Nonprofit Agencies, and Victim Services," in Harold W. Demone, Jr. and Margaret Gibelman, eds., *Services for Sale* (New Brunswick, NJ: Rutgers University Press, 1989), pp. 215-27.

75. Sally Engle Merry, "Wife Battering and the Ambiguity of Rights" in Austin R. Sarat and Thomas R. Kearns, eds., *Identities, Politics and Rights* (Ann Arbor: University of Michigan Press, 1997), pp. 283-84.

76. Herbert Jacob, *Silent Revolution: The Transformation of Divorce Law in the United States* (Chicago: University of Chicago Press, 1988), pp. 8, 30, 41, 45-46, 59-60, 80. See also Lenore J. Weitzman, *The Divorce Revolution* (New York: Free Press, 1985), pp. 15-51, and Steven Mintz and Susan Kellogg, *Domestic Revolutions: A Social History of American Family Life* (New York: Free Press, 1988), pp. 228-33.

77. Ruth R. Faden and Tom L. Beauchamp, *A History and Theory of Informed Consent* (New York: Oxford University Press, 1986), pp. 89-94, 143. Quotation is from p. 94. Not only clinical practice but medical research has been influenced by the ethos of rights and the ethos of democratic participation. See John Gaventa, "The Powerful, the Powerless, and the Experts: Knowledge Struggles in an Information Age," in Peter Park et al., eds., *Voices of Change: Participatory Research in the United States and Canada* (Westport, CT: Bergin & Garvey, 1993), pp. 21-40, and Steven Epstein, *Impure Science: AIDS, Activism, and the Politics of Knowledge* (Berkeley: University of California Press, 1996).

78. Michael J. Lacey, ed., *Government and Environmental Politics* (Washington, DC: Woodrow Wilson Center Press, 1991). See especially the essays by Samuel P. Hays, "Three Decades of Environmental Politics: The Historical Context," pp. 19-80; Thomas R. Dunlap, "The Federal Government, Wildlife, and Endangered Species," pp. 209-32, and Christopher Schroeder, "The Evolution of Federal Regulation of Toxic Substances," pp. 263-313.

79. See Richard Claude, *The Supreme Court and the Electoral Process* (Baltimore: Johns Hopkins University Press, 1970), pp. 147-48. One need not take these

developments as progress for democracy. Political scientist Martha Derthick, for instance, objects that in the reapportionment decisions, "State and local governments and, not incidentally, state and local electorates were stripped of much of their discretion in the critical matter (in a democracy) of defining the meaning of representation." See Derthick, "Crossing Thresholds," p. 69. Of course, if a substantial proportion of the population is denied the vote altogether, the phrase "in a democracy" is not much to go by.

The reapportionment cases, in turn, would become basic to a more aggressive interpretation of voting rights for blacks. The Voting Rights Act of 1965, designed to enforce the Fifteenth Amendment, by 1969 was reinterpreted along Fourteenth Amendment "equal protection" lines. This meant that it would be enforced not only to assure blacks a vote but a "meaningful" vote, and this opened up new arguments about the necessity for redistricting to create one or more congressional districts where a majority of voters would be black. See Abigail Thernstrom, *Whose Votes Count? Affirmative Action and Minority Voting Rights* (Cambridge: Harvard University Press, 1987), p. 25.

80. Amy Bridges, *Morning Glories: Municipal Reform in the Southwest* (Princeton: Princeton University Press, 1997), pp. 181–83, 200.

81. Austin Ranney, *Curing the Mischiefs of Faction: Party Reform in America* (Berkeley: University of California Press, 1975), p. 3. Ranney, a distinguished political scientist, was also an active participant in the process of reform.

82. Geoffrey Cowan, telephone interview and e-mail communication, Jan. 7, 1998. On Fannie Lou Hamer, see Kay Mills, *This Little Light of Mine: The Life of Fannie Lou Hamer* (New York: Dutton, 1993); on the reforms in the Democratic Party, see Byron E. Shafer, *Quiet Revolution* (New York: Russell Sage Foundation, 1983).

83. Graham, *The Civil Rights Era*, p. 363.

84. Burdett A. Loomis, *The New American Politician* (New York: Basic Books, 1988); James L. Sundquist, *The Decline and Resurgence of Congress* (Washington, DC: Brookings Institution, 1981); Paul J. Quirk, "Policy Making in the Contemporary Congress: Three Dimensions of Performance," in Marc K. Landy and Martin A. Levin, eds., *The New Politics of Public Policy* (Baltimore: Johns Hopkins University Press, 1995), pp. 228–45.

85. George Kateb, "The Moral Distinctiveness of Representative Democracy," *Ethics* 91 (1981):360. My account here merely samples the many areas of social life where notions of moral equality, democratic access, and the rights of citizenship have been newly influential since the civil rights movement. One area that deserves more attention is corporate responsibility where initiatives sponsored by civil rights veterans or others inspired by civil rights called to account corporate boards and investors in corporations. This also included a significant, if now languishing, broadcast reform movement. See Robert B. Horwitz, "Broadcast Reform Revisited: Reverend Everett C. Parker and the 'Standing' Case: *Office of Communication of the United Church of Christ v. Federal Communications Commission*," *Communication Review* 2 (1997):311–48.

86. Martin Wattenberg, *The Decline of American Political Parties, 1952–1994* (Cambridge: Harvard University Press, 1996), p. 174.

87. David Butler, cited in ibid., pp. 171–73.

88. Ibid., pp. 90–112.

89. Walter Dean Burnham, "Party Systems and the Political Process," in William Nisbet Chambers and Walter Dean Burnham, eds., *The American Party Systems* (New York: Oxford University Press, 1967), p. 305.

90. A. James Reichley, *The Life of the Parties* (New York: Free Press, 1990), p. 311.

91. G. Calvin MacKenzie, "Partisan Leadership Through Presidential Appointments," in L. Sandy Maisel, ed., *The Parties Respond* (Boulder, CO: Westview, 1994), p. 360.

92. See Reichley, *The Life of the Parties*, pp. 383–85.

93. See Amy Bridges, "Winning the West to Municipal Reform," *Urban Affairs Quarterly* 27 (1992):494–518.

94. The states are Oregon, California, Colorado, Arizona, and Washington in order of the most initiatives. My calculations are made from Table 4.3 in David Magleby, *Direct Legislation* (Baltimore: Johns Hopkins University Press, 1984), p. 71.

95. Speech to California Conference of the Congressional Union, June 1–2, 1915, cited in Inez Haynes Irwin, *The Story of the Woman's Party* (New York: Kraus, 1971), p. 101. Originally published 1921.

96. Richard White, *"It's Your Misfortune and None of My Own": A History of the American West* (Norman: University of Oklahoma Press, 1991), pp. 359–63. See also Paul W. Kleppner, "Politics Without Parties: The Western States, 1900–1984," in Gerald D. Nash and Richard W. Etulain, eds., *The Twentieth-Century West: Historical Interpretations* (Albuquerque: University of New Mexico Press, 1989), pp. 295–338.

97. Gianfranco Poggi, *The Development of the Modern State* (Stanford: Stanford University Press, 1978), p. 133.

98. John J. Coleman, *Party Decline in America: Policy, Politics, and the Fiscal State* (Princeton: Princeton University Press, 1996), pp. 13–14, 35, 45, 68.

99. Nelson Polsby, *Consequences of Party Reform* (New York: Oxford University Press, 1983), p. 54.

100. See Margaret Gibelman and Harold W. Demone, Jr., "The Evolving Contract State," in Demone and Gibelman, eds., *Services for Sale*, p. 26.

101. Steven Rathgeb Smith and Michael Lipsky, *Nonprofits for Hire* (Cambridge: Harvard University Press, 1995), pp. 4–5.

102. Kay Lehman Schlozman and John T. Tierney, *Organized Interests and American Democracy* (New York: Harper & Row, 1986), pp. 75, 81.

The growth of private organizations of various kinds is by some measures even more phenomenal. In 1940, there were 12,500 non-church charitable tax-exempt organizations in the country; by 1990, 700,000, with most of the growth taking place after 1960. Most of these are not membership organizations of any sort but private or family foundations, nothing much more than tax shelters, so the 700,000 figure is not to be taken too seriously. Still, the very notion of a "nonprofit sector" only dates to the contemporary period. This "sector," particularly the larger foundations within it, began to develop self-consciousness as a third force (besides government and the market) in American life, one peculiarly dedicated to the public good, and one with strong

interests in civic participation, at least since the Ford Foundation's major initiatives in community action programs began in 1961. See Peter Dobkin Hall,
Inventing the Nonprofit Sector (Baltimore: Johns Hopkins University Press,
1992), pp. 13, 244, 252.

103. Dallas A. Blanchard, *The Anti-Abortion Movement and the Rise of the Religious
Right* (New York: Twayne, 1996), pp. 61–72, 121–25.

104. Epstein, *Impure Science*, p. 348.

105. Jack L. Walker, Jr. makes this point in *Mobilizing Interest Groups in America:
Patrons, Professions, and Social Movements* (Ann Arbor: University of Michi-
gan Press, 1991), pp. 41–48. The influential theory was classically stated by
Mancur Olson, *The Logic of Collective Action* (Cambridge: Harvard University
Press, 1965).

106. Reichley, *The Life of the Parties*, pp. 236, 256.

107. Ibid., p. 356.

108. Paul S. Herrnson, "The Revitalization of National Party Organizations," in
Maisel, ed., *The Parties Respond*, p. 45.

109. Sig Mickelson, *From Whistle Stop to Sound Bite* (New York: Praeger, 1989), pp.
38–39.

110. Ibid., p. 39.

111. "'Nightline' Pulls Plug on Convention Coverage," *New York Times*, Aug. 15,
1996, p. 19.

112. Byron Shafer, *Bifurcated Politics* (Cambridge: Harvard University Press, 1988),
pp. 151–52. See also Theodore White, *The Making of the President 1968* (New
York: Atheneum, 1969), pp. 301–302.

113. Todd Gitlin, *The Whole World Is Watching* (Berkeley: University of California
Press, 1980).

114. Herbert J. Gans, *Deciding What's News: A Study of CBS Evening News, NBC
Nightly News, Newsweek and Time* (New York: Pantheon, 1979), pp. 68–69,
204–206.

115. Newton N. Minow, John Bartlow Martin, and Lee M. Mitchell, *Presidential
Television* (New York: Basic Books, 1973), p. 8.

116. Timothy Crouse, *The Boys on the Bus* (New York: Ballantine, 1973).

117. Joe S. Foote, *Television Access and Political Power* (New York: Praeger, 1990),
pp. 14–15.

118. Ibid., p. 30. In fact, the networks granted Stevenson and four minor party candidates airtime. When the FCC ruling came down, the networks felt obliged to
offer Eisenhower reply time, but he declined. See Minow, Martin, and
Mitchell, *Presidential Television*, p. 78. They (p. 79) point to a similar episode
in 1964 when President Lyndon Johnson took to television to discuss several
international events within two weeks of the election and Republican candidate Barry Goldwater's request for equal time was turned down by the FCC.

119. See Foote, *Television Access and Political Power*, pp. 141–43.

120. For the narrative, see Minow, Martin, and Mitchell, *Presidential Television*, pp.
67–72. See also Foote, *Television Access and Political Power*, pp. 41–42.

121. Foote, p. 49.

122. April 22, 1985, quoted in Foote, p. 82.

123. Ibid., for Ford, Carter, and Reagan. The Clinton cases took place June 17, 1993 and April 18, 1995.

124. Daniel C. Hallin, *We Keep America on Top of the World* (New York: Routledge, 1994).

125. Mickelson, *From Whistle Stop to Sound Bite*, pp. 161–62.

126. Kiku Adatto, *Picture Perfect* (New York: Basic Books, 1993), identifies the early 1968 usage of the term.

127. Michael Schudson, *The Power of News* (Cambridge: Harvard University Press, 1995), pp. 1–33, 124–41.

128. Mary Ann Glendon, *Rights Talk* (New York: Free Press, 1991), pp. 171–73.

129. Ibid., pp. 5–7. There are many other discussions of rights-talk and a rights-oriented political process, and many of them, though not as extreme as Glendon's, are nonetheless very critical of excesses and distortions in a rights-oriented political process. See Thelen, ed., *The Constitution and American Life*, especially Thomas L. Haskell, "The Curious Persistence of Rights Talk in the 'Age of Interpretation,'" pp. 324–52, and Hendrik Hartog, "The Constitution of Aspiration and 'The Rights That Belong to Us All,'" pp. 353–74; Michael J. Lacey and Knud Haakonssen, *A Culture of Rights: The Bill of Rights in Philosophy, Politics, and Law, 1791 and 1991* (Cambridge: Woodrow Wilson International Center for Scholars and Cambridge University Press, 1991), especially William A. Galston, "Practical Philosophy and the Bill of Rights: Perspectives on Some Contemporary Issues," pp. 215–65, and Alan Ryan, "The British, the Americans, and Rights," pp. 366–439. Critical of rights-talk and other ways of thinking and talking that appear to presuppose a detached or autonomous individual is Michael J. Sandel, *Democracy's Discontent: America in Search of a Public Philosophy* (Cambridge: Belknap Press of Harvard University Press, 1996); a vigorous defense of rights-talk as it has emerged in constitutional law is Harry N. Hirsch, *A Theory of Liberty: The Constitution and Minorities* (Ithaca, NY: Cornell University Press, 1992).

130. Jonathan Rauch, *Demosclerosis: The Silent Killer of American Government* (New York: Times Books, 1994), pp. 80–81.

131. Robert N. Bellah, Richard Madsen, William M. Sullivan, Ann Swidler, and Steven M. Tipton, *Habits of the Heart* (Berkeley: University of California Press, 1985), p. 154.

132. Paul Lichterman, *The Search for Political Community: American Activists Reinventing Commitment* (Cambridge: Cambridge University Press, 1996).

133. Kim Cromwell, "Khamisa's Anguish," *San Diego Magazine* 49 (December 1996): 122–25, 188.

134. Terry Rodgers, "Taking a Stand Against Pollution," *San Diego Union-Tribune*, Oct. 17, 1997, pp. A-1, A-27.

135. William Glaberson, "Killer in 'Megan' Case Sentenced to Death," *New York Times*, June 21, 1997, p. 1.

136. See R. Shep Melnick, *Regulation and the Courts*.

137. David Vogel points to this dynamic in *Kindred Strangers: The Uneasy Relationship Between Business and Politics in America* (Princeton: Princeton University Press, 1996), p. 160.

Conclusion: A Gathering of Citizens

1. Hanna Fenichel Pitkin, "Justice: On Relating Private and Public," *Political Theory* 9 (1981): 327.

2. "Forum: Whatever Became of the Public Square?" *Harper's* 281 (July 1990): 49.

3. On the decline of conversation and gathering places, see Christopher Lasch, "Conversation and the Civic Arts," in his *The Revolt of the Elites and the Betrayal of Democracy* (New York: Norton, 1995), pp. 117–28. For critical responses to intellectuals' complaints about the decline of conversation, see Michael Schudson, "Why Conversation Is Not the Soul of Democracy," *Critical Studies in Mass Communication* 14 (December 1997): 297–309, and David Simpson, "The Cost of Conversation," *Raritan* 16 (1997): 75–85. On scandal, see Suzanne Garment, *Scandal: The Culture of Mistrust in American Politics* (New York: Times Books, 1991). On declining trust in institutions, the standard work is Seymour Martin Lipset and William Schneider, *The Confidence Gap*, 2nd ed. (Baltimore: Johns Hopkins University Press, 1987). On the decline in newspaper readership, see Newspaper Association of America, *Facts About Newspapers 1997* (Vienna, VA: Newspaper Association of America, 1997). This reports that 78 percent of adults read a weekday newspaper in 1970, 67 percent in 1980, 62 percent in 1990, and 59 percent in 1996.

4. "Discourse on the Sciences and the Arts" (1750), in Donald A. Cress, ed., *Basic Political Writings of Jean-Jacques Rousseau* (Indianapolis: Hackett, 1987), p. 17. "We have physicists, geometers, chemists, astronomers, poets, musicians, and painters; we no longer have citizens."

5. For the 1950s, in addition to Robert Dahl, cited in the last chapter, there is David Riesman writing on the suburbs: the new suburbanite "if he is political at all—rather than parochially civic-minded, tending to a 'garden' which includes the local schools and waterworks—he is apt to be an Eisenhower Republican, seldom informed, rarely angry, and only spasmodically partisan." David Riesman, "The Suburban Sadness," in William M. Dobriner, ed., *The Suburban Community* (New York: Putnam's, 1958), p. 377. Or Herbert J. Gans on the lower-middle-class residents of Levittown: "Generally speaking, Levittowners do not take much interest in the national society, and rarely even see its influence on their lives. As long as they are employed, healthy, and able to achieve a reasonable proportion of their personal goals, they have no need for the federal government or any other national agency, and being locals, they do not concern themselves with the world outside their community. Indeed, they might better be described as *sublocals*, for they are home-oriented rather than community-oriented." Herbert J. Gans, *The Levittowners* (New York: Pantheon, 1967), p. 189. Or C. Wright Mills, observing that "the facts of widespread public indifference" overshadow all others in American political life. Many Americans "are strangers to politics. They are not radical, not liberal, not conservative, not reactionary; they are inactionary; they are out of it. If we accept the Greeks' definition of the idiot as a privatized man, then we must conclude that the U.S. citizenry is now largely composed of idiots." C. Wright Mills, *White Collar* (New York: Oxford University Press, 1953), p. 328.

For the 1920s, in addition to Walter Lippmann, already amply cited, there is the observation of political scientist Robert C. Brooks: "The average man necessarily finds most of his energies absorbed by the process of earning a living; the average woman is largely engrossed in household cares. . . . With personal registration every year, and with one or two primaries or elections each year, both of the latter involving long and difficult ballots, many turn aside from politics, except perhaps when an occasional thrilling contest takes place." Robert C. Brooks, *Political Parties and Electoral Problems* (New York: Harper, 1923), p. 429.

For the 1890s, consider E. L. Godkin's contention that "It is simply impossible . . . for a man living in 1897 to feel the same interest in the working of the machinery of his political party as the man living in 1817. The demands of other things on his attention are infinitely greater; so are his opportunities of improving his condition; so is the area over which he may extend his activity." Godkin also writes, and critics of television might heed these remarks: "Nothing is more striking in the reading public to-day, in our democracy, than the increasing incapacity for continuous attention. . . . The diligent newspaper reader . . . gets accustomed to passing rapidly from one to another of a series of incidents, small and great, requiring simply the transfer, from one trifle to another, of a sort of lazy, uninterested attention, which often becomes subconscious; that is, a man reads with hardly any knowledge or recollection of what he is reading." See E. L. Godkin, *Unforeseen Tendencies of Democracy* (Boston: Houghton Mifflin, 1898), pp. 70-71.

6. Robert N. Bellah, Richard Madsen, William M. Sullivan, Ann Swidler, and Steven M. Tipton, *Habits of the Heart* (Berkeley: University of California Press, 1985).

7. For a valuable review and analysis, see Joyce Appleby, *Liberalism and Republicanism in the Historical Imagination* (Cambridge: Harvard University Press, 1992).

8. Robert D. Putnam, *Making Democracy Work: Civic Traditions in Modern Italy* (Princeton: Princeton University Press, 1993), pp. 115, 150.

9. Robert D. Putnam, "Bowling Alone," *Journal of Democracy* 6 (1995): 65-78. For further work that elaborates and deepens the argument and explores what might explain a decline in social capital, see Robert D. Putnam, "Turning In, Tuning Out: The Strange Disappearance of Social Capital in America," *PS: Political Science and Politics* 24 (1995): 664-83; Robert D. Putnam, "The Prosperous Community," *The American Prospect* 13 (Spring 1993): 35-42; Robert D. Putnam, "The Strange Disappearance of Civic America," *The American Prospect* 24 (Winter, 1996): 34-48. Critiques include Nicholas Lemann, "Kicking in Groups," *Atlantic Monthly* 277 (April 1996): 22-26; Michael Schudson, "What If Civic Life Didn't Die?" *The American Prospect* 25 (March-April 1996): 17-20; Theda Skocpol, "Unravelling from Above," *The American Prospect* 25 (March-April 1996): 20-25; Richard M. Valelly, "Couch-Potato Democracy?" *The American Prospect* 25 (March-April 1996); 25-28; William A. Galston, "Won't You Be My Neighbor?" *The American Prospect* 26 (May-June 1996):

16–18; Alejandro Portes and Patricia Landolt, "The Downside of Social Capital," *The American Prospect* 26 (May–June 1996): 18–22; and the entire issue of *The Public Perspective* 7 (June/July 1996), the publication of the Roper Center for Public Opinion Research. For some commentary on the controversy in the general press, see Richard Morin, "So Much for the 'Bowling Alone' Thesis," *Washington Post National Weekly Edition*, June 17–23, 1996, p. 37; Anthony Lewis, "An Atomized America," *New York Times*, Dec. 18, 1995, p. All.

10. Lemann, "Kicking in Groups," pp. 22–26.

11. Warren E. Miller and J. Merrill Shanks, *The New American Voter* (Cambridge: Harvard University Press, 1996), pp. 54–55.

12. Everett C. Ladd, "The Data Just Don't Show Erosion of America's 'Social Capital,'" *The Public Perspective* 7 (June/July 1996): 7.

13. Christopher Jencks, "Who Gives What?," in Walter W. Powell, ed., *The Nonprofit Sector: A Research Handbook* (New Haven: Yale University Press, 1987), pp. 321–39.

14. John F. Helliwell and Robert D. Putnam, "Correction," *PS: Political Science & Politics* 29 (1996): 138.

15. Alexander W. Astin, et al., *The American Freshman: Thirty Year Trends, 1966–1996* (Los Angeles: Higher Education Research Institute, UCLA, 1997), pp. 86–87, 116–17.

16. Jack L. Walker, "Interests, Political Parties, and Policy Formation in American Democracy," in Donald T. Critchlow and Ellis W. Hawley, eds., *Federal Social Policy: The Historical Dimension* (University Park: Pennsylvania State University Press, 1988), pp. 141–70. Walker points to the growth of interest groups and their ability to represent groups the parties ignored and articulate issues the party system denied. He concludes, "We have moved to a higher plateau of political participation from which there is no turning back" (p. 167).

17. Some thinkers might argue that we have moved or should move from a citizenship of rights to a citizenship of difference. For many in academic life who have become disenchanted with the language and institutions of liberalism, a new model must be constructed that respects and celebrates human differences, and they see liberalism as too often insisting that people be treated according to their sameness. There is a long story to be told here, but the end of it is that the celebration of difference is compatible with liberalism. A liberalism of rights insists that people be treated according to their fundamental moral equality as human beings; there is nothing in liberalism to require that people be the same or that they all seek to approximate a white or male or Anglo-Saxon or heterosexual character. Indeed, the lesson of the past quarter century is that the language of the Declaration of Independence or the Gettysburg Address or the Fourteenth Amendment, even if the authors did not imagine their words applying to women or minorities of various sorts, is a language of universalistic values that group after group has successfully claimed as its own. Liberals, in the broadest sense of the term, must either bow to the just demands of groups that demonstrate existing liberalism to have been more narrowly construed in fact than in theory, or else explain why they would defend putting a

given barrier between social practice and the explicit aspirations of the Declaration of Independence or the Fourteenth Amendment.

There are, of course, complicated issues about difference. For instance, some advocates of affirmative action would say that members of minority groups that have suffered past discrimination must be treated differently in order, ultimately, to be treated the same. Just what should follow for law and public policy from the biological differences between men and women is a contested issue. What should follow for law and public policy from the biological differences between children and adults is also contested. These are complex matters, and I do not think traditional American political thought affords any consistent answers. I do not think the concept of rights offers any panacea at all. But neither do any of the versions of post-liberal thought, so far as I can determine. As an empirical matter, the language of public life has not in the slightest abandoned its emphasis on rights. As a normative matter, I do not see a strong case that it should.

18. E. J. Graff, "In & Out in Vermont," *The Nation* 265 (Oct. 20, 1997): 19–20.
19. Jane Mansbridge, "The Role of Discourse in the Feminist Movement," Working Papers of the Center for Urban Affairs and Policy Research, Northwestern University, 1993. See also evidence of changing language in Sally Engle Merry, "Wife Battering and the Ambiguities of Rights," in Austin Sarat and Thomas R. Kearns, eds., *Identities, Politics, and Rights* (Ann Arbor: University of Michigan Press, 1997), pp. 271–306.
20. David Thelen, *Citizenship in the Age of Television* (Chicago: University of Chicago Press, 1996).
21. Steven Mintz and Susan Kellogg, *Domestic Revolutions: A Social History of American Family Life* (New York: Free Press, 1988), pp. 178–79.
22. See note 5.
23. Putnam cites the relevant data. A standard compilation, though dated now, is Lipset and Schneider, *The Confidence Gap*.
24. John T. McGreevy, *Parish Boundaries: The Catholic Encounter with Race in the Twentieth-Century Urban North* (Chicago: University of Chicago Press, 1996), pp. 20–21.
25. Ibid., pp. 218–19.
26. Jay P. Dolan, *The American Catholic Experience* (Garden City, NY: Doubleday, 1985), pp. 435–39.
27. Ibid., p. 453.
28. Andrew M. Greeley, *The Catholic Myth* (New York: Scribner's, 1990).
29. For a more extended argument, see Michael Schudson, *The Power of News* (Cambridge: Harvard University Press, 1995), pp. 169–88.
30. In the early sixties, 21 percent of the population was below the poverty level. This dropped to 11 percent in the early 1970s, then went back up to 14.5 percent by 1992. James Patterson, *America's Struggle Against Poverty, 1900–1994* (Cambridge: Harvard University Press, 1994), pp. 224–25.
31. John M. Blum et al., *The National Experience: A History of the United States*, 8th ed. (San Diego: Harcourt Brace Jovanovich, 1993).

32. David Hackett Fischer reports that what Paul Revere said was, "The Regulars are coming out!" The only thing he clearly did not say was, "The British are coming!" since Revere and all those he warned regarded themselves as British, too. See David Hackett Fischer, *Paul Revere's Ride* (New York: Oxford University Press, 1994), pp. 109–10.

Acknowledgments

I have gone back to school in writing this book. I have unlearned so much of what I thought was certain, and I am deeply grateful to all who have helped me see American society anew.

I am grateful to those audiences who have listened to earlier, struggling versions: Ellen Lagemann and the Center for the Study of American Culture and Education at New York University; Jim Miller and the liberal studies program at the New School for Social Research; Marvin Kalb, Pippa Norris, and the Barone Center at the Kennedy School, Harvard University; fellow members of the "Culture Group" at the University of California, San Diego; Peter Dahlgren and the Journalism and Mass Communication faculty at Stockholm University; John Keane and the Centre for the Study of Democracy at Westminster University; Nicholas Garnham, Colin Sparks, and the communication program at Westminster University, London; David Eason and Middle Tennessee State University's School of Communication; David Sullivan and the

Department of Communication at the University of San Diego; Robert Bellah, Richard Madsen, and their *Habits of the Heart* colleagues who invited me to speak at their conference at the University of California, Berkeley; Bruce Western and the Department of Sociology at Princeton University; Diane Vaughan and the Department of Sociology at Boston College; David Crocker, William Galston, and the Institute for Philosophy and Public Policy at the University of Maryland. I also benefited from presenting my work at meetings of the American Sociological Association, the National Communication Association, and the Organization of American Historians, where Andrew Robertson was especially helpful.

Paul Starr has aided me enormously, as have his colleagues at *The American Prospect*, where, in several brief essays, I was able to try out parts of my argument. The first public version of this work began as a lecture at a wonderful conference Craig Calhoun organized at the University of North Carolina to honor Jurgen Habermas and the English translation of *The Structural Transformation of the Public Sphere*. The proceedings were later published as a book with Craig's elegant introduction that I usually recommend students read before reading Habermas.

I drafted the first chapters of this project during 1992–93 at the Center for Advanced Study in the Behavioral Sciences, where I tried out ideas on a congenial study group that Robert DeMaria and Elizabeth Eisenstein organized and that included Richard Baumann and Josefina Vasquez. My year at the center was supported by a grant from the National Science Foundation (SES-9022192) for which I am grateful. I have benefited from the fine collections and services of the libraries at the University of California, San Diego; the University of California, Los Angeles; Stanford University, and the American Antiquarian Society. I am also grateful to the Museum of American Political Life at the University of Hartford and to its founding curator, Edmund Sullivan, who assisted me there.

The Spencer Foundation provided an indispensable research grant at a formative stage in my writing. I was encouraged to apply for this grant by the late Lawrence Cremin, then the foundation's president. An eminent historian of American education, Cremin believed deeply that education means much more than "schools." He believed that a work that examined how Americans acquire political opinions in the whole range of their life experience—including the experience of political participation itself, was very much within the domain of educational research. I am grateful to the Spencer Foundation for its support and to Lawrence Cremin personally for trusting in the promise of this project.

I have benefited from the advice and ideas of many colleagues around the country through the years. This includes many colleagues in UCSD's Political Science Department, among them Steven Erie, Alan Houston, Gary Jacobson, Sam Kernell, Sandy Lakoff, Arend Lijphart, Sam Popkin, and Tracy Strong.

Colleagues from elsewhere have provided valuable criticism: Joyce Appleby, David Hall, Laura Kalman, Richard Kaplan, David Kirp, Ralph Lerner, Jenny Mansbridge, the late Roland Marchand, Maria Poarch, Jack Rakove, Kay Lehman Schlozman, John David Skrentny, and Robert Wiebe. Jim Boylan kindly read the whole manuscript before it was ready for public viewing. When it reached somewhat more presentable form, Michael Kammen, Robert Putnam, David Thelen, and Alan Wolfe read through the full manuscript and Richard John the first half of it. All of them offered such enormously helpful criticism that I hope there are parts here they will barely recognize!

I've learned something of the triumphs and travails of public life through conversations with my brother Charlie, an appeals court judge in Wisconsin. I also had the pleasure, when he ran for state supreme court, of campaigning with him at the Sheboygan Bratwurst Festival. There's nothing like actually doing electoral politics to remind you of the great highs and lows it can provide minute by minute. Charlie's love has held our whole far-flung family together through the years in difficult circumstances and, of real pertinence to this book, he has lived the life of a good citizen.

Martin Kessler originally signed this project for Basic Books when he was president of that estimable publishing house. When he saw the corporate handwriting on the wall, Martin left Basic for the Free Press. I went with him. Cancer took him from us well before I finished this book. Martin Kessler held up the highest standards for publishing academic work of public significance. He is missed not only by those who knew

him and cared for him, as I did, but also by the many others who benefited from the kind of publishing he believed in. I hope this book is one
he would have been proud of. The Free Press assigned my project to
Bruce Nichols, who accepted the orphan with open arms and has been
diligent, insightful, caring, and perhaps most of all, genuinely interested
in this work from the day he took it on.

I have had the stimulation of colleagues and students in both the
Department of Communication and the Dimensions of Culture program
at Thurgood Marshall College. Robert Horwitz's and Chandra Mukerji's
words of wisdom and encouragement have often helped. Several graduate students have done wonderful work as research assistants at different
points along the way, and let me mention especially Cynthia Chris and
David M. Ryfe.

I thank my wife, Suzie, for her enduring support, even when, with
three kids clamoring for attention, it was by no means easy to encourage
a project so consuming of time, energy, and emotion. Daniel, Jenna, and
Zachary have kept me on track in another way, regularly reminding me
that this is only a book, not a life. I hope, of course, that it is a good one
because I believe in the power of books to open minds, touch hearts, and
challenge the ways people have come to see the world.

In that hope, with that belief, and with my love, this book is for
Daniel, Jenna, and Zachary.

Index